SONGS OF WISDOM AND CIRCLES OF DANCE

McGill Studies in the History of Religions,
A Series Devoted to International Scholarship
Katherine K. Young, Editor

SONGS OF WISDOM AND CIRCLES OF DANCE

Hymns of the Satpanth Ismāʿīlī Muslim Saint, Pīr Shams

Tazim R. Kassam

State University of New York Press

Published by
State University of New York Press, Albany

Printed in the United States of America

For information, address State University of New York Press, State University Plaza, Albany, N.Y., 12246

Cover painting by Tazim Jaffer
Production by Diane Ganeles
Marketing by Nancy Farrell

Library of Congress Cataloging-in-Publication Data

Kassam, Tazim R.
Songs of wisdom and circles of dance : Hymns of the Satpanth Ismāʿīlī Muslim saint, Pīr Shams / Tazim R. Kassam.
p. cm. — (McGill studies in the history of religions)
Includes bibliographical references and index.
ISBN 0-7914-2591-6 (CH: acid-free). -- ISBN 0-7914-2592-4 (PB: acid-free).
1. Islamic poetry, Indic—Translations into English. 2. Sufi poetry, Indic—Translations into English. 3. Ismailites—South Asia—Poetry. I. Title. II. Series.
PK2978.E5K37 1995
297′.43—dc20 94-36269
CIP

10 9 8 7 6 5 4 3 2 1

To my dear parents
Rahim Count Kassam Jivraj
and
Laila Alijah Mawji Esmail Jivraj

Verily you should worship none save Him
and show kindness unto thy parents.
Whether one or both attain old age,
say not harsh words to them but speak to them tenderly
and serve them generously and with humility.
And say:
"O Sustainer! Bestow thy Grace upon them,
even as they cherished and cared for me as a child."
Surah al-Isra Verse 22

Contents

Acknowledgments

First and foremost, I wish to express my sincerest gratitude to Dr. Katherine K. Young. An exacting and generous mentor, it is she who kindled and stoked my interest in the academic study of religions. I am also deeply indebted to Dr. Charles Adams, whose eloquent and lucid lectures on the Islamic tradition remain for me exemplary.

I wish also to acknowledge the Faculty of Religious Studies at McGill University for providing a lively and stimulating intellectual environment for the study of religions. My thanks are due to Deans Joseph McLelland and Donna Runnalls, who lent me timely support over the years, and to Dr. Robert Culley and Dr. Arvind Sharma for their advice during the early stages of this work. Dr. Robert Stevenson played a crucial role in getting me to India to study languages and train in Indian Classical Vocal Music. For this and his affectionate aid in moments of crisis, I am most grateful.

Over the course of my research, I benefited from the assistance of many individuals. I am truly indebted to Mr. Jafferali (Chotubhai) Lakhani and Dr. Bhupendra Trivedi of Bombay for the many hours they spent with me discussing the language and content of the *ginān*s of Pīr Shams. I also wish to recognize the efforts of Dr. Prabha Atre, an accomplished vocalist of the Kirānā style of classical Hindustani Music, who initiated me into the complexities of Indian musical genres and performance. Thanks are also due to Mr. Adam Gacek and Mrs. Zawahir Moir, both formerly at the Institute of Ismaili Studies, London, for sharing their insights on the study of Arabic and Khojkī Ismāʿīlī manuscripts. Last, but not least, I thank Dr. Paul Walker whose probing questions and reflections significantly advanced my appreciation of the history and thought of Shīʿism.

I am deeply honored that the artist, Tazim Jaffer, specially painted the evocative scene on the cover of my book. My rather commonplace map and diagrams were transformed into lovely sketches by Fatima Hirji.

Since this work originated as a doctoral dissertation, I wish gratefully to acknowledge that my doctoral work was supported by the financial assistance, at various times, of the Shastri Indo-Canadian Institute, the Social Science and Humanities Research Council of Canada, the Institute of Ismaili Studies, the Social Science Research Council and the Faculty of Religious Studies at McGill University.

Finally, I would like to acknowledge my brother, Al-Karim Jivraj, for his affection and generosity; and my dear sister and colleague, Zayn Kassam-Hann, for the friendship and courage she has given me over the years. A guide in body and spirit, Zayn initiated me into the realms of Literature, Philosophy, and Ismāʿīlī Studies.

To my beloved parents, Laila and Rahim, I owe a debt of love, honor, and gratitude too profound to tell with words. It is to them that I humbly dedicate this work.

Transliteration

The transliteration scheme used in this work for Arabic and Persian terms is that of the Institute of Islamic Studies (IIS), McGill University. For Sanskrit, Hindi, and Gujarati, I have followed the transliteration scheme given for Sanskrit in Michael Coulson's *Sanskrit: An Introduction to the Classical Language*. These two transliteration systems do not always coincide in their assignment of symbols for specific phonetic values. For instance, the Nāgarī letter श and the Arabic ش are similarly pronounced as "sh" in "sheet," but the first is transliterated "ś" by Coulson and the second "sh" by the IIS system. Whereas the IIS system uses "ch" to represent the Arabic letter چ as in "chant," the Nāgarī letter च for the same consonant is transliterated "c" by Coulson who retains "ch" for the Nāgarī aspirate छ. It may be possible to develop a consistent transliteration system that would uniformly represent phonetically similar or identical letters in the Arabic and Sanskrit alphabets, but this would be at the cost of interfering with the integrity of rather long-established transliteration systems for each of these two language groups. Instead of upsetting these conventions, I have opted to accommodate both transliteration systems. Thus, rather than write the Ar./Per. Shāh (king) as Śāh or, alternatively, change the Skt./Guj. *śabda* (word) to *shabda*, I have decided to retain both "ś" and "sh," although, in pronunciation, they have more or less the same phonetic value.

Nasals have been transliterated according to their classes; for instance, if an *anusvāra* is followed by the retroflex consonant "ṭ," it is transliterated "ṇ," or, if it is followed by the velar "kh," it is transliterated "ṅ." Many Hindi and Gujarati words end with a nasalized vowel. These are indicated with an "ṅ," as in *piyuṅ* (beloved) or *māthuṅ* (head). The *anusvāra* is transliterated as "ṃ" as in *siṃha*.

Whereas in Sanskrit, the short inherent vowel "a" in the last consonant of a word is usually sounded and transliterated, in Hindi and Gujarati, this final "a" frequently goes unpronounced; for instance, *das avatār* (Guj./Hin.) instead of *dasa avatāra* (Skt.), or *saṃsār* (Guj./Hin.) instead of *saṃsāra* (Skt.). An exception to this are words such as *mārga* or *śabda* which end in a conjunct consonant. Accordingly, the final short vowel of Gujarati and Hindi terms has been dropped except when the "a" vowel is pronounced. It should be noted, however, that, in the footnotes to the translations, when words from the *gināns* are cited, they are transliterated precisely as they occur in the Gujarati edition. Foreign words and names of places and languages that are in common English usage, such as Allah, Islam, Delhi, Sind, Baghdad, Punjabi, and so on, have not been transliterated.

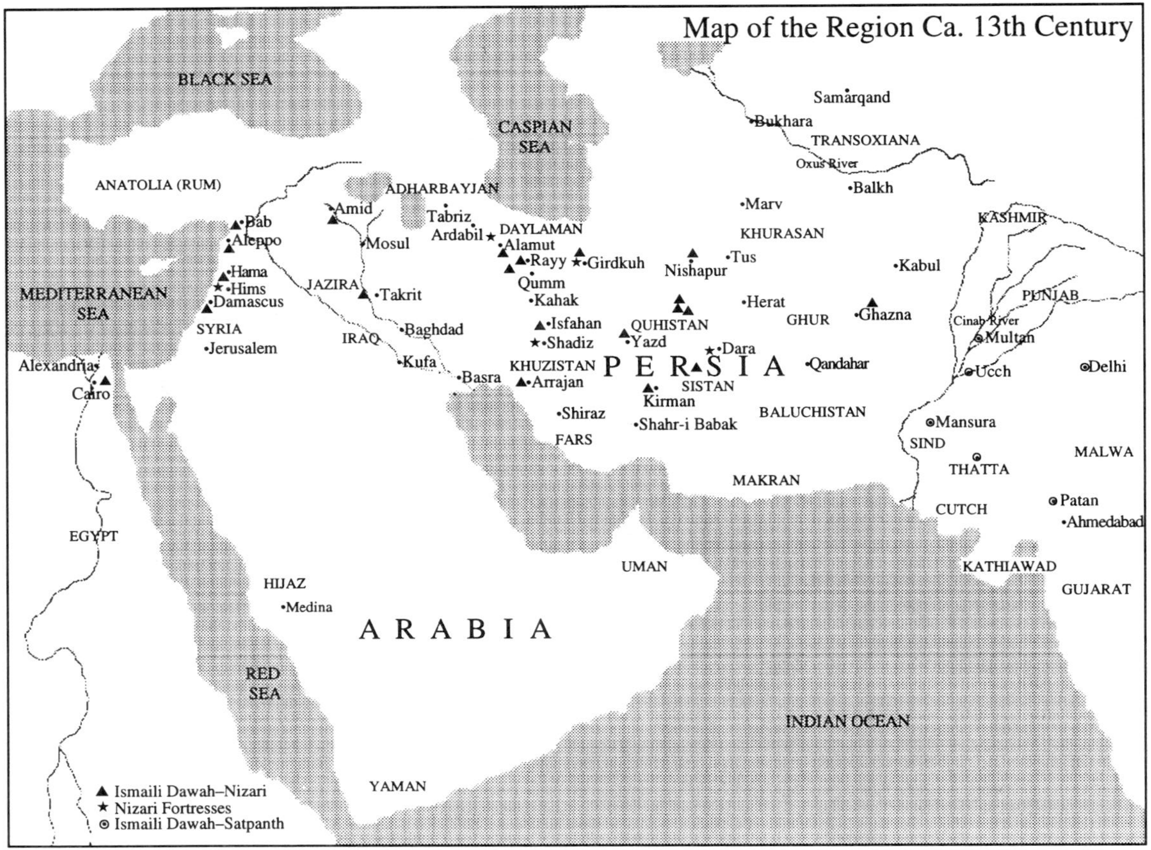
Map of the Region Ca. 13th Century
BLACK SEA
CASPIAN SEA
ANATOLIA (RUM)
MEDITERRANEAN SEA
ADHARBAYJAN
Amid
Tabriz
Ardabil
DAYLAMAN
Alamut
Rayy
Girdkuh
Qumm
Kahak
Bab
Aleppo
Mosul
Hama
Hims
Damascus
JAZIRA
Takrit
SYRIA
Jerusalem
IRAQ
Baghdad
Kufa
Basra
Alexandria
Cairo
EGYPT
Isfahan
Shadiz
KHUZISTAN
Arrajan
QUHISTAN
Yazd
PERSIA
SISTAN
Kirman
Shiraz
FARS
Shahr-i Babak
Samarqand
Bukhara
TRANSOXIANA
Oxus River
Balkh
Marv
KHURASAN
Tus
Nishapur
Herat
GHUR
Ghazna
Kabul
Dara
Qandahar
BALUCHISTAN
MAKRAN
UMAN
KASHMIR
PUNJAB
Cinab River
Multan
Ucch
Delhi
Mansura
SIND
THATTA
MALWA
CUTCH
Patan
Ahmedabad
KATHIAWAD
GUJARAT
HIJAZ
Medina
ARABIA
RED SEA
YAMAN
INDIAN OCEAN
▲ Ismaili Dawah–Nizari
★ Nizari Fortresses
⊙ Ismaili Dawah–Satpanth

Chronology of Events (C.E.)

632	Prophet Muḥammad dies: conflict over successor
661	ʿAlī ibn Ṭālib assassinated
711	Muḥammad ibn al-Qāsim conquers Sind
765	Jaʿfar al-Ṣādiq dies: split between followers of Ismāʿīl and Mūsā al-Qāẓim
883	*Dāʿī* al-Haytham sent to Sind
910	ʿUbayd Allāh al-Mahdī (d. 934) becomes first Fāṭimid caliph
941–958	Controversy over anonymous *dāʿī* in Sind during reign of al-Muʿizz (d. 975)
959	*Dāʿī* Jalam b. Shaybān secures Fāṭimid rule in Sind
976	Amir Sebüktigin begins conquest of India
998–1031	Maḥmūd Ghaznawī conquers Sind
1004	*Dāʿī* Dāʾūd b. Naṣr establishes defense alliance with Ānandpāl
1010	Caliph al-Qādir launches anti-Fāṭimid campaign
1010	Maḥmūd Ghaznawī massacres Ismāʿīlīs in Multān
1011–1025	Ismāʿīlī–Ḥabbārid alliance in al-Manṣūrah
1026	Maḥmūd Ghaznawī massacres Ismāʿīlīs in al-Manṣūrah: ends Arab rule in Sind
1019	Druze declare Fāṭimid caliph al-Ḥākim (d. 1021) divine
1051	Pro-Ismāʿīlī Sūmrahs wrest back Thaṭṭa in Lower Sind from Ghaznawids
1052	Caliph al-Qāʾim sponsors anti-Fāṭimid manifesto in Baghdad
1057	Fāṭimids gain brief control of Baghdad under pro-Fāṭimid Turk, al-Basāsīrī
1090	Ḥasan-i Ṣabbāḥ captures fortress of Alamūt in Daylamān

1092	Niẓām al-Mulk assassinated by an Ismāʿīlī *fidāʾī,* Abū Ṭāhir Arrānī
1094	al-Ghazālī's critique of the Ismāʿīlīs at the behest of Caliph al-Mustaẓhir
1094	al-Muṣtansir dies: split between followers of Nizār and al-Mustaʿli
1100	Nizārīs seize fortress of Girdkūh
1160–1175	Ghūrids attack and destroy Ismāʿīlī supporters in Sind
1164	Ḥasan ʿala Ḍhikrihi al-Salām (d. 1210) proclaims the Qiyāmah
1206–1236	Ismāʿīlī uprisings in Delhi during reign of Illtūtmish and his daughter, Raḍiyya
1210	Jalāl al-Dīn Ḥasan III publicly repudiates the Qiyāmah
1220	Beginning of the Mongol invasion of the Islamic empire
1256–1257	Rukn al-Dīn Khūr Shāh surrenders Alamūt followed by Mongol massacre
1275	Ismāʿīlīs briefly recapture Alamūt

PART I

CHAPTER 1

Gināns: A Wonderful Tradition

Coursing through cultures and time, tuneful verse has given immediate and moving expression to the human longing for the divine. Poetry strung on sweet melodies, sacred hymns and songs bear testimony to the religious life of the devout and to the sonorous and inspiring vocal artistry of saints and minstrels. Such is the *ginān* tradition of the Satpanth Khojahs, Indian successors of the Fāṭimid and Nizārī Ismāʿīlī sect of the Shīʿah Muslims. A heritage of devotional poetry, the *ginān* tradition is rooted in the musical and poetic matrix of Indian culture where, from village street to temple stage, the human voice sings in love divine. Traditionally recited during daily ritual prayers, *gināns* have been revered for generations among the Satpanth Ismāʿīlīs as sacred compositions (*śāstra*). The term *ginān* itself has a double significance: on the one hand, it means religious knowledge or wisdom, analogous to the Sanskrit word *jñāna;* on the other hand, it means song or recitation, which suggests a link to the Arabic *ganna* and the Urdu/Hindi *gānā,* both verbs meaning to sing.[1]

The present *imām* or spiritual head of the "Shia Imami Ismaili Muslims,"[2] His Highness Prince Karīm al-Ḥusaynī Āghā Khān IV, has plainly endorsed and recommended the *ginān* tradition many times to his followers in his directives (*farmān*). During his visit to Dacca in 1960, he described the *gināns* as a "wonderful tradition":[3]

> I feel that unless we are able to continue this wonderful tradition . . . we will lose some of our past which is most important to us and must be kept throughout our lives. Dacca, 17.10.1960

Four years later, he reminded his followers in Karachi of the unique importance of the tradition:

> Many times I have recommended to my spiritual children that they should remember the *Ginans,* that they should understand the meaning of these *Ginans* and that they should carry these meanings in their hearts. It is most important that my spiritual children from wherever they may come should, through the ages and from generation to generation, hold to this tradition which is so special, so unique and so important to my *jamat.* Karachi, 16.12.1964

The Satpanth Ismāʿīlīs regard the *gināns* as a sacred corpus of devotional and didactic poetry composed by their *dāʿīs* or *pīrs* (revered teachers and guides) who came to the Indian subcontinent between the eleventh and twentieth centuries C.E. to preach Ismāʿīlī Islam. Known as Hind and Sind by medieval Muslim geographers at the time, this area stretched from the highlands of Baluchistan to the Bay of Bengal and from Kashmir to Sri Lanka. The landmass is now divided into the nations of Afghanistan, Pakistan, India, Sri Lanka, and Bangladesh. The activities of the Ismāʿīlī *daʿwah* (mission) were mainly concentrated in the northwestern area of the subcontinent, including the provinces of Sind, Punjab, Multan, Gujarat and Mālwā, Kashmir, and present-day Rajasthan, Cutch, and Kāṭhiāwāḍ.

Ginās are thus extant in several Indian languages, among which Gujarati, Hindi, Punjabi, Sarāiki, and Sindhi are prominent. *Ginānic* vocabulary is also peppered with loan words from Persian, Arabic, and Sanskrit. The songs are rich in imagery and symbolism drawn from the spiritual and cultural milieu of the Indian subcontinent. Indeed, they have been so deeply influenced by the distinctive religious idiom and vocabulary of Hindu, Ṣūfī, and Tāntric traditions that their links to Fāṭimid or Nizārī Ismāʿīlism are not easily discerned. The entire *ginān* corpus consists of about one thousand works whose lengths vary from five to four hundred verses.[4] Less than a tenth of this sizable vernacular South Asian Muslim literature has been edited and translated, much less analyzed.

Ritual Performance

The performative context of the *ginās* and their intimate link to the ritual practices of Satpanth Ismāʿīlism demonstrate the central place of this tradition of hymns in the religious life of this South Asian Shīʿite Muslim community. *Ginān* recitation in the daily communal services of the Satpanth Ismāʿīlīs represents a long tradition of liturgical prayer. The religious meaning of these hymns is centered in their ritualized performance. Religious benefit is accrued by the actual vocalization or recitation of a *ginān,* and, thus, it is uncommon for a book of *ginān*s to be silently read in prayer. In the context of Satpanth practice, *ginān*s come to life when they are sung, and to sing a *ginān* is to pray. Singing is thus ritualized into worship, a characteristic feature of the religious setting of India. The *ginān* of the Ismāʿīlī *pīr* is the Satpanth counterpart of the Hindu *geet, bhajan,* or *kīrtan* and forms a continuum in the expressive and inspirational aspects of the North Indian Sant and Bhakti traditions in the context of which poetry, melody, and communal worship fuse to create religious ardor. In terms of their ritual role, *ginān*s function primarily as performative texts or songs inasmuch as the spirit of a *ginān* comes alive when it is being recited.[5]

According to the older religious specialists (*al-wāʿiẓīn*) within the community, the melodies (*rāg*) of *ginān*s were set by their composers to create the proper mood and disposition for prayer. The traditional view is that a *ginān* ought to be recited by heart truly to have effect because singing from a book places undue reliance on an external source and introduces an intermediary between worshipper and God. The most faithful rendition of *ginān*s was once considered to be found in oral memory, not in written manuscripts.[6] Hence, elderly *ginān* teachers of the community (*jamāʿat*) put great emphasis on the memorization of *ginān*s, arguing that, as ritual prayer and invocations, they should issue directly from the heart. Only when thus memorized and internalized would *ginān*s manifest the power of *śabda* (sacred word), a requirement analogous to that held for the efficacious recitation of the Qur'ān and the Vedas.

This unmediated link between the *ginān*s and the believer's heart is stressed, not only by an emphasis on memorization, but also on the correct receptivity or audition of the *ginān*s. A verse from a *ginān* attributed to Pīr Ṣadr al-Dīn describes what impact the recitation of *ginān*s may have on the heart of a devotee:

> *gīnāna bolore nīta nūre bharīyā,*
> *evā haiḍe tamāre harakhanā māejī*
>
> Recite *ginān*s and the self fills with Light!
> Thus will your hearts be made blissful.[7]

*Ginān*s are also believed to have this power to transform and to enlighten if properly attended to. Many stories in the tradition describe the miraculous conversion to Satpanth of Hindus, bandits, wild beasts, and pigeons upon hearing the sweet and melodious words of the *gināns*.[8] This belief in the transformative power of melodic recitation combined with the fervent chorus of congregational singing has been captured in a popular tale about the late Ismail Ganji. Reputedly an impious Ismāʿīlī of Junāgaḍh in Gujarat, he heard a verse of a *ginān* one evening in the *jamāʿat khānah* which so touched him that he burst into tears. Immediately, he repented his wayward ways and began a new life. So thoroughly did he reform himself that he was eventually appointed chief minister in the court of the ruler of Junāgaḍh.[9]

As an integral part of their communal worship, the recitation of *gināns* in the religious life of the Satpanth Ismāʿīlīs has served the multiple purposes of prayer, expressing devotion, and imparting the teachings of Satpanth. It is not surprising, therefore, that *gināns* are a deeply cherished tradition. G. Allana describes an attachment widely shared in the Satpanth Ismāʿīlī community for this tradition of devotional singing:

> Ever since my early childhood, I recall hearing the sweet music of the *ginans*. When I was a little boy, my mother, Sharfibai would lift me, put me in her lap and sing to me the *ginans* of Ismaili Pirs. She had a very serene and melodious voice. I did not understand, then, as to what they were all about. I loved my mother, as well as her enchanting voice. My initiation into the realms of poetry and music was through the *ginans*.[10]

Later on, Allana describes the stirring and uplifting mood created by his mother's predawn recitations of *gināns* in the *jamāʿat khānah* (hall of prayer or assembly):

> Everybody listened to her bewitching voice, singing a *ginan*. No other person, as is normally customary, dare join his or her voice with hers to sing in a chorus. . . . The fragrance of that spiritual atmosphere still lingers in my mind. . . . The weight of life's burdens dissolved.[11]

Gināns are recited daily in the *jamāʿat khānahs* during morning and evening services. Unlike the Ṣūfī practice of *samāʿ* or the Hindu *kīrtan*, however, *ginān* recitation is not (presently) accompanied by any musical instruments.[12] A member of the congregation, male or female, who knows how to recite *ginān*s is usually called upon by the *mukhī* (chief of ceremonies) to lead the recitation. Although singers may vary in how they embellish the tunes, in general, they follow a simple and uniform melody. In most instances, *ginān* tunes can be learned without difficulty, and singers rarely have any formal musical or voice training. However, good singers are easily identifiable by their melodious voices, tuneful renderings, and correct pronunciation. Beautiful recitation is praised and encouraged, and it is not uncommon for individual members of the congregation to express personally their feelings of appreciation to *ginān* reciters. On special festivals, reputed reciters who can sing a large repertoire of *ginān*s, and who have been noted for their moving delivery, are called upon to sing. These individuals, however, do not collectively constitute a special or distinct class of performers within the *jamā*ʿ*at* (congregation).[13]

While the recitation of a *ginān* constitutes a ritual in itself, *ginān*s also play a vital role in the conduct of other rites of worship performed by Satpanth Ismāʿīlīs in their *jamā*ʿ*at khānahs*. This intimate relationship to rituals is indicated by the classification and arrangement of *ginān*s found in several *ginān* manuscripts and printed editions. Specific *ginān*s are indicated for different times and types of prayer, for special occasions, and for various religious ceremonies. Evening prayers, for example, usually commence with *ginān*s that emphasize the importance of prayer during the auspicious hours of sunset.[14] Certain *ginān*s that dwell upon mystical themes are recommended for the *subhu sādkhak* (literally, the quester before dawn). These *ginān*s are recited before or after periods of meditation in the early morning hours. *Ventījo ginān*s are recited for the sake of supplication or petition for divine mercy. *Ghaṭpāṭ ginān*s accompany the ritual of drinking holy water, and a subcategory of these are sung when the water is actually sanctified. Similarly, select *ginān*s are recited at funeral assemblies, during the celebrations of Navrūz (the Persian New Year), and to commemorate the installation of the Imām of the time (*ḥāḍir imām*). Thus, a native taxonomy of *ginān*s has been developed within the tradition for specific occasions and ritual usage.[15]

The recitation of *ginān*s is not restricted to worship but permeates the personal and communal life of the Satpanth Ismāʿīlīs. Frequently, social functions and festive occasions commence with a recitation of a Qur'ānic verse followed by a few verses of a *ginān*. Various councils that administer to the religious and secular needs of the community may similarly begin their meetings with a *ginān* recitation. In addition to sponsoring *ginān* competitions to encourage beautiful recitation and correct pronunciation, the community occasionally holds "special concerts or *ginān mehfil/mushā'iro* . . . during which professional and amateur singers recite *gināns* to musical accompaniment."[16] With the arrival of the tape recorder in the modern world, many *mushā'iras* as well as individual singers have been recorded, and it is not uncommon to find prerecorded *ginān* audio tapes constantly replayed at a Satpanth Ismā'īlī's home to fill it with an atmosphere of devotion and invoke blessings (*barakah*) upon the household.

The significance of *gināns* in the Satpanth Ismā'īlī tradition derives from this nexus among devotional song, ritual worship, and sacred community.[17] The recitation of *gināns* marks off sacred time and space by creating a feeling of "majestic pathos and beauty,"[18] while it also gives expression to a sense of communal identity and fraternity. Binding its participants to an experience of listening, singing, and feeling, this performative aspect of the *ginān* tradition has played a crucial role in sustaining the spirit of the Satpanth tradition and its teachings.[19]

Historical Significance

Given its vital role in their daily religious life, clearly the modern Ismā'īlī community cannot be understood without a historical appreciation of the significance of the *ginān* tradition and of the evolution of Satpanth Ismā'īlism in the Indian subcontinent. Not only has this cumulative tradition been pivotal to the genesis of a unique South Asian Shī'ite Muslim subculture through the conversion and intermarriage of Ismā'īlī Muslims with Hindus, it has also sustained and preserved a small and generally beleaguered religio-ethnic community over a period of some eight centuries. Furthermore, the successful creation and establishment of the Satpanth Ismā'īlī community in the region of the Indian subcontinent has had economic ramifications that have helped firmly to secure the institutional foundations of the contemporary Ismā'īlī community. Despite this role, it is a disquieting fact that scholarship on this Shī'ah Muslim sect has yet to appreciate fully the religious and historical significance of Satpanth Ismā'īlism.

It has been rightly remarked that the Ismā'īlīs are "a tiny minority of a minority within the Muslim faith."[20] The sect is estimated to be about eight percent of the Shī'ah branch of Islam, itself comprising a mere fifth of the Muslim world. The Ismāʿīlīs form an international community of about fifteen million people spread across more than twenty-five countries. As a result of successive emigrations throughout their history, Ismāʿīlī communities are to be found in many different parts of the world.[21] There are three main subdivisions within the present worldwide Ismāʿīlī community based on ethnic origin, a common history, and cultural tradition: Middle Eastern, Central and East Asian, and South Asian. For many centuries, however, fearing persecution on account of their religious identity, the Ismāʿīlīs of Central and East Asia (Afghanistan, Tajikistan, and Chinese and Russian Turkestan) and parts of the Middle East (Syria, Iran, Lebanon, Iraq, and Kuwait) have lived in secrecy. Hence, to date, little is known about the regionally specific religious practices and traditions of these Ismāʿīlī communities.

Of the tributaries of successors of the Fāṭimid and Nizārī Ismāʿīlī tradition, the most visible is the Satpanth Ismāʿīlī community of the Indian subcontinent whose offspring are found in South Asia (Pakistan, India, Indonesia), Africa (Kenya, Tanzania, Uganda, West and South Africa) and the West (Europe, Britain, Canada, Australia, and the U.S.A.). Mainly descendants of the Khojahs (the name of the Indian converts to Satpanth),[22] these Ismāʿīlīs have played a prominant role in shaping modern Ismāʿīlī history, and in building up its numerous institutions. While this is slowly changing, Ismāʿīlīs of South Asian descent currently occupy the most influential and high-ranking positions of Ismāʿīlī regional and international councils, and constitute the main economic base of the community.

As political changes occur in Central and East Asia, Russia, and the Middle East, it has become increasingly apparent that, since the decline of the Fāṭimid empire, pockets of Ismāʿīlīs have managed quietly to survive in many discrete areas, and they have embraced over the centuries aspects of their cultural and linguistic environment.[23] However, the existence of this plurality of Ismāʿīlī traditions has yet to have an impact on the prevailing religious structures and mores of the modern Ismāʿīlī community. The prevalent ritual and devotional ethos found among the Ismāʿīlīs today in religious centers and prayer halls across the globe continues to be that of Satpanth Ismāʿīlīsm, the form of Ismāʿīlīsm that evolved in the Indian subcontinent.[24] From showcase Ismāʿīlī edifices, such as the Ismaili Centre at Cromwell Gardens in London and the monumental Burnaby *jamāʿat khānah* in Vancouver, to simpler places of prayer and communal gathering spread across East Africa, Pakistan, and the Indian subcontinent, with the exception of the central *duʿa* which is recited in Arabic, religious ceremonies are conducted mainly in Gujarati or Urdu and follow the practice of the Satpanth tradition. In a world marked by constant and dramatic changes, particularly in the last two centuries, this heritage of Satpanth Ismāʿīlī devotions and practices has provided a liturgical language of continuity, stability, and cohesion to an otherwise scattered and often oppressed religious minority.

As noted earlier, despite the formative historical role of the Satpanth tradition, it has barely received the scholarly attention it deserves. This book is but a small step towards remedying this situation. Too little is known about the foundations of this stream of Ismāʿīlī Islam and how it spread from the Middle East to the Indian subcontinent through the deft maneuvers of Ismāʿīlī *pīrs* or preacher-poets. To investigate this early period, I have focused attention on the *ginān*s attributed to one of the first preachers of the tradition, Pīr Shams. Next to an obscure figure who may have preceded him called Satgūr Nūr, Pīr Shams appears to have played a seminal role in the establishment of Ismāʿīlism in Sind. Part II of this work makes available for the first time a complete translation of an anthology of 106 *ginān*s attributed to this venerable Ismāʿīlī *dāʿī* of the twelfth century.[25]

In the first part of this book, I advance a theory of the origins of Satpanth that significantly revises current views concerning the formative period of the Satpanth Ismāʿīlī tradition. In general, the successful spread of Ismāʿīlī ideas in the Indian subcontinent has been viewed in terms of the literary activity and preaching of the *pīrs* which gave rise to the *ginān* tradition. That is, the Ismāʿīlī *pīrs* supposedly won converts to Ismāʿīlī teachings, which they called *satpanth* (true path), by conveying them in hymns using Hindu symbols and themes. However, a careful reconstruction of the historical period marking the entry of Ismāʿīlism into the Indian subcontinent and a cautious but trenchant reading of allusions preserved in the *ginān*s associated with the name of Pīr Shams strongly suggests that the origin of Satpanth Ismāʿīlism was a much more complex affair involving not just religious but also political realities. I will attempt to demonstrate that, in addition to the inspirational oral teachings of the *pīrs* embodied by the *ginān* tradition, a number of social and political factors played a crucial role in giving birth to the unique form of Ismāʿīlism called Satpanth.

CHAPTER 2

Satpanth Ismāʿīlism in the Context of Ismāʿīlī Studies: Marginal Territory

The Neglect of Satpanth Ismāʿīlism

Scholarship in Islamic Studies has made far greater advances in the study of Sunnī Islam than in that of the Shīʿah minority. In his bibliographic review of sources on Shīʿism, Wilferd Madelung observes that "scholarly literature on Shīʿism is still limited and uneven. There is no comprehensive survey of Shīʿism in its full range."[1] Whereas some progress has been made in this area in the last half century, the study of Islam continues, by and large, to be a study of its Sunnī interpretations and expressions. In recent times, when the Shīʿah have received scholarly attention, this has generally been in the context of political movements and of religious fundamentalism.

The problems of the study of Shīʿism originate, however, within the broader development of the history of Islam. Long-held misconceptions about the Shīʿah can be traced to early Sunnī works on heresies that propagated views of the Shīʿah as a radical, misguided, and heterodox branch of Islam.[2] For a long time, western scholars of the Islamic tradition accepted and presented as normative such Sunnī-centred interpretations of Islam. They also exaggerated and further embellished the latter's prejudiced accounts of the Shīʿah with their own fantasies. For this and other reasons, the field of Shīʿī studies still lags far behind Sunnī studies.

In particular, the Ismāʿīlīs, a subsect of the Shīʿah, have for centuries been the target of Sunnī and Twelver Shīʿī aspersion.[3] In his discussion of this problem, Marshall Hodgson says, "The world has usually heard about the Ismāʿīlīs from their enemies."[4] Consequently, Ismāʿīlism has suffered major problems of misrepresentation both within and outside Islam.[5] Accused from the beginning of *bid*ʿ*a* (innovation) and *ghuluww* (extremism) for their religious views, especially their doctrine of *imāmah,* Sunnī chroniclers commonly referred to the Ismāʿīlīs by the insulting epithet *mulḥid,* "a Muslim term of abuse for a religious deviant or heretic."[6] Since the mid-twentieth century, positive strides have been made to correct these misperceptions by scholars such as Wladimir Ivanow, Henri Corbin, and Marshall Hodgson who based their work on Ismāʿīlī sources and challenged older myths and fallacies.

This is the broader framework of a more pointed issue. While Shīʿism and the various subsects of the Shīʿah, including the Ismāʿīlīs, now have a place on the map of Islamic studies, there are still unusual gaps to be found in the area marked Ismāʿīlism. There is considerable discrepancy as to which periods or aspects of Ismāʿīlī history have drawn scholarly attention. What we find is that whereas the first half of Ismāʿīlī history is richly detailed, scholarship on its later periods tends to be very sketchy. Some scholars have argued that "meager sources" are responsible for these sharp contrasts of clarity and obscurity that exist with regard to its different phases of history.[7] Yet, as will be shown in the case of Satpanth Ismāʿīlism, for which primary sources are plentiful, even very recent overviews of Ismāʿīlī history have uniformly skimmed over or altogether ignored this phase.

Satpanth Ismāʿīlism: A Nonexistent Category?

The fact that the Satpanth period of Ismāʿīlī history has received negligible attention in Ismāʿīlī studies is especially puzzling because it spanned some eight centuries—well over half the life of the sect. It seems obvious that an appreciation of the broader movement of Ismāʿīlism is impossible without an adequate understanding of such a major period of its historical evolution, one, moreover, which forms the bedrock of its modern manifestation. Yet, key surveys of the history of the Ismāʿīlī sect essentially disregard or dismiss the Satpanth tradition.

To illustrate this fact, examination follows of four recent surveys of Ismāʿīlī history written by specialists in the field in the latter half of this century whose explicit purpose was to provide a comprehensive overview of the sect: Wladimir Ivanow's *Brief Survey of the Evolution of Ismailism* [1952][8]; an article coauthored by Aziz Esmail and Azim Nanji titled "The Ismāʿīlīs in History" in *Ismāʿīlī Contributions to Islamic Culture* [1977][9]; Wilferd Madelung's article on "Shiism: Ismāʿīlīyah" in the *Encyclopedia of Religion* [1986][10]; and finally, Farhad Daftary's recent volume, *The Ismāʿīlīs: Their History and Doctrines* [1990].[11] Notwithstanding the singular and praiseworthy contributions of each one of these scholars to the field of Ismāʿīlī studies as a whole, still one observes notable lacunae in their writings. To ascertain the place and treatment of Satpanth Ismāʿīlism in their works, we ask the following questions. Firstly, how much attention do they give to the Satpanth phase of Ismāʿīlī history? Secondly, where do they place it within the broader history of the sect? Finally, what is their interpretation and overall assessment of this phase?

Let us begin with Wladimir Ivanow, the pacesetter of Ismāʿīlī studies in this century. Four years before he wrote his *Brief Survey*, Ivanow published a seminal monograph on Satpanth Ismāʿīlism which, in many ways, set the framework and agenda for subsequent *ginān* scholarship.[12] In that monograph, Ivanow investigates the reasons for the success of the Ismāʿīlī *daʿwah* in the subcontinent and surveys the literature and religious practices of Satpanth. Observing that the greatest impediment to the spread of orthodox Islam "was connected with its conservatism of forms," he attributed the success of the Ismāʿīlī preachers to the following strategies:

> Either by intuition, or sound and clever reasoning, the Nizari Ismaili missionaries devised . . . methods depending on two principles. One was their bold tactics in separating the meaning and spirit of Islam from its hard Arabic shell. The other was their concentration of efforts on a few definite castes.[13]

His analysis of Ismāʿīlī preaching in the Indian subcontinent was to influence all subsequent interpretations of Satpanth literature, in particular, his theory that the Ismāʿīlī preachers, or *pīrs*, deliberately explained "the high ideals of Islam in the familiar terms of the ancestral religion and culture of the new converts,"[14] which in the case of the Satpanth Ismāʿīlīs was mainly Hinduism. Ivanow recognized this tactic in Satpanth literature and felt the *ginān* tradition had effectively constructed a

> bridge between Ismailism and Hinduism which permitted the new ideas to enter that entirely different world of Hindu mentality.[15]

Given his fairly extensive and penetrating analysis of Satpanth, it is astonishing to discover, therefore, that, in his ninety-one page

Brief Survey, Ivanow devotes but three pages to the subject of Ismāʿīlism in the Indian subcontinent.[16] Why, despite his obvious acquaintance with the scope and influence of this tradition, did he offer such an unusually terse discussion of Satpanth Ismāʿīlism in his subsequent survey of the history of the sect? This same question may be asked of Esmail and Nanji. Their doctoral dissertations on Satpanth Ismāʿīlism notwithstanding,[17] they offer a mere paragraph of comment to this subject in their thirty-page article, two-thirds of which is devoted to the period leading up to the Mongol invasion (1256 C.E.) and the fall of Alamūt. Similarly, Madelung offers a column of comment to the subject in his fourteen-page subsection on the "Ismailiyyah," and Daftary touches briefly on Satpanth under the dubious title "Indian Nizārism" in his otherwise monumental book, *The Ismāʿīlīs.*

All of these important surveys focus attention principally on the history of the Ismāʿīlīs until the Nizārī period and give scant coverage to the following eight centuries of the sect. This, despite the fact that several of these authors were intimately familiar with the history, primary sources, and religious practices of the so-called "post-Alamūt" Satpanth Ismāʿīlī tradition. Why then do their surveys not elaborate more fully on this period of Ismāʿīlī history? Should one deduce from this obvious neglect that the authors considered the Satpanth phase to be rather marginal to the overall history of the Ismāʿīlī sect? Certainly, their cursory treatment of this phase implies it was relatively unimportant.

This leads to the second question, namely, where do the scholars place Satpanth Ismāʿīlism within the broader development of the Ismāʿīlī sect? An analysis of how the above authors plot the development of Ismāʿīlī history and distinguish among its different periods and phases reveals another startling fact: Satpanth Ismāʿīlism has no formal place in their schemes. That is, there is no separate classification for the Satpanth phase that indicates clearly that it is a unique and distinctive period apart from, for example, the Nizārī period or the Fāṭimid period. This point can be illustrated by examining how the surveys characterize the different stages of Ismāʿīlī history.

Ivanow's stated purpose in his *Brief Survey* is to provide a general overview of the evolution of Ismāʿīlism and to help "the intending student of Ismailism to introduce some order or system into the material which he has to handle."[18] He introduces such an order or system by distinguishing among five main periods:

1. *Incubation period (632–909 C.E.):* "On which very little reliable information is available," but which led to the establishment of the Fāṭimids in Egypt.

2. *Fāṭimid period (909–1100 C.E.):* "when the Ismaili movement and its literature attained their full development."
3. *Alamūt period (1100–1400 C.E.):* "the period of life and death struggle, during which great concessions were made to popular tendencies."
4. *Anjudān period (1400–1600 C.E):* "a kind of renaissance . . . a revival of spirit and activity in the Persian Ismaili community."
5. *Modern period (1700–):* "characterised by accelerated cultural advancement and re-orientation."[19]

According to Ivanow, the main purpose of the Ismāʿīlīs in history was to realize the theocratic ideal at the heart of Shīʿism, namely, to restore the prerogative of the first Shīʿite *imām,* ʿAlī, and his successors to govern and guide the Muslim *ummah* through the divinely appointed institution of imāmate. He asserts that this Shīʿī aspiration to establish the *imām's* leadership over the *ummah* was a pragmatic and a feasible program during the formative period of Islam. However, as early attempts of the Shīʿah to secure the rights of their *imāms* to the caliphate failed repeatedly, a key Shīʿī theme emerged, namely, the concept of the *mahdī* or messiah *imām* who would rise to vindicate the Shīʿah and fill "the earth with equity and justice."[20]

In Ivanow's judgment, the climax of the Ismāʿīlī movement was attained during the Fāṭimid period when "the grand dream of a theocratic Islam might well have succeeded."[21] Moreover, the reign of the Fāṭimids was a victory not only in political terms; Fāṭimid patronage of trade, learning, and culture forged a cultural hegemony that was to have a lasting impact on Islamic civilization. Given these achievements, Ivanow singles out this period to represent the peak of Ismāʿīlī history. For various reasons, however, the Fāṭimid venture ultimately failed. The Nizārīs, one of its beneficiary subgroups, had already established a foothold in northern Persia, and continued to cherish the dream of an Ismāʿīlī state under the sovereignty of the *imām.* Spearheaded by Ḥasan ibn al-Ṣabbāḥ from the fortress of Alamūt, the Nizārīs were able to rally crucial support for the Ismāʿīlī cause. They sustained a social and political struggle against the powerful Saljūqs for 160 years,

> by the end of which there were all the signs of their having won the day legalizing their position in the world of Islam. It was only the overwhelming calamity of the Mongol invasion which swept them away.[22]

This was the second moment in their history, according to Ivanow, when the Ismāʿīlīs might have succeeded in attaining their theocratic aspirations. However, the Mongol destruction of Alamūt in 1256 C.E. marked a turning point, and, for all practical purposes, he claims that the Ismāʿīlī political program was put to rest, and thenceforth, the Ismāʿīlī movement became passive and apolitical. It went underground, adopted *taqīyah,* and forked into various, independent streams that developed their own local histories and traditions.

Undoubtedly, the excitement of Ismāʿīlī history for Ivanow is the sect's resolute and repeated attempts to assert the political sovereignty of its *imāms.* His historical narrative is driven by the sect's revolutionary enterprise, and this is the defining benchmark for his assessment of the course of Ismāʿīlī history. Given the importance placed on the sect's insurgent political career, which he assumes to be its raison d'être, Ivanow pays greatest attention in his book to the Fāṭimid and Alamūt periods and heaps praise on the Fāṭimids for their military, intellectual, and cultural achievements.

Esmail and Nanji's article similarly highlights the eminence of the Fāṭimid period of Ismāʿīlī history noting both the political successes of the Fāṭimids and their "most brilliant and outstanding" intellectual achievement.[23] Like Ivanow, the authors also divide their discussion of Ismāʿīlī history into five periods (the formative period, the period of Fāṭimid rule, the Ismāʿīlīs of Alamūt, the post-Alamūt period, and the modern period), except their scheme subsumes Ivanow's Anjudān period under the heading "post-Alamūt." Again, the criterion for distinguishing among various periods of Ismāʿīlī history is its political fate. Thus, for instance, both the studies by Ivanow and by Esmail and Nanji employ the term "Alamūt" rather than the term "Nizārī" to refer to Ismāʿīlism before the Mongol invasion. The name of the fortress that housed the central headquarters of scattered Nizārī Ismāʿīlī cells of resistance in northern Persia during the eleventh and thirteenth centuries, Alamūt was a majestic symbol of Ismāʿīlī power.

The categories used by Madelung in his subsection on the "Ismāʿīlīyah" in his article on "Shiism" to designate the major periods of Ismāʿīlism appear to define the total history of the sect in terms of its accomplishments during the Fāṭimid period. His tripartite division of Ismāʿīlī history into pre-Fāṭimid, Fāṭimid, and post-Fāṭimid implies that the Fāṭimid period was the benchmark and centerpiece of Ismāʿīlism. Madelung's scheme is a fine example of how scholarship can inadvertently normatize and privilege a particular expression within the historical diversity of a religious movement. The prefixes "pre-" and "post-" imply that Fāṭimid Ismāʿīlism is to be taken as the focal point in relation to which the rest of Ismāʿīlism ought to be assessed. This categorization of Ismāʿīlī history presents the Fāṭimid period as the axis and climax of the Ismāʿīlī movement. The question is not whether the achievements of the Fāṭimid period were remarkable, but whether scholars may use it as the defining point of Ismāʿīlī history.

In this respect, Ivanow's scheme is conceptually sharper and respects the uniqueness and integrity of each phase. Although Ivanow judges the intellectual achievements of the Fāṭimid phase more favorably than the rest, still he insists that each period of Ismāʿīlī history ought to be examined and assessed within its own historical context and not in comparison to another phase. According to Madelung's scheme, the tacit yardstick for understanding Ismāʿīlī history is the Fāṭimid period, thus fostering the view that the Fāṭimids represent the normative core of Ismāʿīlism.

As the most recent, thorough, and carefully documented discussion of the subject, Daftary's study of Ismāʿīlism is of special interest since, as he himself points out, modern strides in Ismāʿīlī studies have at last made it "possible to convey an overall view of the evolution of Ismāʿīlism."[24] In his introduction, Daftary offers the criteria he has used in order to draw distinctions among various phases of Ismāʿīlī history. Asserting that, while it is difficult to select any specific order of phases in the history of Ismāʿīlīs,

> it is, however, possible on the basis of a mixture of chronological, doctrinal, geographical as well as literary and ethnological considerations, to distinguish five phases, some running parallel to others.[25]

He does not, however, elaborate on these criteria in his discussions of different phases. In actual fact, his book treats Ismāʿīlism strictly in terms of its chronological development and includes, where appropriate, detailed discussions of the origin and development of its major doctrines. The stated purpose of his book is "to cover all the major phases and events in the development of Ismāʿīlism."[26] Accordingly, he schematizes Ismāʿīlī history as follows: Early Ismāʿīlism (c. 700–900 C.E.); Fāṭimid Ismāʿīlism (c. 900–1100 C.E.); Mustaʿlian Ismāʿīlism (c. 1100–present); Nizārī Ismāʿīlism of the Alamūt period (c. 1100–1256 C.E.); and post-Alamūt Nizārī Ismāʿīlism (c. 1250–present). In addition to the Nizārīs of Alamūt, Daftary also discusses at length the history of the Mustaʿlians, the other stream of

Ismāʿīlism that followed the split after the Fāṭimid Imām, Mustanṣir bi'llāh (d. 1094 C.E.). Otherwise, his scheme repeats the same general pattern as those of Ivanow and Esmail and Nanji. The following diagram summarizes the schemes that have been discussed:

Schemes of Ismāʿīlī History

C.E.	Ivanow	Esmail/Nanji	Madelung	Daftary
632	Incubation	Formative	pre-Fāṭimid	Early Ismāʿīlism
700				
800				
909	Fāṭimid	Fāṭimid	Fāṭimid	Fāṭimid
1000				
1094	Alamūt	Alamūt	post-Fāṭimid	Nizārī/Mustaʿlian
----- 1256	--------------	post-Alamūt	----------------	post-Alamūt
1300				Early
1400	Anjudān			Anjudān
1500				
1600				
1700				
1800	Modern	Modern		Modern
1900				
Present				

What do these schemes reveal? If the assumption is that the Ismāʿīlī venture is a political movement rooted in an attempt to establish a Shīʿī theocracy under the *imām,* then clearly those phases of its history that manifested vigorous political activity would receive the most attention. This much is evident from the above chart. Common to all four surveys is the fact that post-Alamūt Ismāʿīlism is dealt with more or less as one major phase. While it is the longest phase, it is given the least coverage, thus leaving a major part of Ismāʿīlī history obscure. Madelung's tripartite division of Ismāʿīlī history lumps into one category the entire period from 1094 C.E. up to the present, effectively discounting the discrete and complex course of Ismāʿīlī history since the Fāṭimids under the label "post-Fāṭimid Ismāʿīlism."

As we probe into this issue of the mapping of Ismāʿīlī history, what should by now be conspicuous by its absence is the category of Satpanth Ismāʿīlism. Despite the authors' cognizance of this historical phase and its complexities, not one of them identifies Satpanth as a distinctive period of Ismāʿīlī history in their surveys. Even Ivanow, the first scholar to focus academic attention on the subject with his monograph on Satpanth,[27] fails to recognize it as a unique phase preceding and running parallel to the Anjudān period. All the authors encrypt Satpanth Ismāʿīlism under the "post-Alamūt" category and render it invisible. We must conclude by this exclusion of Satpanth in their formal schemes that the authors did not regard it to be of much importance to the broader development of the Ismāʿīlī sect. To repeat, this assessment is difficult to grasp given the fact that, not only is the Satpanth period one of the longest continuous phases in Ismāʿīlī history, but it also forms the bedrock of the modern Ismāʿīli community.

The final question, namely, the authors' interpretation and assessment of Satpanth, will give us a few clues as to why Satpanth has not been highlighted in their schemes of Ismāʿīlī history. Acknowledging the long history of Satpanth in his monograph on the subject,[28] Ivanow explains that Ismāʿīlism established itself in India by making use of doctrines that "formed a transition between Ismailism, Sufism and Hinduism."[29] This comment should be read in the context of Ivanow's view that, after the Fāṭimid period, Ismāʿīlī theology deteriorated:

> When the Fatimid organization collapsed, popular exuberant enthusiasm swept away the results of three long centuries of theological work, and the "Great Resurrection" in Alamūt sanctioned a new, popular version of Ismailism.[30]

Drawing a distinction between religion in an urban versus a rural, agrarian setting, Ivanow held that, during the middle period of the Islamic world (ninth to twelfth centuries), the more literate, educated part of society was concentrated in urban areas. By contrast, "in the vast tracts of rural and tribal territories such men [of learning] were very rare,"[31] and so the outlook of the peasant populations was generally narrow, unsophisticated, and susceptible to superstitious beliefs.

Thus, following nineteenth-century distinctions between rational–classical as opposed to superstitious–popular traditions, Ivanow shared the bias that philosophical religious texts were culturally superior to oral tradition, mythology, and folklore. Accordingly, he drew attention to the dual nature of Ismāʿīlī philosophy, even in the Fāṭimid period, such as its "remarkable sobriety of tone and reasoning," on the one hand, which coexisted with "speculations of the most fantastic kind," on the other. He then traced these contrasts to the opposition between town and village. "This contrast between the highest urban culture of the time and the illiteracy of the masses," especially in Fāṭimid times, is used to explain the development of two parallel streams of speculation, that of the state-affiliated literati and that of the populists who mingled with simple folk.[32]

His judgment of Satpanth as "popular" Ismāʿīlism was based on speculations on how such doctrines might develop in rural contexts. Ivanow notes that, while the uneducated "man in the village" would have had little interest in abstruse philosophy, his religious enthusiasm would easily have warmed to ideas that some extraordinary mysteries were being revealed to him. "What possibly fertilized for him such speculations was a variety of home-made simplifications and beliefs which could substantially modify the original doctrines."[33] He further explains that these "home-made simplifications" were the work of the "small fry," the rank-and-file Ismāʿīlī missionaries who, lacking the talent "to conceive and develop original and extensive schemes,"[34] instead made use of older, half-remembered religious ideas and infused them with Ismāʿīlī content. In other words, they created a potpourri of syncretic religious doctrines that succeeded in fueling popular religious sentiment.

Inasmuch as it drew attention to the question of the influence of urban versus rural contexts on the development of two parallel streams of religious expression in Ismāʿīlism, Ivanow's analysis was important. However, his low opinion of the culture of the masses adversely colored his otherwise insightful exposition and limited his appreciation of the so-called populist's own idiom. A case in point is his explanation of the missionary's role as a purveyor of populist notions alongside philosophical Fāṭimid doctrines:

> The rank and file Ismaili missionaries who were in direct contact with the masses probably experienced great difficulty in standing between these two opposed ideologies. . . . It is most probably for this reason, that we find concessions to popular belief in the works by less qualified authors.[35]

Thus, while favoring the rational and systematic religious discourse that flourished under the patronage of the Fāṭimids, Ivanow thought that the Nizārī period sanctioned "concessions" and a populist trend that inevitably led to syncretistic, haphazard, and corrupt doctrinal formulations. Satpanth Ismāʿīlism, which he felt indiscriminately mixed Ṣūfī, Hindu, and Ismāʿīlī ideas, was thus seen as the culmination of this process of deterioration in intellectual rigor. His scorn for the peasant mentality that he thought nourished the

Satpanth tradition is obvious in his skepticism regarding its literature's historical reliability:

> This particularly applies to Satpanth with its Hinduistic basis. The Indian mind is notoriously unhistoric, and its polymeric and syncretic perception is aggravated by intense hyperbolism in expression.[36]

Undermining his own judgment of the lax nature of the work of the Ismāʿīlī preachers, Ivanow concedes in the same monograph that the Ismāʿīlī *pīrs* of India solved "with remarkable tact and intuition" their challenge of "rendering the process of transition from Hinduism to Islam . . . as easy and smooth as possible."[37] Interestingly, despite their intellectual limitations, they were able to lay "the foundation of a new cultural group which in itself bore the seeds of further great progress."[38] Having reached this significant conclusion, Ivanow still failed to give due place to the Satpanth phase in his *Brief Survey*. One can only speculate that his cynical view of Satpanth as the final stage of the deterioration of Ismāʿīlī doctrines since the Fāṭimid period was responsible for this neglect.

In his mere column of comment on Ismāʿīlism in the Indian subcontinent, Madelung reiterates Ivanow's judgment concerning the lack of theological substance or philosophical refinement in the Satpanth tradition. He curtly dismisses its literary heritage of *gināns* with the following remark:

> They include hymns, religious and moral exhortation, and legendary history of the pirs and their miracles, but contain no creed or theology. Islamic and Hindu beliefs, especially popular Tantric ones, are freely mixed. While idol worship is rejected, Hindu mythology is accepted.[39]

The assertion that disparate ideas have been "freely mixed" in the *gināns* thus yielding a careless syncretism is premature. In studies of two major works attributed to Pīr Shams, the *Garbīs* and the *Brahma Prakāśa,* I have found the contrary to be the case.[40] On careful analysis of the *gināns,* one detects purposeful connections and a creative interdependence of Hindu and Islamic ideas. The characterization of *ginān* literature as a hodgepodge of syncretic and folk ideas "highly coloured by Hinduism"[41] helps to make it appear to be far less appealing as a focus of scholarly study than the theologically rigorous and "pure" Ismāʿīlī texts of the Fāṭimid period.

Esmail and Nanji's article dispenses with Satpanth in a mere paragraph, and it is unclear why these authors did not elaborate on a period of Ismāʿīlī history whose significance their own previous research clearly recognizes. Their decision to curtail a discussion of Satpanth may be due to its association with Hinduism, an issue that has sparked controversy for the modern Ismāʿīlī community as it attempts to dispel doubts regarding its fundamentally Islamic identity.[42] In their only comment on Satpanth Ismāʿīlism, the authors skirt any explicit mention of Hinduism. Rather, they acknowledge the influence of Hindu ideas in the development of this phase of Ismāʿīlī history indirectly, as follows:

> The doctrines contained in the *ginān* literature constitute a markedly Nizārī and mystical vision of Islam. In addition, the cosmological myths and eschatological ideas prevalent in India were utilized by the pīrs in order to provide a locally intelligible expression to fundamental Ismāʿīlī principles.[43]

The above interpretation suggests a seamless continuity between Nizārī and Satpanth ideas, so that Satpanth appears to be nothing less than Nizārī Ismāʿīlism couched in Indian myths. This view is highly problematic as it obscures the fact that the Satpanth phase of Ismāʿīlī history represents a truly distinctive linguistic, cultural, and religious milieu from the preceding Arabo-Persian and Middle Eastern tradition. The assertion that Ismāʿīlī *pīrs* who went to preach in the subcontinent *translated* Nizārī doctrines using "cosmological myths and eschatological ideas prevalent in India" deserves to be carefully tested and critiqued. As a sect with a history of creative responses to context, it is equally possible that the *pīrs evolved* a religious sensibility in the Indian environment that addressed Ismāʿīlī aspirations from *within* the context of a profoundly different cultural and spiritual milieu.

Esmail and Nanji also present Satpanth as being part of a more mystically oriented, post-Alamūt trend in Ismāʿīlī history:

> Henceforth, the individual search for inner, spiritual transformation received increasing emphasis in the articulation of the faith. . . . In India, the Ginān literature exhibited the same quest for mystical illumination . . . and inner mastery.[44]

From this statement, one might infer that the main feature of Satpanth Ismāʿīlism is an emphasis upon an inner, mystical recognition of the *imām's* spiritual reality. What becomes obscured by this assertion, therefore, are those facets of the Satpanth tradition that have evolved out of a Hindu ethos, namely, communal worship, religious narrative, a song tradition, and the complex ritual practices of Satpanth Ismāʿīlism.

In his two-page summary of the major phases of Ismāʿīlī history at the beginning of his book, Daftary identifies the last period as:

> The post-Alamūt phase of Nizārī Ismāʿīlism, from the second half of the 7th/13th century to the present time. This covers three distinct periods; namely, the obscure early post-Alamūt, the so-called Anjudān, and the modern periods.[45]

Beyond the general inadequacy of the category "post-Alamūt Nizārīsm," note his complete lack of reference to the Satpanth tradition. He merely adds the vague comment, "Later, the Nizārīs achieved new successes in the Indian subcontinent and Central Asia,"[46] which barely acknowledges the long and vital tradition of the Satpanth Ismāʿīlis. As the most comprehensive and duly acclaimed treatment of Ismāʿīlī history, Daftary's voluminous work presumably had the benefit of the small but growing academic writing on the subject of Satpanth. Yet, his work fails to reflect the current state of scholarship on Satpanth Ismāʿīlism or Ismāʿīlism in the Indian subcontinent.[47]

Particularly perplexing is Daftary's use of the awkward phrase "post-Alamūt Indian Nizārīsm" to refer to Satpanth Ismāʿīlism, although he himself states that Ismāʿīlism in India was self-identified as Satpanth or True Path.[48] There are two problems with this odd designation. Firstly, it suggests again an unequivocal and seamless continuity between Nizārī and Satpanth Ismāʿīlī ideas which, as cautioned earlier, is questionable. It is not clear to what extent, if at all, "Nizārism" is taught by Satpanth Ismāʿīlism in the manner that is implied by the term "Indian Nizārism." Secondly, by calling Satpanth Ismāʿīlism "Indian Nizārīsm," the originality and particularity of the Satpanth tradition is compromised. Even a modest exposure to Satpanth literature reveals that Nizārī Ismāʿīlism and Satpanth Ismāʿīlism do not share a similar religious language and symbol system in the way that Fāṭimid and Nizārī Ismāʿīlism do. By referring to Satpanth as "Indian Nizārism," Daftary follows Esmail and Nanji in assuming that Satpanth Ismāʿīlism is a straightforward substitute for or translation of Alamūt Nizārism.

As for his opinion of Satpanth literature, he iterates the views of

Ivanow and Madelung, namely, that its philosophical or theological contribution to Ismāʿīlī thought was minimal. He mentions that, while the "Indian Nizārīs" developed their own distinctive literary heritage, the *ginān*s, "they did not produce any elaborate theological or philosophical treatises nor did they translate the Persian and Arabic texts of other Nizārī communities into their own languages."[49] For one thing, this observation quite undoes his designation of Satpanth as "Indian Nizārism" for it is true that whereas the Ṭayyibī Ismāʿīlīs in India (the Fāṭimids were split into the Nizārī and Ṭayyibī sects) continued to develop a theological tradition inherited from their Yamanī ancestors, there is little linguistic or intellectual continuity between the Satpanth–Nizārī or Satpanth–Fāṭimid religious and literary expressions.

Reasons for the Neglect of Satpanth Ismāʿīlism

Evidently then, the history of scholarship in Ismāʿīlī studies has been partial to certain areas. Why do these otherwise seminal surveys of Ismāʿīlī history share a common disregard for the Satpanth phase? It is important to emphasize that this critique in no way means to suggest that scholarly attention to Fāṭimid or Nizārī Ismāʿīlī history be curtailed, nor that these phases are not intrinsically interesting and worthy of detailed study. Indeed, they are, and, given the paucity of research on Shīʿism and Ismāʿīlism in general, scholarship on any aspect of their history and development is vital. Rather, the main purpose here is to draw attention to a problem *within* the field of Ismāʿīlī studies and to make plain that study in this field has failed to focus upon certain key areas. In particular, it is meant to expose the neglect that prevails in the area of Satpanth Ismāʿīlī studies even at the semantic level of recognizing it as an integral category.

As the preceding analysis has shown, surveys of Ismāʿīlī history and doctrine tend to focus on the period leading up to the thirteenth century as if no significant developments took place in the sect thereafter. Why has this later period, and specifically, the Satpanth tradition that emerged and was elaborated during it, been treated as a rather marginal part of the Ismāʿīlī movement? How can we explain the scholarly dismissal of such a major period of Ismāʿīlī history?

The irregular course of Ismāʿīlī studies may be rooted in a hidden set of assumptions which have hindered or retarded a critical appreciation of the Satpanth tradition. I suggest that an interpretive grid of questionable premises and dichotomous thinking has governed and constrained the orientation of scholars towards their materials: orthodox versus heterodox, classical versus folk, and political versus religious.

Much has already been written about the bias in scholarship, especially in Islamic studies, towards the so-called higher or classical expressions of Islamic civilization as against its local, folk, or popular forms.[50] Older studies of folk Muslim practices and traditions for the most part manifest a superior and contemptuous attitude toward popular culture, which was perceived to be an aberration of a purer tradition for consumption by "commoners," that is, those low in intellect and high in passion and fantasy. The interest in popular culture as a genuine and vital social expression is a relatively recent development in Islamic scholarship and has manifested itself under the rubric of Islamic expressions in local contexts. This renewed interest in local, vernacular Islamic formations (once pejoratively called "folk" Islam) has been positively influenced by the perspectives of cultural anthropology and the social sciences, and there now exists a range of valuable studies of indigenous, popular Islamic expressions.[51]

By and large, the agenda of Islamic studies, in common with other religious specializations that grew out of orientalist scholarship, has been dictated by the cultural productions of the elite class, the so-called *ashrāf,* thus privileging the "great" traditions over the "little" traditions of the *ʿawāmm* or common folk. This situation is evidenced by the greater attention and volume of scholarship devoted to the classical heritage of Islam, undoubtedly a legacy of eighteenth- and nineteenth-century ideas that the "classical" was superior and that "beginnings" embraced the essence of a tradition. These notions have since been criticized and revised, and modern scholarship on Islam, particularly under the influence of the history of religions' perspective, avoids such characterizations. Nevertheless, interpretations still exist that consider the classical, textual traditions of Islam as normative, the standard by which all other Islamic traditions must be measured, and, consequently, local Muslim traditions are condemned as mere adulterations.

It is important to note that this differential judgment of classical and folk not only exists in scholarship but is also native to thinking within Islam. Scholars often uncritically accept moral judgments made by particular Muslim communities about which Muslim theology or practice is sound and which is corrupt. These internal evaluations that label some traditions as pure and others as impure are polemical, and their purpose is to define hierarchies and to establish patterns of authority. Truth claims legitimizing certain traditions and rejecting others serve the interests of specific groups and help to perpetuate them within a social system. In other words, claims of religious orthodoxy and authenticity are intimately related to assertions of power. Thus, when scholars tacitly recommend such claims, they may inadvertently collude with internal polemical voices that lay claims to truth and authority within their specific religious groupings.

The classical–folk dichotomy has had particularly negative implications for the study of Satpanth Ismāʿīlism. Given that Satpanth literature is written in Indian vernaculars and not in the classical languages of Islam, this fact automatically relegates it to a subordinate position under the categories of "folk," "popular," and "syncretic." Unlike Turkish or Urdu, which enjoy more prestige as semiclassical languages, the Indian dialects used in the *ginān*s, whose form, style, and symbolism are folkloric, are felt to be lesser vehicles for literary and intellectual expression. Further, the literature draws from several sources, which fact compromises its "purity." Its mythical, didactic, and ritual content locate it centrally within the popular religious movements of India. As an oral and folk tradition, Satpanth Ismāʿīlism is thus easily dismissed as a "hodge-podge," "superstitious," and "historically unreliable" tradition.

The classical versus folk dichotomy also creates a linguistic bias that has adversely affected scholarship on Ismāʿīlism (and Islam) inasmuch as Arabic and Persian sources have been regarded as the more sophisticated and authentic writings, whereas literatures in other languages are deemed to be of lesser consequence. It is this kind of linguistic prejudice that is transparent in Daftary's criticism that the Khojahs neither learned nor attempted to translate their Fāṭimid or Nizārī heritage.[52] To judge as a shortcoming the fact that they did not learn Arabic is to suggest that Ismāʿīlī literatures in Arabic and Persian stand as the singular authentic sources of Ismāʿīlī doctrines.

This is the kind of problem that emerges when one phase of Ismāʿīlī (or Islamic) history is used as a yardstick for another. Such ahistorical comparison can lead and often has led to some difficult and fruitless conclusions. For instance, Ivanow stresses that the Fāṭimid philosopher-*dāʿī* was intellectually and morally superior to the Satpanth's miracle-working *pīr*; and both Madelung and Daftary join him in his view that the *ginān*s are devoid of cosmological or theological doctrines so amply found in Fāṭimid Ismāʿīlism. However, the urbane textual and intellectual achievements of Fāṭimid Ismāʿīlism belong to a particular context and set of circumstances as do the oral and poetic achievements of Satpanth Ismāʿīlism. The question is not which one of these is inferior or superior, but what light historical scholarship can shed on understanding religious data in relation to their specific settings.

Also linked to the classical–folk dichotomy are assumptions concerning what is orthodox and heterodox within Ismāʿīlism. As in the larger Islamic context, so in the Ismāʿīlī context, whatever departs from the Arabo-Persian norm inadvertently adds up to heterodoxy. This would appear to be a particularly suitable judgment of the Satpanth Ismāʿīlī tradition given its apparent Hindu content. What could be farther away from the strict iconoclasm of orthodox Islam than congenial habitation with the mythical whimsy of Hinduism?! From this perspective, an Islamic sect with Hindu influences must, by definition, be suspect and regarded as heterodox, syncretic, and corrupt.

Accordingly, to explain the somewhat awkward existence of Satpanth Ismāʿīlism, Ismāʿīlī scholars have regularly interpreted it to have been an expedient means of conversion (and thus tolerated temporarily). That is, they have argued that Satpanth was a suitable and necessary strategy assumed for the purpose of conversion. While it may be true that the strategy of religious accommodation and syncretism was an important factor in the etiology of Satpanth, the problem with this interpretation is that it divests the tradition of its religious authenticity. To interpret Satpanth mainly as a clever conversion strategy is to take away from it the religious meaning and social implications it has held for those who have practiced it for some eight centuries. Precisely such mismeasure has provided justification for the neglect of Satpanth studies within the sect's own research institutions. In recent times, it has become increasingly difficult for scholars both within and outside the Ismāʿīlī community to gain access to Satpanth Ismāʿīlī materials. This trend is likely to continue given the sect's contemporary interest in locating and asserting its identity more centrally within the larger Muslim *ummah*.

Also key to the orthodox versus heterodox problem is the question of power. To what extent does the political success of the Fāṭimids add emphasis to the assertion that their literature was "classical," their doctrines "orthodox," and their culture the "epitome" of the Ismāʿīlī venture? How much of the prestige of these achievements derives from the political grandeur of the Fāṭimid period? As we have seen, scholars have repeatedly emphasized the political ambitions of the Ismāʿīlīs, as the rise of Shīʿism was tied to the question of authority and leadership over the Muslim *ummah*. In this light, the Shīʿah have often been depicted as a sect focused on revolt, revolution, and the subversion of Sunnī orthodoxy. This characterization is even more emphatically applied to the Ismāʿīlīs who tenaciously held on to their ambitions to secure the claims of the imāmate. Therefore, perhaps it should not be surprising that the highest point of Ismāʿīlī history has been identified with those moments when the imāmate could exercise political authority.

The determination of the key phases of Ismāʿīlī history according to the political fortunes of the Ismāʿīlī sect becomes transferred, with unfortunate consequences, onto the broader developments within the sect, including its literature and thought. Hence, the doctrinal development of the sect is shown to follow a course parallel to the rise and fall of Ismāʿīlī power. Furthermore, since the appeal of Ismāʿīlī history lies primarily in those periods when it came closest to attaining a theocratic ideal, periods when the sect appears to have been politically dormant have drawn less attention. Thus, scholarly emphasis on the political aspects of Ismāʿīlism may help to explain the predominance of research on Fāṭimid and Nizārī Ismāʿīlism and the comparative neglect of the seemingly more quiescent phases such as Satpanth Ismāʿīlism. Undoubtedly, such a focus on the political career of the Ismāʿīlī movement has compromised a deeper appreciation of its religious history. It is worth asking whether these surveys of Ismāʿīlism would have ended so abruptly in the thirteenth century had their schemes been determined, not by the quest for an Ismāʿīlī state, but by the changing shape of Ismāʿīlī religious doctrines.

This then is the grid of interlocked assumptions that has contributed to setting the agenda for Ismāʿīlī studies. In conclusion, it appears that Satpanth Ismāʿīlism has been marginalized within Ismāʿīlī studies because (a) it is a *folk* Islamic tradition, (b) it is a *heterodox* development within Ismāʿīlism, and (c) it appears to have little *political* interest. These factors combined have rendered Satpanth, in the minds of some scholars, to be rather inconsequential to the larger picture of Ismāʿīlī history and, hence, undeserving of sustained and carefully focused scholarly attention.

CHAPTER 3

Rethinking the Emergence and Significance of Satpanth Ismāʿīlism

*Ginān*s in the Courts: Beginnings of a Historical Study of Satpanth

The historical study of the *ginān* literature began in the present so-called modern period of Ismāʿīlism. The start of this phase is marked by the transference of the residence of Āghā Khān I, the 46th Imām, Ḥasan ʿAlī Shāh, from Persia to India in 1845 C.E. The *imām's* move brought to a head tensions within the Satpanth (also referred to here as Khojah) community that led to three major court battles: the Sarjun Mīr case in 1848 C.E.; the Khojah case in 1866 C.E.; and the Hājī Bībī case in 1908 C.E. A scrutiny of these cases reveals that three interlinked issues were at stake: What precisely was (a) the extent of the *imām's* religious authority? (b) the religious identity of the Khojah sect? and (c) the status of the *gināns?* These cases are significant to Satpanth Ismāʿīlī studies because the court's judgment was to rest on investigations concerning the origins, history, and religious literature of the Satpanth Khojahs. The specific circumstances of the cases, the evidence used in defense of rival positions, and, most critically, the judgment rendered by the justices, all these factors played a vital role in shaping subsequent stances towards and interpretations of Satpanth Ismāʿīlism within the community as well as in Ismāʿīlī scholarship.

Well before Āghā Khān I arrived in Bombay, there was dissention within the Satpanth Khojah Ismāʿīlī community. As early as 1829 C.E., a Khojah by the name of Habib Ibrahim refused to submit to the *imām* the customary tithe called *dasond* and subsequently challenged the latter's rights to receive such dues. Āghā Khān I dispatched his maternal grandmother Mari Bibi, with an emissary,

Mirza Abdool Cassim, who together visited the Ismāʿīlīs in Bombay and vigorously defended the *imām's* right to the tithes. Ibrahim, along with his partisans who numbered twelve—hence, they were called the *Bārbhāī* or twelve brothers—stuck fast to their position and lost membership in the community in 1830 C.E. Five years later, they repented and were readmitted, but only after pledging to pay their arrears in *dasond* and publicly attesting that the *imām's* authority on religious matters was final.

In 1846 C.E., Āghā Khān I moved his headquarters (*darkhānah*) to India, and, during his brief two-year stay in Calcutta, another quarrel transpired. This time it had to do with the inheritance rights of Khojah women, and the dispute led to the Sarjun Mīr Case of 1847 C.E. The Āghā Khān supported women's right to inherit property as prescribed in the Qur'ān, while his opponents insisted on maintaining the prevalent practice among the Satpanth Khojahs at the time, namely, of observing the less equitable Hindu rights of female inheritance. During the trial, the Satpanth Khojahs displayed a rather muddled sense of their own roots, history, and religious identity, so the exasperated Judge Erskine Perry decided it best to uphold the status quo. Thus, he ruled in favor of the Bārbhāī Khojahs who wanted to maintain their current practice of Hindu inheritance, which considerably limited women's rights to inherit property, and against the Āghā Khān who defended these rights for Muslim women. Judge Perry says:

> Although they call themselves Musalmans, they evidently know but little of their prophet and Quran. . . . To use the words of one of themselves, they call themselves Shīʿīs to a Shīʿī, Sunnīs to a Sunnī, and they probably neither know nor care anything as to the distinctive doctrine of either of the great divisions of the Musalman world.[1]

Obviously, this confusion of religious identity presented a problem for the British judge, for, without sufficient certitude that the Khojahs were either Hindu or Muslim, how was he to adjudicate which of the two traditional rules of inheritance should apply? On the other hand, what the judge perceived to be a conundrum of religious identity among the Satpanth Khojahs was, in fact, a demonstration (and consequence) of a longstanding Ismāʿīlī practice of *taqīyah* or religious camouflage as a method of self-protection. It seems that, over the centuries, this practice had effectively created a sense of multiple identities among the Satpanth Ismāʿīlī Khojahs, identities which made them adaptable to hostile circumstances and which, deliberately and sometimes opportunely, left the question of precise classification and characterization quite nebulous.

Recognizing the changed circumstances of his community under the British, however, Āghā Khān I realized that such ambiguity would be a serious liability for his followers, and he thus launched a process of religious and social reform. He took several strong measures to

> crystallize the identity of the Khojah Ismāʿīlīs. He eliminated certain prevailing Hindu customs, such as the observance of the Hindu Law of inheritance, and some Sunnī burial and marriage customs.[2]

In 1861 C.E., he even published a letter declaring his wish that his Satpanth Khojah Ismāʿīlī followers openly embrace the Shīʿah Imāmī creed of his ancestors. He reassured them that their religious freedom would be protected in the Indian subcontinent under British law and, therefore, that they could relinquish those Hindu and Sunnī religious practices that had hitherto helped them to conceal their identity for fear of persecution. He directed the Satpanth Khojahs to stop performing marriage ceremonies, funeral rites, and ablutions in Sunnī or Hindu form and to bring them into line with general Shīʿī practice. The letter was circulated among his followers, who signed it to confirm their allegiance to him as their *imām* and to agree to comply with his wishes.

But the first Āghā Khān's attempts to define and sharply refocus the Satpanth Khojah's identity as a Shīʿah Ismāʿīlī sect by adjusting their religious and social practices was met immediately with strong resistance, and older antagonisms resurfaced. The Bārbhāī, headed by Ibrahim's son, Ahmed Hubibhoy, again raised their voices in dissent and showed their defiance by refusing to submit their religious dues. Asserting that the Khojahs had been Sunnī Muslims all along since their conversion to Islam, they argued that the Shīʿah *imām,* therefore, had no rights to their dues which they had been submitting in the past, not as tithes, but as charitable donations for the welfare of the community. Accordingly, it was up to community elders to decide how these funds were to be administered, and the Āghā Khān's control over Khojah funds and properties was thus declared illegal. Asserting that, since the Satpanth Khojahs were Sunnīs, who do not accept the claims of the Shīʿah *imām,* the Āghā Khān was entitled neither to Khojah monies nor to an absolute religious authority over the regulation of their customs and ceremonies. Thus, the Bārbhāī filed suit demanding that

> the Imam may be restrained from interfering in the management of the trust property and affairs of the Khoja community or in the election and appointment of the Mukhi Kamadhias, from excommunicating any Khojas or depriving them of the various privileges appertaining to membership; from celebrating marriages in the Jamatkhana; from demanding or receiving from any Khoja any oblation, cess, offerings, etc., in the alleged spiritual or temporal capacity.[3]

This case hinged on one crucial question: What exactly was the religious identity of the Khojahs since their origin? Both sides agreed that the Khojahs had been converted by Pīr Ṣadr al-Dīn from Hinduism to Islam. The Bārbhāi, however, claimed that Pīr Ṣadr al-Dīn was a Sunnī and had converted the Khojahs to Sunnī Islam. The Āghā Khān I, on the other hand, claimed that Pīr Ṣadr al-Dīn was an Ismāʿīlī *dāʿī* who had converted the Khojahs to Shīʿah Ismāʿīlism and that, from the beginning, they had professed allegiance to the hereditary Shīʿah *imām*. Thus, the resolution of the case pivoted on determining whether the Khojahs were Sunnī or whether they were Shīʿah Muslims.

It was in this tense context that the *ginān* tradition of the Satpanth Khojah Ismāʿīlīs was catapulted into public attention. In 1866 C.E., specific *ginā**ns*** were presented as evidence in the British High Court of Bombay to vindicate the hereditary rights of the *imām* over his Khojah community. In what became famously known as the Khojah Case, Judge Sir Joseph Arnould ruled in favor of the *imām*, having concluded that the Khojahs were:

> A sect of people whose ancestors were Hindus in origin, which was converted to and has throughout abided in the faith of the Shīʿah Imāmī Ismāʿīlīs and which has always been and still is bound by ties of spiritual allegiance to the hereditary Imāms of the Ismāʿīlīs.[4]

What is remarkable is that a specimen from the Satpanth literature of the Khojah Ismāʿīlīs was admitted in court as authoritative textual evidence to defend the *imām's* claims, effectively validating this religious corpus as an appropriate basis for historical judgment. Justice Arnould considered *ginānic* testimony pivotal to his verdict, for which he had to determine such historical questions as who were the Shīʿah as distinct from the Sunnīs, who was the Āghā Khān, and what was the Khojahs' relationship to the Āghā Khān? As the religious literature of the Khojahs, the *ginān*s were thus upheld as suitable evidence to demonstrate that the community had indeed venerated the Āghā Khān's ancestors for many centuries. In thus legally establishing the *imām's* rights and status, however, the court's verdict did not quell the voices of dissent among his Khojah followers and, thereby, bring an end to the challenge of the authority of the Āghā Khāns.

The third court case, called the Hājī Bībī Case, was filed some four decades later in 1908 C.E. against Āghā Khān III, Sir Sulṭān Muḥammad Shāh, by his first cousin, Hājī Bībī, daughter of his uncle, Junghi Shāh. She and her supporters, mainly composed of members from the Āghā Khān's extended family, asserted that they had equal claims to the religious offerings made to the Āghā Khān. In their view, the tributes paid to Āghā Khān III by his followers were meant to provide for the needs of his relatives who had joint title over his estate and property. They also maintained that, when the Khojahs had converted to Shīʿah Islam, they had become Ithnā ʿAsharīs, not Ismāʿīlīs.

Now it is interesting to note that, in every instance, contested rights over property and religious dues fueled the disputes. Even in the case of the inheritance rights of Khojah women, the problem was property and, accordingly, the material interests of power and privilege. To solve the problem of who had authority to manage these various assets, the court first had to determine who was their rightful owner. Since the property under discussion was of a religious nature, the court also had to ascertain the purpose and meaning of the religious dues.

What is intriguing is that, depending on the claims being made, the litigators asserted either that the Satpanth Khojahs were, in truth, Hindus (to circumvent Muslim laws of female inheritance), Sunnīs (to obtain communal control of religious dues), or Ithnā ʿAsharīs (to gain joint ownership of the Āghā Khān's estate). The disputes were clearly motivated by self-interest, but to what extent were they also an outcome of a crisis of identity among the Satpanth Khojahs? As already noted, Justice Perry was exasperated by the fact that the Khojahs seemed to know little about their own history and showed even less self-awareness of their apparently polymorphous religious identity. Evidently, the syncretism of the Satpanth Khojahs' religious ideas and practices was complicated enough that it was a legitimate question to ask, "Were they Sunnī or Shīʿah, Ismāʿīlī or Ithnā ʿAsharī, Hindu or Muslim?" Moreover, the determination of this question of identity was not merely a matter of theoretical interest but would have immediate religious, economic, and political ramifications for the various claimants. And none had as much to lose as Āghā Khān III, for whom the answer to this question would have been crucial. If the judgment ruled in his favor, it would safeguard his property rights; but, more fundamentally, it would legally affirm and endorse his religious status and authority both within and outside the Satpanth Khojah community. A positive ruling would put a seal on the religious identity of the Satpanth Khojahs as Shīʿah Muslims and as the followers of the lineal descendants of the Nizārī Ismāʿīlī *imāms* of Persia who at that time was the Āghā Khān III.

Two important points emerged from the court's historical investigations. Firstly, it was noted that the Ismāʿīlīs had routinely enjoined and practiced *taqīyah* or religious concealment as a precautionary measure against persecution at the hands of their enemies, particularly the Sunnīs, who viewed their religious doctrines as heresy and treason. Ismāʿīlīs thus had a long history of hiding their true beliefs and practices, and they often adopted non-Ismāʿīlī practices as a protective cover. Secondly, the court observed that the traditional Ismāʿīlī methods of conversion included the process of religious tolerance. Ismāʿīlī missionaries sought

> to make converts by assuming to a great extent the religious standpoint of the person whom they desired to convert, modestly hinting a few doubts and difficulties and then, by degrees, suggesting as the only possible solution of these the peculiar tenets of their own system.[5]

In other words, the Ismāʿīlī *pīrs* were trained to attract believers through an approach of religious acceptance, gentle persuasion, and gradual indoctrination. Using a cordial but deliberate approach, first they won the confidence of potential converts or supporters to their cause by conceding the truth of the formers' religious tenets. Then, they gradually led them to see how these tenets were essentially imperfect or false. (Elsewhere, I have illustrated how this selective strategy of partial acceptance and rejection is manifest in a specimen of Satpanth Ismāʿīlī literature.[6])

After reconstructing a sketchy historical background of the Nizārī *daʿwah's* activity in India, the court still had to determine whether Pīr Ṣadr al-Dīn was a Sunnī or Shīʿī Muslim. According to traditional accounts that prevailed among the majority of the Khojahs, Pīr Ṣadr al-Dīn had been sent from Khurāsān by the Nizārī *imām,* Islām Shāh (d. ca. 1480 C.E.), and had converted many Hindus to Ismāʿīlism to whom he gave the title Khojah (from the Persian *khwājah* for lord, master).[7] The minority Khojah faction maintained otherwise, namely, that Pīr Ṣadr al-Dīn was a Sunnī and converted the Hindus to Sunnī Islam. Three arguments were advanced in support of the first position. First, if Pīr Ṣadr al-Dīn was a Sunnī, instead of performing pilgrimages and making homage to the Āghā Khān and his ancestors, why did the Khojahs not venerate Pīr Ṣadr al-Dīn at his shrine in Ucch? Second, if the Pīr had indeed preached a Sunnī form of Islam, why was there substantial evidence that the Khojahs had been submitting tithes and religious offerings to the Āghā Khān's ancestors for generations? Third, and most decisively, how could the *ginān Das Avatār,* considered to be the most sacred poem of the Khojah scriptures, have been composed by a Sunnī given its teachings? The majority Khojah position arguing in favor for the Āghā Khān concluded, therefore, that Pīr Ṣadr al-Dīn could not have been a Sunnī Muslim.

The court first established the fact that the *Das Avatār* was part of the ancient religious literature of the Khojahs and was regularly recited in their prayer assemblies throughout the region. Composed of ten parts, the last section of the work, in particular, was greatly esteemed by the Khojahs and routinely recited during preburial rites for the deceased. It was in this final section that the first Shīʿite Imām, ʿAlī, was identified as the awaited tenth *avatār.* The court mused that if, indeed, Pīr Ṣadr al-Dīn had composed this *ginān* and introduced it among the Khojahs as a great religious work—its importance had been established by its universal use and reverence among the Khojahs—then, it may hold the key to the true religious identity of the Khojahs. Justice Arnould explained as follows how the Hindus were converted by the *pīrs* of the Ismāʿīlī *daʿwah:*

> What is Dasavatar? It is a treatise in ten chapters containing (as, indeed, its name imports) the account of ten avatars or incarnations of the Hindu God Vishnu; the tenth chapter treats of the incarnation of the Most Holy Ali . . . it is precisely such a book as a Dai or missionary of the Ismailis would compose or adapt if he wished to convert a body of not very learned Hindus to the Ismaili faith. It precisely carries out . . . the standing instructions to the Dai . . . viz, to procure conversion by assuming, as in great part true, the

> religious standpoint of the intended convert. This is exactly what the book does: It assumes the nine incarnations of Vishnu to be true as far as they go, but not the whole truth, and then supplements the imperfect Vishnuvite system by superadding the cardinal doctrine of the Ismailis, the incarnation and coming manifestation (or Avatar) of the "Most Holy" Ali.[8]

Hence, he ruled that, based on the authority of the *ginān* literature, the Āghā Khān was the true spiritual head and hereditary *imām* of the Satpanth Khojahs, who were, at root, a Shīʿah Ismāʿīlī Muslim sect of converted Hindus. As for the existence of Hindu, Sunnī, and Ithnā ʿAsharī practices among the Khojahs, he accounted for them thus:

> The Khojas have observed these practices . . . out of Takiyah—concealment of their own religious views and adoption of alien religious ceremonies out of dread of persecution for religion's sake.[9]

That the authority of the *gināns* should have thus been invoked in defense of the *imām's* legitimacy is noteworthy and yet also ironic. For while the *ginān* tradition helped to establish in an official, public, and legal British setting that the Satpanth Khojahs were Shīʿah Ismāʿīlīs, the ambiguities integral to the syncretic composition of the sect's religious identity would not be resolved nor cleared by this ruling. In due course, the same sacred tradition that had been invoked by the British court of law to establish that the Satpanth Khojahs were Shīʿah Ismāʿīlī Muslims would be used by Sunnī Muslims to repudiate that the Satpanth Khojahs were Muslims at all since their religious literature, the *gināns,* contained Hindu myths and ideas.

The public and legal recognition of the *gināns* as an authoritative source for confirming the sect's religious identity further endorsed and reinforced the tradition's status within the community; but, by its very exposure, the *ginān* tradition and, by extension, the Satpanth Khojah Ismāʿīlīs had became vulnerable to attack by "orthodox" Muslims who derided its Hindu–Muslim mixture as un-Islamic. The public exposure of the Khojahs' religious literature which, thus far, had been so carefully guarded turned out to be a mixed blessing. Under British law, the religious rights and freedoms of the Satpanth Ismāʿīlīs were protected, but this protection was to be short-lived.

The birth of India and Pakistan, marked as it was by intense Hindu–Muslim strife, reintroduced age-old fears. The eventual assertion of a Sunnī Islamic state in Pakistan awakened old anxieties as the Satpanth Khojahs faced renewed threats of persecution.[10]

It is clear, therefore, that the emergence in the last century of a public discourse on the subject of the religious literature of the Satpanth Khojah Ismāʿīlīs, namely, the *ginān* tradition, occurred in an atmosphere constrained by legitimate fears, age-old tensions, and competing vested interests. Investigations and assessments of this religious corpus of poetry were undertaken, not for purely academic interest, but were precipitated by a context of serious political and economic complexities. The confusing nature of the tradition itself did not ameliorate the situation. But it is an ironic twist that the very tradition that nurtured the religious life of the Satpanth Khojahs for so many centuries, and that had successfully been used to establish the link of this South Asian Muslim community with the Nizārī Ismāʿīlī *imāms,* once it became exposed, turned into fodder for ultraconservative Muslim groups wishing to question the community's Muslim identity. To some extent, this reversal of affairs helped to demonstrate the validity of the sect's centuries-long fears of persecution.

Consequently, subsequent attitudes toward the *ginān* tradition, both within the community itself but also affecting Satpanth Ismāʿīlī scholarship, have invariably been fashioned within a crucible of constraints. As the Satpanth Khojah Ismāʿīlīs continue to affirm their ties to Shīʿah Islam, a process spurred by the first Āghā Khān two centuries ago, they also clumsily struggle to protect a heritage which, once exposed, has invited rebuke. The community's steady restoration of an "Islamic" identity under the direction of the Āghā Khāns has resulted in a reconstructive process wherein the Satpanth heritage is being presented as simply a convenient strategy of conversion and a single strand among many diverse developments of Ismāʿīlism. Thus recast as the "Indian phase" of Ismāʿīlism, the Satpanth literature of the Khojahs, while still widely recited and heard today in *jamāʿat khānahs* around the world, runs the risk of being interpreted as a mere relic of a past era whose utilitarian purpose and historical and cultural particularity thus makes it increasingly irrelevant. A growing awareness of the presence of "non-Khojah" Ismāʿīlī traditions that evolved in Syria, Afghanistan, Tajikistan, Central Asia, and China has accelerated this trend of telescoping Satpanth within the broader historical development of Ismāʿīlism more generally. Given this broader perspective, and because of its intrinsic nature—

vernacular in linguistic idiom, syncretistic in religious ideas and practices, and folkloric and mythopoetic in form—the Satpanth tradition also stands to become marginalized within the sect itself.[11] The stance of the Institute of Ismaili Studies in London towards the Satpanth Ismāʿīlī tradition reflects this development within the community.[12]

Satpanth Ismāʿīlism: A Reinvestigation of its Origins

To date, a true appreciation of the historical significance and role of Satpanth Ismāʿīlism has not been achieved. To recognize the true importance of this development in Ismāʿīlī history, I think it is necessary to reopen the question of the origins of the Satpanth Ismāʿīlī tradition in the Indian subcontinent. Satpanth Ismāʿīlism is strikingly different from both Fāṭimid and Nizārī Ismāʿīlism. Various studies of its *ginān*s have demonstrated the indigenous roots of the Satpanth heritage and its embrace of Indian dialects, culture, and religious worldview.[13] The deep influence of Hindu Vaiṣṇavism and Bhakti, Tantrism, Ṣūfism, and other religious currents in India on the expression of Satpanth Ismāʿīlism has been generally explained by what may be termed the "conversion theory."[14] According to this widely-held theory, the goal of religious conversion adequately accounts for the origin and formal expressions of Satpanth Ismāʿīlism. The *ginān* heritage is thus postulated as being the consequence of the *daʿwah,* or preaching activities of the Nizārī Ismāʿīlī *pīrs* in the Indian subcontinent. The *pīrs* allegedly succeeded in attracting converts into their fold through the *ginān*s which they composed to convey their beliefs using religious myths and symbols that were familiar to the Indian environment. Hence, the general view is that the Satpanth tradition was developed by the Nizārī *dāʿīs* or *pīrs* essentially to spread the *religious* teachings of the Ismāʿīlī *daʿwah.*

Since the time of the public discussions of the *ginān*s in the British Courts in India before independence, it has thus been typical to argue that, in order to ease the transition of potential converts from Hinduism to Ismāʿīlī Islam, the *pīrs* adopted the strategy of accommodating indigenous religious mores and concepts. Satpanth's form and content were thus deliberately derived from the Indian milieu, and this method of accommodation or assimilation successfully won converts to Ismāʿīlism.[15] This interpretation has set the broad parameters for any discussion of Satpanth Ismāʿīlī literature and has determined the approach and analysis of most works on the *ginān* tradition.

A secondary and much less explored explanation for the Indian nature of Satpanth Ismāʿīlism is that it was also a means of *taqīyah* (religious dissimulation), a way to protect new converts to Ismāʿīlism from persecution both at the hands of the Hindus and the hostile Turkish Sunnī rulers of the Indian subcontinent.

In light of the *ginān*s attributed to one of the earliest Ismāʿīlī *pīrs* of Satpanth, Pīr Shams, I believe we must reengage this question of why Ismāʿīlism developed in the Indian subcontinent into the specific form called Satpanth. There can be no doubt that the *ginān* literature has played a vital role in the religious life of Satpanth Ismāʿīlism. What needs to be reconsidered, however, are the beginnings of Satpanth. What role did this literary corpus actually play in the conversion of Hindus and other Indians? Was the *ginān* tradition developed primarily for the sake of conversion? Is it reasonable to explain the formation of the Satpanth Ismāʿīlī community chiefly on the basis of the religious teachings in the *ginān*s? Did Satpanth exist before the *ginān*s, or did it arise along with the evolution of this sacred corpus? Could there have been motivations other than religious conversion that instigated the *pīrs*' activity and strategy? Likewise, what nonreligious factors attracted converts to the path that the *pīrs* were inviting them to? And finally, why did the *pīrs* adopt the strategy of indigenization to achieve their objectives?

I would like to argue that *religious* considerations account only partially for the successful emergence of the Satpanth Ismāʿīlī community. In the following pages, I will endeavor to show that there may have been other equally important political and social incentives that spurred the development of Satpanth Ismāʿīlism and its specifically Indian form. In dispute here is the position that religious conversion in and of itself holds the key to the formation of Satpanth Ismāʿīlism. This suspicion is aroused by the existence of some important but unresolved questions.

Firstly, why is it that, when the Fāṭimid Ismāʿīlī *daʿwah* sent its emissaries to Sind to spread Ismāʿīlī teachings in the ninth century, a strategy of compromise was seldom applied for conversion? In fact, it was quite explicitly rejected, for when an unknown *dāʿī* admitted to using such an approach, it was sharply censured by the Fāṭimid hierarchy. Why would the Ismāʿīlī *daʿwah* decry local accommodations in one historical context and unabashedly encourage them in another? Secondly, by the twelfth/thirteenth century, Ṣūfism had already gained ground in India, and it was certainly much closer in perspective to Nizārī Ismāʿīlism than was Hinduism. Yet, why did the Ismāʿīlī *pīrs* in India choose to express their teachings in terms of

Hindu Vaiṣṇavism and not Ṣūfī Islam? Why did Ismāʿīlism in India not evolve into a Ṣūfī *tariqah?* Thirdly, how is one to explain the wide gap in forms, both in terms of literary expression and ritual practices, that exists between the religious traditions of Nizārī Ismāʿīlism and Satpanth Ismāʿīlism? Established patterns of religious life tend to be highly conservative and self-preserving, especially in periods of sudden or dramatic change. In unfamiliar contexts, traditional ways are usually asserted more strictly because they help to maintain the psychological structures of religious identity. Typically, therefore, in unknown territory one would expect considerable reluctance to allow variations of religious forms or practice, as leniency could easily lead to assimilation and loss of identity.

How can Satpanth be a *translation* of Nizārī Ismāʿīlism, as it is generally projected to be, when it exists in so distinctive a form? Why did the Nizārī *pīrs* choose to convey Ismāʿīlī teachings in Indian vernacular languages and religious images and beliefs when Muslim languages and cultural norms were commonplace in the areas of Sind and northwestern India? Why, in sum, did the *pīrs* decide to advance a form for Ismāʿīlism in India which, for all intents and purposes, *appears* to have little in common either with its antecedent historical traditions or with normative types of Islam as such?

Surely religious conversion could not have been the sole motive for initiating a tradition that would stand in such contrast to its religious predecessors and that could, in the long term, develop away from them. Moreover, given the fact that the Ismāʿīlīs claimed that the rightful leadership of the Muslim *ummah* (community) belonged to their *imāms,* why would the sect have risked submerging itself into the fabric of Indian religious life, which, in so many respects, was the antithesis of iconoclastic and priestless Islam? These questions are not sufficiently accounted for by the religious conversion theory alone.

Based on a careful review of historical events, I will argue that the reason why the Ismāʿīlī *daʿwah* developed such an indigenized form of Ismāʿīlism in the Indian subcontinent was not only religious but also sociopolitical. The shape that Ismāʿīlism took in India was intimately linked to events occurring at the centre of the *daʿwah*—first in Cairo, then in the sphere of Alamūt—as well as those in the local context of Sind and northwestern India. The beginnings and formation of the Satpanth phase of Ismāʿīlism in the Indian subcontinent coincided with the period from the end of the reign of the Fāṭimid caliph al-Mustanṣir bi'llāh to the Mongol destruction of the

Nizārī Ismāʿīlī headquarters at Alamūt, that is, from about 1094 C.E. to 1256 C.E. From this point onwards, given the collapse of the organizational center at Alamūt and the consequent political and material losses of the Nizārī *daʿwah,* dispersed Ismāʿīlī locales became responsible for charting their own courses in history. That is to say, the policies and development of *daʿwah* activity in the Indian subcontinent or Syria or Central Asia could no longer be guided with a uniform hand by a strong central *daʿwah* located at Alamūt but, rather, was shaped by the force of events, sociopolitical realities, and cultural complexes closer at hand.

The outline of my argument is as follows: I will briefly cover the political history of Ismāʿīlism up to the destruction of Alamūt in order to show how the form of the *daʿwah* in Sind and northwestern India was closely monitored and directed by the center of the *daʿwah,* installed first in Cairo in North Africa, then Yaman, and finally, Alamūt. I will also show how social and historical realities in the Indian subcontinent combined to provide fertile ground for the development of an indigenous form of Ismāʿīlism. Further, I will outline how events affecting the *daʿwah* in the traditional Islamic lands as well as events in the subcontinent promoted—and perhaps even determined—the development of a specifically Indian form of Ismāʿīlism. Finally, I will argue that, with the collapse of Alamūt, the *daʿwah* in India had no recourse but fully to develop Satpanth Ismāʿīlism in order to safeguard its own survival.

This historical sketch will sweep over a period of some six centuries, from the time of Prophet Muḥammad's death in 632 C.E. to the Mongol invasion of Alamūt in Persia in 1256 C.E. It will be shown that the development of Ismāʿīlism in the Indian subcontinent was closely connected to events taking place in the remoter, central regions of the Islamic and Ismāʿīlī world. Whereas Stern[16] and others have dismissed any link between Fāṭimid Ismāʿīlism in Sind in the ninth to eleventh centuries, and the later development of Satpanth Ismāʿīlism in India in the twelfth century, I will argue that the evidence appears to suggest the contrary. It seems that these two phases and forms of Ismāʿīlism were linked by Nizārī Ismāʿīlī activity, and it may be possible to trace with some accuracy the period during which Satpanth Ismāʿīlism was conceived. I will demonstrate that Satpanth emerged out of the throes of a political and religious crisis, and argue that had Ismāʿīlism not been thus reshaped in India, the sect's very survival would have been at stake. Finally, this section will also uncover why, as Maclean astutely observed, "the frequently vented causal argument which holds that Hindus converted to Ismāʿīlism in Sind as a simple consequence of congenial similarities in ideological themes would appear to miss the mark."[17]

The Roots of Sunnī–Shīʿī Ismāʿīlī Tensions in Early Islam

The Ismāʿīlīs, as mentioned earlier, are a subsect of the Shīʿah branch of Islam that claims that the Prophet Muḥammad explicitly designated his cousin and son-in-law, ʿAlī ibn Abī Ṭālib, to succeed him as the rightful leader of the nascent Muslim community or *ummah.* According to the majority of the Shīʿah, the office of imāmate is hereditary and passes down through the progeny of ʿAlī and his wife Fāṭimah, daughter of the Prophet, by explicit designation (*naṣṣ*) generally to the eldest son.

The Sunnīs reject this claim and maintain that Muḥammad had left the question of leadership to the consensus (*ijmāʿ*) of the community's elders who, accordingly, elected Abū Bakr as the first caliph. The venture of Islam, then, began with a crisis of leadership over the Prophet's successor and led to a cleavage that eventually solidified into the Shīʿah and the Sunnī branches of Islam. This was an issue of serious consequence because, after the *hijrah* (migration to Medina), Prophet Muḥammad himself had led the early Muslim community, not only in religious matters, but in economic and political ones as well. Muḥammad's career in Medina was, in many respects, an articulation of the Islamic ideal of a theocratic state.

Over the course of Islamic history, the Sunnīs and the Shīʿah each resolved differently the dilemma of providing for both the religious and political aspects of the Prophet's authority.[18] Broadly speaking, the Sunnī solution divided the Prophet's dual function into two: the office of the caliphate was to safeguard the Islamic state, and the Qur'ān and the Prophet's *sunnah* or example were to constitute the sources of Islamic law. The Shīʿah, on the other hand, insisted that these two functions remain joined in the person of the *imām* whose authority, like the Prophet's, was construed to be both spiritual and temporal. While accepting the Qur'ān and the *sunnah* as sources of religious authority, the Shīʿah maintained that only the *imām* of the time possessed the special knowledge or *ʿilm* to interpret Revelation.

The six centuries following these early disagreements over the Prophet's successor bear witness to the internal struggles within the Islamic world over the issue of political and religious authority.

From the start, the Shīʿah, the party of ʿAlī, suffered setbacks. When ʿAlī finally became the fourth caliph, he was assassinated (d. 661 C.E.); the rights of his elder son, Ḥasan (d. 669 C.E.) were abdicated; and Ḥusayn, his younger son, was brutally dismembered in Karbalāʾ (d. 680 C.E.). These successive attacks against the *ahl al-bayt,* or family of the Prophet, crystallized the Shīʿah movement and intensified its determination *to seek justice and avenge the usurped position of its imāms.* It was partly in response to these early infractions and violence that the die was cast, and the Shīʿah cause developed its revolutionary complexion. The Ismāʿīlīs, in particular, were to sustain for the longest period the political resolve to rectify the injustice that they felt had been done to their *imāms* and to reclaim for them their legitimate position within the *ummah.*

As has been stated, the office of imāmate was construed from the time of ʿAlī and his sons as hereditary. Inevitably, over the course of Shīʿī history, differences of opinion arose over the issue of succession, as a result of which the Shīʿah have splintered into many subsects distinguished by their line of *imāms.* The Ismāʿīlī sect emerged from a split that occurred in 765 C.E. following the death of the fifth Imām, Jaʿfar al-Ṣādiq. The group that followed his elder son, Ismāʿīl al-Mubārak, are the Ismāʿīlīs, while those who supported Ismāʿīl's younger brother, Mūṣā al-Qāẓim, are known as the Twelvers (Ithnāʿ Asharī). With each split came further antagonisms, revenge, and reprisals. A period of intense hostility towards the Shīʿah in general, the four Ismāʿīlī *imāms* succeeding Jaʿfar feared for their lives and went into hiding. During this time, they secretly organized their followers into a sophisticated organization called the *daʿwah.* The word *daʿwah* primarily means invitation or call to Islam. In the Ismāʿīlī case, however, it also refers to a highly organized, hierarchically structured, religio-political network that, not only promoted its political cause, but also articulated, elaborated and transmitted Ismāʿīlī teachings.

The outreach activity and diplomatic maneuvers of the *daʿwah* gradually won significant grass-roots support for Ismāʿīlī claims in Persia, Yaman, North Africa, and even as far away as Sind and culminated in the foundation of the Fāṭimid Ismāʿīlī state. In 910 C.E., the twelfth Ismāʿīlī Imām, ʿUbayd Allāh al-Mahdī (d. 934 C.E.), was proclaimed the first Fāṭimid caliph and *amīr al-muʾminīn* (commander of the faithful) in Ifrīqiya (Tunisia). This action marked "the opening phase of the Ismāʿīlī attempt to give concrete shape to their vision of an Islamic society."[19]

The Fāṭimid Dynasty and Its Relations to Sind

During Fāṭimid rule, the power and influence of Ismāʿīlism stretched beyond Egypt to include parts of Palestine, Syria, the Hijāz, Yaman, Persia, Sind, and Sicily in the Mediterranean. Regarded as the most illustrious period of Ismāʿīlī history, Fāṭimid power extended over two centuries and stimulated an efflorescence in trade, scholarship, art, and statecraft. What is of particular interest here about the Fāṭimid enterprise is its links with the Indian subcontinent. Around 883 C.E., before the Fāṭimids came to power, the famous Ismāʿīlī *dāʿī,* Abū al-Qāsim ibn Hawshab Manṣūr al-Yaman, had established an Ismāʿīlī base in Yaman. In that same year, he sent his nephew, al-Haytham, to spread the Ismāʿīlī *daʿwah* in Sind.[20] Less than a century later, the chief jurist of the Fāṭimid Caliph al-Muʿizz, Qāḍī al-Nuʿmān (d. 974 C.E.), recorded in his *Risālat iftitāḥ al-daʿwah* (written ca. 957 C.E.) that the *daʿwah* in Sind was doing well.[21]

When the Fāṭimid *daʿwah* reached the subcontinent, Sind had both a Muslim and a non-Muslim population. Muslims had begun to visit India as early as the time of the third Caliph, ʿUthmān (644–656 C.E.). Pro-Shīʿī sentiments were present in Sind as early as 649 C.E. when al-Ḥākim al-ʿAbdī, a partisan of ʿAlī, raided Mukrān. The advent of Islam in the subcontinent was marked by the conquest of Sind by Muḥammad ibn al-Qāsim in 711–712 C.E. Muḥammad seized the area from the coast all the way up to Multān along the Indus river. During his time, the main centers of Sind, al-Manṣūrah, and Multān (Multān was the name of both a town and the surrounding region) were established.[22] Although the Sunnī Arabs made no attempt at converting the local populace, much of the indigenous Buddhist population of Sind eventually became Muslim for economic reasons.[23] It seems that the area of Upper Sind or Multān also had some previously settled Arabs with ʿAlid (supporters of the first Shīʿī *imām,* ʿAlī) sympathies. In 871 C.E., Yaʿqūb ibn Layth was appointed ruler of Sind by the ʿAbbāsid caliph and his pro-Shīʿī views may have helped the spread of Shīʿism in Sind.[24] The geographer and historian, Masʿūdī, records in 915 C.E. that he found several descendants of ʿUmarī ʿAlids in the region of Multān.[25] After Yaʿqūb's death (878 C.E.), Sind was divided between two independent Arab chiefs. The Banū Sāma ruled Multān, and the Quraysh Ḥabbārids governed al-Manṣūrah. While these dynasties were Sunnī, both areas appear to have been hospitable toward the Shīʿah. Thus, by the time the Fāṭimid Ismāʿīlī *daʿwah* reached Sind in 883 C.E., Sind already had a local population of Arab Muslims comprised both of Shīʿah and Sunnī, as well as indigenous Muslims comprised mainly of converted Buddhists.

During the expansion of the Fāṭimid empire, its vassal states were in close touch with the central *daʿwah* in North Africa. Events that occurred in distant regions of the Fāṭimid empire were communicated to the center, which, in turn, radiated news within the *daʿwah* network. Thus, although the empire's dispersed vassal states were semi-independent, the central *daʿwah* in North Africa appears to have ensured that these states operated under the framework and policies issued from the Fāṭimid headquarters. By the tenth century, the Islamic world stretched more or less from North Africa to Tibet, and news travelled quickly, especially regarding events taking place in the central Islamic lands of Iraq and Persia.

Although at the peak of its success the Fāṭimid empire briefly extended over a vast area, it never attained the ultimate goal of hegemony over the Islamic world. The Fāṭimid caliphate failed to overthrow the ʿAbbāsid caliph in Baghdad and to unite the Muslim world under a Shīʿah *imām-khalīf*. Indeed, soon after the Fāṭimid conquest of Egypt (969 C.E.) and the transference of the caliphate to Cairo from Ifrīqiya (Tunisia, where the Fāṭimid caliphate was first proclaimed in 909 C.E.), the resources of its *daʿwah* were consumed in the constant struggle to maintain and consolidate lands already existing under the Fāṭimid empire.

While the Fāṭimid period is regarded to be the most illustrious in Ismāʿīlī history, it was not immune to problems and conflicts. From the start, the Fāṭimid caliphate faced internal and external challenges. The focus here will be on those problems that were to be of some consequence to the Ismāʿīlīs in Sind. The very birth of the Fāṭimid state precipitated internal divisions. In 899 C.E., Ḥamdān Qarmaṭ, a powerful Ismāʿīlī *dāʿī* who had won a considerable Ismāʿīlī following in lower Iraq, broke off from the *daʿwah,* then centred in Syria, when the Fāṭimid caliph ʿUbayd Allāh declared himself as the *imām.* According to Ḥamdān Qarmaṭ, ʿUbayd Allāh's claim repudiated the pre-Fāṭimid Ismāʿīlī belief that Muḥammad b. Ismāʿīl would return as the *mahdī* (messiah) to restore truth and justice in the world. His faction, named Qarmaṭī after him, refused to accept that ʿUbayd was the expected *mahdī* and rejected the claims of the Fāṭimid caliphs to the imāmate, which the Qarmaṭīs maintained had come to an end with Muḥammad b. Ismāʿīl.[26]

This defection proved fatal in the long run to the Fāṭimid goal of capturing the eastern heartlands of Islam where the ʿAbbāsids were centered. Although the Caliph al-Muʿizz (ruled 953–975 C.E.)

made special efforts to regain the allegiance of the Qarmaṭīs and had some success in Khurāsān, Sīstān, and Mukrān, dissenting groups continued their vigorous anti-Fāṭimid and anti-ʿAbbāsid activities in lower Iraq, Daylamān, Ādharbayjān, and Baḥrayn. They succeeded in thwarting several attempts by the Fāṭimids to secure Syria fully, from which base the Fāṭimids might have launched a successful attack on Baghdad. Although the Fāṭimid Ismāʿīlīs and the Qarmaṭī Ismāʿīlīs were foes at the time, in relation to the Sunnī ʿAbbāsids both sects were subversive elements and pro-ʿAlīd. Thus, Sunnī writers and chroniclers regularly but erroneously identified the two by the same label, namely, "Qarmaṭī," and the Fāṭimids were invariably blamed for Qarmaṭī excesses, such as their desecration of Mecca and the slaughter of pilgrims making the *ḥajj* in 930 C.E.

The influence of the Qarmaṭīs, however, was far-reaching. This is evident from the views held by an unknown *dāʿī* in Sind, who attracted the attention and displeasure of the Fāṭimid caliph, al-Muʿizz. While few details are known about the actual operation of the early Fāṭimid *daʿwah* in Sind, some clues exist that give an impression of its approach and both its gains and losses. An interesting incident survives about one of al-Haytham's successors, an anonymous *dāʿī* who worked in Sind between 941–958 C.E. during the reign of al-Muʿizz. This *dāʿī* had succeeded in converting a Muslim prince[27] in the region, as well as a large group of non-Muslims described by al-Nuʿmān in his *Majālis waʾl Musāyarāt* as *majūs* (Zoroastrians; in this case, more likely, a reference to Hindu sun-worshippers). However, the *dāʿī's* beliefs and methods of conversion stirred up considerable controversy at the Fāṭimid headquarters.

According to the famous Fāṭimid *qāḍī*, al-Nuʿmān, the *dāʿī* introduced the following "reprehensible innovation" to accomplish his task:

> He won a great number of Zoroastrians (*majūs*) for the *daʿwa,* while they were still keeping their religion and had not previously become Muslims. He allowed them to follow their earlier practices.[28]

Apparently, the Caliph al-Muʿizz "did not like the *majūs* retaining their old views and thought the *dāʿī* disloyal for holding that the Fāṭimids were of Qaddāḥid origins," a view propagated by the Qarmaṭīs.[29] Evidently, this unnamed *dāʿī* had incurred the displeasure of al-Muʿizz for two reasons: firstly, for improperly converting the *majūs,* and secondly, for holding incorrect Qarmaṭī views concerning the Fāṭimid caliph's claim to the imāmate.[30] As Nanji explains, Fāṭimid territories were widely scattered and posed a challenge to the central *daʿwah* in North Africa which attempted to

> provide a common basis for their heterogenous and widely-scattered adherents. The diversity of such adherents was potentially a seed-bed of a wide variety of heterodox beliefs, particularly in the case of Sind, where the converts brought with them a deeply-rooted background of wide practices.[31]

al-Muʿizz seems to have disapproved of the *dāʿī's* concessionary method of spreading the *daʿwah* and insisted on a more strict adherence to Islamic practice and tradition. It appears that, at the time, the conversion to the Ismāʿīlī cause was a two-step process. First, the convert became a Muslim. Later, after proper initiation, the convert would swear allegiance to the Ismāʿīlī *imāms.* In any case, the anonymous *dāʿī's* breach was serious enough that the *daʿwah* headquarters planned on having him removed. The *dāʿī,* however, died in a riding accident, and the matter was closed. Based on the official exchanges between the center in North Africa and the *daʿwah* in Sind, what this incident seems to underscore is that the Fāṭimid *daʿwah* discouraged assimilation, adaptation or compromise in religious practices and doctrines.

The suspect *dāʿī* was succeeded in 965 C.E. by Jalam b. Shaybān who brought to an end the dynastic rule of the Banū Sāma, secured Fāṭimid rule in Multān, and openly proclaimed the sovereignty of al-Muʿizz.[32] For four decades (965–1005 C.E.), the *khuṭba* (Friday sermon) in Multān was recited in the name of the Fāṭimid caliphs, displacing their rivals, the ʿAbbāsids of Baghdad. The Fāṭimid Caliph al-Muʿizz wrote to Shaybān praising him for his victory but also commending him for destroying an idol and its temple and building a mosque at the site.[33] Maclean has convincingly argued that this could not possibly have been a reference to the famous sun-temple in Multān and notes that, "In any case, it is clear that the Ismāʿīlīs of Multān did not pursue a policy of temple or image destruction."[34] Even if, as Maclean suggests, the letter from al-Muʿizz had propagandist motives, what is worth noting is that the caliph's official approval of Jalam's strict prohibition of Hindu elements was consistent with his denunciation of the syncretic and more compromising attitude of Jalam's predecessor. Thus, it is reasonable to conclude that, at the earliest stage of the Ismāʿīlī *daʿwah* in the subcontinent, indigenization and religious accommodation were not a part of its conversion strategy. On the contrary, the official policy of the *daʿwah* seems to have positively discouraged assimilation or tolerance of local religious elements.

The other constant challenge faced by the Fāṭimid caliphate was opposition to ʿAlīd claims from the ʿAbbāsid caliphate that was bolstered first by the Shīʿī Būyids and later by the Sunnī Saljūq Turks. As we have noted, by the time that the Fāṭimids came to power, the Ismāʿīlīs had already developed the elaborate organization of the *daʿwah* to rally support for their *imāms'* claims. The *daʿwah* continued its activities in earnest during the Fāṭimid period, and small gains were made in Iraq and Persia. Its activities, which included the prolific writings of contemporary Fāṭimid *dāʿīs,* revived interest in Ismāʿīlism among pro-Shīʿīs such as the Twelvers. Rulers of a few towns in ʿAbbāsid territories began to transfer their allegiance to the Fāṭimid caliph, al-Ḥākim bi-Amr Allāh (ruled 996–1021 C.E.), and were subsequently threatened by the ʿAbbāsid caliph al-Qādir. Fearing the growing Fāṭimid influence in the region, al-Qādir launched an anti-Ismāʿīlī propaganda campaign in 1010 C.E. and invited the theologians and scholars of Baghdad to prepare a manifesto discrediting the Fāṭimid caliph's claim to being a descendant of ʿAlī. This declaration of the Fāṭimids as imposters and the Ismāʿīlīs as heretics was read in mosques throughout the ʿAbbāsid empire. Al-Qādir also commissioned the leading Sunnī theologians of Baghdad to write works castigating the Fāṭimids as the enemies of Islam and denouncing Ismāʿīlī teachings as blasphemy.[35]

While one cannot say without more detailed historical investigations that al-Qādir's manifesto *directly* led to the killing of Ismāʿīlīs, it is worth noting that, after the manifesto, these massacres began to occur with increasing frequency. The manifesto openly sanctioned anti-Ismāʿīlī aggression in the Islamic heartlands and set into motion a wave of anti-Ismāʿīlī episodes. It is not a mere coincidence that the Ismāʿīlīs in Sind were massacred by Maḥmūd Ghaznawī the same year that Baghdad issued the manifesto against the Fāṭimids. In Ifrīqiya, Ismāʿīlīs were increasingly persecuted by Sunnī Berbers, a fact which culminated in the attack and massacre of the Ismāʿīlīs of Qayrawān, Tripoli, Mahdiyyah, and Tunis in 1016 C.E.[36] Three decades later, the Fāṭimids permanently lost Ifrīqiya when the local Zīrid rulers transferred their allegiance to the ʿAbbasīds in 1048 C.E.

Another development that occurred at this time, weakening the Fāṭimids and affecting the Ismāʿīlīs in Sind, was a controversy over the Fāṭimid caliph, al-Ḥākim bi-Amr Allāh. Towards the latter half of his reign (996–1021 C.E.), some *dāʿīs* began to preach the divinity of al-Ḥākim. The official Fāṭimid *daʿwah* vigorously opposed this interpretation and summoned its esteemed *dāʿī*, al-Kirmānī, to Egypt to compose treatises refuting such ideas. al-Ḥākim himself became reclusive and spartan towards the end of his life and mysteriously disappeared in 1021 C.E. While Kirmānī's writings were widely circulated and seem to have checked the spread of these problematic doctrines, the dissident *dāʿīs* held to their ideas and formed the Druze religion, winning a small following in Syria. They actively proselytized between the years 1021–1043 C.E. after which time neither conversion nor apostacy was allowed. During this short time, however, the Druze *daʿwah* managed to extend its reach as far as Sind, for in 1033 C.E., soon after the massacre of the Ismāʿīlīs in Multān, the Druze leader, al-Muqtanaʿ, wrote to the Fāṭimid *dāʿī* Sūmar Rājabāl asking him to lend his support to their cause. Although the Fāṭimid *daʿwah* distanced itself from Druze ideas, the latter's teachings concerning the divinity of al-Ḥākim merely added fuel to Sunnī antipathy for the Ismāʿīlīs. That negative Ismāʿīlī stereotypes continued to flourish and spread to all corners of the Islamic lands is attested to by the massacre of Ismāʿīlīs as far away as Bukhārā and Transoxiana under the Qarakhānid ruler, Bugrā Khān, in 1044 C.E.[37]

Meanwhile, the Fāṭimid Ismāʿīlī state in Sind had not survived for long. In 976 C.E., the Ghaznawid leader, Amīr Sebüktigin, attacked India. He invaded part of western Sind and forced the Hindu king, Jaypāl, out of his Hindūshāhī territory, annexing the region extending from Kābul to Peshāwar. Rulers of Mukrān, which is the region adjacent to Sind on the southwest side, also transferred their allegiance to Sebüktigin. The Ismāʿīlīs of Multān were thus vulnerable to Ghaznawid forces on the whole western flank. Multān was subsequently invaded, but its ruler, the Fāṭimid *dāʿī* Shaikh Ḥamīd, succeeded in securing a truce with Sebüktigin.[38]

Unlike his father, however, Sebüktigin's successor, Maḥmūd Ghaznawī, was a sworn enemy of the Fāṭimid Ismāʿīlīs. He continued his father's advance on India and in 1001 C.E. defeated Jaypāl's forces in Peshāwar. Three years later, he conquered the Hindu ruler of Bhāṭiyah, a region east of Multān. Fearing Multān would be next in the order of attack, its Fāṭimid governor, Abū al-Fatḥ Dā'ūd b. Naṣr, entered into a defense alliance with Anandpāl, successor of the Hindūshāhī king, Jaypāl. This alliance may also have included other Indian dynasties of the northwest.[39]

In 1005 C.E., Maḥmūd Ghaznawī invaded Multān with the avowed purpose of defending Sunnī orthodoxy and purging the Ismāʿīlīs from the region for their alleged apostacy. Anandpāl attempted to block Maḥmūd's advance to Multān but was defeated. Ismāʿīlī forces capitulated after withstanding the Ghaznawid attack for a week. Fined an indemnity of twenty million dirhams, Dāʾūd b. Naṣr was made a tributary to the Ghaznawid *sulṭān*. In four years, however, Maḥmūd returned, and in 1010 C.E. he captured and imprisoned Dāʾūd and brutally massacred the Ismāʿīlīs in Multān and surrounding areas. Contemporary reports vividly describe this mass genocide that included various kinds of mutilation and bloodshed. According to Mubārak Shāh, "so many Ismāʿīlīs were killed at Multān that a stream of blood flowed through the Lahore Gate and Maḥmūd's hand stuck to the hilt of the sword."[40]

It is noteworthy that Maḥmūd of Ghazna attacked the Ismāʿīlīs of Multān in 1010 C.E., the same year as al-Qādir's anti-Fāṭimid manifesto, and massacred them expressly to purge these so-called apostates from *dār al-islām*. Maclean rightly points out that "through his actions in Multān, Maḥmūd could emphasize (vis-à-vis the Shīʿī Daylamites) his role as the primary defender of Sunnī orthodoxy within the ʿAbbāsid empire, a basis for the legitimization of Ghaznawid rule."[41] Indeed, this pattern of expunging Ismāʿīlīs to win caliphal approval and territorial authority became typical and was used with equal success by the Saljūqs, Ghūrids, and Īl-Khāns (Mongols who converted to Islam), as well.

Around the same time, another local ruler of Sind based in Manṣūrah, a Ḥabbārid Arab whose name was probably Khafīf, is said to have converted to Fāṭimid Ismāʿīlism.[42] It is likely that after the Multān massacre what remained of the Ismāʿīlī population became concentrated in al-Manṣūrah, which already had a large ʿAlid community. Knowing that his state was also vulnerable to Maḥmūd's invasion, the Ḥabbārid Arab ruler seems to have allied his forces with the remaining Arab Ismāʿīlīs. It is not certain whether or not the Ḥabbārids actually proclaimed the Fāṭimid creed, but Manṣūrah became the center of Ismāʿīlī activity for the next fifteen years. In 1026 C.E., however, the combined forces of the Ismāʿīlīs and Ḥabbārids were completely crushed when Maḥmūd Ghaznawī, on his return from his desecration of the Hindu temples of Somnāth, brutally annexed al-Manṣūrah and Lower Sind, thus bringing to a close the era of Arab rule in Sind.

Subsequent to the conquest of the Sunnī Ghaznawids, anyone mildly suspected of Ismāʿīlī connections was killed. Maḥmūd's own *vazīr* (minister) Hasnak, who accepted a cloak from the Fāṭimid Caliph al-ʿAzīz in Egypt, was put to death in 1032 C.E. by Maḥmūd's son and successor, Masʿūd, allegedly for conspiring with the Ismā-

ʿīlīs. The Ghaznawid attack left the surviving Arab Ismāʿīlī community in Sind in complete disarray. During this uncertain period, rival Ismāʿīlī interests surfaced. There is, for instance, the epistle mentioned earlier from the Druze leader, al-Muqtanaʿ, in 1033 C.E. to the *shaykh* Ibn Sūmar Rājabāl "asking him to espouse the Druze cause."[43] That Fāṭimid Ismāʿīlī activity still continued is evidenced by letters written to the *daʿwah* in Yaman by the Caliph al-Mustanṣir (d.1094 C.E.) that confirm appointments of *dāʿīs* for Sind.[44] Thus, for instance, according to traditions preserved by the Bohorās, a subsect of the Fāṭimid Ismāʿīlīs in Sind, a certain *dāʿī* called ʿAbd Allāh was sent from Yaman in 1067 C.E. and allegedly succeeded in converting the Rājput king of Gujarat, Jayasingh Siddharāja (1094–1143 C.E.) in Anhilwāḍa Pāṭan.[45]

A few observations can be made about this early period of the Fāṭimid Ismāʿīlī *daʿwah* in Sind. Before the arrival of the Ghaznawids, it seems that the Arabs in Sind, whether Sunnī or Shīʿah, lived in relative accord. Their relations appear to have been cemented by a common livelihood of exports and trade, Arab culture and ethnicity, and the faith of Islam. It is interesting to note that, unlike the Fāṭimid Ismāʿīlīs, the early Sunnī Arab rulers of Sind made no effort to convert the local populace, perhaps not wishing to lose the aristocratic status they enjoyed as a result of revenues (*kharāj* or land taxes) that were levied higher for non-Muslims than non-Arab Muslims (called *mawālī*).[46] As Maclean has demonstrated, the significant conversion of Sind's Buddhists to Islam had a basis in their experience of economic deprivation relative to the Arab merchants and aristocrats.[47]

The Fāṭimid *daʿwah* appears to have focused its efforts on first winning the support of pro-ʿAlīd Arab Muslim compatriots and then winning over local Hindu chiefs. That is, early Fāṭimid power in both Multān and Manṣūrah was linked to an Arab Muslim base, and Fāṭimid rule was established either by converting existing Arab Muslim rulers or by securing political alliances with them. There is no indication that the Sunnīs and Shīʿah of Upper Sind harbored overt hostilities. On the other hand, it was not until the devastation of Multān that the Arab Ḥabbārids of al-Manṣūrah joined ranks with the Fāṭimid Ismāʿīlīs. This alliance (or allegiance) was undoubtedly motivated by the desire to protect the Arabs of Sind against their Turkish aggressors. Ethnicity and vested interests thus combined to form solidarity, subordinating the question of religious loyalties.

With the Ghaznawid invasion under Amīr Sebüktigin around 980 C.E., the whole pattern of power in the region of Sind was altered. Although the Ghaznawids expressed special antipathy for the Ismāʿīlīs in order to endear themselves to the caliphate in Baghdad, practically no ruler in the region of northwestern India was spared Ghaznawid aggression. This included the Hindu states adjacent to Multān which were also attacked in the name of Islam as being comprised of idol-worshipping infidels. To protect themselves, the Fāṭimids of Multān struck up alliances with both Hindu and Sunnī Arab rulers in the region. While this joining of interests did not ultimately succeed in defeating the Ghaznawids, it must certainly have opened up a new chapter of close relations between the Ismāʿīlīs and Hindu chieftains, especially once the Arab base that the Fāṭimids had formerly built upon was destroyed by the successive massacres undertaken by Maḥmūd Ghaznawī.

As we have noted, the Multān and al-Manṣūrah massacres left the Fāṭimid *daʿwah* in disarray. The Druze split in Cairo reverberated in Sind and must have caused further confusion. It is most likely that the Hindus and Ismāʿīlīs of Upper Sind fled south from the Ghaznawids and took cover in the region called Thaṭṭa among the local Sindhi tribes. The chiefs of these formerly Hindu tribes had long intermarried with Arab settlers; over time, they had made influential connections through kinship relations, thereby securing wealth and land.[48] However, they also retained certain Hindu customs such as commensality. It is from this group that the Sūmrah dynasty emerged. We can surmise that some Sūmrahs had already converted to Fāṭimid Ismāʿīlism since Shaykh Sūmar Rājabāl, who probably belonged to this Sindhi tribe, was addressed as the chief *dāʿī* by the Druze from whom he received an epistle to espouse their cause.

Abbas Hamdani believes that the early Sūmrah rulers had close contacts with the Fāṭimid Ismāʿīlī *daʿwah* after the Ghaznawid devastation of Multān and al-Manṣūrah and that, after the Fāṭimid schism following al-Mustanṣir in 1094 C.E., they threw their support behind the Nizārīs,[49] rather than defecting groups such as the Druze or Qarmaṭī. Over time, intermarriages may have occurred between the Ismāʿīlīs and Hindus who fled from Upper Sind and the local population that was already of mixed Sindhi–Hindu and Arab–Muslim lineage. In fact, the seeds of incorporating Hindu elements into Ismāʿīlī identity, which is at the heart of the community later called Satpanth Ismāʿīlism, may well have been sown in the fertile ground of the Sūmrahs with its tradition of intermarriage, trade, and political alliance between Sindhis and Arabs.

Within two decades of Maḥmūd's attack, the Sūmrahs repossessed Lower Sind from the Ghaznawids in 1051 C.E. and ruled for about three centuries. Sūmar Rājabāl and his successors made concentrated efforts to regain the areas of Multān and al-Manṣūrah, probably using Lower Sind as their base. Although existing evidence tends to support the Ismāʿīlī affiliations of the Sūmrahs, it is interesting that contemporary Sunnī writers do not accuse them of Ismāʿīlī (or Qarmaṭī) connections, but they do note that the Sūmrahs retained many Hindu customs.[50] As much of the Arab base of the Fāṭimid Ismāʿīlī forces in Upper Sind was destroyed by the Ghaznawid attacks, it is possible that, given a context of intense anti-Ismāʿīlī hostilities, the Sūmrahs did not make a point of declaring their Ismāʿīlī connections. This may have been viewed as an application of *taqīyah* by the Fāṭimid *daʿwah*. Due to the political events in Sind, the Fāṭimid center in Cairo no doubt felt it necessary to relax somewhat the stringent requirement that the Indian *daʿwah* conform to strictly Islamic practice and tradition. At any rate, the continued practice of Hindu customs, thanks to the Hindu origins of the Sindhi tribes that evolved into the Sūmrah dynasty, and the practice of dissimulation are ways to explain why the Sūmrah Muslims were not immediately suspected of Ismāʿīlī sympathies.

We shall return to the history of Sind shortly, but first it is necessary to examine other events occurring in the larger Ismāʿīlī world. It was during the Fāṭimid caliph al-Mustanṣir bi'llāh's long reign of some sixty years (1036–1094 C.E.) that internal rivalries within the Fāṭimid state came to a climax and ultimately led to its demise. Court intrigues between his ministers and rivalries among the Berbers, Turks, Arabs, and Daylamīs in the Fāṭimid army culminated in open warfare in Cairo in 1062 C.E. Egypt also faced an economic crisis when famine and food shortages resulted after seven years of drought between 1065 and 1072 C.E. The Fāṭimid caliphate was considerably weakened by these problems.

In the meanwhile, as the Islamic heartlands were being subdued by the Saljūqs who defeated the Ghaznawids in 1038 C.E., the Fāṭimid *daʿwah* was making progress in scattered regions in Iraq and Persia. Once again, fearing the Ismāʿīlīs' growing influence, the ʿAbbāsid caliphate sponsored another anti-Fāṭimid manifesto in 1052 C.E. The Saljūqs, declaring themselves champions of Sunnī Islam, advanced on to Baghdad and in 1055 C.E. successfully won the ʿAbbāsid capital from the Shīʿī Būyids. When Ṭughril was declared *sulṭān* in 1056 C.E. by the ʿAbbāsid caliph, al-Qā'im, he announced his plans to destroy the Shīʿī Fāṭimids in Egypt and Syria. However, *daʿwah* activities had peaked during the time of al-Mustanṣir under the astute direction of his *dāʿī*, al-Mu'ayyad fī'l-Dīn al-Shīrāzī, and the very year after Ṭughril became *sulṭān*, pro-Fāṭimid Turks under their leader, al-Basāsīrī, took over Baghdad where for a brief spell of two years the *khuṭba* was pronounced in the name of the Fāṭimid caliph al-Mustanṣir bi'llāh.[51]

This success in Baghdad, though short-lived, must have been exuberantly celebrated across the Fāṭimid Ismā'īlī domain, for it marked for the first time after the caliphate of Ḥazrat 'Alī a historical realization of the *imām's* rightful position over the Islamic *ummah.* It should be noted that the seizure of Baghdad (1057 C.E.) came soon after the repossession of Lower Sind by the Sūmrahs (1051 C.E.), and the latter must have been cheered considerably by this event. (It is interesting to note that a prominent theme in the *ginān*s of Pīr Shams is the promise of help from Iraq or the West, and it may be speculated whether this is, in fact, a remnant of the memory of this victory.)

At any rate, by 1060 C.E., the Saljūqs had conquered Fāṭimid Syria, and in 1070 C.E., the custodians of Mecca abolished the Shī'ī *adhān* (call to prayer), pronouncing the *khuṭba* for the 'Abbāsid caliph and the Saljūq *sulṭān,* thus effectively ending Fāṭimid rule in the Hijāz. Clearly, the territorial extension of the Fāṭimids was in rapid decline. In Yaman, however, the *da'wah* succeeded in winning the support of the Ṣulayḥid dynasty. The Ṣulayḥid Queen, al-Malika al-Sayyida, maintained close relations with Fāṭimid caliph al-Mustanṣir and supervised renewed efforts to strengthen the *da'wah* in India. Henceforth, the Ṣulayḥids remained in charge of the *da'wah* in India, selecting and dispatching *dā'īs* there with al-Mustanṣir's approval. We have noted, for instance, that the *dā'ī* 'Abd Allāh and others were sent to Gujarat from Yaman in 1067 C.E.[52]

By the end of al-Mustanṣir's life, however, the Fāṭimids were under constant attack in the Islamic east, and the situation in Cairo had deteriorated considerably. In 1072 C.E., the head of the Persian *da'wah* in Iṣfahān, 'Abd al-Malik b. 'Aṭṭāsh, appointed Ḥasan-i Ṣabbāḥ as *dā'ī.* The Fāṭimid *da'wah* in Persia, which maintained close contact with the chief *dā'ī* Badr al-Jamālī in Cairo, had won small pockets of supporters from Kirmān to Ādharbayjān. Ḥasan-i Ṣabbāḥ intensified efforts to establish a military base in Daylamān, which culminated in the capture of the virtually impregnable fortress of Alamūt in 1090 C.E. This date would mark in retrospect the beginning of the Nizārī Ismā'īlī state and a policy of open revolt against the Saljūq regime.[53]

The Saljūq empire was consolidated during the reign of Arp Arslān (1063–1073 C.E.) with the help of his *vazīr,* the celebrated Niẓām al-Mulk. After Ḥasan-i Ṣabbāḥ captured Alamūt, Niẓām, a sworn enemy of the Ismā'īlīs, ordered the general Abū Muslīm to kill Ḥasan. Abū Muslīm did not succeed and was himself later killed by an Ismāʿīlī in 1095 C.E. However, with the support of the ʿAbbāsid caliphate, the *vazīr* engineered more anti-Fāṭimid propaganda in Baghdad, and himself wrote against the Ismāʿīlīs or the *bāṭiniyya* in his *Siyāsat-nāma.* His fear was not misplaced for, after encouraging Malikshāh to order armies against the Ismāʿīlīs of Quhistān and Rūdbār in 1092 C.E., Niẓām al-Mulk was assassinated the same year by Abū Ṭāhir Arrānī, the first Ismāʿīlī *fidāʾī* (one who risks one's life for the *daʿwah*). The most serious and sophisticated denunciation of the Ismāʿīlīs, however, came from the pen of the famous Sunnī theologian, Abū Ḥāmid Muḥammad al-Ghazālī (d. 1111 C.E.), who at the request of al-Mustaẓhir, Malikshāh's successor, composed a treatise in 1094 C.E. known as *al-Mustaẓhirī* which systematically refuted the so-called doctrines of the Bāṭinīs (believers in the *bāṭin* or esoteric, hidden meaning of the Revelation).[54]

Indeed, the year 1094 C.E. was to mark another cleavage in Ismāʿīlī history. al-Mustanṣir died that year, and the Fāṭimid *daʿwah* split into two branches. The Fāṭimid Ismāʿīlīs in Syria and Persia threw their support behind the Fāṭimid caliph's elder son, Nizār, and came to be known as the Nizārī Ismāʿīlīs. The younger son al-Mustaʿli, however, was installed as his successor to the throne in Cairo and, when Nizār revolted, al-Mustaʿli had him killed. Thenceforth, the Persian Ismāʿīlīs effectively cut all relations with Cairo, referring to themselves as *al-daʿwa al-jadīda,* the new mission or teaching. Yaman, however, remained faithful to al-Mustaʿli; and as the Ṣulayḥids had supervised the *daʿwah* in the Indian subcontintent, presumably they continued to influence loyalties in the region. The question is, therefore, whom did the Sūmrahs support? Hamdani is convinced that they allied themselves with the Nizārī *daʿwah* since, as the later Satpanth tradition shows, the Nizārīs were more accommodating of local customs, whereas the Ṭayyibi Bohrās, directed from Yaman, were not assimilative. To this we might add that the Sūmrahs may also have preferred the alliance with the Nizārīs because, unlike the apolitical Ṭayyibi Bohrās, the Nizārīs were actively engaged in political maneuvers and wielded the powers of a scattered state from their base in Alamūt.

Connections of the Nizārī State in Alamūt with Political Events in Sind and the Formation of Satpanth

Marshall Hodgson's classic work on the Nizārīs reveals in detail their quest for an independent state.[55] Between 1090 C.E., when Ḥasan-i

Ṣabbāḥ seized Alamūt, and 1256 C.E., when Rukn al-Dīn Khūr Shāh surrendered it to the Mongols, the Nizārī Ismāʿīlīs struggled to maintain a confederation of self-governed states amidst an intensely hostile Sunnī environment. It has been shown that, by the time of the Nizārī–Mustaʿlī split, the Fāṭimid Ismāʿīlīs had been subjected to repeated and harrowing persecution, and their doctrines publicly distorted and vilified. The Ismāʿīlīs were widely denounced as *mulāḥida* (heretics) or *ḥashīshiyya* (assassins and/or smokers of ḥashīsh),[56] and the Sunnī overlords, whether Saljūqid or Ghaznawid, had license to attack and kill them at will.

This period of Islamic history has been noted for its volatility, political fragmentation, constantly shifting loyalties, and warring independent kingdoms. Under the system of *iqṭāʿ* or land grants instituted by Niẓām al-Mulk, the *sulṭān* had parcelled out the Saljūq empire to *amīrs* or commanders from whom revenues were collected.[57] The Saljūq *amīrs* were themselves in constant battle to expand their own vassal states. They were also embroiled in intrigues over the sultanate so that the heartlands of the Islamic world were more or less in a chronic state of confusion and civil war. In this context of widespread chaos and Sunnī enmity, the Nizārīs developed their own program of revolt. As Daftary explains, "The Persian Ismāʿīlīs adopted precisely such a piecemeal strategy in their efforts to subdue the Saljūq domains, locality by locality, stronghold by stronghold, and leader by leader."[58]

Following the atomized nature of power in the region, the Nizārī response was to capture discrete strongholds and towns and form a network or cluster of fortresses or *dār al-hijrahs* (places of refuge) that they fortified and defended. While widely dispersed, these various Nizārī outposts were centrally coordinated from Alamūt so that, in contrast to the Saljūq empire, a distinctive feature of this decentralized Nizārī state was its cohesion and precise coordination of revolt. Nizārī methods of securing key strongholds across the region demonstrated a variety and expediency of means, a characteristic that would be manifest again in their approach to the *daʿwah* in India. Their methods ranged from diplomacy and persuasion to military maneuvers and political assassination. It was this last strategy, however, for which they would become renowned, abhorred, and truly feared.[59]

While murder for political advantage or power was a widespread phenomenon among the rival Turkish dynasties of this period, the Nizārī Ismāʿīlīs were singled out and stigmatized for their assassinations, which Marshall Hodgson argues were neither random nor senseless, but carefully calculated attacks occasioned by "very specific defense or retaliation."[60] The stealth, suddeness of attack, and highly selective and prominent targets of the suicidal missions of the Nizārī *fidā'īs* earned them a terrible reputation. Already beleaguered by persecution and hatred, the Nizārī Ismāʿīlīs perfected this stealthy technique of targetting key officers and used it with success. Not surprisingly, this drew the grim retaliation of repeated mass murders of Ismāʿīlīs, even in cases where Ismāʿīlī *fidāʿīs* were not involved. Increasingly, in a mood of hysteria and witch-hunting, the Ismāʿīlī *fidāʿīn* came to be wrongfully accused of all kinds of assassinations. As Hodgson sums up,

> The reaction of the Muslim community at large to the Nizārī threat was violent and unanimous. All who did not share in the Nizārī revolt—Twelver Shīʿahs as well as Sunnī—united to resist it. . . . The violence of the reaction . . . [was] expressed at its fullest in the recurrent massacres of Nizārī colonies.[61]

It is not necessary to list here the succession of pathetic massacres, sometimes in retaliation for assassinations, sometimes in battle over strongholds, but more frequently as a matter of course, that the Nizārī Ismāʿīlīs suffered in Persia.[62] The point to be made is that, although the Nizārīs withstood the Saljūqs and later the Khwārazmians in western Persia for 166 years, it is certain that with such unrelenting persecution their numbers had dwindled considerably by the time of the Mongol invasion.

To be sure, the situation of the Ismāʿīlīs was already delicate and vulnerable when they captured Alamūt in 1090 C.E. The division among the Fāṭimids following al-Mustanṣir's death four years later left the Ismāʿīlīs in Persia with a smaller force of men to draw upon. This weakened situation was to be followed by more than a century and a half of sustained warfare and bloodshed. The Nizārīs withstood these attacks mainly as a result of their astute leadership and remarkable unity and cohesion, but it is reasonable to surmise that a toll had been exacted upon the Nizārī population. Still, given their impressive fortresses and strongholds that were scattered in northern Persia in the highlands of Daylamān, Rūdbār and Qūhistān, and the regions of Kirmān and Sīstān, the Nizārīs continued to represent a center of power for the Ismāʿīlīs, including those in Sind.

To what extent did the Nizārī Ismāʿīlī *daʿwah* or the new dispensation (*al-daʿwa al-jadīda*), as it declared itself to be, continue to covet the long-held Fāṭimid Ismāʿīlī goal of Shīʿī hegemony over the Islamic world? Did the Nizārī *daʿwah* consider this to be a realistic goal? It is clear that the immediate concern of Ḥasan-i Ṣabbāḥ and his successors was to establish an independent Nizārī state to ensure that the Ismāʿīlīs had a safe harbor, the power and autonomy for self-rule, and a place in which to give shape to their own vision of a just society. But this goal represents a retreat from the ideal of supremacy over the whole *ummah*. Given the circumstances, a reorientation of goals appears to have taken place during the Nizārī period: empire building was replaced *de facto* by the more attainable goal of a self-governed Ismāʿīlī state. But how did the Nizārīs accept the fact that their ideal of presiding over *dār al-islām* may have failed, and, more importantly, how did they face the realization that this aspiration had perhaps altogether gone out of reach? Accordingly, how did *al-daʿwa al-jadīda* reshape the Nizārī Ismāʿīlī quest for sovereignty and justice?

The answers to these questions can be found in the development of Nizārī Ismāʿīlī leadership and ideology. As noted earlier, Nizār, the elder son of al-Mustanṣir, was killed soon after his younger brother, al-Mustaʿli, became caliph. According to later Nizārī sources concerning the veracity of which there has been debate, Nizār's infant son or grandson was smuggled out of Cairo and secretly delivered to Ḥasan-i Ṣabbāḥ at Alamūt where he and his sons lived in anonymity.[63] In the *imām's* absence, Ḥasan-i Ṣabbāḥ came to occupy the high rank of *ḥujjah* or proof of the *imām's* existence. Hodgson points out, however, that neither Ḥasan-i Ṣabbāḥ nor his two successors at Alamūt actually named any *imāms* after Nizār and that there is no indication of an official doctrine at the time that the *imāms* were in hiding or that the heads of Alamūt were in secret contact with them.[64] Rather, *Haft Bāb-i Bāba Sayyidnā*, a work attributed to Ḥasan-i Ṣabbāḥ, predicts the coming of the *Qāʾim* who would bring justice and truth to the world and would complete the cycle of *imāmah*—a typical Shīʿī position that came to be invoked whenever an *imām* was physically hidden or absent.

Hodgson discusses this issue at length and doubts that Nizār had any descendants. In his view, the story of hidden *imāms* with whom the *khudāwands* or lords of Alamūt had been all along in secret contact was a later fabrication.[65] Whatever may be the truth, in 1164 C.E., the fourth head of Alamūt, Muḥammad b. Buzurg Ummīd's son, Ḥasan II, declared himself to be, not a *dāʿī* nor a *ḥujjah*, but the hidden, anticipated *imām* himself who would bring justice on earth.[66] Ḥasan II's sons also held tenaciously to this claim that they were descendants of Nizār and the Fāṭimid caliphs.[67]

What is relevant to this discussion is the contrasts in ideology and policy demonstrated by the heads of Alamūt who effectively exercised supreme authority over the Nizārī *daʿwah* during the course of more than 150 years. Nizārī Alamūt went through three phases.[68] The first phase (1090–1162 C.E.) was the establishment of the Nizārī state by Ḥasan-i Ṣabbāḥ whose policies were faithfully followed by his two successors. The second phase (1162–1210 C.E.) was initiated by Ḥasan II ʿala Ḍhikrihi al-Salām who claimed he was the awaited Nizārī *imām*. Ḥasan II declared the arrival of the *Qiyāmah* (Resurrection or the Last Day when humanity would be judged and, accordingly, be committed to eternal hell or paradise), and suspended all loyalty to Islamic norms or *sharīʿah*. The third phase (1210–1256 C.E.), established by Jalāl al-Dīn Ḥasan III, consisted of a strict return to *sharīʿah*, and attempts at reconciliation with the Sunnī world. It is necessary to assess more carefully the implications of these changing orientations.[69]

During the first phase of Nizārī history, the practice of *sharīʿah* was strictly enforced, so much so that Ḥasan-i Ṣabbāḥ had his own son killed for drinking wine.[70] The bone of contention between the Sunnī and Shīʿī worlds at this time does not appear to have been over the practice of *sharīʿah*, which evolved from the basic principles of the Qurʾān and *ḥadīth* as sources of divine guidance in human affairs. While the Shīʿah and the Sunnīs had different traditions of *ḥadīth* and slightly variant readings of the Qurʾān, what decisively separated them was the Shīʿah insistence that absolute religious authority and interpretation of these primary sources was vested only in the *imām*. The Shīʿah, and especially the Ismāʿīlīs, had elaborated in different philosophical terms the special nature of esoteric interpretation or *taʾwīl* that was the prerogative only of the *imām*, at the basis of which was the principle that only he possessed knowledge of the Qurʾān's *bāṭin*, the inner reality or essence of Revelation. The attack against the *bāṭiniyya* by Ghazālī and others was, at heart, an attack against the notion of a singular, divinely sanctioned religious authority and, more important, against the special privileges to which such claims would thus entitle the *imām*. That this particular guidance and knowledge of the will of God was not directly accessible to all Muslims, but had to be transmitted and interpreted through the special office of an *imām*, went against the so-called egalitarianism of Sunnī Islam.[71]

Over the course of their history, the Ismāʿīlīs were consistently attacked for their esoteric doctrines concerning the *imām's* special knowledge or teachings (*taʿlīm*), which involved initiation, hierarchy, absolute allegiance, hidden truths, and so forth. Whether as *taʿ*-

līmiyya or *bāṭiniyya,* the Ismāʿīlī and general Shīʿī insistence on the imāmate as the custodian of spiritual secrets and of Muḥammad's *wilāyah* or proximity to God did not always endear them to the Sunnīs who sought more accessible and clear-cut ways of determining God's will.

Now, during the period after the death of al-Mustanṣir and the start of the Nizārī *daʿwah,* it seems clear from Ḥasan-i Ṣabbāḥ's strict practice of *sharīʿah* and observance of general Islamic ordinances that the Nizārī Ismāʿīlīs were consonant with the Islamic *ummah* at large. Certainly, it would have been impossible to assert any influence over the *ummah* without being in close harmony with prevalent Islamic norms. It is evident that during the Fāṭimid period, al-Muʿizz consciously safeguarded his followers' Islamic roots and identity, for a common ground with their fellow Muslims was essential if the Ismāʿīlīs were to be successful in convincing the former of the necessity and legitimacy of the guidance of the Shīʿah *imāms.* Thus, we see that he insisted that the *daʿwah* strictly follow Islamic patterns of law and worship when it propagated Ismāʿīlī ideas.

By the time Ḥasan II ʿala Ḍhikrihi al-Salām assumed leadership of the Nizārī *daʿwah,* it must have become increasingly obvious, however, that the sovereignty over the *ummah* that the Ismāʿīlīs had cherished for their cause would not come to pass any time soon. It has been suggested that the declaration of the *Qiyāmah* was thus "a spiritual rejection of the outside world,"[72] and a final rebuttal against Sunnī Islam. That is, by declaring the *Qiyāmah* and relieving his followers of the duty to observe *sharīʿah,* Ḥasan II repudiated the sacred law and posed it as being an empty shell of ritualism bereft of spirit. The true believers, he declared, would be able to apprehend the truth and the will of God directly through the *imāms.* The obligations of *sharīʿah* were reinterpreted and reconfigured through *taʾwīl* or esoteric hermeneutics so that, for instance, instead of performing the five daily ritual prayers, the Nizārīs were to be in constant prayer by always recollecting God in their hearts. This suspension of the obligation of the *sharīʿah* marked a sharp break, ritually and symbolically, from the wider *ummah* that had spurned and ridiculed the Nizārī claims. At the same time, however, the declaration of the *Qiyāmah* assured the Nizārīs that a spiritual resurrection had taken place in which they had been vindicated, for only those who followed the *imām* and recognized his inner reality would know God and were privy to the *bāṭin* or spiritual realities, whereas the enemies of the *imām,* in rejecting his knowledge and guidance, had been cast into spiritual hell or nonexistence.[73]

It is worth noting that hitherto Ismāʿīlī philosophers had seldom deprecated the *sharīʿah* in their works nor suggested that it was merely a hollow shell concealing a superior truth. Why would Ḥasan II have made such a bold move, one that, as Hodgson observes, would have further estranged the Ismāʿīlīs from the Sunnīs and other groups of the Shīʿah? As he points out, the Sunnīs would care little for the higher reality of spiritual awareness promised by the Resurrection nor for the claim that Ḥasan was the *Qāʾim* (lit., "riser," the messianic *imām*). However,

> they would care that now the Ismāʿīlīs had in fact done that villainous deed they had been long accused of doing, thrown off the shackles of the law . . . and from now . . . to be called *Mulḥid,* "heretic". . . (for) they have now rejected those universal forms of law which held the Islamic community together.[74]

In fact, the disastrous consequence of this declaration was probably realized by one of Ḥasan's successors, Jalāl al-Dīn, less than half a century later, and at a time when his community faced imminent attack by the fierce, Sunnī-inclined Mongols. Not only did Jalāl al-Dīn revert to the strict practice of *sharīʿah* but, in response to his circumstances, he went so far as to identify himself and the Nizārīs as Sunnīs, a tactic which proved successful inasmuch as it saved the lives of his Nizārī followers.

Why, then, did his grandfather, Ḥasan II, make such an incomprehensible move? Firstly, as noted earlier, Ḥasan II's father, Muḥammad b. Buzurg Ummīd, was the *dāʿī* or lord of Alamūt, whereas Ḥasan II was claiming to be the *imām* himself. How was he to validate this claim? If Ḥasan II was the *imām,* he had to be the promised *Qāʾim* or messiah of the *Haft Bāb-i Bāba Sayyidnā* who would bring justice and truth to earth. As we have suggested, by the time of Ḥasan II, it must have been obvious to him that the establishment of justice and truth, which meant the *imām's* supreme authority over *dār al-islām,* was a remote if not an impossible prospect. As Daftary points out,

> The announcement of *qiyāma* was in fact a declaration of independence from the larger Muslim society and, at the same time, an admission of failure of the Nizārī struggle to take over that society; for the *qiyāma* declared the outside world irrelevant.[75]

This was a bold retreat from the earlier Fāṭimid and Nizārī assertions of revolution to change the world and set things aright. In retrospect, one is inclined to read the *Qiyāmah* as an "admission of failure," but, at the time of its declaration, quite the opposite meaning was intended, namely, the ultimate success and vindication of the *daʿwah*. For, the abandonment of the goal of dominion over the Muslim world did not necessarily preclude a plan to secure a limited dominion over an Ismāʿīlī state. Conceivably, Ḥasan II ʿala Ḍhikrihi al-Salām might still have been able to entertain hopes of bringing justice and truth to Ismāʿīlīs by gaining control of small regions including Sind. Nonetheless, even if the declaration signalled a contraction—not a complete withdrawal—of political aspirations, the doctrine of *qiyāmah* marked a turning point in Ismāʿīlī history.

As the promised *Qāʾim*, Ḥasan had to deliver on his promise of truth and justice to his followers to retain their support. He had to reward their sacrifices, to vindicate their support of his claim as *imām* and to fulfill their expectations that the righteous Shīʿī *imām* had been ultimately victorious. This he did by parting the physical realm from the spiritual and asserting that the latter was superior and then proclaiming a Resurrection in which the Nizārīs had won supremacy in the spiritual world. To their satisfaction then,

> The Nizārīs envisaged themselves in spiritual Paradise, while condemning the non-Nizārīs to the Hell of spiritual non-existence. Now the Nizārīs had the opportunity of being collectively introduced to Paradise on earth, which was the knowledge of the unveiled truth; the Nizārī Imām was the epiphany (*maẓhar*) of that unchangeable *ḥaqīqa*.[76]

Ḥasan II effectively translated success from the theater of the temporary and mundane to the more permanent and, therefore, superior realm of the spiritual. And, in that realm, the Ismāʿīlīs had achieved victory through their *imām*, for it was only by the recognition of his true nature that they had been given entry into Paradise and received divine felicity. The concept of *Qiyāmah* skillfully transferred the ideal of dominion over *dār al-islām* from the lower world of bodies to the higher world of souls and relieved the *imāms* of the necessity to find completion of their office in temporal terms. That is to say, regardless of whether the *imām* was the caliphal head of the *ummah* or not, his spiritual authority was confirmed, and he had unveiled his true reality as the *maẓhar* or epiphany of God. At the same time that the political role of the *imām's* office was thus subordinated to the religious, this did not mean that the imāmate could not, at a moment's notice, rekindle his caliphal rights over the *ummah.*

The declaration of *Qiyāmah* in 1162 C.E. essentially spiritualized an aspiration that for centuries had been materially sought. It created an opening, a window in the space of which religious forms were represented as fluid signs. It is most likely that Satpanth Ismāʿīlism, which was conceived in embryonic form by the forging of alliances and marriages with the Sūmrahs, was given even greater impetus, if not legitimacy, at this time when the Nizārīs rejected their formal solidarity with mainstream Islamic symbols. Moreover, an indication that the *daʿwah* in India was both active and under political stress is evidenced by the fact that, when the Ghūrids attacked Sind first in 1160 C.E. and then again in 1175 C.E., the historian Jūzjānī notes that they "delivered Multān from the hands of the Qarmaṭians," in other words, the Ismāʿīlīs. Hamdani suggests that the fifth or sixth Sūmrah chief, Khafif or Unar, ruled Multān at the time.[77] It appears that the Sūmrahs had successfully restored their power in Multān with help from the "West," that is, from the forces of the Nizārī *daʿwah* in Alamūt or Persia. Further, since the Ghūrid incursions against the Ismāʿīlīs in Multān began around the time of Ḥasan II ʿala Ḍhikrihi al-Salām, his promise that as the Qāʾim he would bring about justice and truth would have been extremely important to the Ismāʿīlīs in Sind.

Minhāj Jūzjānī mentions in the *Ṭabaqāt-i-Nāṣirī* that Muḥammad Ghorī's father, the Ghūrid *sulṭān,* ʾAlāʾ al-Dīn, at the end of his life (circa 1160 C.E.) had cordially received emissaries from Alamūt whom he treated "with great reverence; and in every place in Ghūr they sought, secretly, to make proselytes."[78] This, says the chronicler, left a slur on his reign which his successor, Muḥammad Ghiyās al-Dīn, immediately redressed by putting to the sword all the "Mulāḥidah of Alamūt."

> In every place wherein the odour of their impure usages was perceived, throughout the territory of Ghūr, slaughter of all heretics was commanded. . . . Ghūr, which was a mine of religion and orthodoxy, was purified from the infernal impurity of the Karāmiṭah depravity by the sword.[79]

The Ghūrids also "attacked and devastated Quhistān, forcing the submission of Nizāris there."[80] Nonetheless, the Ismāʿīlīs must have persisted in Multān because fifteen years later Muḥammad's brother, Shihāb al-Dīn, again attacked Multān and Ucch and "delivered it from the hands of the Karāmiṭah."[81] From this we can surmise that, at the time of the Ghūrids, the Nizārī Ismāʿīlī *daʿwah* was quite active in the northwestern regions of the Indian subcontinent. The Nizārīs even attempted diplomacy to win the sympathy of the Sunnī Ghūrids. This overture backfired, and they were hunted down instead. The Nizārī *daʿwah* was correctly perceived by the Ghūrid Turks to be a real threat and, indeed, Shihāb al-Dīn was assassinated by a Nizārī in 1206 C.E. The Sūmrah chiefs in Sind, one of whom ruled Multān, were doubtless in close but secret contact with the Nizārī *daʿwah.* As Jūzjānī notes, the emissaries from Alamūt who visited 'Alā' al-Dīn around 1160 C.E. were suspected of secretly spreading Ismāʿīlism "in every place in Ghūr." Presumably, this referred to the lands annexed by the Ghūrids, including Sind.

It was around this time in 1164 C.E. that Ḥasan II declared the *Qiyāmah* doctrine. Now, it is important to recall that sectarian Ismāʿīlī sources written in Gujarati at the turn of this century claim that Ḥasan II sent the first *pīrs* of the Satpanth *daʿwah* to India between 1162 and 1166 C.E.[82] A number of factors point to the likelihood, therefore, that the impetus for what in the future would evolve into Satpanth Ismāʿīlism gained considerable momentum and endorsement during this period. Firstly, Ḥasan's *Qiyāmah* doctrine allowed scope for such syncretic innovation; secondly, hostilities from Sunnī rulers in India were growing more intense and recurrent; thirdly, other strong rivals such as the fast-growing Ṣūfī *ṭarīqahs,* the Mustaʿlī Ismāʿīlīs, and local Hindu chiefs aligned with Sunnī rulers had to be contended with; and fourthly, the Nizārīs already had an indigenous environment within which to evolve a complex religious identity as a result of their long history with or identification as the Sindhi Sūmrahs. The following discussion will elaborate upon these ideas.

The Birth of Satpanth Ismāʿīlism

Whereas the Nizārīs were allied to or had merged with the Sūmrahs in Sind, the Ṣulayḥid Ṭayyibīs of Yaman maintained a fairly strong hold on the Cambay or Gujarat area. That the Nizārīs and Mustaʿlīs were sworn enemies after the 1094 C.E. schism is confirmed by the fact that Ḥasan-i Ṣabbāḥ had Mustaʿli's son, the Fāṭimid caliph al-Āmir, assassinated by a *fidāʾī* in 1124 C.E. in Cairo. The Ṣulayḥids maintained that al-Āmir had had a son by the name of Ṭayyib, and, hence, their *daʿwah* came to be known as the Ṭayyibī *daʿwah.* Over time, a large segment of the Hindu trading caste called *bohrā* (derived from the Gujarati *vohorvuṅ*—to trade) became Mustaʿlī Ṭayyibī Ismāʿīlīs. Thus, the Ṭayyibīs of India are also known as the Bohorās.

It may be recalled that during the time of the Fāṭimid caliph al-Mustanṣīr, the Ṣulayḥids had been assigned the responsibility of overseeing the *daʿwah* in India. After the Nizār–Mustaʿli split, since the Ṣulayḥids were already in control of the Fāṭimid *daʿwah* in the region, their attempts to win particularly the Arab Indian following over to their side would have been relatively easy. However, that the Sūmrahs became allies of the Nizārīs strongly suggests that Alamūt continued to pursue its own *daʿwah* activities in the region of Sind after the death of al-Mustanṣīr. Had they spread their activities into Gujarat, they would have faced their entrenched rivals, the Ṭayyibī Ismāʿīlīs.

It has been mentioned that there is a record of several *dāʿīs* appointed to preach in Sind preserved in the *Sijillāt al-Mustanṣirriyā*, which contains letters written by the Fāṭimid caliph al-Mustanṣīr to the Yamanī *daʿwah*. According to the Ṭayyibī Bohorā tradition, one of them, a *dāʿī* called ʿAbd Allāh, was sent in 1067 C.E. and allegedly converted the Rājpūt Hindu king of Gujarat, Siddharāja Jaisingha (1094–1143 C.E.) whose capital was Anhilwāḍa Pāṭan. It is interesting to note that, in the Satpanth tradition, Pīr Satgur Nūr, allegedly the first *pīr* of Satpanth, is claimed to have converted this same king. However, there is little evidence to suggest that either of these two figures converted the king, for he remained a faithful Śaivite Hindu till death. Nonetheless, contemporary Muslim writers praise Jaisingha for his generous treatment of Muslims who were free to worship in their own mosques.[83] Hollister even suggests that Siddharāja was to some extent influenced by Islam since "he asked for burial instead of cremation," although he "died as a Hindu."[84] At any rate, Siddharāja Jaisingha's reign has been celebrated as the most glorious of Rājput Gujarat, and

> In popular imagination, Siddharāj himself was the founder of *all* the important communities in Gujarat—no less than *three* Muslim *pirs* are reported to have converted him to their own particular sect.[85]

It is possible that many Arab Muslims, including the Fāṭimid Ismāʿīlīs, found amnesty among these Hindu kingdoms. What the above traditional accounts suggest is that, after the Ghaznawid invasion of 1030 C.E., the Fāṭimid *daʿwah* probably made special efforts to build alliances with and win the loyalty of local Hindu chieftains.

After the 1094 C.E. split, both the Nizārīs and Mustaʿlīs continued this policy but with different emphasis and accommodations. According to Hamdani, the Mustaʿlī Ṭayyibīs, who remained further south near the coastal regions of Cambay "exercised a thorough Arab influence" on its community.[86] He continues:

> We find in their Daʿwa in Gujarat people with Arabic names, and literature written mainly in Arabic. The local Hindu tradition was abandoned and the process of Arabicising had gone very deep. But in the case of the Sūmras, except for their hereditary Arab names (some of them) we find a considerable Hindu cultural influence.[87]

Most likely, the Arab-identified Multānī Ismāʿīlīs in Sind found a much more familiar atmosphere among the Ṭayyibīs in the Gujarat region than among the Sūmrahs who held onto some Hindu manners and customs in Lower Sind.

Hence, of the two branches of Ismāʿīlism in India, the Mustaʿlī Ṭayyibīs in Gujarat would have been more quickly and easily identified with their Fāṭimid predecessors and, were, therefore, much more exposed and vulnerable to persecution by Sunnī dynasties in the North. The Ṭayyibīs adopted an apolitical stance and did not pursue territorial expansion. Instead, they concentrated their *daʿwah* activities in the more hospitable environment of the Cambay region from which they kept in close touch with their headquarters in Yaman and continued their seafaring trade. There may be a close parallel, in fact, between the conversion of the Hindu *bohrā* or trading caste to Ṭayyibī Ismāʿīlism and the earlier Buddhist conversions to Arab Islam, since both were linked to an elevation of status through increased trade and Arabization. The distance of the Bohorās from the sultanate in North India and their lack of territorial ambitions may have helped to protect them initially from the North Indian Sunnī dynasties for some two centuries. However, with the Khaljī conquest of Gujarat in 1298 C.E., followed by successive Tughluqid attacks, persecution increased with such intensity that by the fifteenth century, "the Ṭayyibīs observed *taqiyya* very strictly, adhering outwardly to many of the Sunnī formalities."[88]

On the other hand, it seems clear that the Nizārī branch of the Fāṭimid *daʿwah* continued to court political goals, as evidenced by the presence of the Nizārī *daʿwah* in Multān and Ucch and its connections or identification with the Sūmrahs who were centered in the Thaṭṭa district in Lower Sind. In their attempts to recover Upper

Sind, the Nizārīs had to face not only the Ghūrids but also the Ṣūfīs whose missionary activities had increased substantially. However, though references are made to Nizārī presence in the regions held by the Ghūrids, on the whole, it appears that their *daʿwah* worked "behind the scenes." Undoubtedly, the Nizārīs instigated sporadic indigenous uprisings that the Ghūrids encountered from local Hindu or converted Hindu tribes. For instance, there is an intriguing reference to a rebellion by the Sankurān tribe near Multān, a year after Shihāb al-Dīn massacred the Ismāʿīlīs in Multān in 1175 C.E. According to Jūzjānī, "most of the Sankurān tribe were manifestly confessors of the Kur'ān creed . . . but, as they had stirred up rebellion, they were put to death."[89] It is also worth noting that when Shihāb al-Dīn attacked Ucch, the other major center of Nizārī activity, he was confronted by a Rājah of the Bhaṭī Hindu tribe "which previously held a large part of Sind."[90]

It is reasonable to hypothesize that after the Ghaznawid massacre and the Fāṭimid schism, the Sūmrahs, who supported the Nizārīs rather than the Mustaʿlians, struck up alliances with other local Hindu chieftains whose kingdoms were also being ravaged by the Sunnī dynasties of the North. As Zahid explains, the Nizārī *daʿwah*

> realized the difficulty of recovering the lost following [of Fāṭimid Ismāʿīlīs] in the face of internal dissensions, hostile orthodox Turkish rulers and *ṣūfī* missionaries. Therefore, they decided to win support among the non-Muslims by creating the impression that the Ismāʿīlī beliefs were akin to local Hindu beliefs.[91]

If our reconstruction of the Sūmrah identity is correct, this amalgam had already been forged in the crucible of Arab–Hindu Ismāʿīlī interactions of the preceding century. The emergent identity could now be put to further political use. In other words, by winning the support of more Hindu chieftains, a successful extension of Ismāʿīlism as Satpanth could procure crucial *political* benefits for the Nizārīs.

An important question, however, is how would such an alliance with the Nizārīs have benefited the Hindu local rulers and chieftains? After all, like the Turkish *ghāzīs* or warriors who were devastating their temples and plundering their coffers in the name of Islam, the Nizārīs, too, were Muslim. As Maclean questions, "Without the presence of some additional motivating factor, it is not clear why certain groups of Hindus would abandon their own ideological system for another with a number of similar themes."[92] In this respect, the Sūmrah dynasty, which had long intermarried with the Arabs yet retained various Hindu customs and manners, must have played an important intermediary role with other Hindu tribes. The Sūmrahs would also have preserved the memory of the grandeur of the Fāṭimid dynasty in its heyday and, by the twelfth century, the Nizārīs had themselves established a reputation as a formidable power centered at Alamūt. Thus, it would not have been difficult for the Sūmrahs to reassure or convince local Sindhi and Hindu chiefs and tribes that alliance or solidarity with them and the Nizārīs would be a political advantage. There appears, therefore, to be sufficient evidence to back the interpretation that "the support given the *daʿwah* by certain sectors of the Hindu population can be seen as an attempt to come to terms with the same historical tensions resulting from the refeudalization of Sind."[93]

Interestingly, the clues revealing the reasons why local Hindu rulers may have been interested in the Nizārīs were found in the *gināns* attributed to Pīr Shams, and these will be discussed in greater detail in the next chapter. But, in brief, various *gināns* repeatedly mention that help against the "enemy" or "demon" was imminently expected from Daylamān, the West, or Iraq and that this (military) support would arrive under the supervision of the Shāh, the Qā'im (messiah *imām*), the long-awaited *avatār* (savior). There are a sufficient number of allusions in the *gināns* to support the hypothesis that the Nizārī call or *daʿwah* (invitation) appealed to the local Hindu chiefs precisely because it offered them hope of a powerful ally "from the West" who would overcome the oppression of the Turks. The fact that the Nizārīs presented this hope in a religious framework that had already integrated many aspects of Hinduism and accommodated the cultural sensibilities of the Hindus must surely have made the proposition of an alliance more tempting. Besides, once the Hindus had overcome their Sunnī oppressors and freed their lands, they would still have been at liberty to reassert their older beliefs and customs.

An incident of an uprising in Delhi by the "Qarmaṭī" or "Malāḥidah" in 1206 C.E. shows that the Nizārī *daʿwah* remained in an active political mode in India at least until Alamūt was demolished by the Mongols. The Mongol hordes began their advance towards the Muslim East around 1220 C.E., and, while estimates vary, by 1260 C.E. they had reportedly killed some eight million Muslims from Samarkand to the Indus River. Nizami says, "India was the only country where refugees could find both security and livelihood."[94] Anticipating the Mongol threat to Alamūt, the incident in Delhi betrays that the Nizārīs may have been seriously planning to seize the seat of Muslim power in India. Before the revolt in Delhi, they had attempted to kill the *sulṭān* Illtūtmish (d. 1236 C.E.) in the mosque during Friday prayers, but the king escaped.[95] Taking advantage of the political instability in Delhi during the first year of the reign of his daughter, Queen Raḍiyya, a troop of "Mulāḥidah heretics of Hindustan" headed by a learned Turk, Nūr al-Dīn, again assembled in Delhi publicly criticizing the Sunnī *ʿulamāʾ*. Then, they attacked the Muslims in the Jāmiʿ Masjid during Friday prayers.[96] The revolt was repressed, but what is interesting is that these so-called heretics, or Nizārīs, had collected at Delhi

> from different parts of the territory of Hind, such as Gujarāt, and the country of Sind, and the parts round about the capital, Dilhī, and the banks of the rivers Jūn and Gang.[97]

The regional spread of the rebels suggests a fairly extensive arena of covert activity as well as an advanced degree of organization in order to mobilize forces from various parts of Hind and Sind. Also, it is important to note that the troop largely consisted of an indigenous Nizārī following. Hamdani says that the principal Ismāʿīlī force in Sind was that of the Sūmrahs and that "Sindhi Ismāʿīlīs had formed the main bulk of the people who revolted at Delhi under Nūr Turk."[98] According to him, the Sūmrahs must have summoned the help of the Ismāʿīlīs in Gujarat. Had it not been for the destruction of Alamūt, it seems highly probable that the Nizārīs would have continued their attempts to seize power in India.

The Collapse of Alamūt and its Implications for Satpanth

However, events in the Eastern Islamic lands dictated otherwise. The consequences of Ḥasan II's declaration of the *Qiyāmah* in 1164 C.E. were to be severe. This decisive break from the Sunnī world backfired, and *Qiyāmah* Nizārism was ostracized as being utterly un-Islamic, a consequence clearly understood by Ḥasan's grandson, Jalāl al-Dīn. Thus, while the *Qiyāmah* had succeeded in buttressing Ḥasan II's position as *imām*, by the time Jalāl al-Dīn Ḥasan III came to office, the violent reaction from the Sunnī world that Ḥasan II had supposedly declared irrelevant had made it intolerably relevant. His declaration had only helped to deepen an already entrenched

Sunnī suspicion of the "esotericists" and to add fuel to Sunnī persecution of the Ismāʿīlīs.

Soon after he assumed office in 1210 C.E., Jalāl al-Dīn Ḥasan III publicly repudiated the doctrine of *Qiyāmah,* declared his solidarity with Sunnī Islam, and ordered his followers to practice *sharīʿah* strictly in line with the Sunnī way.[99] He established contacts with the ʿAbbāsid caliph al-Nāṣir and various Sunnī rulers informing them of his reform. He also had mosques built in every Nizārī town to underscore uniformity with Sunnī worship and invited Sunnī theologians and jurists to preach to his Nizārī followers. These measures succeeded in convincing the caliph at Baghdad of Ḥasan's newly acquired orthodoxy, and the latter issued a decree in 1211 C.E. confirming his conversion to Sunnī Islam. Consequently, Ḥasan was accorded the status of *amīr,* and his territorial rights were recognized by the ʿAbbāsid caliph "who showed him all manner of favours."[100]

The Nizārīs seem to have accepted this behavior without question, interpreting it as a form of total *taqiyya* or religious dissimulation. Daftary observes that "Ḥasan's new policies had obvious political advantages for the Nizārī community and state, which had survived only precariously."[101] The key, in my view, lies not in the first half of this statement, but in the second. For indeed, had the Nizārīs merely sought political advantage, the adoption of Sunnism should have taken place much earlier. Rather, by this stage, the very existence of the Nizārī community seems to have been at stake, so much so, that further attacks on them might have proven fatal.

Thus, Jalāl al-Dīn's reorientation bought time and offered the Nizārī Ismāʿīlīs temporary relief from the incessant attacks of their enemies. The Ghūrid attacks against Ismāʿīlīs in Quhistān stopped, and Ismāʿīlīs in Syria actually received assistance from the Sunnī Ayyūbids to fight the Franks. Ḥasan III played an active role in military alliances with the ʿAbbāsid caliph against the Khwārazmians. Having gained the confidence of Sunnī rulers and the caliph in Baghdad, it appears that Ḥasan III's son, ʿAlāʾ al-Dīn Muḥammad III, relaxed somewhat the strict identification with Sunnism. However, the pro-Sunnī orientation declared by Ḥasan III was never formally renounced by Alamūt.

By the time ʿAlāʾ al-Dīn Muḥammad III came to power in 1221 C.E., the lands of Islam were experiencing the shockwaves of the Mongol invasion. The Mongols had already destroyed the Khwārazmian empire, crossed the Oxus valley, and seized Balkh. Many Sunnīs sought refuge in the Nizārī fortresses of Quhistān and Rūdbār. Muḥammad III made several diplomatic attempts towards peace with the Mongols, but they were rebuffed and scorned. Also, despite the Nizārīs' show of Sunnī affiliation, many Sunnī *ʿulamāʾ* (scholars, theologians) distrusted their sincerity. Some of these scholars occupied influential positions in the Mongol retinue and incited the Mongols against the Nizārīs. In 1252 C.E., the first task entrusted to Hülagü Khān by the Great Khān Möngke, instigated by the Sunnī Muslims at his court, was to destroy the Nizārī state; only then should he proceed to capture the rest of the Islamic lands and force the submission of the ʿAbbāsid caliphate in the capital, Baghdad.[102] When Rukn al-Dīn Khūr Shāh succeeded his father in 1255 C.E., he gave strict orders to his followers to abide by the *sharīʿah.* Like his father, Rukn al-Dīn made several attempts to submit to the Mongols peacefully, and several letters were exchanged. Ironically, at the very point when Ismāʿīlī revolutionary activity was at its lowest, and the Nizārīs seemed most secure vis-à-vis the Sunnī world, the marauding Mongols led by Hülagü Khān in 1256 C.E. would strike them their final blow.

The Nizārī Ismāʿīlī state had a poignant end. Alamūt and its lords fell as a result neither of heroic battles lost nor of a lack of skills and wherewithal. Rukn al-Dīn Khūr Shāh's diplomatic maneuvers to forestall the reputedly savage devastation of the Mongols worked against him. In exchange for the peaceful release of his subjects, he agreed to have his generals submit their fortresses and to surrender. Hülagü insisted that Rukn al-Dīn Khūr Shāh surrender himself, but the *imām* held on to his relatively secure position at Alamūt, and Hülagü, growing impatient, made plans for attack. Finally, upon the urgings and advice of his scholar-guest, Naṣīr al-Dīn Ṭūsī, Imām Rukn al-Dīn Khūr Shāh surrendered. Hülagü had promised amnesty if Rukn al-Dīn Khūr Shāh would cooperate by ordering his men to yield their citadels. Virtually all Nizārī fortresses were expeditiously dismantled by Hülagü on Rukn al-Dīn Khūr Shāh's orders, after which Rukn al-Dīn, his family, and his followers were roundly slaughtered. Juwaynī's boast that Hülagü Khān had succeeded in wiping out the Ismāʿīlīs came very close to the truth. As Hodgson explains,

> Meanwhile, the Sunnī Muslims persuaded the Mongols to destroy the whole Ismāʿīlī people so far as they could. . . . The men of Kūhistān were summoned to great gatherings—presumably on the pretext of consultation—and slaugh-

> tered. The slave markets of Khurāsān were glutted with Ismāʿīlī women and children, denied the privileges of Muslims.[103]

This fatal event left surviving Nizārīs—and there could not have been many—in a state of complete shock and confusion. Though weakened to the extreme, the Nizārīs still attempted over the next two decades to restore their strongholds in Rūdbār and Qūhistān but failed. Finally, in 1270 C.E., their prized and impregnable fortress at Girdkūh in Daylamān capitulated. Along with their fellow Persians, those Nizārīs who were able to slip away probably fled to neighboring India to escape the cruelty of the Mongol hordes who systematically exterminated civilian populations in Persian towns along their march from Alamūt to Baghdad. As curtly stated by I. P. Petrushevsky, "This mass-killing was a complete system . . . and had as its goal the planned destruction of those elements of the population that were capable of resistance."[104]

Surely at the end of this wholesale massacre and destruction, the priority of the Nizārīs must have shifted to sheer survival. If in the mid-twelfth century Satpanth was envisaged by the *daʿwah* at Alamūt as an expeditious political strategy, at the fall of Alamūt a century later it would have represented a haven of escape, and an indispensible refuge. The Mongol catastrophe had devastated the Nizārīs and brought to a complete halt their active social and political program for an independent Ismāʿīlī state.

However, without their tangible power networks and fortresses in the West, if discovered, the Nizārī-affiliated Sūmrahs would also have been vulnerable to the extreme in India. Undoubtedly, the Nizārīs who swelled the ranks of the Ismāʿīlīs in Sind had to make a crucial decision at this painful historical juncture. By 1270 C.E., to have been identified either with their Fāṭimid or with their Alamūt forebears would have been suicidal, given the incessant Sunnī reprisals against the *mulāḥidah* (which, no doubt, received renewed vigor with the Il-Khān's embrace of Sunnī Islam). To survive, the Ismāʿīlīs clearly had to take cover under the guise of a Sunnī or some other non-Fāṭimid and non-Nizārī identity. The *daʿwah* in India had already succeeded in planting the seeds of an indigenous identity and establishing an ethnic base. In the course of the Nizārī *daʿwah's* long association of some three centuries with the Sūmrahs and other local Hindu tribes, the essential contours of Satpanth Ismāʿīlism must have gradually taken shape. It is plausible that the seeds of the Satpanth tradition were sown at the time of Ismāʿīlī–Hindu alliances around 1005 C.E., when the invasions of Amīr Sebüktigin, followed by those of his son, Maḥmūd Ghaznawī, brought them together. However, not until the declaration of the *Qiyāmah* in 1164 C.E. is it likely that Satpanth gained its religious and political legitimacy. The final demise of Alamūt, and the consequent need both for camouflage and sanctuary, would submerge these initial political underpinnings of the Satpanth tradition; thereafter, the safer route for the survival and propagation of Ismāʿīlism was political pacifism and religious anonymity in the guise of a Hindu–Muslim syncretic sect.

In giving up its political ambitions, the *daʿwah* in India would safeguard the survival of the Indian Ismāʿīlī community. After the devastation of Alamūt, the only real choice for Ismāʿīlī endurance in Sind in the face of Sunnī oppression was to vanish, which the Ismāʿīlīs did under the ostensibly Hindu–Muslim syncretic identity of Satpanth Ismāʿīlism. Having become marginal to the extreme, had the Ismāʿīlīs in Sind clung to their much maligned Nizārī past, they would certainly have risked extinction. To survive, they legitimized the nascent Satpanth community that had been built upon political alliances and intermarriage, and, by thus aligning themselves with Hindu elements, they were able to enlist native resources and sympathy. This was achieved through a sustained and creative application of the age-old Ismāʿīlī technique of *taqīyah* (religious dissimulation) which involved, in this instance, a combined process of indigenization, adhesion, and syncretism. We may call this strategy the chamelion technique, that is, using camouflage for the sake of self-preservation and regeneration.

In addition to *taqīyah,* however, another principle that may have enabled the Ismāʿīlīs in India to follow such a remarkable course of action was their hermetic tradition based on the dialectic between the *ẓāhir* and the *bāṭin,* the exoteric and the esoteric. This dialectic has worked in opposing directions depending upon the historical circumstances of this sect. When it was important to emphasize uniformity, as was the case in the Fāṭimid period, the antinomian pull of the esoteric or *bāṭin* was restrained. On the other hand, when religious forms became restrictive or potentially dangerous, the outer or *ẓāhir* was subordinated to its inner meaning or *bāṭin,* as in the case of the Satpanth Ismāʿīlīs in the subcontinent for whom it must have been crucial to relinquish *sharīʿah* in order to hide their Muslim identity. At the doctrinal level, as long as new forms and symbols delivered the essence or *bāṭin* (called *sār* in the *ginān*s) to the seeker, the replacement of older forms of practice was justified. By thus appealing to this dialectic between *ẓāhir* and *bāṭin,* the Ismāʿīlīs periodically attached and detached the symbolic and ritual forms of religious life from inner, spiritual realities as they saw fit. It is not surprising that such an inherently unpredictable principle provoked intense suspicion and antipathy from orthoprax-minded Muslims.

In summary then, contrary to the opinion that Satpanth Ismāʿīl-ism developed mainly to promote religious conversion, I have attempted to demonstrate that the key factors for its evolution into this Indic form were rooted in historical circumstances that ultimately forced post-Alamūt Ismāʿīlīs in Sind to find inconspicuous ways by which to survive. The Nizārī Ismāʿīlīs had suffered successive setbacks leading up to their final defeat in 1256 C.E. Now, not only did the Ismāʿīlīs in Sind (indigenous or refugees who fled from the Mongol debacle) have to disappear from public view, they also had to find unobtrusive methods of survival. It is probably for this reason that, despite their affinity to Ṣūfī *ṭarīqahs* such as the Chishtī order, they did not pursue nor adopt a similar form so as to remain a safe distance away from mainstream Sunnī Islam, which would surely have continued to massacre the Ismāʿīlīs had their presence been suspected. Instead, the solution of the Satpanth tradition, that externally appeared to be Hindu but was internally recognizable as Ismāʿīlī, created a safe harbor; it also fashioned the social and cultural bridge that would facilitate Hindu crossings to Satpanth, thereby allowing for the continued growth of this sect. In addition to the early marriage of the Nizārī cause with the Sūmrahs, what made possible the transition and transformation from Nizārī to Satpanth Ismāʿīlism was the practice of *taqīyah* and the Ismāʿīlī concept of the relationship between form and spirit, *ẓāhir* and *bāṭin*.

Before closing this section, a few observations are necessary. Scanning Ismāʿīlī history, one notices over the course of its development a significant number of shifts in policy, method, and doctrine. The only constant in all this change is the principle that change be in deliberate response to context and circumstance. As one author states, "The Ismāʿīlīs were noted for making changes in their policies according to circumstances."[105] Circumstance, however, was weighed or assessed in terms of the goals of the *imām* or the heads of the *daʿwah*. Thus, al-Muʿizz and Ḥasan-i Ṣabbāḥ shared in common the belief that Ismāʿīlīs had to assert a central role in the Islamic *ummah* and, accordingly, took care that in exoteric matters of the *sharīʿah,* they were in consonance with mainstream Islamic practice. On the other hand, Ḥasan II ʿala Ḍhikrihi al-Salām rejected this framework and introduced his own assessment of the meaning of justice in history. Although the declaration of the *Qiyāmah* and the suspension of the *sharīʿah* tacitly conceded that the goal of Ismāʿīlī sovereignty was no longer realistic, in terms of the future of the sect, this offered it a new life by redefining its goals and its successes in spiritual and ultimate terms.

Also, the rupture with the Islamic *sharīʿah* asserted in practical terms the Ismāʿīlī philosophical distinction between the *ẓāhir,* or the visible form of faith, and the *bāṭin,* or its internal reality. This distinction facilitated the separation of one from the other without fear of the loss of the *bāṭin* or the essentials of the faith. Hence, the practice of *taqīyah* was defensible on religious terms, and it has been consistently invoked in Ismāʿīlī history during periods of persecution or sociopolitical aggression. The virtual identification of the Nizārīs with the Sunnīs towards the end of Alamūt period starkly betrayed the degree to which the sect had become weakened and marginal, for, in spite of its being a state, its only way of surviving was through total religious dissimulation. As seen in the discussion of developments in Sind after the 1094 C.E. split, the Nizārī Ismāʿīlī cover in the subcontinent was not to be Ṣūfism nor Sunnism, but Satpanth.

Finally, it is important to draw attention to the vital link that existed between the Ismāʿīlī technique of masking religious identity and of striking up political alliances. It is clear that the self-presentation of the Ismāʿīlīs was invariably linked to those forces in the environment which the *daʿwah* felt would advance its cause. For instance, the Fāṭimid *daʿwah* in Sind maintained an Arabo-centred personality, and its first mission was to gain the alliance of the pro-Shīʿah Muslim Arab rulers of the region. We have noted that during the time of al-Muʿizz, with Arab rule firmly in place, conversion of the indigenous population was regarded to be first a process of islamization, and then of ismāʿīlization. It would appear that conformity with general Islamic patterns was desirable and encouraged.

Only later, when this Arab base was demolished by the Ghaznawids, did the *daʿwah* reorient itself to local Hindu or Sindhi–Arab chieftains, and, accordingly, indigenous religious and cultural elements were accommodated. Thus, we find that some form of dissimulation and compromise was already at work among the Sindhi–Arab Muslims who became the Sūmrahs. The Sūmrahs in Lower Sind do not appear to have made a show of their Fāṭimid, and later Nizārī, connections, and retained many Hindu customs. Further South, traditions about ʿAbd Allāh and Satgur Nūr converting the Gujarati king Siddharāja emphasize this refocusing of interest on establishing a more indigenous power base. A similar pattern is evident in the Persian *daʿwah* which aligned itself with pro-Shīʿī Persian elements which were already anti-Turkish, anti-Saljūqid, and anti-ʿAbbāsid–Sunnī. A systematic study of the precise configuration of these religious, political, and ethnic alliances cannot be undertaken here but would help explain considerably the shifts in policies and doctrine observed through the course of Ismāʿīlī history. Clearly, the form that Ismāʿīlism developed in the Indian subcontinent was intimately connected with historical and political circumstances, although this form eventually evolved into the complex social and religious framework of Satpanth Ismāʿīlism. In conclusion, the investigations of this chapter confirm Maclean's suspicion quoted earlier, namely that "the frequently vented causal argument which holds that Hindus converted to Ismāʿīlism in Sind as a simple consequence of congenial similarities in ideological themes would appear to miss the mark."[106]

CHAPTER 4

Pīr Shams: Problems of Historical Identity

This chapter will focus on reconstructing the historical identity of the Ismāʿīlī preacher, Pīr Shams Sabzawārī, who belongs to the foundational period of Satpanth Ismāʿīlism and to whom is attributed the collection of *ginān*s translated in this work. He is, at once, one of the most celebrated and most enigmatic figures of the tradition. A charismatic personage representing the prototype of a holy man possessed of sacred lore and miraculous powers, he has acquired a substantial layer of folklore and oral tradition which depicts him variously as a powerful yogi, a miracle worker, and a Muslim *faqīr*.

The Gujarati edition of the Anthology translated in Part II provides a hagiographic account of Pīr Shams titled, "A Short Life-History of Our Twenty-Third Pīr—Ḥaḍrat Pīr Shams al-Dīn Sabzawārī." In brief, the hagiography describes his place of origin (Sabzawār), the *imām* who commissioned Pīr Shams to preach (Imām Qāsim Shāh), the scope of his travels (from Badakhshān through the Hindukush, the Pāmir mountain ranges, Kashmir, and on to India), and his various adventures and miracles of conversion along the way (bringing down the sun to cook some raw meat, defeating the famous Ṣūfī master, Bahāʾ al-Dīn Zakariyya, etc.).[1] True to motifs that are typical of the genre of legends and hagiography, the account boasts of Pīr Shams Sabzawārī's spiritual powers that are displayed in his heroic defeat of his foes, in his superiority over other famous holy men, in his far-flung travels that encompass many lands, and in his healing powers that win him great fame. It is worth noting that many details in the hagiography, which will be discussed later, coincide with references found in the *ginān*s of the Anthology attributed to Pīr Shams including, for instance, the names of towns, regions, persons, dates, and allusions to political intrigues.

The vivid hagiographic materials surrounding this Ismāʿīlī *pīr* is made all the more complex and interesting since,

> what is now told about the saint is a mixture of memories of at least three different eminent persons who possessed one and the same name—Shamsu'd dīn Muhammad.[2]

There has been, in other words, considerable confusion about the identity of Pīr Shams, for the heterogenous material associated with him has "acquired for him many identities."[3] The legends, myths, and folkloric motifs that have collected around the name of Shams suggest a conflation of the identities of three separate individuals who lived between the mid-twelfth and early fourteenth centuries: the mystic–poet Jalāl al-Dīn Rūmī's famous mentor, Shams-i Tabrīz; the Ismāʿīlī Imām, Shams al-Dīn Muḥammad, son of the last *imām* of Alamūt, Rukn al-Dīn Khūr Shāh; and the Ismāʿīlī preacher, Pīr Shams, the alleged composer of many *ginān*s of Satpanth literature. Since these key figures were proximate to each other in time and region, Ivanow suspects that

> a "Sind to Qonya" legend was produced which . . . incorporated various folklore motifs and religious relics of many nations residing between those extreme [geographic] points.[4]

Ivanow notes that legends of Shams were not only abundant in northwestern India, where the latter's shrine is located in Multān, but that they were also widely circulated and extremely popular among the Ṣūfī *darwishes* of Persia and in the northern areas of Afghanistan and Tibet.

Such a body of material would be of vast interest both to students of folklore and hagiography. However, what is relevant here is the light it may shed on the question of the identity of the Ismāʿīlī preacher Pīr Shams, who is claimed to have composed many *ginān*s. Ivanow and Nanji have carefully sifted through some of this material and weighed it in relation to other historical evidence. They have reached the conclusion that three distinct figures by the same name of Shams al-Dīn existed and that the Pīr Shams of the Satpanth tradition was neither the mystic Shams-i Tabrīz nor the *imām* Shams al-Dīn Muḥammad. Both scholars also conclude that little by way of historical fact can be known about the actual life and work of Pīr Shams. Dismissing outright the value of traditional oral or sectarian materials, Ivanow says "there is nothing by way of history of real events around which the legends have developed."[5] With a similar attitude of incredulity towards the dates mentioned in connection with Pīr Shams in the Satpanth *ginān* literature, he says "it would hardly be necessary to argue that all of them are based on pure fantasy."[6] Even Nanji, who does not "summarily dismiss the accounts of the gināns as a source of history,"[7] finally concludes after reviewing his evidence that "the historical personalities of the early pīrs remain dim and obscure."[8] Thus, there is little agreement or certainty on such fundamental questions as to the approximate dates and areas of activity of Pīr Shams. In the words of Jamani, who offers the most recent review of the problem, "Despite all of the clarification offered . . . the personality who is credited with having set the Nizari Ismāʿīlī daʿwa [in the Indian subcontinent] in motion . . . remains an enigma."[9]

While it may not be possible to recover a true image of the historical personality of the *ginān* composer Pīr Shams, nor to ascertain with any precision his specific travels and activities, I still think it is worth carefully investigating what Nanji has styled the "historicizing tradition"[10] that developed around this *pīr* in the *gināns* for what this tradition might reveal about the beginnings of the Satpanth *daʿwah*. As is well known in studies of folklore and oral literature, it is not uncommon for sacred tradition to fuse accounts of origins stretching over several generations under a key figure who becomes a culture hero.[11] Thus, the stories in the *gināns* associated with Pīr Shams, who was a primary architect of Satpanth, may register some important clues regarding its beginnings. In fact, an examination of the testimony preserved in the *gināns* translated in this study has revealed some interesting insights about this pivotal phase of the Satpanth *daʿwah* in the Indian subcontinent. At the very least, the patterns, allusions, and evidence recorded in these sources seem to suggest that the main activities of Pīr Shams most likely took place during the last century of the Nizārī state prior to the fall of its headquarters in Alamūt. The internal evidence also appears to support the theory advanced in the previous chapter regarding the political underpinnings of Satpanth Ismāʿīlism.

The Problem of Multiple Identities

This chapter will first review the controversy regarding the multiple identities of the Ismāʿīlī poet–preacher, Pīr Shams, and the various claims regarding his dates and areas of activity. Then, it will analyze the internal evidence on Pīr Shams that exists in the *ginān*s attributed to him. In particular, several narratives in the *ginān*s will be investigated for clues regarding the situation and strategy of the early *daʿwah*. Although the emerging picture may reflect essentially the subjective and normative historical consciousness of Satpanth concerning its origins, nonetheless, it may also display a dim memory of the complexity of forces with which the *daʿwah* had to contend. Placed within the context of a historical understanding of the region and the larger Ismāʿīlī world, these accounts may provoke some interesting questions and, even perhaps, yield a few insights into the foundational phase of Satpanth Ismāʿīlism.

It has been noted that the identity of Pīr Shams came to encompass three distinct historical personalities. The confusion of Pīr Shams with Shams-i Tabrīz stems from oral traditions associated with a mausoleum in Ucch, a short distance from Multān.[12] A region long associated with Ṣūfism, it is not surprising that tales of the famous Ṣūfī mystic who so enamored Rūmī became entwined with the exploits of this Ismāʿīlī *pīr* whose activities were also centered in Multān. For generations, this shrine in Ucch has been venerated as that of the famous Ṣūfī master, Shams-i Tabrīz.

Local informants state that the mausoleum was erected by Pīr Ṣadr al-Dīn, the grandson of Pīr Shams in 1330 C.E.[13] A plaque on the mausoleum bears an inscription recording the demise of Pīr Shams as the year 1356 C.E.,[14] which date is quoted in a sectarian Satpanth source, *Noorun Mubin* by Ali Chunara.[15] Ivanow, however, doubts the plaque's authenticity since "the ancient shrine has been on many occasions rebuilt, repaired . . . so that nothing, or very little of the original building is left."[16] Nanji, too, distrusts the value of any dates or inscriptions found on the tomb, arguing that any original markings were probably lost as the shrine underwent successive periods of neglect and repair.[17] Although an official government plaque on the tomb presently states that it belongs to the Ismāʿīlī saint, Pīr Shams, the sway of oral tradition is amply illustrated by the fact that local inhabitants and pilgrims insist that the shrine, itself called "Shāh Shams," contains the remains of the Ṣūfi saint, Shams-i Tabrīz.[18]

Shams-i Tabrīz

A cloud of mystery surrounds the life of Shams-i Tabrīz, the enigmatic spiritual mentor and beloved of the famous mystic, Jalāl al-Dīn Rūmī (1207–1273 C.E.). In R. A. Nicholson's words, this figure "flits across the stage [of history] and disappears tragically enough."[19] All that is known about Shams-i Tabrīz (d. circa 1247 C.E.), whose hagiography depicts him as an antinomian Ṣūfī who defied all conventions, is that he arrived in Qonya around 1244 C.E. where he met Rūmī.[20] Rūmī was deeply impressed with the *pīr* and became his disciple. This incited the jealousy of Rūmī's own admirers who took to rebuking Shams. After three years, Shams-i Tabrīz suddenly disappeared, and, by some accounts, he is reported to have been tragically murdered by the son of one of Rūmī's disciples.[21] Although there is some doubt as to the precise date that he was killed, it is certain that Shams-i Tabrīz died long before Rūmī (d. 1273 C.E.). Both their tombs are in Qonya on a site that has served for centuries as a Ṣūfī center of the Turkish Mevlevi (from Rūmī's title, *mawlānā* or master) order of *darwishes*.

Ivanow notes that, according to popular tales in Sind, Shams-i Tabrīz did not die in Qonya but escaped with Rūmī to Multān "walking on foot over the sea."[22] He was not, however, left in peace even in India, so he yanked off the skin of his entire body by tugging on his ponytail and flung this at his persecutors. He then proceeded to Multān where he acquired some raw fish or meat and asked the local inhabitants to cook it for him. They refused, whereupon Shams-i Tabrīz ordered the sun to cook the meat. The sun obliged him and began to descend, scalding the earth with its heat. The terrified Multānis begged Shams to send it back, and so he did, but storytellers explain that this is why the sun has remained closer to Multān than to any other place on earth, and that is why Multān is the hottest place in the world. Local inhabitants point to a Hindu temple called Keshavpurī as the site where this miracle is believed to have taken place.[23]

A similar tale is preserved in the *gināns* attributed to the Pīr Shams of Satpanth. It is in this realm of the imaginary and the miraculous that Shams-i Tabrīz becomes firmly identified with the Ismā'īlī composer of *gināns* whose activities centred around Multān. As Multān was the seat of ancient solar cults, including Hindu and Zoroastrian, the existence of such a tale was not unusual. In fact, an ample stock of popular stories about moving or otherwise controlling the sun exist in the region.[24] Moreover, since the name Shams means "sun," this further facilitated puns, word play, and the idea that Shams was an incarnation of a solar deity. At any rate, the question remains, was the Ismā'īlī Pīr who was buried at Ucch the same person as Shams-i Tabrīz? Were these two men separate figures who had some connection? And, if Pīr Shams were Shams-i Tabrīz, how would the existence of two tombs—the one in Multān and the other in Qonya—be explained? Ivanow ultimately says, "All my attempts to solve this strange problem have so far failed."[25]

Imām Shams al-Dīn Muḥammad

A twist is added to this puzzle with another claim that Shams-i Tabrīz was, in fact, none other than the son of the last Ismāʿīlī *imām* of Alamūt.[26] Nūr Allāh al-Shūstarī in his *Majālis al-Mu'minīn* (written circa 1610 C.E in India) traces the ancestry of Shams-i Tabrīz to Ismāʿīlī roots.[27] An interesting refutation of this claim has been advanced by Ahmad Akhtar in an article, "Shams Tabrīzī: Was he Ismailian?"[28] According to Akhtar, the claim that Tabrīzī was an Ismāʿīlī *imām* is made by appealing to a genealogy which proves that Shams-i Tabrīz was the son of ʿAlāuddīn or Jalāluddīn, both names of Alamūt *imāms.* He traces the source of this information to Daulatshāh who wrote *Tadhkirat al-Shuʿarā* and upon whom even the careful scholar R. A. Nicholson relied for details concerning Tabrīzī's life. However, Akhtar attempts to discredit Daulatshāh as a reliable source and points out that even E. G. Browne observed of the latter's work, "This is an entertaining but inaccurate work, containing a good selection of historical errors."[29] After consulting the older and, in his estimate, more reliable accounts of Aflākī and Jāʿmī, Akhtar concludes that the real name of Tabrīzī's father was Muḥammad bin ʿAlī bin Malikdād or Malīk Dā'ūd and not ʿAlāuddīn or Jalāluddīn. Thus, he concludes, "The alleged claim of Shamsuddīn being an Ismailian is absolutely unfounded."[30]

There is, however, another reason why it is likely that Shams-i Tabrīz and the Ismāʿīlī Imām are not one and the same person. Scholars generally concur that a son of Imām Rukn al-Dīn Khūr Shāh, the last ruler of Alamūt, was secretly escorted out of his father's castle, Maimun Dīz, around 1256 C.E. when the Imām realized that there was no way of averting the impending attack of the Mongols.[31] Although in his *Tarīkh-i Jahāngushay,* which extols the victories of his patron, Hülagü Khān, Juwaynī (1226–1283 C.E.) claimed that Hülagü had succeeded in bringing an end to the Shīʿī line of *imāms,* Hodgson has pointed out that Juwaynī's boast was not to be trusted, since he was a special enemy of the Ismāʿīlīs.[32] There is some uncertainty regarding the Imām Shams al-Dīn Muḥammad's date of birth. Whereas Ivanow thinks he was born in 1252 C.E., which means that he was only four years old when he was smuggled out of the Nizārī fortress, Maimun Dīz, other sources variously claim that the Imām was seven (b. 1248 C.E.) or twenty-one years old (b. 1235 C.E.) when he escaped.[33] According to Ivanow, Imām Shams al-Dīn died around 1310–1311 C.E.[34] Now, if Shams-i Tabrīz died around 1247 C.E., and if Imām Shams al-Dīn was born between 1235–1252 C.E., it is impossible that the two could have been the same person. Even if the earliest estimated birth of 1235 C.E. is accepted, had Imām Shams al-Dīn Muḥammad been the mystic Shams-i Tabrīz, the latter would have met Rūmī when he was barely nine years old!

According to Mumtaz Sadikali, Shams al-Dīn escaped Maimun Dīz with his uncle Shāhinshāh and went to Ādharbayjān.[35] Ritter notes that the child was carefully hidden, and "He and his successors either remained in complete seclusion or they appeared in disguise as Sufi Shaikhs."[36] To remain incognito, it seems that the Imām lived as a Ṣūfī in various towns in Ādharbayjān including Ardabīl, Ahar, Tabrīz, and Angoda. He adopted the profession of silk-making and embroidery and, hence, also came to be known as Shams Zardozī (Shams, the embroiderer). In his *Khiṭābāt-i ʿĀliya,* Pīr Shihāb al-Dīn Shāh (d. 1884 C.E.) explains that the confusion between Imām Shams al-Dīn Muḥammad and Shams-i Tabrīz developed because the Imām had briefly lived in Tabrīz, where his handsome countenance had earned him the epithet, "Sun (*shams*) of Tabrīz."[37]

The Imām Shāhīs' Shams

In addition to the identification of Pīr Shams with Shams-i Tabrīz, and the identification of Shams-i Tabrīz with Imām Shams al-Dīn Muḥammad, there is yet a third identification of Pīr Shams and Imām Shams al-Dīn Muḥammad. In the sectarian sources of the Imām Shāhīs, a branch of Satpanth that split off in the sixteenth century,[38] the *ginān Satveṇiji Vel* composed by Nar Muḥammad Shāh identifies Pīr Shams not only with Shams-i Tabrīz, but also with Imām Shams al-Dīn Muḥammad, son of Imām Rukn al-Dīn Khūr Shāh.[39] Characteristically, Ivanow describes the sectarian work as "a kind of legendary history of the imāms and the pīrs, in rather florid and bombastic style, chiefly dealing with miracles."[40] The *Satveṇi* goes on to describe Imām Shams as having relinquished his throne to his son Qāsim Shāh in 1310 C.E. in order to come to India to spread the *daʿwah,* which he did disguised as a *pīr*.[41]

Ivanow doubts the veracity of this claim, arguing that, if Imām Shams really did abdicate his position as *imām* and take on the mantle of *pīr,* he would have been at least sixty years of age by the time he began to preach in India. Instead, he theorizes that the *Satveṇi* account among the Imām Shāhīs had been created to legitimize Nar Muḥammad Shāh's claim to the imāmate. Since only the sons in the bloodline of an *imām* may receive the investiture of the imāmate, Ivanow speculates that it would have served Nar Muḥammad Shāh's self-interest to endorse or even fabricate a genealogy that traced his father, Pīr Imām Shāh, to the Ismāʿīlī Imām Shams al-Dīn Muḥammad. The fortuitous coincidence of the name of Pīr Shams with that of the Imām Shams would have facilitated such a forged theory of descent.[42]

What conclusions can be drawn from this discussion of the three Shams al-Dīns? Was Pīr Shams Sabzawārī of the *ginān*s the Ismāʿīlī Imām or the Ṣūfī shaykh? And what is the real identity of the person buried in the tomb in Multān? It seems plausible that the identification of Pīr Shams Sabzawārī with Imām Shams al-Dīn was contrived to boost Nar Muḥammad Shāh's claims to the imāmate. There also seems to be sufficient evidence that the child, Imām Shams al-Dīn, narrowly escaped from Alamūt and that he lived in secrecy. However, it seems highly improbable that he would have relinquished his office as *imām* to take on the duties of a *pīr*. As for the identification of Imām Shams al-Dīn with Rūmī's mentor, Shams-i Tabrīz, the latter would have had to be only seven or twelve years old when he was allegedly killed by Rūmī's followers. It seems unlikely, therefore, that Imām Shams was Shams-i Tabrīz.

The question remains, however, whether Pīr Shams Sabzawārī—the Ismāʿīlī preacher—was none other than Shams-i Tabrīz. Except for the interlude of his three-year association with Rūmī, not much is known about this Ṣūfī saint. The hagiographic image of both Pīr Shams and Shams-i Tabrīz fits that of an itinerant, antinomian, and wonder-working *qalandar* (wild, ecstatic *ṣūfī*) figure. Ivanow mentions an interesting reference in Jāʿmī's *Nafaḥāt al-Uns* (completed in 1476 C.E.) to an alleged meeting between the famous saint of Multān, Bahā' al-Dīn Zakariyya (d. 1277 C.E.) and Shams-i Tabrīz. Could this have been, in fact, a reference to Pīr Shams? The *ginān*s attributed to Pīr Shams describe a similar confrontation between him and Bahā' al-Dīn Zakariyya. Nanji does not make much of this matter:

> The confrontation with Bahā' al-Dīn Zakariyyā is a commonly diffused motif used in this case to illustrate the contrast between a wandering "qalandar" type ṣūfī and the established type of ṭarīqa ṣūfism of Bahā' al-Dīn. In the Ismāʿīlī context the confrontation was also meant to exemplify the superiority of the daʿwa and the dāʿīs over other similar forces and figures standard in the milieu.[43]

Both points are valid, but in addition, the confrontation (real or fictional) may capture the memory that either Pīr Shams himself or the early *daʿwah* confronted a very serious threat in the activities of the Sūfī *tarīqah* founded by Bahāʾ al-Dīn in Multān. It may be recalled that Sind, and particularly the area of Multān, had long been a vital zone of *daʿwah* activity. The establishment in Multān of a Suhrawardī order headed by Bahāʾ al-Dīn would thus have represented a major challenge to the early *daʿwah,* especially as this Ṣūfī *ṭarīqah* had close connections with the Delhi sultanate.

At any rate, the reference by Jāʿmī to an alleged meeting between Bahāʾ al-Dīn Zakariyya and Shams-i Tabrīz does not help resolve the question of whether or not the Ismāʿīlī *pīr,* Shams Sabzawārī, was, in fact, Shams-i Tabrīz. Nor can we be sure if the two identities had already been merged by the time Jāʿmī wrote his work. The only remaining clue is the tomb in Qonya which, if it is truly that of Shams-i Tabrīz, would rule out the possibility that he and Pīr Shams were the same figure. Ivanow's investigations led him finally to conclude that the person buried at the shrine in Ucch was not Shams-i Tabrīz, but an independent personage known as "Sayyid Shamsu'd-dīn Sabzawari . . . an eminent Ismaili missionary who converted a large number of Hindus,"[44] namely, the figure referred to as Pīr Shams in many *gināns* of the Satpanth Ismāʿīlīs.

Assuming, then, that the tomb in Ucch belongs to the Ismāʿīlī preacher, Pīr Shams Sabzawārī, let us now turn to the question of dates, provenance, and origin. The caretakers of the tomb or *mutawallī* who claim to be descendants of Pīr Shams preserve a manuscript containing a *shajara* (a genealogical tree) and life stories of various *pīrs.*[45] Ivanow also observes that the *shajara* is devoted mainly to the genealogy of the Sayyids who own the shrines and who claim to be descendants of the *pīrs.*[46] Jan Vansina has pointed out that genealogies "are of direct relevance to the social structures of today,"[47] and Ivanow alludes to this role of the *shajara* in maintaining the claims of the shrine-keepers. Thus, at first, he discounts the information in the *shajara* as "utterly unreliable,"[48] but later he modifies this view.

Although the genealogy contained in this *shajara* was "perverted and corrupt," not only was it the earliest that Ivanow had been able to find for Pīr Shams, but the dates given in it were the same as those given for him in *Khātima Mirʾāt-i Aḥmadī,* a famous history of Gujarat composed by ʿAlī Muḥammad Khān between 1748 and 1761 C.E., and the only known non-Nizārī source containing the genealogy of the Satpanth Ismāʿīlī *pīrs.*[49] This leads Ivanow to reckon that the dates given in the shrine's *shajara* were probably the most reliable dates available on Pīr Shams.[50] This list traces the *pīr's* lineage to the Shīʿī Imām Jaʿfar al-Ṣādiq and indicates that his family hailed from Sabzawār. It also states that Pīr Shams was born in the town of Ghazni in 1165 C.E., that he came to the province of Multān in 1202 C.E. (at the age of 37), and that he died there in 1277 C.E. (at the ripe old age of 112 years).[51] As Ivanow notes, the *shajara* thus extends the life of Pīr Shams from *before* the Ghūrid invasions to two decades *after* the fall of Alamūt which attributes to him an unusually long life.[52] If the *shajara* is to be trusted, Pīr Shams would have thus lived and preached in the region mainly during the half century before the fall of Alamūt (1256 C.E.).

In addition to the *shajara* in possession of the shrine-keepers and the genealogy found in *Khātima Mirʾāt-i Aḥmadī,* other sectarian genealogies of the *pīrs* of Satpanth have been preserved by the Khojah Ismāʿīlīs and the Imām Shāhīs. Misra feels that "the value of these genealogies for historical research is not very great."[53] However, if carefully handled, they could reveal important information, such as names of the *pīrs,* their relative importance, their probable sequence of activity, and continuities or lapses in the *daʿwah.* Several lists of genealogies exist amongst the Ismāʿīlīs, some of which have been reproduced by Misra.[54] In the older *duʿa* or daily prayer of the Satpanth Khojahs, it was customary to recite a list of the Ismāʿīlī *imāms* beginning with Ḥaḍrat ʿAlī, followed by another list of Ismāʿīlī *dāʿīs* and *pīrs.* According to Nanji, such lists of *pīrs* and *imāms* also existed among non-Khojah Ismāʿīlīs. One such list was discovered by the Russian scholar A. Semenov, who traced it to a seventeenth-century Persian Ismāʿīlī.[55]

Although the popular conception among the Satpanth Ismāʿīlīs is that Pīr Shams was the second *dāʿī* to be sent from Persia to preach in India after Pīr Satgur Nūr, in the genealogy of Ismāʿīlī *pīrs,* Pīr Shams is actually listed as the fifteenth *pīr* after Satgur Nūr. This leads Nanji to speculate that either Shams belonged to a much later period of the Satpanth *daʿwah* or that Satgur Nūr's name was deliberately advanced in the genealogy to make him appear as a "foundational" figure of the Ismāʿīlī *daʿwah* in India.[56] Another explanation, following Nanji's cue that the list did not necessarily imply lineal descent but spiritual descent, is that the names listed between Satgur Nūr and Pīr Shams may refer to other contemporary *dāʿīs* who operated in northwestern India during the Alamūt period. Nonetheless, the genealogies preserved by the Khojah Ismāʿīlīs, like the *shajara* at the shrine, indicate that the predecessor of Pīr Shams was Ṣalāḥ al-Dīn, who is also said to be the father of Pīr Shams. For instance, the *ginān Satvarṇi Vaḍi,* verse 127 mentions Ṣalāḥ al-Dīn as the name of the father of Pīr Shams. It also indicates that both men descended "from a line engaged in propagating the daʿwa on behalf of the Imāms of Alamūt."[57]

Pīr Shams al-Dīn b. Ṣalāḥ al-Dīn Sabzawārī

What tentative conclusions can be drawn from the above discussion regarding the origin and date of Pīr Shams? Firstly, there is no reason to doubt that a person named Pīr Shams was indeed a historical entity. Were we to accept Ivanow's view that the *shajara* preserved at the tomb of Pīr Shams is the most trustworthy of the evidence in this category, at the very least we may surmise that Pīr Shams was born in Ghazni in the middle of the twelfth century, that his family hailed from Sabzawār, that he travelled eastward to Multān from where he conducted his activities, and that he was buried in a town nearby called Ucch in the second half of the thirteenth century. The man buried in the tomb at Ucch in Multān is most likely Pīr Shams al-Dīn Sabzawārī, an Ismāʿīlī poet–preacher who played an instrumental role in the formation of Satpanth Ismāʿīlism. The genealogies provided by Nanji, Misra, and Gulshan Khakee all list his immediate predecessor's name as Ṣalāh al-Dīn, who was possibly his father.[58]

It is this Ismāʿīlī figure, Pīr Shams al-Dīn Sabzawārī, whose legacy and works have been preserved in the *ginān* tradition. The conflation of his identity may signal a personage whose activity and influence had been so powerful that, as is the case with culture heroes and founding figures in general, his hagiographic image was exaggerated to assume superhuman proportions. This is confirmed by the fact that this very Shams "was also regarded as a great Sufic saint, and it is in this capacity that he is now looked up to by many Muhammadans of all schools."[59] Beyond this, what we know about Pīr Shams is legendary. We turn, therefore, to examine the internal evidence preserved in the *ginān* literature.

Gināns: Internal Evidence on the Problem of Identity

It has been noted that the activities of the Ismāʿīlī *daʿwah* in the Indian subcontinent catalyzed the unique indigenous form of Ismāʿīlism called Satpanth and its religious literature called *ginēns,* a word derived from *jñāna,* the Sanskrit term for sacred knowledge or wisdom. The significance of this religious literature in the formation, history, and life of this sect cannot be overstated. For well over seven centuries, the *ginān* tradition has exercised the role and status of *śāstra* (sacred scripture) in the religious life of Satpanth Ismāʿīlism, and *ginān* recitation continues to be an integral and vital part of its daily ritual and devotional practices today. The composition of this body of vernacular poetry has been traditionally ascribed to the Satpanth *pīrs,* poet–preachers sent from Persia to win sympathy for Ismāʿīlī teachings and engagements in the region.

For generations, the *ginān* tradition has been the focus of intense veneration among the Satpanth Ismāʿīlīs. As Ali Asani says, "For those who revere them, the *gināns* are the embodiment of truth, the keys to eternal happiness."[60] This is typically the sentiment that most religious and oral societies express towards their sacred traditions. The perennial problem for the scholar is how to balance the claims of sacred tradition with the demands of historical investigation. That Ivanow felt this dilemma, and that he recognized the intensity of attachment the Khojah Ismāʿīlīs felt towards their tradition, is manifest in his "profound apologies to those for whom the legends may be dear."[61] Since attention now turns to the *gināns* attributed to Pīr Shams for what may be relevant to an understanding of his role and activity or, failing this, to an understanding of the situation of the early *daʿwah,* a few remarks concerning the nature of the evidence represented by Satpanth literature are appropriate.

Ivanow's genuine concern that his scholarship may distress or otherwise perturb his Ismāʿīlī friends is partly explained by his attitude towards their religious literature. It has already been noted that Ivanow had little regard for the popular religious imagination or for its folklore. He says,

> It is an indisputable fact that religious tradition generally is very little concerned with historical reliability, seeking in the past only for instructive examples, or vindicating certain religious or moral principles. This particularly applies to Satpanth with its Hinduistic basis. The Indian mind is notoriously unhistoric. . . . All this . . . belong[s] to the sphere of belief, or religious legend, not history.[62]

Ivanow is certainly correct in maintaining that sacred traditions are not the same thing as documented histories. The purposes, goals, and methods of each are distinct. Where their paths cross, however, is on their common fascination with what really happened in the past: when, how, and why. It is not possible here to enter into the subject of the relationship and distinction between history and tradition, but it is necessary to question Ivanow's sweeping claim that "there is, of course, almost nothing in the way of history of real events around which the legend [of Pīr Shams] has developed."[63] By declaring traditional materials as useless, his statement only succeeds in discounting completely the potential value of tradition (oral or written) for an understanding of the past.

Materials in oral tradition, folklore, myth, and sacred stories are neither "true" nor "false" in any absolute historical sense. Various disciplines such as cultural anthropology, folklore, religious studies, and psychoanalysis have evolved complex approaches to these materials to cull from them the meaning that they have had for their own societies as well as in terms of literature as such.[64] The challenge for the historian is how to sift through these kinds of sources to glean what may potentially be of historical value. In his study of *Oral Tradition as History,* Jan Vansina has demonstrated that such materials are usually grounded in reminiscences, hearsay, or eyewitness accounts of contemporary events which, depending upon the criterion of truth that exists within a given society, will be communicated over time more or less faithfully.[65] Whether the content is considered to be factual or fictional, whether the narrative form is epic or poetry, whether the society has checks and balances to reward precise or to punish imprecise memorization, and whether a written record of oral performances exists alongside the tradition, all these considerations affect and determine the degree of accuracy with which these sources preserve a memory of the past.

In the case of *ginān* literature, much more research will be necessary before any of these larger issues are resolved. Many areas remain obscure and perplexing. Little, for instance, is known about the actual process of *ginān* composition and transmission. Although the traditional explanation is that the *pīrs* from Persia composed the *gināns,* did these early Persian-speaking *pīrs* personally compose this Indian vernacular poetry which "requires expert knowledge of several Indian languages?"[66] Or did they have local disciples who received their teachings and then creatively fashioned them into a poetic form? Are there linguistic, literary, and narrative clues within the *gināns* to help determine such things?

Another subject that requires careful investigation is the condition and value of extant *ginān* manuscripts. Nanji has suggested that *gināns* may have begun as an oral tradition, but that by the sixteenth century there was already a written manuscript tradition existing alongside the oral tradition.[67] As Asani has noted, until extant *ginān* manuscripts have been collected, reconditioned, catalogued, and made accessible to scholars, it will be impossible to grasp the process by which *gināns,* if they began as oral traditions, came to be recorded and, further, to know how much of the earliest compositions has been preserved faithfully over centuries of transmission.[68] Like Ivanow, Asani is highly skeptical and believes that several centuries of transmission have "riddled extant *ginān* texts with corruptions and distortions."[69] However, the exact nature of these variations, whether they are typical errors encountered in the process of copying manuscripts or whether they represent more serious and willful editorial changes, and the frequency of one or the other within the *ginān* corpus as a whole, will not be known until many more specimens of this tradition have been studied.

These questions obtain no less for the *gināns* that have been translated in this study. The individual hymns in the printed Gujarati volume of *gināns* attributed to Pīr Shams were collected from various manuscripts which were then destroyed early this century.[70] Unfortunately, there are no *ginān* manuscripts for any *pīr* dated earlier than the mid-eighteenth century; moreover, most extant *ginān* manuscripts are in very poor condition. It remains questionable if it is even possible to trace the history of the transmission of individual *gināns* in their manuscript form. Annemarie Schimmel, for example, concedes that it may never be possible to reconstruct the original texts from extant manuscripts. Nevertheless, she thinks that the writings of the Ismāʿīlī *pīrs* may actually

> constitute the oldest extant literary expression of Sind. Although it is next to impossible to reconstruct the original texts of their religious, mystically tinged poetical sermons and prayers, parts of the later Ismāʿīlī literature in Kacchi, Gujerati, and a few pieces of Sindhi are of such archaic a character that we may accept some of them as genuinely ancient witnesses of the language of the Lower Indus Valley.[71]

Thus, not all questions of antiquity, authorship, and transmission can be resolved by manuscript study alone. Linguistic and substantive criteria also need to be developed to differentiate among different layers in the *ginān* tradition. It is possible that *gināns* attributed to a certain *pīr* may have been composed at a later date and posthumously ascribed to him. In some cases, internal evidence makes this clear,[72] but, in other cases, a number of issues, such as different recensions and variants, the nature of the language, historical allusions, thematic content, and so forth, must be assessed in tandem to determine the question of origin, authorship, and authenticity.

In addition to textual issues, what must also be factored into an analysis of materials in the *gināns* is the oral dimension of this tradition, that is, its orality in terms of its composition, ritual practice, and formal transmission. A perspective must be articulated that considers the meaning and relevance of such concepts as authorship, authority, and authenticity in the context of this religious literature. It is noteworthy that even Asani, a textual scholar of the *gināns,* has been forced to question the purely textual and philological approach to the *ginān* tradition that he himself applied to the hymn, *Būjh Nirañjan.* He goes so far as to claim that "the application of conventional canons of textual criticism involving the tracing of transmission lines to an ideal archetype or autograph is futile and inappropriate."[73] Consequently, however, he casts very serious doubts on the authorship, authenticity and integrity of the *ginān* tradition as a whole. In this respect, Nanji's approach is more balanced. While the oral nature of *gināns* must be taken into account and while the possibility of revision, interpolations, and updating in the transmission of *ginān* manuscripts must be carefully considered, these should be done "without exaggerating the degree to which this *alteration* was done (italics mine)" since "adherents would be loath to alter or pervert what was in their eyes a 'sacrosanct' tradition coming from their pīrs."[74]

In sum, it is important to qualify that the following analysis of the poems attributed to Pīr Shams is to make a beginning in the study of this rich reservoir of religious literature but that, while it is outside the scope of this work, studies dealing in depth and in tandem with textual, linguistic, and manuscript issues and the ritual, contextual, and oral–compositional nature of the *gināns* attributed to Pīr Shams must be pursued as well. At this stage, while cognizant of the unresolved problems surrounding the *ginān* manuscript tradition,[75] an analysis of the Gujarati printed version (which is the standard version currently in use) will nonetheless prove useful to the task at hand. The translations and analysis of the *gināns* attributed to Pīr Shams Sabzawārī provided in this study proceed on the assumption that the *gināns* are likely to be more well-preserved in substance than Asani's comment might suggest for the reasons given below.

Several arguments lend support to the view that until recently, the tendency to preserve carefully their Satpanth literature will have been greater than any inclination to edit or admit changes into it.

Vansina has pointed out that it is necessary to evaluate a group's attitude towards its oral or sacred tradition to ascertain how carefully the group will transmit it. For instance, according to the criterion of facticity, "Factual traditions or accounts are transmitted differently—with more regard to faithful reproduction of content—than are fictional narratives such as tales, proverbs and sayings." Vansina goes on to add, "The criterion hinges on the notion of truth, which varies from one culture to another and which must be studied."[76]

Now, it has been noted that Satpanth tradition strictly maintains that the *ginān*s were composed by Ismāʿīlī *pīrs* who were *authorized* to do so by the *imām*. The traditional understanding of the office of *pīr* is that it embodies a special status and charisma that was not available to any Ismāʿīlī except through exemplary service and spiritual advancement. Only the class of individuals that was given the authority of this office could preach and compose *ginān*s. This was a deeply ingrained belief among the Satpanth Ismāʿīlīs and formed the basis of their claim that *ginān*s were elevated compositions worthy of scriptural status or *śāstra*. Thus, the claim that the *pīrs* composed the *ginān*s has long been understood in literal terms. It is thought that the very words and tunes of the hymns were the miraculous work of the *pīrs* sent from Persia. In sermons given in the *jamāʿat khānah,* older preachers would often draw an analogy between the *ginān*s composed by the Ismāʿīlī *pīrs* and the inspired utterances of the Vedic *ṛṣis* or seers. In other words, *pīrs* were thought of not merely as poets but as divine seers and inspired men possessing spiritual knowledge. Accordingly, like the Vedas (the *ginān*s of Pīr Shams, for instance, frequently refer to themselves as Veda), the words of the *ginān*s are deemed to be holy and to possess the power to heal, to protect, to convert, and to enlighten.[77] Given this attitude toward their religious literature, it is clear why the Satpanth Khojahs "would be loath to alter or pervert" their *ginān*s, "a sacrosanct tradition coming from their pīrs."[78]

Despite all good intentions to reproduce as faithfully as possible this sacred literature which is believed to have been composed by a special class of spiritual guides (the *pīrs* or *gurus* as they are also called in the *ginān*s), other formal elements are required to show that their messages and teachings may have remained relatively free from careless mistakes or deliberate alterations in transmission. In the case of the *ginān*s, this evidence is to be found in their literary form combining poetry and melody, both of which greatly enhance the chances of faithful reproduction. To be reproduced exactly, a poem must be memorized, and it is unlikely to change from recitation to recitation, unless the poet has license to do so. In the case of sacred poetry, due to the potency inherent in its very words, the tendency will be to safeguard the exact form as far as possible. Inevitably, small variations may occur over time, but the actual degree of change in exact wording will depend on the frequency of recitation, which generally helps to increase fidelity, and on the controls for maintaining faithful performance in the form of reward and punishment. Thus, in a context such as the *jamāʿat khānah,* where faithful recitation is expected, reciters can be reprimanded for mispronunciation or interpolations.[79] The structure of poetic form assists in memorization, but the addition of melody greatly enhances recall. Vansina notes, "One of the poets actually explained that the melody serves as a means to remember words," a sentiment that I have also heard expressed by *ginān* singers.[80] Thus, songs increase a group's ability faithfully to transmit messages over time, since poetry and melody both function as mnemonic devices.

Based on the attitude of the Satpanth Khojahs towards their tradition, as well as the actual formal elements of that tradition, one can see that the tendency towards preserving the *gināns* intact outweighs the tendency towards tampering with them. Two more arguments for preservation of form can be found within the *gināns* themselves: secret teachings and special messengers. As will become clear in the analysis of the material, a recurrent theme in the *gināns* attributed to Pīr Shams is that the teachings of Satpanth were to be practiced privately, or in secret, and that these teachings would be conveyed in the form of *gināns* recited by his two messengers or disciples, Candrabhāṇ and Surbhāṇ. Generally speaking, esoteric and highly secret messages entrusted to specific individuals for transmission are likely to be more carefully preserved and safeguarded.[81] Also, teachings that are transmitted in the context of initiation or secret ceremonies are treated as special and sacrosanct. Oral transmission is particularly effective when the need for secrecy is acute; to safeguard and control the accuracy of transmitted materials and the messages that they contain, select members are usually assigned to perform this task. Based on the accounts in the *gināns,* there is substantial evidence that this is what may have happened in the context of Satpanth.

A concern for secrecy and preservation is revealed, in fact, by the invention of a special script to record the *gināns* and to keep them accessible only to a private circle of adherents.[82] According to Satpanth tradition, Pīr Ṣadr al-Dīn, the next major *pīr* after Pīr Shams, invented the Khojkī script which is based on proto-Nāgarī letters. This script may have served a number of functions, including preserving the *pīrs'* teachings; providing an exclusive but common means of communication among converts living in the contiguous regions of Sind, Punjab, and Gujarat; and acting as a source of cohesion for a linguistically diverse religious group.[83] What is particulary significant in this context is that

> Khojkī may have served the same purpose as the secret languages, such as the so-called *balabailān* language, utilized by Muslim mystics to hide their more esoteric thoughts from the common people.[84]

Thus, not only was the tradition later preserved in writing but also in a secretive script emphasizing a concern for faithful transmission. In conclusion, the above reasons suggest that consideration should be given to the likelihood that the *gināns* in their extant form may still reflect and preserve more rather than less their essential motifs and contents at the origin of their composition.

The *Gināns* on the Life and Times of Pīr Shams

We now turn to an analysis of the materials in the *gināns* attributed to Pīr Shams that may shed some light on the question of his life and times. As previously noted, scholars such as Ivanow have rejected as totally invalid any testimony preserved in the *gināns*. However, such an extreme stance may not be reasonable. Certainly, given the nature of this tradition, caution must be exercised in treating narratives in the *gināns* as historical accounts. On the other hand, Nanji has made an important observation that is amply confirmed by the *gināns* translated in this study, namely, that the *ginān* tradition demonstrates a definite proclivity to "historicize" about the past.[85] That is, there is clearly a "historical intention" in the *ginān* accounts, where the past is used as an argument, a proof of legitimacy, or to teach a lesson relevant to the present.[86] The preponderance of actual place names, of identifiable historical persons, and, in some instances, of the mention of specific dates in the *gināns* suggests a serious concern with history or what Vansina has called "facticity" within the tradition. Ivanow was himself struck by this but found such precision and remarkable historicity suspicious and prematurely dismissed it as "nothing but a poetical device which inspires no confidence."[87]

What is of special interest here, then, are those narratives in the *ginān*s of Pīr Shams that attempt to communicate a concrete sense of the past and which refer to specific dates, places, names, and events. At the outset, it is worth noting the differences in tone and imagery between the narratives in the *ginān*s that describe the activities of Pīr Shams and that of the short hagiographic "Life-History" that prefaces the Gujarati edition of the Anthology translated here. Interestingly, the *ginān*s themselves are far less hyperbolic in tone and imagery, a fact that has important implications. It appears that existing alongside the bare contours of the life of Pīr Shams mentioned in the *ginān*s were more detailed oral accounts of his life known to his associates and disciples. After his death, these details may have been orally transmitted from one generation to the next, giving rise to a hagiographic tradition which was no doubt elaborated upon according to religious and cultural expectations. Given the more restrained and conservative tenor of the *ginān*s, it does not seem as if many of these hagiographic elements were reincorporated into them. (Accordingly, one can hypothesize that *ginān*s with highly embroidered accounts betray a later period of composition.)

Dates

In our earlier discussion concerning the dates of Pīr Shams, it was noted that, according to the genealogy preserved at his tomb, Pīr Shams was born in Ghazna in 1165 C.E. and buried in Ucch in 1277 C.E. Now there are several dates mentioned in the *ginān*s attributed to Pīr Shams that advance his life by at least half a century. The earliest date appears in the fifth verse of *Surbhāṇaji Vel,* which states that Pīr Shams visited his disciple Surbhāṇ in s. 1175, that is, 1118 C.E.[88] The next date occurs in the *ginān* sequence called *Joḍīlo* (see translation in the Anthology). Verse 25 of Ginān number 77 (henceforth, the *ginān* number and verse will be cited as follows: 77:25) states:

> In the year Samvaṭ 1178 on the last day of the month of Kārtik,
> The Guru established himself; the day was Tuesday. 77:25

Zawahir Noorally interprets this verse to mean that the Pīr established his center of preaching on this date (1111 C.E.).[89] The verse occurs in the context of a story about the Pīr's conversion of a Hindu town, and the date given marks the time when the king and his subjects were initiated into Satpanth. The next two dates are cited in

Candrabhāṇaji Vel; it notes that Pīr Shams came to Cīnab in s. 1200/1143 C.E. and that Candrabhāṇ converted to Satpanth in s. 1207/1150 C.E.[90]

Now what is to be made of these dates, one of which includes the day and month as well? Why was it so important to record the date of these stated conversions and meetings with the disciples? If these dates are to be trusted, how do we account for the dates preserved in the *shajara* which place Pīr Shams a century later? It is rather difficult to answer these questions. There is no obvious reason to suspect that these dates were concocted. Could the dates be markers of events associated with *dāʿīs* who preceded Pīr Shams? Either Pīr Shams did, in fact, preach in India during the first half of the twelfth century or he did not, in which case, one can only speculate that perhaps he had a predecessor whose activities have been attributed to him. The connection of these dates with his two disciples only serves to complicate matters further.

If the dates are trustworthy, it would mean that the main activity of Pīr Shams in Sind immediately preceded the Ghūrid invasions of the Ismāʿīlī areas in Multān which began in 1160 C.E., and which ended with Muḥammad Ghori's capture and slaughter of the Ismāʿīlīs in Multān's capital, Ucch, in 1175 C.E. Whether Pīr Shams was born in Ghazna in 1165 C.E. and came to India in 1202 C.E., or whether he was already in India by 1118 C.E., both the *shajara* and the *ginān* dates imply that his activities in Sind preceded the fall of Alamūt. In other words, in all likelihood his activities and preaching took place at a time when the Nizārī Ismāʿīlī *daʿwah* was still a vigorous political operation. If this were the case, has some memory of this context been preserved in the *gināns* attributed to him? Is there any evidence in the *gināns* that indicate directly or implicitly that Pīr Shams was engaged in political activity?

Place Names

To answer this question, let us examine a few *gināns* in the Anthology attributed to Pīr Shams that refer to places in the general area associated with Ismāʿīlī presence in Sind, namely, Multān, Cīnab, Ghazni, and Ucch.[91] This discussion and analysis will limit itself to those details that may be of relevance to the life and work of Pīr Shams or of his time and will focus on accounts centered in and around Multān. Nonetheless, it will sufficiently demonstrate that there is a great deal of rich material embedded in the *gināns* that may be of some historical value.

Twelve *ginān*s in the Anthology make reference to Multān and a town called Cīnab, which most likely refers to Multān itself[92] (since Multān is "the city on the Cīnab river").[93] What is most striking about this group of *ginān*s is their battle and fort imagery and the secret alliance that exists between a Queen Surjādevī and Pīr Shams through his two disciples. According to these *ginān* narratives, Pīr Shams came from the region of Alamūt (Daylamān) to Multān where he settled. From Multān, the Pīr proceeded to Ghazni taking along with him two youths, Candrabhāṇ and Surbhāṇ.[94] These two disciples accompanied Pīr Shams wherever he went, and they feature regularly in his various adventures. In fact, upon closer inspection of the various stories, they function typically as mediating or messenger figures between the Pīr and his opponents or allies.

The constant presence of these two diminutive figures, which, from a literary standpoint, act as a foil to heighten the stature of the Pīr, signals their importance in the narratives. Candrabhāṇ and Surbhāṇ were the Pīr's two arms, so to speak, inasmuch as he instructed them to communicate messages to his devotees or to teach new recruits the beliefs and practices of Satpanth. But, lest their significance be missed, several *ginān*s simply declare the "fact" that they were his true disciples (*dāsa*) and devotees (*bhakta*). For instance,

> Two brothers Candrabhāṇ and Surbhāṇ
> were the disciples (*cela*) of Pīr Shams
> Of a common ancestor, they were devotees (*bhagat*)
> of the present age (*kalyug*). 2:1

The authorization of their status is significant particularly since it is clear that they actually function in several narratives as the Pīr's surrogates. An interesting *ginān* which recounts a dialogue between Pīr Shams (in the form of a parrot) and one of his female devotees (a queen called Surjādevī) confirms this special connection between the Pīr and his two disciples. She asks him to tell her about the appearance and approach of the "two travellers" whom he is sending to her. Pīr Shams replies:

> "O Queen, both of them live with me;
> They will come reciting the *ginān*s of the Guru;
> As for their caste, they are servants/devotees (*dāsa*)." 15:2

Surjādevī then says she will bring together her circle of eight to this meeting and beseeches him to teach all. The Pīr then speaks of a place (of happiness) that existed before there was either earth or sky:

> Queen Surjā asked, "What is the key to that place, O Swāmī
> Reveal to us some sign, some name by which to realize it." 15:7

This theme of secret signs and keys is pervasive throughout and creates the impression that a special code existed which the characters used to communicate messages. It is possible, for instance, that the various unknown characters named in the *gināns,* as well as the repeated reference to mythical characters, represented some kind of secret code language. In any case, the Pīr assures her that his disciples will come and show her the path. It is worth stressing that Pīr Shams seems to be in secret communication with the queen and reveals to her the signs by which she will recognize his messengers, who, in turn, will give her the "keys" to release or freedom. Further, the queen appears to have collected together a small group of followers who await further instruction from the Pīr.

Another *ginān* narrative describes just such a promised meeting between the Pīr's disciple and the queen. Surbhāṇ has been sent to Surjādevī who lives in the home of a demon–king. His mission is thus fraught with danger, for he has entered the "demon's land" or enemy territory to meet his master's devotee (*dāśī*) [10:1]. The queen emerges from her private quarters when Surbhāṇ announces he has been sent by the Guru. She urges,

> "Standing on my feet, I, the Queen plead!
> O Swāmī, have mercy upon us!
> Carry us safely across to the other shore. 10:6
>
> "If you [promise to] recollect Shāh Pīr," [replied Surbhāṇ]
> We will assure you and give you our word of honor. 10:7

He teaches her that to attain "the other shore" (that is, security, peace, salvation, happiness), she must swear an oath of allegiance and repeat "Shāh Pīr," an epithet of the *imām.* As the messenger is about to depart, Surjādevī's group appears and entreats him quickly to return to "Deliver us to the other shore!" Tension and intrigue surface in this poem. In addition to religious salvation, the metaphor of crossing over safely to the other shore may imply release from a temporal state of fear and insecurity.[95] We learn that the queen is married to a "demon" in the city of Cīnab [10:16] and that she is a secret follower (and, possibly, an informant) of Pīr Shams. The appeal that the queen and her small gathering make for assurances to be delivered across to the other shore may be both literal and symbolic. That is, this may be a plea for imminent rescue as well as eternal salvation. At any rate, the disciple takes a pledge from the queen and promises that

> "You will attain the supreme boon of Heaven!
> You will enter that glorious City of Immortality (*amrāpūri*)!"
> Surbhāṇ read aloud from the scriptures (*śāstra*)
> Pīr Shams had made such a promise (*kol*). 10:14

And what was this promise? That Pīr Shams and the *imām* or Shāh, as the latter is generically titled in the *ginān*s, would come to the fort in Multān and liberate them.[96] This promise and prediction of the arrival of the Shāh or *imām* is reiterated in several *ginān*s. The common motif that runs through them all is that the Shāh, bearing his sword, Dhulfikār, and mounted on his horse, Duldul, would arrive in Multān from the West (several *ginān*s are more specific and refer to Iraq or Daylamān) with a large army equipped with powerful weapons to attack and vanquish the evildoers, capture their forts, and install the rule of the righteous.[97] For instance,

> In the city of Delhi, Sāheb Rājā will capture the fort and rule;
> When the Sāheb arrives, the wicked will flee and the
> pious will rule. 2:1
>
> The Shāh will come to Multān in Jambudvīpa with the Pāṇḍavas
> Attacking the wicked, the Shāh will expel them and
> himself rule. 2:2

In fact, the Shāh, who promises freedom from the oppressor, is none other than the awaited tenth *avatār* of Viṣṇu.

> Naklankī [*avatār*], the bearer of light, has become manifest!
> He, the Shāh, rides on the mount of Duldul. 4:2
>
> As pledged, the Shāh will bring justice:
> His hands will seize the three-edged sword. 4:3

There is a strong emphasis on the expectation of the Shāh's arrival, the promise of justice, and the inevitable expulsion of "wicked infidels." The battle imagery and the promise of victory against the unjust underscores the political dimensions of the role of the Shāh as *avatār*. Succor is to come, not only in terms of the state of spiritual freedom, but as concrete victory over an oppressive enemy. In one *ginān,* a curious interjection records:

> The Shāh has sent us a message
> He has captured the fort and razed it to the ground. 11:20

To continue with the drama of Queen Surjādevī, what precisely was her mission? What were the disciples of Pīr Shams conveying to her, and vice-versa? We can surmise that the messages were not restricted to religious teachings from an episode where the relations between king and queen reach a climax. The queen has a confrontation with her husband, the so-called demon–king referred to in the *ginān*s as Kaliṅga, who stands for an enemy of the Pīr or the *daʿwah*. It would seem that Surjādevī has attempted for some time to convince her husband–king to "convert" to their side, for she says,

> O King! For ages and ages I have kept on telling you
> That you, O Kaliṅga, are performing evil deeds! 47:11

However, having had no success, she warns her king:

> Flee! Flee, O demon Kaliṅga! My Master is coming
> from the West.
> Ninety battalions will be crushed under his horse's shoe!
> Alas! When your army is conquered before
> your very face,
> Who will rescue you then, I do not know. 47:1
>
> From the West will beat the claps of many drums.
> They will beat to signal the thunders of war!
> My Shāh will cry out his orders across the three worlds;
> They will instantly herald him as the Sultān. 47:2
>
> Harken! Horses vigorous in step and chariots
> the speed of wind!
> And elephants all beautifully decked out for the Shāh,
> Wielding thirty-six weapons, the man who is Nakalaṅkī
> will mount,
> And in fourteen worlds will resound the hail:
> Victory! Victory! 47:3

Not to be outstripped by his queen, the king replies angrily:

O Queen! I have three times as many forts all
in splendid shape!
Indeed, within their walls the gods earn their living. . . .
My army has more than a million strong, nay infinite
is its number!
By contrast, a trifle indeed is the army of your Shāh! 47:6-8

Clearly, this was no puny sovereign, and the forces and wealth of his kingdom appear to have been substantial. Somewhat foolhardily, Surjādevī continues to challenge him with praises of the Shāh who will soon come to destroy him. The king must have been generous, for, instead of promptly punishing her for treason, he merely rages at her disloyalty, woefully crying:

O Queen! You eat, drink and make merry at the expense
of my wealth.
And then you dare to swear, "My Shāh is this and
my Shāh is that!"
Oh! Is there such a one here in this city of Cīnab
Who can bring my Queen back to her senses? 47:10

In a fit of temper, the king mounts his steed and rides off to fight the Shāh. There is no indication in the poem itself who wins, but another *ginān* predicts that at the crooked fort at Cīnab, "Kaliṅga will be beheaded." [39:14] Another verse says

At Cīnab, yes at Cīnab, you can hear the tenth demon [cry];
Surjā's husband did not return. O Brother, so be it. 8.29

We surmise from references to a large following at Cīnab and its chaste woman, Surjādevī, that, according to Satpanth tradition, the Shāh had been victorious over the demon–king. We may never know whether this actually happened, but the account may still hold political significance. For, it is plausible that the narrative marked an event in the emergent period of the *daʿwah* in India when a local Hindu kingdom was wrested away by the Sūmrahs who received the help of reserve forces from Alamūt. An interesting question is why did the queen have such strong Ismāʿīlī sympathies in contrast to her husband–king? Quite possibly, this may have been an instance of the practice of intermarriage to gain political alliances. An arranged marriage of an Ismāʿīlī woman (such as the daughter of a Sūmrah chief) with a Hindu king would have been one way to create social and political connections and to rally support around the Ismāʿīlī cause without undue strife. It would seem, then, that this method did not always work. At any rate, the above narrative is an important testimony, even if couched in the form of a heroic religious tale, that when the *daʿwah* did not succeed by peaceful means in striking up alliances to advance its cause, on occasion, it may have had to engage in warfare with local Hindu kingdoms.

While it is not possible to present and analyze all the details in the *gināns* attributed to Pīr Shams, what becomes quickly apparent is the abundance of allusions, nuances, metaphors, and narrative episodes that communicate the following themes which suggest the context in which the *daʿwah* operated and the Ismāʿīlī message was spread: secret missions; conspiracy and alliances; promises of victory and reward; relief from oppression; help as military enforcements; tithe to support the cause; plotted rebellion; the Shāh as refuge and savior; tests of faith; loyalty and sacrifice as prerequisites to salvation. To illustrate, several *gināns* eulogize the need for and examples of self-sacrifice or martyrdom:[98]

> Tear out the roots of evil, O Brother,
>   and the soul will stay pure!
> Sever your head and submit it willingly to the Guru;
> Then, the Gurunara will become your helper. 26:3
>
> For the sake of my soul, I have relinquished all;
> I have come to take refuge in you. 33:8
>
> Hear, O Brother! Listen, O Friend!
>   What did he do for the sake of his soul?
> O Friend, he cut off his head and sacrificed it,
>   yes, he cut his head off. 46:4

These verses may indeed reflect a readiness to sacrifice oneself to the Guru or *imām's* cause. They are balanced by frequent assurances that one's true reward lies in the attainment of eternal life in the hereafter. The kingdom of the Sāheb is *svarga* (heaven), *amarāpūri* (City of Immortality), and *vaikuṇṭha* (abode of Viṣṇu).

> If you follow our orders, you will attain
>   the City of Immortality;
> There you will gain endless happiness and protection
>   of the Lord. 61:11

Those who followed the Guru's words
attained Heaven (*vaikuṇṭha*);
Recognize our devotees, for they are our servants. 71:1

But equally, there are many assurances that salvation is not only heavenly but earthly, inasmuch as military help is anticipated from the Shāh who lives in the West and who promises a just and liberated society.[99] In addition to the verses noted above with reference to Surjādevī, the following oath is noteworthy:

Yes Sir! There ʿAlī will come with Dhulfikār from the West;
No one will dare challenge him face to face. 41:39

Yes Sir! There Pīr Shams, the soldier of ʿAlī, says:
The sky will thunder with hundreds of weapons of the Shāh!
The Sāheb of countless wanderers will mount his horse—
And nothing will be able to arrest his speed. 41:45

Now what can be made of these patterns? Should one simply interpret these stories of conflict and battle as part of the narrative ethos found within Hindu Epic and Purānic literatures? Were these tales merely the exaggerated claims proliferated by Hindu or Muslim rulers to valorize themselves and promote their own interests? To be sure, there is ample evidence in both Muslim and Hindu epic literature of such tales that brag about the heroic strength and deeds of a king. Nonetheless, it may be unwarranted to dismiss the accounts in the *ginān*s merely as fantastic tales modelled after the epic tradition and created mainly for self-authentication and for the pious edification of converts. Just as it is evident that Hindu concepts and symbols are deliberately used in the *ginān*s to convey a message of faith that, in the final analysis, leads the believer to the savior figure of the *imām* (as Shāh, Sāheb, Guru, or Swāmī), it may be argued that the motifs and imagery drawn from the Hindu epic literature could have been self-consciously used as a vehicle to couch, and thus to preserve in memory, actual events and incidents that occurred in the early *daʿwah* in Sind. Although the *ginān* tradition is permeated with Hindu concepts, myths, and sentiments found within the Indian milieu, the tradition as a whole possesses a remarkable internal consistency and integrity which suggests that the composers of this literature were not randomly adopting and embracing indigenous beliefs and practices. On the contrary, the resulting syncretism of their work, as I have argued elsewhere, is not a careless hodgepodge, but a carefully crafted alliance and synergy of ideas.[100]

Accordingly, it would be inappropriate completely to discount as incredulous the *ginān* narratives just because of their similarity to the idiom of the Hindu epic tradition. Such a view has led some scholars prematurely to conclude that there can be nothing of historical value in the *ginān* literature.[101] The narratives may be neither historical nor mythical *per se*, but this does not preclude the possibility of considering them as allegorical or symbolic in nature. That is, they could allude to historical situations of real conflict that existed in the early *daʿwah,* albeit in the dramatic form of an idealized character set that represents friends and foes.

Approached from this perspective, the *ginān* narratives suggest that there was perhaps much more complexity at the ground level of the *daʿwah's* activity than has been thus far recognized. Although one cannot conclude from Surjādevi's story that Ismāʿīlī *dāʿīs* and preachers regularly worked on local rulers through their wives, the occasional application of this strategy is not inconceivable. Such an approach of gaining influence, striking alliances, and seizing control of kingdoms was not unknown at the time. There is a very interesting incident which demonstrates the reverse of the process, that is, a Hindu queen is enticed by the prospect of being Queen of the Kingdom by marriage to a Muslim monarch if she agrees to conspire against her Hindu husband–king. In Henry Raverty's translation of the *Ṭabakāt-i Nāṣirī,* he states in his notes that, after Multān was captured from the Ismāʿīlīs in 1175 C.E., the Ghūrid Sulṭān Muʿizz al-Dīn went on to seize Ucch. He then gives Ferishta's account of the battle as follows:

> As he knew that to overcome that Rājah in battle and capture the fort would be arduous, he dispatched a person to the wife of the Rājah, who was despotic over her husband, and cajoled her, and promised, saying: "If, by your endeavours, this city shall be taken, having contracted marriage with you, I will make you Malikah-i-Jahan. . . ."[102]

Raverty notes that the Rājah was a chief of the Bhaṭī tribe and that, according to Ferishta, the ploy worked, and the Sulṭān did marry the queen's daughter. Both queen and daughter were made Muslims and sent to Ghazni for further instruction, where they died unhappy, "from not having obtained the enjoyment of the Sulṭān's society."[103] It is impossible to reach any conclusions with this information, save that Muslim rulers used this tactic of the promise of marriage with some success.

The question has been raised earlier whether the *pīrs* dispatched from Persia themselves composed the *ginān*s or whether they had their local disciples compose them. The accounts of the disciples of Pīr Shams seems to suggest that they may have played a key role in shaping the *ginān* tradition. In several *ginān*s, the Pīr instructs his disciples to teach his devotees and new followers the practices and doctrines of Satpanth. Other *ginān*s bear testimony that they did:

> [Surbhāṇ] related to her the Guru's wisdom (*ginān*)
> And they meditated on its teaching (*veda*) . . .
> "We will impart to you the principles of religion (*dharma*),
> But lady, you are the mistress in a demon's house." 10:4
>
> Hari came to the province of Daylamān
> and then settled in Multān;
> Vimras, Hari's devotee recited *ginān*s in honor
> of the Guru. 14:3
>
> "Come to Multān both of you, O King and Queen!
> I will send you two messengers after
> six months have passed." 28:68
>
> They all bowed at the Guru's feet and confessed
> all to him:
> "Show us, O Swāmī, all about the fellowship of truth." 68:10
>
> "Our devotees are examples of wisdom (*ginān*)—
> they will teach you;
> They are Vimras and Surbhāṇ; they will give support
> of the truth. 68:11

It is possible that the actual names of the disciples, Candrabhāṇ and Surbhāṇ, are pseudonyms which convey this idea of composition. Candrabhāṇ may literally refer to "one who knows *chand* or meter" and Surbhāṇ to "one who knows *sur* or melody." Certainly, this would help to explain the teachers' familiarity with the Hindu material. At the very least, the composers of the *ginān*s may have been assisted by the Sūmrahs or Hindu converts, who would have been well-acquainted with Hindu ideas and mores. It is also conceivable that the early *pīrs* used their disciples not only as messengers, teachers, and composers, but also as translators of their own messages.

There are several accounts in the *ginān*s that relate the conversion of Hindu chiefs and kings, followed by their subjects. For instance, a narrative set in a town called Bhoṭnagar describes episodes leading to the allegiance of a Gaekwāḍ king called Devsiṅgh.[104] Another narrative describes rulers who are devout followers of the Pīr, for instance, Rājā Manaśudha and Rāṇī Radīyā in a town called Prem Pāṭaṇ.[105] The preponderance of references to people of power and high social status, that is, to rulers and kings, in the *ginān*s is striking. Nanji thinks that the conversion of rulers should be interpreted at a symbolic level and not as a testimony of historical actuality because in contrast to the earlier Fāṭimid *daʿwah* in Sind, the Nizārī *daʿwah* in the Indo–Pak subcontinent was, subsequent to the fall of Alamūt, quietist and nonpolitical in orientation.[106] This view is iterated by Christopher Shackle and Zawahir Moir who go on to firmly assert a position that this investigation counters, namely, that after the destruction of Multān by Maḥmūd Ghaznawī,

> While it seems probable that the practice of *taqiyya* would have allowed an Ismaili tradition to continue locally, *this never resulted in any subsequent attempt to regain local political power on the Fatimid pattern* (emphasis mine).[107]

On the contrary, if the Nizārī *daʿwah* had begun its activities in the Indo–Pak region well *before* Alamūt's fall, it may still have been sufficiently active in Sind politically to establish a vassal state or to reclaim the stake of its predecessors, the Fāṭimids. The preponderance of relations with rulers and their conversions in the *ginān*s suggests that there is more to these narratives than legitimation and the pious edification of converts. Given the historical context, it is possible to recognize in these stories covert messages of political alliance. If the Nizārī *daʿwah* had seriously entertained political ambitions right until the moment of Alamūt's destruction, it is reasonable to expect that it would have continued to channel its energies into winning the favor and support of local chieftains wherever it could.

Assuming that the early beginnings of Satpanth were both political and religious but that after Alamūt's devastation, Satpanth was forced underground, and had to adopt a more inward, spiritual, and quiescent expression, do the *ginān*s reflect this change and, if so, how? I have argued thus far that there are a number of *ginān* narratives, particularly the ones associated with Multān, that indicate a situation of tension, intrigue, and promise of imminent help. These poems preponderantly focus upon actual battle scenes and on the victory expected through the impending arrival of the Shāh, who is represented as the savior–*avatār*. It is clearly this promise of success that is at the bottom of many alliances made with the Pīr, who gives repeated assurances and pledges of military aid. The practical dimensions of these promises are, however, very easy to miss since they are couched in the language of religious salvation.

It is, in fact, possible to detect a slight difference between those *ginān*s in which liberation is clearly associated with victory over an enemy and those in which it refers primarily to religious salvation. That is, there are *ginān*s in the Anthology of Shams, specifically, the series of songs called the *Garbīs*[108] which, unlike the *ginān*s connected with Surjādevī, promise salvation almost exclusively in terms of the hereafter. A different strategy is used in these *ginān*s to make the case for the Shāh compelling. Whereas in the above *ginān*s the appeal of the Shāh rests in the military prowess by which he will vanquish oppressors and evildoers, in the *Garbīs* the case is built up in terms of a litany of souls that were saved by the Shāh and his *pīrs*. Salvation in this context is unambiguously a spiritual freedom, not a political liberation (an echo of Ḥasan II's declaration of *Qiyāmah*). Since the language of salvation is found in both instances, it is not surprising that the shift in focus from political to spiritual would be imperceptible, for the political foe is depicted as the devil—who could be viewed both as a real oppressor and enemy or as the personification of evil as such. With the passage of time and as the tradition relinquished its political aspirations, it is likely that these numerous allusions to military aid in the *ginān*s came to be interpreted purely in symbolic terms as representing victory over evil. Thus, the memory that the earliest allegiances were inspired by promises of worldly as well as spiritual victory would have been submerged.

To make this point, we take a brief look at the *Garbīs*. A caveat should be made, namely, that internal evidence in this cycle of twenty-eight *ginān*s attributed to Pīr Shams suggests that they may either belong to a later date or have acquired later additions and interpolations. The most obvious indication of this is the presence of the names of *imām*s and *pīrs* who lived between the fourteenth and eighteenth centuries. They are Imām Qāsim Shāḥ[109] (d. ca. 1370 C.E.) [or Qāsim ʿAlī Shāh? (d. ca. 1750 C.E.)], Imām Isḷām Shāh[110] (d. ca. 1440 C.E.), Pīr Ṣadr al-Dīn[111] (d. ca. 1450 C.E.), Pīr Ḥasan Kabir al-Dīn[112] (d. ca. 1500 C.E.), and Imām Shāh Nizār[113] (d. 1722 C.E.). For instance,

> Who holds authority at present?
> We disclose his name—Shāh Nizār! 82:14

Serve the light of the Satgur!
Know he is Lord Qāsim Shāh. 83:17

One *ginān* cites the names of two *imāms*:

O Careless Ones! Believe in the Light of Qāsim Shāh
He is the legitimate heir, the true *imām*
in this age of Kalyug. 92:7

O Careless Ones! Divine light shines in Śrī Islām Shāh!
Recognize the Lord when you see him. 92:9

In all such references to the *imām*, it seems that the purpose of the verses is to identify the name of the current *imām*. It is possible that the existence of three different names which came to coexist in this manner is a result of manuscript transmission, that, whereas one name was crossed out and rewritten, the other was not. In any case, the presence of these names raises questions about the printed version of the *Garbīs*.

The main purpose here, however, is to show that there is a subtle but significant reorientation in the *Garbīs'* approach to the meaning of salvation and in the justification for following the *imām*. Briefly, the *Garbīs* consist of a sequence of twenty-eight folk songs ranging from eighteen to twenty-two verses each. The word *garbī* has several meanings. In Gujarat, the *garbī* is a popular folk dance akin to another dance form called the *rāsa*, in which dancers move around in a circle singing and keeping rhythm by clapping their hands and feet. Originally, the word *garbī* referred to an earthen pot with holes on the sides which was used by Hindus as a receptacle for lamps celebrating their deity's luminous presence. Typically, devotees would sing and dance circling around the lamp pot to honor the deity of which it was the receptacle. Women often danced with the pots on their heads. The actual songs sung on such occasions were also called *garbīs*.

The *Garbīs* attributed to Pīr Shams form a narrative about conversion. Woven into the narrative are long sections of instructions and exhortations so that only eight poems actually describe any dramatic actions or scenes. Briefly, the story of the *Garbīs* is as follows. Pīr Shams comes to a town called Analvāḍ to find the villagers celebrating the festival of *nortā*. This is most probably the festival of Navarātrī, which literally refers to the "nine nights" of worship and devotion to the Hindu goddess Durgā or *mātā bhavānī* (the fearsome

Mother). The scene is a veritable spectacle of festivities, with five-hundred Hindus dancing and thirty-six *paṇḍits* chanting the Vedas.

The Pīr watches them worship and adore their idols and is angered by the image worship. As a strategy to stop it, he decides to join in the dance and to sing his own *garbīs*. Night after night, he returns to sing and dance, all the while admonishing the Hindu worshippers for paying homage to idols made of mere stone. Instead, he preaches to them the principles of *sat panth*, the True Path. Finally, one night a *brahmin* called Śaṅkar leaves the *garbī* dance in disgust. (The narrator has a gloss that poor Śaṅkar lacked *puṇya* or merit.) The rest of the crowd, however, remains to listen to the Pīr because (again the narrator explains) it has realized the secret, namely, that he, Pīr Shams, is a saint (*deva*—lit., god). The first ones to realize this truth are the remaining thirty-five *brahmin paṇḍits*. Their hearts transformed, they abandon their religious scriptures (*purāṇ*), and there is great rejoicing as they beat their seven drums and cry *jay! jay!* (Victory! Victory!). The villagers, meanwhile, are stunned by this spectacle.

The Pīr (referred to as Guru) continues singing his songs of wisdom (*ginān*s), and, soon enough, word spreads and the princes of the land arrive and join in the dancing. News of the spectacle reaches the king who, with his ministers, comes to hear the much talked-about Guru. Impressed with the latter's miraculous conversion of the *brahmins*, the king, too, prostrates himself at the Guru's feet. Again, the villagers are astonished. In this manner, then, the priests, king, queen, townsfolk, and various religious ascetics such as the *jogis*, *sannyāsis*, and *vairāgīs* all prostrate themselves at the Guru's feet and abandon their gods (*deva*) and scriptures (*śāstra*). A small mountain of strings piles up as the *brahmins* break off and discard their sacred threads. The dancers throw away their *garbī* lamps, which they have worshipped all these nights, into the sea. The Guru then makes them drink holy water (*pāval*) to purify them of past sins. He appoints a leader (*mukhī*) to oversee this new religious community, which is blessed by the sudden vision (*dīdār*) of the Lord (*nar*) Qāṣim Shāh. Their hearts are filled with divine light (*nūr*), and the story ends with a scene of general rejoicing with the Pīr's songs of wisdom (*ginān*) and circles of dance (*garbī*).

Now, what is of interest here is the method by which Satpanth is made attractive in the *Garbīs* to this society of Hindus. It is important to note that the *Garbīs* construct a religious framework for conversion and that the poems focus upon the superiority of the religion that the Pīr is offering to them. Several elements ultimately combine into defining this True Path, or *sat panth*, as the Pīr calls it in the *Garbīs*. The configuration of religious elements in the context before the Pīr's arrival undergoes a major change by the end of the narrative, but without dramatic upheaval. In the first instance, there is the festival of Navarātrī, the nine days before the celebration of Daserā, when the Goddess Durgā, here referred to as *mātā bhavānī* (fearsome Mother), is worshipped. Hindus, gathered in a temple compound in a town called Analvāḍ, are worshipping *śakti*, the female principle of the Lord Śiva. There is, besides the *garbī* lamp pot, a stone and clay image of the goddess in the temple that they adorn and worship. Their ritual is characterized by revelry and dancing (*garbī*) to the accompaniment of song (*gīt*), as well as the recitation of heroic tales (*kathā*) by the *brahmin paṇḍits* from their sacred scriptures (*śāstras*).

Interestingly, all these elements that initially stand out in the narrative are the very ones that are finally rejected (see illustration). As the Pīr recites his *garbī* songs, he invokes by way of association other elements intrinsic to the Hindu milieu, including Hindu theories of salvation and Hindu mythology. In other words, the Hindu worldview remains present in the new path that the converts adopt. Common religious motifs such as the ideal of salvation or liberation from rebirth (*mukti*); the attainment of bliss in heaven (*vaikuṇṭha*); the destruction of the effects of past deeds (*karma*); the accumulation of merit (*puṇya*); the saving powers of deities, saints, and *avatār* figures; and the traditional veneration for sacred word and scripture (*śāstra*); all these familiar notions are invoked.

But, although many aspects of the Hindu worldview are retained, they are deliberately used as the scaffolding for a new concept of faith. Satpanth *also* rejects, reorganizes, and redefines these and other elements internal to the Hindu context. Thus, the Guru tells the Hindus to throw away their idols, which are mere stones, but he entices them with the hope of salvation by conjuring up the image of millions of gods and godlings such as the *yakṣas* and *meghas*, the *kinnars* and *devas* who are all in heaven (*vaikuṇṭha*) attending upon and serving the *guranar* or *satguru* who is none other than the *avatār* of Viṣṇu, the bow-wielder (*sāraṅgapāṇa*) identified as ʿAlī, the first Shiʿite *imām*. Likewise, the Pīr exhorts the Hindus to pay heed to the *sār* or essence of their *śāstras* whose last *Veda* is the Qur'ān, the message of which he has conveyed in the *gināns*. While retaining the prominence of the Vedas and Purāṇas, the *Garbīs* reject their pertinence and pronounce them to be archaic, whereas their essence has been freshly expressed in the *gināns*. The Qur'ān is proclaimed as the conclusive Veda, and the *gināns* as the inspired words of the *pīrs*

The Garbīs of Pīr Shams

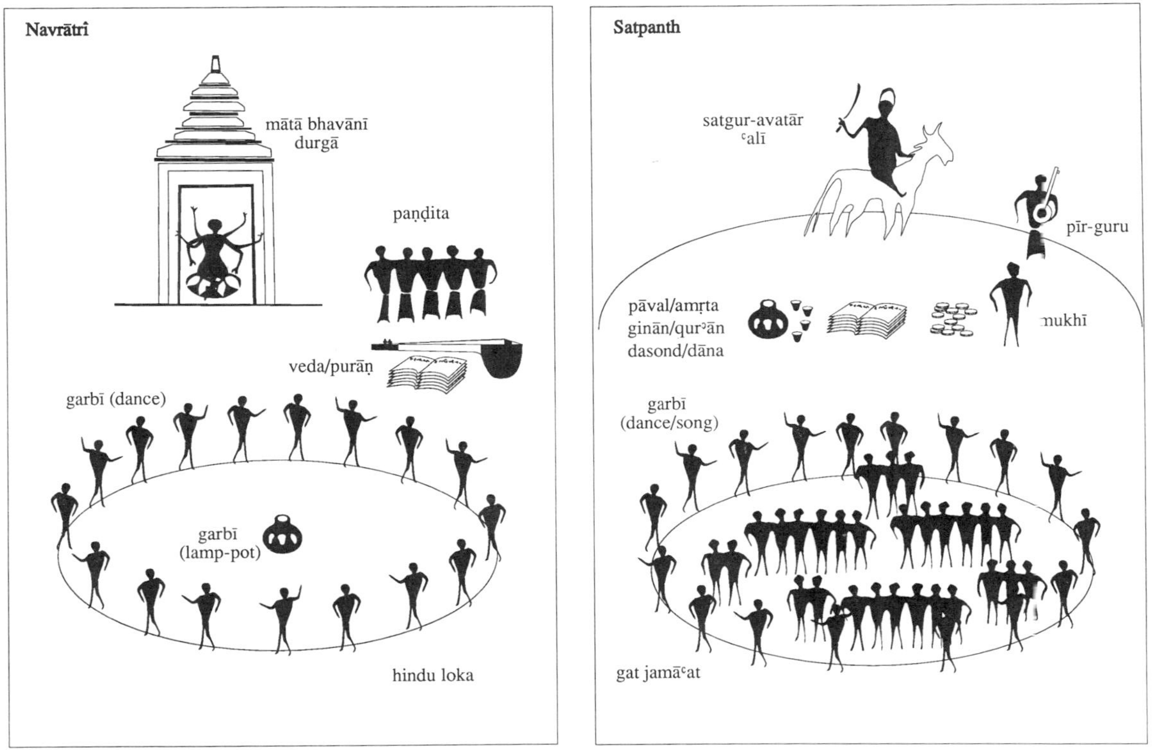

capture the gist of the Qur'ān's teachings. Satpanth is, therefore, the True Path, and the crowning phase of Hinduism (a claim not much different from the Qur'ānic assertion of itself as the last Revelation, and of Islam as the perfection of the religion of the *ahl al-kitāb* or People of the Book).

In a process much like the *lexique technique* employed by Kabīr in his popular phrase, *rāma rahīm kṛṣṇa karīm,* the *Garbīs* succeed in creating an emotional and cognitive bridge by the juxtaposition and association of Hindu and Ismā'īlī concepts. The coexistence of vocabulary such as *avatār* and *nūr, purāṇ* and *kurāṇ, sat dharma* and *dīn* by their very proximity construct a religious language mutually recognized by Hindus and Satpanth Ismā'īlīs alike.

In all this, what should have become abundantly clear is that the exclusive focus of the *Garbīs* is religious conversion, practice, and salvation. The Hindus who accept the Pīr's teaching are portrayed as consciously renouncing their former idols, sacred texts, priests, and rituals of worship and voluntarily adopting Satpanth as their new religion (*dharma*) with its own locus (*satgur–avatār*), its own scripture (*ginān*), its own religious official (*mukhī*), and its own set of rituals (the drinking of holy water or *pāval,* the paying of tithe or *dasond,* and the congregational prayer or *satsang*). Yet, although this True Path is taught in the *Garbīs* as a *new* path, it is also presented as a continuation of an ancient one. That is, Satpanth is shown to be rooted in and vindicated by the primordial Hindu tradition of which it is considered to be the ultimate expression.

Finally, what makes this work a rather good specimen of an inward orientation and quiescent stage of Ismā'īlism is that not only has it little war imagery, but that salvation is truly understood as the salvation of souls. To illustrate:

> The *imāms* are from light; they are
> ever present in the world. 82:15
> Listen to this true wisdom and serve [them]; 82:16
> Then you will reach the other shore
> and attain Heaven (*svarga*). 82:17

This focus on the salvation of souls is underscored by lists in the *Garbīs* of those persons and souls saved by the *avatār–imām*; they include figures in Hindu mythology such as Dhruva, Hariścandra, and the five Pāṇḍava brothers. There are a number of verses that repeat the following claim and promise:

Rather, serve Sāheb, the Creator, with firm faith— 81:06
He who saved in this age of Kalyug twelve crore
devout souls. 81:16
He who in this last period will save countless
brave believers. 81:17

Moreover, the *imāms,* who have saved countless souls and rewarded the true and righteous, were none other than the famous *avatārs* of Hindu mythology. Among these savior figures are also *pīrs,* namely, Pīr Ṣadr al-Dīn and Pīr Ḥasan Kabir al-Dīn.

Five crore [were saved] by Prahlād
who recited the name of Narsiṃha. 89:07
Seven crore [were saved] by Hariścandra
who was saved by Śrī Rāma. 89:08

Twelve crore pious [were saved] by truth
in this age of Kalyug. 89:11
Their rescuer was Pīr Ṣadr al-Dīn;
he saved them all by himself. 89:12

Numerous will come together with
Pīr Ṣadr al-Dīn, some twelve crore 91:11
Countless crore will come with Guru Ḥasan Shāh
who upheld the Vedas. 91:12

This kind of enumerative list of souls saved, that is, ferried across to the other shore[114] (*pahele pār*), occurs several times in the *Garbīs*. An image is created of a heaven filled with divine light (*nūr*) where millions of enlightened souls congregate by the Ganges and where the 124,000 prophets are also gathered [91:13]. The interiorization of salvation as eternal life in a heavenly abode of bliss is emphasized by the repeated use of the symbol of divine light or *nūr* which would fill the pure souls.

The gathering is filled with the saints (*awliyā*)
who bear divine light. 94:12
The gathering radiates with the *Gurunar*
who is full of divine light. 94:13

O Hindus! On and on why wander in circles?
Drink in the pure light. 96:10
O Hindus! He who lives in Kahak city is the Sāheb—
giver of boons. 96:13

O Hindus! Attaining heaven (*vaikuṇṭha*)
you will reign in eternal bliss. 96:14

The theme of promises made by the Pīr in the Multān *ginān*s continues in the *Garbīs*, but this promise is no longer in the form of receiving military aid from the West nor being rescued by the Shāh. Rather, the promise is reconceived as the act of showing the path to and *revealing* the true reality of the Shāh. Thus, the *Garbīs* declare,

We have come up to your door,
[now] recognize us! 101:12
We have kept our promise,
[now] what have you to say? 101:13
Countless of souls have not been saved,
why remain with them? 101:14

The *pīr* made a promise and he came—
see how he showed them the path! 106:14
The *pīr* explained this word by word
to those who would accept Satpanth. 106:16
They were saved, man and woman,
when Pīr Shams spoke his thoughts. 106:17

Accordingly, the ultimate object of religion as depicted in the *Garbīs* has become the attainment of the divine vision (*dīdār*) and reality of the *imām*. Thus, the Pīr declares

Who enters the religion of Satpanth attains freedom
and the divine vision. 99:15

If your earnings are honest and pure,
you will enter Heaven's (*svarga*) gate. 105:16
O believers, attain the divine vision (*dīdār*)
and your sins will vanish. 105:18

Salvation in the *Garbīs*, therefore, is primarily a spiritual reality, and the one who holds the key to this state of eternal bliss is the *avatār–imām*, the path to whom only the *pīrs* could reveal.

To conclude, then, if the narratives in the *ginān*s can be construed to mirror reality at some level, mistily reflecting clues about social, cultural, and historical context, it seems that some interesting patterns emerge upon closer inspection of the *ginān*s attributed to Pīr Shams. There is sufficient evidence to argue that the *ginān*s display an unusual degree of interest in historical memory. This effort at realism goes to the point of citing specific dates, places, and historical personalities. For instance, there is an unusual verse in the *ginān* titled *Janāzā* (coffin or corpse) which records that the day that the Pīr departed Multān was a Thursday, the 17th day of Vaiśakhī [25:23]. One explanation of this mysterious record suggests that it marks the day when the Pīr died and that, since then, a fast has been observed on Thursdays.[115] Other verses in the same *ginān* describe how his followers wept when his time to depart neared and how they then carried his coffin off to Ucch where he was buried [25:21, 24].

It is also possible to detect contrasts in the *gināns* attributed to Pīr Shams. We have noted that the *gināns* associated with Multān are consistently connected with fort and battle imagery and predictions of victory over a menacing demon–king. The imagery of conflict in Cīnab (possibly another name for Multān) is portrayed in great detail in the *gināns*. Delhi, too, is cited in one *ginān,* and this remnant may have some remote connection with the unsuccessful revolt (referred to in the previous chapter) of the Ismāʿīlīs in 1236 C.E. headed by a Nūr Turk during the reign of Illtūtmish's daughter, Raḍiyya.[116] There are scattered references to Ghazni[117] where the Pīr first came to preach as a Muslim *faqīr* from Daylamān.[118] *Ginān*s that refer to Ucch generally concern the conversion activities of the Pīr and his disciples.[119] The contest between the Ṣūfī saint of Ucch, Bahā al-Dīn Zakariyya, and Pīr Shams, who cursed the former with a pair of horns, is related in another *ginān.*[120]

What, if anything, can be made of all this material? What is the source of these allusions and motifs? Could it be possible that they were derived from the environment experienced by the early *daʿwah?* The unusually consistent battle imagery, the abundant place names, and the repeated promises made in the *gināns* attributed to Pīr Shams depict a period of real tension and peril. It seems very likely, therefore, that many *gināns* associated with his name originated during a period of political conflict. The recurrent forecast that the Shāh would come from the West to seize Multān and save Cīnab with well-armed battalions signals that the area was then under the control of the "wicked," that is, the opponents of the *daʿwah.* Except for Bahā' al-Dīn Zakariyya, the opponents identified in the *gināns* are mainly Hindu including a figure who evidently was considered to be a rather powerful Hindu monarch. If we do allow, for the sake of discussion, that these allusions in the *gināns* had some connection with the Ismāʿīlī troubles in Multān, firstly, they must refer to a time when the Ismāʿīlīs, though under serious threat, also had a high probability of gaining back control of the region. The promise of reinforcements from Alamūt, and the predicted outcome of the Shāh's sovereignty, could only have been made when Alamūt was still in power and when the local Hindu and Sindhi allies of the Ismāʿīlīs, such as the Sūmrah dynasty, were still an effective force. After the decline of Alamūt in 1256 C.E. and the fall of the Sūmrahs by the end of the fourteenth century, pretensions to Ismāʿīlī sovereignty would have been meaningless.

Based on the above clues, there appears to be some reason to speculate that the Nizārī *daʿwah* did attempt to rally the support of Hindu kingdoms but that some chieftains remained disinterested in striking up alliances. These activities of the *daʿwah* may have coincided with or shortly preceded the waves of Ghūrid incursions against the Ismāʿīlīs of Multān that took place from 1160 C.E. till 1175 C.E., when Muḥammad Ghori supposedly stemmed Ismāʿīlī influence in the area. Yet, as long as the Nizārī state under Alamūt existed, the Ismāʿīlī mission in Sind could have entertained realistic hopes that Multān eventually would be won back. This would, in turn, place Pīr Shams well enough within the time of Alamūt rule to account for his confidence in offering military reinforcements and predicting actual victory.

Ansar Khan points out that "during the 13th and 14th century, the Ismāʿīlī Sūmrah chiefs were dominant in Sind and, therefore, concerted efforts were made to win back the lost territory in Multan."[121] This period is somewhat later than our own analysis would suggest, but it supports the drift of the internal testimony in the *ginān*s apropos political conflict. That is, while Muḥammad Ghori may ostensibly have put an end to Ismāʿīlī rule in Multān in 1175, the Ismāʿīlī Sūmrahs and their allies in Sind may have kept up hopes of restoring Ismāʿīlī control over the region. In an earlier discussion of battle imagery surrounding Multān and Cīnab, I suggested that the positive forecasts found in the *ginān*s could only have been made had confidence existed that the Ismāʿīlīs possessed sufficient political force to regain power over the area.

In sum, the above points combine to suggest that Pīr Shams was an Ismāʿīlī *dāʿī* who came to Western India from Ghazna in Sabzawār and that he worked to establish Ismāʿīlī affiliations in Sind from a basis in Multān during the Alamūt period at a time when the Ismāʿīlī alliance with the Sūmrahs was secure. The tomb in Ucch, Multān, most likely belongs to this Ismāʿīlī *pīr*.

As for the dating of Pīr Shams, it has been noted that the dates that are cited in the *ginān*s (1118 C.E., 1143 C.E., and 1150 C.E.) differ from the dates given in the genealogy or *shajara* (1165–1276 C.E.)

preserved by the keepers of his shrine by almost half a century. These dates may be associated with the activities of earlier *dāʿīs*. However, the fact that they have been mentioned in connection with the two disciples of Pīr Shams complicates matters. That these dates may not be completely reliable is suggested by the inconsistency between the fact that, on the one hand, the *ginān*s constantly refer to these two disciples as the "two youths" and, on the other hand, the dates posit a gap of some thirty-two years between the time when Surbhāṇ allegedly received Pīr Shams (1118 C.E.) and when Candrabhāṇ converted (1150 C.E.).

The dates given in the *shajara,* though they overextend the life of Pīr Shams (perhaps to make it coincide with that of the Ṣūfī saint and rival of the Ismāʿīlī *daʿwah,* Bahāʾ al-Dīn Zakariyya, who died in 1277 C.E.), appear to be worth serious consideration for the following reasons. Firstly, since the birthdate of Pīr Shams given in the *shajara* is 1165 C.E., this would mean that the life and activities of Pīr Shams followed the declaration of the *Qiyāmah* in 1164 C.E. If Pīr Shams did play a seminal role in the articulation of Satpanth Ismāʿīlism, and this appears to have been the case, the declaration of the *Qiyāmah*—which effectively disengaged the formalities and ritual accoutrement of the faith from its essential principles—would have made this innovative articulation of Satpanth both possible and permissible.

Given the internal evidence of alliances and political conflict attached to his activities in Multān, as well as our knowledge of the history of Sind in the twelfth century, it seems reasonable to suggest that the major activities of Pīr Shams took place in the latter half of the twelfth century. The testimony preserved in the *ginān*s alluding to political conflict, fort imagery, and victory over an insurgent Hindu king suggest the possibility that Pīr Shams was engaged in the region around the time of the Ghūrid invasions which culminated in Ismāʿīlī massacres in 1175 C.E. The allusions in the *ginān* narratives depict a situation both of conflict and difficulty (hence the plea for "liberation") and a promise of help, victory, and security. The time between the Ghūrid attacks on Sind and the fall of Alamūt would have been filled with a similar tension and ambiguity. On the one hand, the Ismāʿīlīs in Sind, with their Sūmrah base, were under attack, but, on the other hand, their center in Alamūt represented a well-known and established power base which held forth the promise of liberation.

It has been shown that the *Garbīs,* which are also attributed to this *pīr,* seem to capture a quieter phase of the Satpanth Ismāʿīlī *daʿwah's* activity. Not only do these poems associate Pīr Shams with historical persons who lived between the fourteenth and eighteenth centuries, but, in contrast to the Multān–Cīnab narratives, they attach a clearly other-wordly, religious significance to salvation. It is likely that as the area of Multān was increasingly subjugated, and as Ṣūfī orders such as the state-affiliated Suhrawardī *ṭarīqah* gained ground in the region, the Ismāʿīlīs migrated south towards Lower Sind and Gujarat. The setting of the narratives in the *Garbīs,* a place called Analwāḍ—which may be the town Anhilwāḍ in Gujarat—is in consonance with the fact that the subsequent center of Ismāʿīlī activity moved away from northwestern India and towards the regions of Mālwā, Kāṭhiāwāḍ, and Gujarat.

The *ginān*s attributed to Pīr Shams that refer to his activities around the Multān area also contain allusions that suggest that he preached during the eve of the growing presence of rival Ṣūfī *ṭarīqahs* in Multān. While it is unclear whether Pīr Shams actually confronted the Ṣūfī saint, Bahāʾ al-Dīn Zakariyya, the legendary contest between the two records the threat that institutionalized and state-affiliated Ṣūfism may have posed to the Satpanth *daʿwah* during this period. That the Ismāʿīlīs did not utterly relinquish their political ambitions in the region is evidenced by their unsuccessful attempt to seize control in Delhi, the political center of North India, in 1236 C.E. under the reign of Queen Raḍiyya. Whether she was the same Queen Radīyādevī who is mentioned in the *ginān*s attributed to Pīr Shams is impossible to ascertain; however, this may be a clue that his life extended to this period and that Pīr Shams had some connection with this uprising.

It is inevitable that there is much by way of speculation here, given the nature of our sources and the lack of other historical information on this figure or the Ismāʿīlī *daʿwah* in Sind at the time. Based on the preceding analysis of the *ginān*s attributed to Pīr Shams and what we know about the historical context in the Indian subcontinent and Persia between the eleventh and thirteenth centuries, and pending the discovery of further materials, we may tentatively conclude the following. The Pīr Shams of the *ginān*s in the Anthology translated here was a *pīr* of the Nizārī Ismāʿīlī *daʿwah* who played a critical role in advancing the latter's political aspirations in Sind, as well as in setting and articulating the religious foundations of Satpanth Ismāʿīlism. Most likely, this figure hailed from Sabzawār, came to India as a youth, and lived between the mid-twelfth and mid-thirteenth centuries. His principal area of activity radiated from a base in Multān, and he lies buried in Ucch in a tomb popularly known as "Shāh Shams."

Conclusion: Recovering History and Tradition

In his *farmān* quoted at the beginning of this study, the present *imām* of the Ismāʿīlīs, Prince Karīm al-Ḥusaynī, refers to the *ginān*s as a "wonderful tradition" and expresses his concern to his followers that it be continued else the community would "lose some of our past which is most important to us."[1] As the pronouncement and counsel of the supreme authority of the worldwide community of Ismāʿīlīs on matters of faith and practice, this message deserves attention. Why does the spiritual leader of this Shīʿite sect regard the *ginān*s to be a wonderful tradition? What of the past do these hymns preserve that ought to be of significance to his followers?

Before the full dimensions of what is "so special, so unique, and so important" about the *ginān* tradition can be known, a great deal more scholarly research on this subject must be undertaken. Unfortunately, Satpanth Ismāʿīlism has received scant attention in the field of Ismāʿīlī studies, which has concentrated itself mainly on the period leading up to the Alamūt catastrophe. Although the Satpanth phase has spanned over half the life of this sect, specialists in Ismāʿīlī studies still persist in ignoring it in their schemata of Ismāʿīlī history. We have endeavored to show that this neglect may be traced to a set of biases that finds greater interest and legitimacy in the political, the orthodox, and the classical aspects of religions. The centuries of Ismāʿīlī history that are most thoroughly investigated are thus also the centuries during which Ismāʿīlīs pursued a vigorous intellectual, social, and political program to secure a theocratic basis for the imāmate. Further, this earlier period of Ismāʿīlī history belonged to an intellectual, cultural, and linguistic milieu that Hodgson identifies as the Islamicate world. As part of this classical, Arabo–Persian centered ethos, such illustrious Ismāʿīlī thinkers as Abū Yaʿqūb al-

Sijistānī, Ḥamīd al-Kirmānī, al-Mu'ayyad fi'l-Dīn al-Shīrāzī, and Nāṣir-i Khusraw have drawn considerable interest.

On the other hand, Satpanth Ismāʿīlism, a post-Alamūt development unfortunately characterized as apolitical, heterodox, and folkoric, has long been regarded as the declining phase of the Ismāʿīlī movement and, hence, has not attracted equal attention. Furthermore, the syncretic nature of this development and its deep indebtedness to Hindu ideas and culture has even led some scholars to question its very identity as a legitimate expression of Islam. Such bias has not only retarded the study of Satpanth Ismāʿīlism, it has also governed the interpretation of what little is known of this tradition. Many theories and interpretations of Satpanth Ismāʿīlism and its literature are problematic.

For example, one repeatedly reads the view that Satpanth literature was the means by which Ismāʿīlī *pīrs* or preachers converted Hindus to Nizārī Ismāʿīlism. This has led to the dubious characterization of the *ginān*s as conversion literature. Clearly, the oral teachings of the *pīrs* played a crucial role in the establishment of Satpanth, and this is expressed in the traditional belief that the very words spoken by the *pīrs* were holy and inspired and that it was the magic of these utterances and sweet hymns that led the Hindus to recognize the True Path or *satpanth*. Such genuine awe and affection for the teachings of the *pīrs* is clearly understandable from the believer's standpoint.

Without diminishing the rhetorical and didactic role of the *ginān*s, however, it is essential to investigate what other practical conditions assisted in the establishment of Satpanth Ismāʿīlism. The notion that, as conversion literature, *ginān*s were solely responsible for convincing Hindus to convert to Ismāʿīlī Islam is untenable. Even were we to accept that the *ginān*s were recited by the *pīrs* as their chosen form of teaching, and that the *pīrs* were themselves charismatic figures, in and of itself, this is not sufficient to explain the fact of conversion as a significant shifting of faith commitments and an assumption of new social mores and religious orientations. It is, therefore, necessary to investigate, in tandem with the *pīrs* religious teachings, what other social, historical, and political realities contributed to their success.

Related to this problematic paradigm of conversion is the usual explanation given for the intermixture of Hindu and Muslim ideas in the *ginān*s, namely, that the *pīrs* used Hindu symbols, myths, and language essentially to convey Nizārī Ismāʿīlī teachings. The mixing of various Hindu, Tantric, Vaiṣṇava, and Ismāʿīlī ideas in the *ginān*s has been construed as an expedient strategy employed by the *pīrs* for closing the gap between their Persian Nizārī Ismāʿīlī religious heritage and the Hindu background of their Indian converts. The syncretism in the *ginān*s, which Ivanow refers to as a hodgepodge, was thus accepted and tolerated for the sake of conversion. Such an interpretation leads to the problematic position, firstly, that having established Satpanth Ismāʿīlism the *ginān* tradition has outlived its function and is thus no longer relevant and, secondly, that it ought to be discarded given its non-Islamic "impurities."

I have attempted to show that the syncretism in the *ginān*s is not a haphazard mishmash of Hindu and Muslim ideas.[2] On the contrary, the *ginān*s intricately weave Hindu and Ismāʿīlī ideas together to fashion a religious sensibility that holds them in dynamic and fertile tension. That is to say, the view that the Hindu influences in the *ginān*s were merely opportunistic overlooks the fact that Satpanth Ismāʿīlism evolved into an integral tradition of beliefs, rituals, and commitments that authentically spoke to and inspired the religious life of generations of Indian Ismāʿīlīs. Interpretations of *ginān*s that characterize it as a superimposition of "a Shiʿite, Ismaili form of Islam on a Vaiṣṇava Hindu substructure"[3] or as the diffusion of Ismāʿīlī Islam through its vernacularization in the Indian context lose sight of this religious and social integrity. Such analysis fails to acknowledge that Satpanth Ismāʿīlism forged a new ethos that drew in full measure from two streams of inspiration to create a religious and cultural synthesis that sustained this fledgling community for several centuries to full maturity.

Another questionable view is that Satpanth Ismāʿīlism was not linked to the earlier Fāṭimid Ismāʿīlī *daʿwah* in Sind and, furthermore, that Satpanth Ismāʿīlism was at root, a quietistic, meditative, and mystically oriented development that arose *after* the downfall of Alamūt when all political aspirations of the Ismāʿīlīs were shattered. A closer investigation of the historical circumstances in Sind and the greater Ismāʿīlī world at the eve of Satpanth Ismāʿīlism, as well as a careful scrutiny of the testimony of its sacred tradition about its own beginnings has shown, however, that the above assumptions need to be revised. I have argued in this book that the roots of Satpanth Ismāʿīlism are, in fact, far more complex than has been hitherto recognized. The explanation that religious conversion was achieved primarily through the literary creativity of the *pīrs* is too simplistic and fails to address the sociological and political dimensions in the creation and emergence of a new ethnic religious community. This study has tried to bring to light some of the social and political factors that were at play at the embryonic stage of Satpanth Ismāʿīlism and to show that its formation was closely connected to historical events in Sind and in the Ismāʿīlī territories.

To summarize briefly, this research reveals that the seeds of an indigenous form of Ismāʿīlism, which later came to be called Satpanth, were probably planted in the first half of the eleventh century. With the threat posed by the invading Ghaznawids at the end of the tenth century, the Ismāʿīlī practice of alliance with Hindu kingdoms to face a common oppressor began around 1001 C.E. with the pact made between the Fāṭimid governor of Multān, Abū al-Fatḥ Dā'ūd b. Nasr, and the Kashmir king, Anandpāl. While it is clear that the Fāṭimids did not encourage a policy of religious accommodation, it seems that they did succeed in gaining the allegiance of indigenous Sindhi groups who had already converted to Islam and intermarried with Arab Muslims. The Sūmrahs were one such group and, as we know, they seem to have retained several Hindu customs.

After the brutal Ghaznawid massacres of the Ismāʿīlīs in Sind between 1010 and 1025 C.E., both in Multān and al-Manṣūrah, the ethnically Arab Ismāʿīlī population in the region was sharply reduced. That Fāṭimid activity continued in the region is evident from letters of the Fāṭimid caliph, al-Mustanṣir, confirming appointments of *dāʿīs* from Yaman. With the split of the sect after the caliph's death in 1094 C.E., the Fāṭimid *daʿwah* in India fell into the hands of the Ṣulayḥids, and this *daʿwah,* which later came to represent the Ṭayyibis, was apolitical, Arab-based, and active principally in the Cambay or Gujarat region. The fact that less than a century later the Ghūrids came to Upper Sind in 1165 C.E. to destroy the Ismāʿīlīs in Multān suggests, however, that a politically active current of Ismāʿīlism was still present in Sind after the Nizārī–Mustaʿli split. This faction was probably led by the Sūmrahs, who seem to have supported the Nizārī Ismāʿīlīs in Persia after the split. The evidence also suggests that the local Sindhi forces which rallied around the Nizārī Ismāʿīlī cause were composed of a network of minor Hindu kingdoms facing a common oppressor, namely, the Sunnī conquerers who established the Delhi sultanate. Thus, whereas the Ghaznawids had attacked an ethnically Arab-based Ismāʿīlī population between 1010 and 1025 C.E., by the time the Ghūrids attacked Multān again between 1165 and 1175 C.E., the Ismāʿīlī forces were predominantly comprised of indigenous chiefs and their resources, and possibly some reinforcements from the Nizārī state.

I propose that the period between the Sūmrah recapture of Lower Sind in 1051 C.E. and the Ghūrid attack of the Ismāʿīlīs in

Multān in 1165 C.E. was the crucible in which the social basis of an indigenous Ismāʿīlī community was forged through intermarriages, political alliances, and a common cause requiring mutual trust and material support. The social interaction and intermixture of customs and identities resulting from such alliances would have, no doubt, created fertile ground for the exploration and exchange of religious and cultural ideas. These primary alliances and a mixed Sūmrah identity came to form the nucleus of the Satpanth Ismāʿīlī community.

Now, whereas the Nizārī Ismāʿīlīs in Persia would have comprehended the value of political alliances with Sindhi Hindu kingdoms, it is another question whether they would have comprehended or welcomed the new evolution of religious ideas gestating within the Sūmrah–Ismāʿīlī nucleus in Sind. The declaration of the *Qiyāmah* by Ḥasan II ʿala Ḍhikrihi al-Salām in 1164 C.E., therefore, may not have been only to establish his own claim to imāmate; it may also have been a prescient legitimization by the head of Alamūt of what already was in process under the *daʿwah* in Sind. At any rate, the separation of form from spirit implied by the doctrine of *Qiyāmah* would have permitted and given impetus to a nascent Indian–Ismāʿīlī, viz. Satpanth, identity in Sind. Even though many Hindu concepts and practices were embraced by this new religious formation called Satpanth, the ingenuity of the *pīrs* in India was in their deft integration and celebration of core elements of an Ismāʿīlī identity within this framework. This they did by their pivotal placement of Satpanth as the culmination of Hinduism and the Ismāʿīlī *imām* as the long-awaited, tenth *avatār* of Viṣṇu.

Without the allusions found in the *ginans* of Pīr Shams, there would have been little reason for this author to suspect the political foundations of Satpanth Ismāʿīlism newly illuminated in this study given its later development. The fatal end to Ismāʿīlī power that occurred with the destruction of Alamūt decisively hid these origins. By evolving an identity that was integral to the Indian environment, Satpanth Ismāʿīlism survived and flourished in India. It is conceivable that the Ismāʿīlīs of Sind subsequent to the Mongol disaster continued to hold some political aspirations, but with the Ismāʿīlī exodus from Persia, coupled with the growing influence of state-aligned Ṣūfism in the area, these aspirations must have been short-lived. The evolving Satpanth Ismāʿīlī identity—with its organic relationship to Hinduism and the Indian environment—helped to shield this sect, which otherwise would have risked extinction had its true Shīʿah Ismāʿīlī identity been known.

The theme of liberation which was at the heart of its origins, and, at least initially, also embraced a political ideal, was easily transformed into a quest for spiritual emancipation. In analyzing the *gināns* attributed to Pīr Shams, this shift has been demonstrated. Clearly, in order that the vulnerable nascent community would survive, Satpanth Ismāʿīlism and the *ginān* tradition had to evolve toward a more inward, pacifist, and mystically oriented form. The literature preserves dimly through sacred narrative and the language of symbols an image of this liberation movement and how the Satpanth *pīrs* faced the challenge of their changed circumstances. The wealth of allusions to rivalry, intrigue, and battle coupled with promises of aid and victory from the West in the *gināns* attributed to Pīr Shams suggest that he himself, however, belonged not to the later quietistic period of Satpanth but to its initial activist, formative period. Based on the consonance between these allusions and external events occurring in Sind and the Nizārī Ismāʿīlī state, we have concluded that Pīr Shams lived and worked during the decades prior to the destruction of Alamūt and at a time when the Nizārī Ismāʿīlīs were still in power.

This study has attempted to cull what may be found in the *gināns* about the past that is of relevance to an understanding of Ismāʿīlī history. In helping raise questions about its origins, the investigation has been rewarded with some critical insights. But what of the claim that it is a wonderful tradition? This points to another aspect of the *ginān* literature that may offer a rich and fruitful area of inquiry. A corollary of the conversion theory is the unproven assertion that Satpanth Ismāʿīlism is an Indian form of Nizārī Ismāʿīlism. This premise has fostered analyses which essentially conclude that Nizārī Ismāʿīlī ideas were merely grafted onto a Ṣūfī, Tantric, or Vaiṣṇava substratum of religious ideas or, conversely, that works from the latter sects were simply appropriated with minor adjustments into the Satpanth corpus of sacred literature. If one were to seek (following Cantwell Smith's phenomenological approach to religion)[4] the meaning of Satpanth Ismāʿīlism on its own terms, one might discover the categories that make up its internal system of coherence, as well as the principles of selection at the basis of the syncretism in Satpanth Ismāʿīlism. This understanding, however, is possible only if the specific configuration of religious ideas and symbolism of Satpanth is understood as it is self-constructed, and not by the yardstick either of Fāṭimid or Nizārī concepts.

What becomes quickly apparent through a sustained and systematic analysis of the *ginān* literature is that it is an integral part of a larger religious system of ritual performances and symbolic relationships that construct a totality encompassing a sacred community and its worldview. The elements of Satpanth religion, ritual, and social patterns of behavior that define and construct the reality of this sect are to be found imbedded in its sacred literature. It is thus not surprising that the British court was able to establish the identity of the sect based on the evidence of the *gināns*. The critical role of the *gināns* in articulating the central concepts of Satpanth, as well as its requisite duties, is evident in the *gināns* of Pīr Shams which convey teachings on the topics of the *avatār*, the *ghaṭpāṭ* ceremony, and the paying of the tithe or *dasond*. The *gināns* have articulated, to borrow from Clifford Geertz, a "machinery of faith" and "systems of significance" for Satpanth Ismā'īlism.[5]

However, as the Satpanth counterpart of the Hindu *veda* or *śastra*, the *gināns* of the *pīrs* go much beyond evolving a worldview and furnishing the ritualistic and symbolic components necessary to maintaining an indigenous religious community. As a musical, literary, and inspirational tradition, the *gināns* constitute a religious performance that sustains the primary dimension of religious experience. For the faithful, this means reaching beyond thought and deed to express and celebrate, through hymn and invocation, the pathos and devotion that feeds a religious life. It has been noted that for centuries the recitation of *gināns* has been an intrinsic part of daily Satpanth worship. In addition to understanding the rich content of the *gināns*, what also needs to be carefully investigated is the performative aspects of this heritage, including the nature of its melodies and their modes of transmission, its various contexts of performance, and the impact of modern conditions on its ritual role and significance. These few areas will constitute, I hope, the focus of future research in the area of Satpanth Ismā'īlī studies.

Notes

Chapter 1

1. See Gulshan Khakee, "The *Dasa Avatāra* of the Satpanthi Ismailis and Imam Shahis of Indo-Pakistan" (Harvard: Ph.D. diss., 1972), 3. This *double entendre* is a recurrent feature of the *ginān* tradition. Note the parallel in the term Qur'ān which also has the dual meaning of "recitation" and "revelation."

2. This is the name officially used by the sect today.

3. *Ginan-e Sharif: Our Wonderful Tradition* (Vancouver: Ismailia Association for Canada, n.d.), i.

4. Two decades ago, based on a list compiled by Alibhai Nanji of Hyderabad, Azim Nanji estimated the total number of *gināns* to be about eight-hundred. See Azim Nanji, *The Nizārī Ismā'īlī Tradition of the Indo-Pak Subcontinent* (New York: Caravan Books, 1978), 10. Nagib Tajdin, a private collector of *ginān* manuscripts, has discovered several unpublished *gināns* in his collection and believes the number to be much higher. Ali Asani recently revised the estimated number of *gināns* to "approximately one thousand hymn-like poems." See Ali. S. Asani, *The Harvard Collection of Ismaili Literature in Indic Languages: A Descriptive Catalog and Finding Aid* (Boston: G. K. Hall & Co., 1992), 6.

5. For an elaboration of the aural dimensions of scripture, see William Graham, *Beyond the Written Word: Oral Aspects of Scripture in the History of Religion* (Cambridge: Cambridge University Press, 1987); Harold Coward & David Goa, *Mantra: Hearing the Divine in India* (Chambersburg: Anima Books, 1991); and *Sacred Sound: Music in Religious Thought and Practice,* ed. Joyce Irwin, JAAR Thematic Studies 50/1 (Chico: Scholars Press, 1983).

6. Asani notes that "even after being recorded in Khojkī, the community's special script, oral knowledge of *ginānic* texts was still necessary to ensure correct reading of an ambiguous alphabet." See Ali S. Asani, "The

Ismaili Gināns as Devotional Literature," *Devotional Literature in South Asia: Current Research 1985–1988*, ed. R. S. McGregor (Cambridge: Cambridge University Press, 1992), 104.

7. *Collection of Gināns composed by the Great Ismaili Saint Pir Sadrudin (Mahān Ismāīlī Santa Pīr Sadardīn Racit Gīnānono Saṅgraha)* (Bombay: Ismailia Association for India, 1969), 61. Translation mine.

8. For instance, see Ginān 68, 70, and 91 translated in Part II of this work.

9. *The Great Ismaili Heroes* (Karachi: Prince Alykhan Religious Night School, 1973), 98–99.

10. G. Allana, *Ginans of Ismaili Pirs: Rendered into English Verse* (Karachi: Ismailia Association for Pakistan, 1984), 1. I owe my own love of music and poetry to my father, Huzurmukhī Rahim Count Kassam Jivraj, who is an admired *ginān* reciter.

11. Ibid., 2.

12. An interesting question is whether musical accompaniment was permitted in the past. I have been informed by a reliable source that, in 1975 at the first International Convention of Ismailia Associations, it was resolved that no musical instruments would be allowed to accompany *ginān* recitation in the *jamāʿat khānah*. This suggests that the recitation of *gināns* to the accompaniment of music may have been in practice in some areas. Modern strictures against holding *ginān mehfils* or musical recitals of *gināns* within the *jamāʿat khānah* space is probably part of the modern trend toward islamization. For a discussion of this trend, see Ali S. Asani, "The Khojahs of Indo-Pakistan: The Quest for an Islamic Identity," *Journal of the Institute of Muslim Minority Affairs*, vol. 8, no. 1 (1983): 31–41, and Diamond Rattansi, "Islamization and the Khojah Ismāʿīlī Community of Pakistan" (McGill University: Ph.D. diss., 1987).

13. This does not preclude the possibility that they may have done so in the past.

14. Typically sung are selected verses from the ginān *Anant Akhāḍo* attributed to Pīr Ḥasan Kabīr al-Dīn. The first line of the work warns, "O Seekers, do not fail to observe the time of *sandhyā* (evening prayer)!" (*āshāñjī, sandhyā velā tame mata koī chūko*). *Sandhyā*, lit. union, juncture, may refer to the hour of sunrise, noon, and sunset; special prayers of this name, that is, *sandhyā*, are commonly offered by the Brahmins at these times. See J. A. Dubois, *Hindu Manners, Customs and Ceremonies*, trans. H. Beauchamp (Delhi: Oxford University Press, 1906), 251–270.

15. That this scheme is still observed was verified by al-Wāʿiẓ Rai Amiraly Amlani who has prepared a "List of Ginans for Recitation on Various

Occasions," for the Ismaili Tariqah and Religious Education Board of Canada.

16. Asani, "*Ginānsas Devotional Literature,*" 106.

17. Non-Ismāʿīlīs are not allowed to participate in the services held at the *jamāʿat khānahs.* This exclusion emphasizes the identity of the Satpanth Ismāʿīlīs as a sacred community bound by a common allegiance to the *imām.*

18. Wladimir Ivanow, "The Sect of the Imam Shah in Gujerat," *Journal of the Bombay Branch of the Royal Asiatic Society,* 12 (1936): 68.

19. These remarks are based on fieldwork on *ginān*s and on interviews with members of the *jamāʿat.* As an insider to the tradition with exposure to Ismāʿīlīs in East Africa, India, Britain, and North America, I am also able to draw on my personal observations of Satpanth practices in these areas.

20. Raymond B. Williams, *Religions of Immigrants from India and Pakistan* (Cambridge: Cambridge University Press, 1989), 186–188.

21. Ibid.

22. According to Satpanth tradition, Pīr Ṣadr al-Dīn gave the converts the honorable title of *khwājah* (lord, master). However, the term *khojah* is not restricted to Satpanth Ismāʿīlī converts, but it is also commonly used to designate Muslim converts in the subcontinent. See Nanji, *The Nizārī Ismāʿīlī Tradition,* 74, 206; and the article by Wilferd Madelung, "Khodja," *Shorter Encyclopaedia of Islam* (Leiden: E. J. Brill, 1961), 256.

23. Pockets of Ismāʿīlīs have lived in communist areas of Central Asia, as well as in the Middle East for long periods, but have remained in *taqīyah* (dissimulation, disguise) to escape political and religious oppression. In the last half century, an increasing number of them have emerged and renewed their contacts with the present *imām,* Prince Karīm Āghā Khān IV.

24. A growing number of Ismāʿīlīs from Afghanistan, Iran, and Northern Pakistan are immigrating to the West. Their traditional songs are occasionally included during religious festivals, but the daily prayer services conforms to Satpanth Ismāʿīlī practice.

25. See Chapter IV for a detailed discussion on the dating of Pīr Shams.

Chapter 2

1. Wilferd Madelung, "Shiism: Ismāʿīlīyah," *Encyclopedia of Religion,* vol. 13, ed. Mircea Eliade (New York: Macmillan, 1986), 247.

2. For instance, see Abū Muḥammad Ibn Ḥazm's *Kitāb al-fiṣal fi'l-*

milal, partial Eng. transl. I. Friedlaender, "The Heterodoxies of the Shiites in the Presentation of Ibn Ḥazm," *Journal of the American Oriental Society,* 28 (1907): 1–80 & 29, (1908): 1–183; ʿAbd al-Karīm al-Shahrastānī's *Kitāb al-milal wa'l-niḥal,* partial Eng. transl. A. K. Kazi & J. G. Flynn, *Muslim Sects and Divisions* (London: Kegan Paul International, 1984).

3. The short title *Ismāʿīlism* is used to refer to the Shīʿah sect of the Imāmī Ismāʿīlī Nizārī Satpanth Muslims, including their total historical tradition. Specific Ismāʿīlī periods or other Ismāʿīlī sects (e.g., Ṭayyibī) will be precisely identified.

4. Marshall G. Hodgson, *The Order of Assassins: The Struggle of the Early Nizārī Ismāʿīlīs Against the Islamic World* (The Hague: Mouton & Co., 1955), 22. Also see the discussion in Bernard Lewis, *The Assassins: A Radical Sect in Islam* (London: Weidenfeld & Nicholson, 1967).

5. For a detailed review of this problem, see Farhad Daftary, *The Ismāʿīlīs: Their History and Doctrines* (Cambridge: Cambridge University Press, 1990), 1–31; and also Farhad Daftary, *The Assassin Legends: Myths of the Isma'ilis* (London: I. B. Tauris & Co. Ltd., 1994).

6. Daftary, *The Ismāʿīlīs,* 5.

7. Ibid., 3.

8. Wladimir Ivanow, *Brief Survey of the Evolution of Ismailism* (Leiden: E. J. Brill, 1952).

9. Aziz Esmail and Azim Nanji, "The Ismāʿīlīs in History," *Ismāʿīlī Contributions to Islamic Culture,* ed. S. H. Nasr (Tehran: Imperial Academy of Philosophy, 1977), 227–260.

10. Madelung, "Shiism," 243–247.

11. Daftary, *The Ismāʿīlīs,* 435ff.

12. Ivanow, "Satpanth," *Collectanea,* vol. 1 (Leiden: E. J. Brill, 1948), 1–54.

13. Ibid., 21.

14. Ibid.

15. Ibid., 22.

16. Ivanow, *Brief Survey,* 19–21.

17. Azim Nanji's dissertation was subsequently published as a book, *The Nizārī Ismāʿīlī Tradition of the Indo-Pak Subcontinent* (New York: Caravan Books, 1978); Aziz Esmail, "Satpanth Ismailism and Modern Changes Within It: With Special Reference to East Africa" (University of Edinburgh: Ph.D. diss., 1972).

18. Ivanow, *Brief Survey,* preface.

19. Ibid., 29–30.

20. Ibid., 2.

21. Ibid., 16.

22. Ibid., 17.

23. Esmail and Nanji, 237.

24. Daftary, *The Ismāʿīlīs,* xvi.

25. Ibid., 29.

26. Ibid., xvi.

27. Although Ivanow was unable to read the primary sources since he did not know Gujarati and Hindi, he overcame this limitation by working with an interpreter.

28. Ivanow, "Satpanth," 19.

29. Ibid., 20.

30. Ibid., 30.

31. Ibid., 31.

32. Ibid., 34.

33. Ibid.

34. Ibid., 35–36.

35. Ibid., 36.

36. Ibid., 3–4.

37. Ibid., 27.

38. Ibid.

39. Madelung, "Shiism," 257.

40. See Tazim R. Kassam, "Syncretism on the Model of the Figure-Ground: A Study of Pīr Shams' *Brahma Prakāśa,*" *Hermeneutical Paths to the Sacred Worlds of India,* ed. Katherine K. Young (Atlanta: Scholars Press, 1994), 231–242; and "Syncretism or Synthesis: The Narrative *Ginān*s of Pīr Shams," unpublished paper presented in Boston at the Annual Meeting of the American Academy of Religion, 1987.

41. Aziz Ahmed, *An Intellectual History of Islam in India* (Edinburgh: Edinburgh University Press, 1969), 24–25.

42. See Asani, "The Khojahs of Indo-Pakistan," 31–41; Rattansi, "Islamization and the Khojah," and Azim Nanji, "*Sharīʿat* and *Haqīqat:* Continuity and Synthesis in the Nizārī Ismāʿīlī Muslim Tradition," *Sharīʿat and Ambiguity in South Asian Islam,* ed. Katherine P. Ewing (Berkeley: University of California Press, 1988), 63–76.

43. Esmail and Nanji, 252.

44. Ibid., 254.

45. Daftary, *The Ismāʿīlīs,* 30.

46. Ibid., 31.

47. For a complete review of the literature on Satpanth Ismāʿīlism and the *ginān* literature, see Chapter III, Tazim R. Kassam, "Songs of Wisdom and Circles of Dance: an Anthology of Hymns by the Satpanth Ismāʿīlī Saint, Pīr Shams" (McGill University: Ph.D. dissertation, 1992), 52–87.

48. "Nizārīsm . . . in India became designated as Satpanth, that is Sat Panth, the True Path." Daftary, *The Ismāʿīlīs,* 478.

49. Ibid., 442.

50. See especially Asim Roy's *The Islamic Syncretistic Tradition in Bengal* (Princeton: Princeton University Press, 1984), and Dietmar Ruthermund, ed. *Islam in South Asia* (Weisbaden: Franz Steiner Verlag, 1975).

51. An important work of this genre continues to be Clifford Geertz's *Islam Observed: Religious Developments in Morocco and Indonesia* (Chicago: University of Chicago Press, 1968). Also notable for a range of approaches are Richard Eaton, *Sufis of Bijapur* (Princeton: Princeton University Press, 1978); Donald B. Cruise O'Brien & C. Coulon, eds., *Charisma and Brotherhood in African Islam* (Oxford: Clarendon Press, 1988); Robert W. Hefner, *Hindu Javanese: Tengger Tradition and Islam* (Princeton: Princeton University Press, 1985); Ewing, ed., *Sharīʿat and Ambiguity* (1988); and Roy, *Islamic Syncretistic Tradition* (1984).

52. Daftary, *The Ismāʿīlīs,* 442, n. 17.

Chapter 3

1. Syed Mujtaba Ali, *The Origin of the Khojāhs and their Religious Life Today* (Wurzburg: Buchdruckerei Richard Mayr, 1936), 51.

2. Rattansi, 16.

3. "The Khoja Case 1866—A Paraphrase," Typewritten manuscript (Ismailia Association, Quebec, n.d.).

4. Asaf ʿAli Asghar Fyzee, *Cases in the Muhammadan Law of India and Pakistan* (London: Clarendon Press, 1965), 545.

5. "The Khoja Case," 10.

6. Kassam, "Syncretism on the Model of Figure-ground" and "Syncretism or Synthesis."

7. Nanji, *The Nizārī Ismāʿīlī Tradition,* 94.

8. Fyzee, 504–5.

9. Ibid., 539.

10. Although not widely publicized, periodic attacks against Khojah Ismāʿīlīs and their literature have occurred in Pakistan since the days of partition. For a detailed discussion of this context of religious and political tensions, and the consequent islamization of the Khojahs, see Rattansi, "Islamization and the Khojah."

11. Rattansi's work is particularly valuable for its exposition of the conflict and ambiguity that has been created around the *ginān* tradition within the modern Khojah Ismāʿīlī community.

12. The premiere research institution of the Ismāʿīlīs, since its founding in 1977, except for collecting and preparing a catalogue (now mysteriously lost) of its *ginān* manuscripts, the Institute of Ismaili Studies has not encouraged nor deliberately pursued much research on the Satpanth tradition. The *ginān* manuscript collection is no longer accessible except by special permission. Under its ambitious publications program, to date, no works have been published on the history or religious symbolism of the *ginān* tradition.

13. For instance, see Ivanow, "Satpanth," (1948); Khakee, "The *Dasa Avatāra,*" (1972); and Hasina Jamani, "*Brahma Prakāsh:* A Translation and Analysis" (McGill University: M.A. thesis, 1985); Ali S. Asani, *The Būjh Nirañjan: An Ismaili Mystical Poem* (Cambridge: Harvard Center for Middle Eastern Studies, 1991); Asani, "Gināns as Devotional Literature," (1992).

14. The first proponent of this theory was Wladimir Ivanow, in "Satpanth," (1948). It has been accepted as the standard interpretive model in all subsequent studies of Satpanth Ismāʿīlism. For instance, see Nanji, *The Nizārī Ismāʿīlī Tradition* (1978); Asani, *The Būjh Nirañjan* (1991); and most recently, Daftary, *The Ismāʿīlīs* (1990).

15. The conversion theory implies, of course, that, since the form of Satpanth was *instrumental,* once its aims were attained, it was dispensable. Given the current trend of islamization among Ismāʿīlīs worldwide, the dispensable or irrelevant theory has taken root, particularly among Western educated circles and within the Ismāʿīlī leadership. This has caused signifi-

cant heartache and a backlash among traditional segments of the community that remain attached to the ritual and devotional modalities of Satpanth Ismāʿīlism.

16. To quote: "The later phases of the history of Ismāʿīlism in Sind and in India stand in no direct connection with this first successful attempt to establish territorial rule in Sind." Samuel M. Stern, "Ismāʿīlī Propaganda and Fatimid Rule in Sind," *Islamic Culture*, 23 (1949), 303.

17. Derryl N. Maclean, *Religion and Society in Arab Sind* (Leiden: E. J. Brill, 1989), 157.

18. For an excellent discussion of this problem, see Hamid Dabashi, *Authority in Islam* (London: Transaction Publishers, 1989).

19. Azim Nanji, "Ismāʿīlism," ed. S. H. Nasr, *Islamic Spirituality: Foundations* (New York: Crossroad, 1987), 180.

20. Ismail K. Poonawala, *Biobibliography of Ismāʿīlī Literature* (Malibu: Undena Publications, 1977), 34.

21. Abbas Hamdani, *The Beginnings of the Ismāʿīlī Daʿwa in Northern India* (Cairo: Sirovic, 1965), 1.

22. Annemarie Schimmel, *Islam in the Indian Subcontinent* (Leiden: E. J. Brill, 1980), 3.

23. For a detailed discussion, see Maclean, *Religion and Society.*

24. Hamdani, 3.

25. Maclean, 126.

26. Daftary, *The Ismāʿīlīs,* 125.

27. Probably an ʿUmarī ʿAlid, see Maclean, 132.

28. Samuel M. Stern, "Heterodox Ismāʿīlism at the time of al-Muʿizz," *Bulletin of the School of Oriental and African Studies,* 17 (1955): 15.

29. Hamdani, 2, n. 12. See following page for an explanation of Qaddāḥid.

30. Daftary, *The Ismāʿīlīs,* 180. Perhaps the *dāʿī*'s leniency would have been tolerated had it not been for his Qarmaṭī-like views on the nature of the office of al-Muʿizz and his Fāṭimid forebears. It seems that the *dāʿī* taught that the Fāṭimid caliphs were successors of the *dāʿī* Maymūn al-Qaddāḥ and that the *qāʾim* or Imām–*messiah* would appear during the reign of al-Muʿizz. For more details, see Maclean, 133.

31. Nanji, *The Nizārī Ismāʿīlī Tradition,* 35.

32. Daftary, *The Ismāʿīlīs,* 180.

33. Stern, "Ismāʿīlī Propaganda," 301.

34. Maclean, 137.

35. Daftary, *The Ismaʿilis,* 194.

36. Ibid., 191.

37. Ibid., 213.

38. Hamdani, 4.

39. Maclean, 138.

40. Ibid., 139, see note 39.

41. Ibid., 139.

42. Daftary, *The Ismāʿīlīs,* 180.

43. Hamdani, 8.

44. John N. Hollister, *The Shia of India* (London: Luzac & Co., 1953), 267.

45. Nanji, *The Nizārī Ismāʿīlī Tradition,* 58.

46. Ansar Zahid, "Isma'ilism in Multan and Sind," *Journal of the Pakistan Historical Society,* 23 (1975): 37.

47. Maclean, 22–77.

48. Hamdani, 8.

49. Ibid., 15.

50. Maclean, 142.

51. Daftary, *The Ismāʿīlīs,* 205.

52. Ibid., 210; Hollister, 267.

53. Daftary, *The Ismāʿīlis,* 336–340.

54. Ibid., 220, 341–2.

55. Hodgson, *Order of Assassins.*

56. Ibid., 133–137.

57. For an incisive analysis of the *iqtāʿ* system and the social disorder it bred, see Marshall Hodgson, *The Venture of Islam: Conscience and History in a World Civilization,* vol. 2 (Chicago: University of Chicago Press, 1961), 49–55.

58. Daftary, *The Ismāʿīlīs,* 352.

59. See Daftary, *The Assassin Legends.*

60. Hodgson, *Order of Assassins,* 112.

61. Ibid., 121.

62. In 1091 C.E., Yūrūn Tāsh massacred Ismāʿīlīs around Alamūt, Rūdbār, and Quhistān; in 1093 C.E., the Ismāʿīlīs in Iṣfahān were massacred and thrown into the bonfire, an act repeated in 1101 C.E.; also in 1101 C.E., Barkiyāruq and Sanjar massacred Ismāʿīlīs in Quhistān; in 1107 C.E. Shāhdiz was seized by Tapar and the Nizārīs destroyed; between 1109–1118 C.E., Alamūt was under siege by Shīrgir; in 1124 C.E. 700 Nizārīs were massacred at Āmid; etc; these killings followed a vicious cycle, with greater or lesser frequency. Cf. Daftary, *The Ismāʿīlīs,* 340–341, 354–363, 404–405.

63. Ibid., 350.

64. Hodgson, *Order of Assassins,* 66.

65. Ibid., 62–68.

66. This theme of justice–savior is also prominent in the *ginānṣ* attributed to Pīr Shams, namely, that the *imām,* as the long-awaited tenth savior or *avatār* of Vaiṣṇavism, will rescue the world from the wicked and restore justice.

67. This includes the present Ismāʿīlī *imām,* His Highness Prince Karīm Āghā Khān IV.

68. Daftary, *The Ismāʿīlīs,* 335.

69. For specific discussions of *taʿlim* and *qiyāmah,* see Hodgson, *Order of Assassins,* 52–61, 160–181.

70. Ibid., 51.

71. For a discussion of Sunnī egalitarian piety, see Hodgson, *Venture of Islam,* vol. 1, 315–330.

72. Daftary, *The Ismāʿīlīs,* 335.

73. Ibid., 388.

74. Hodgson, *Order of Assassins,* 157.

75. Daftary, *The Ismāʿīlīs,* 389.

76. Ibid.

77. Hamdani, 12.

78. Jūzjānī, Minhāj al-Dīn ʿUthmān b. Sirāj, *Ṭabakāt-i-Nāṣirī: A General*

History of the Muhammadan Dynasties of Asia, trans. Henry G. Raverty, vol. 1 & 2 (Delhi: Oriental Books Reprint, 1881), 363.

79. Ibid., 365

80. Daftary, *The Ismāʿīlīs,* 404.

81. Jūzjānī, 449.

82. For instance, see A. J. Chunara, *Noorun Mubin* (Bombay: Ismailia Association for India, 1951); Syed S. Darghawala, *Tawārīkh-i-Pīr* (Navsari: Published by author, 1914); Jaffer Rahimtoola, *Khojā Komno Itihās* (Bombay: Published by author, 1905).

83. S. C. Misra, *Muslim Communities in Gujerat* (London: Asia Publishing House, 1964), 3.

84. Hollister, 270.

85. Misra, 9.

86. Hamdani, 15.

87. Ibid.

88. Daftary, *The Ismāʿīlīs,* 300.

89. Jūzjānī, 451.

90. Ibid., note 3.

91. Zahid, 49.

92. Maclean, 157.

93. Ibid.

94. Khaliq A. Nizami, *Some Aspects of Religion and Politics in India During the Thirteenth Century* (Bombay: Asia Publishing House, 1961), v.

95. Hollister, 349; also Jūzjānī, 624, note 2.

96. Jūzjānī, 646; Hollister, 350.

97. Ibid., 646.

98. Hamdani, 13.

99. Daftary, *The Ismāʿīlīs,* 405.

100. Ibid.

101. Ibid., 406.

102. Marshall Hodgson, "The Ismāʿīlī State," *The Cambridge History of Iran,* vol. 5, ed. J. A. Boyle (Cambridge: Cambridge University Press, 1968), 480.

103. Ibid., 482.

104. I. P. Petrushevsky, "The Socio-Economic Condition of Iran under the Īl-Khāns," *The Cambridge History of Iran,* vol. 5, ed. J. A. Boyle (Cambridge: Cambridge University Press, 1968) 484.

105. Zahid, 47.

106. Maclean, 157.

Chapter 4

1. For a translation of the full account, see Appendix A.

2. Wladimir Ivanow, "Some Muhammadan Shrines in Western India," *Ismaili: Golden Jubilee Number,* reprint January 21 (1936), 5.

3. Jamani, 22.

4. Ivanow, "Satpanth," 12.

5. Ibid.

6. Ibid., 13.

7. Nanji, *The Nizārī Ismāʿīlī Tradition,* 50.

8. Ibid., 69.

9. Jamani, 26.

10. Nanji, *The Nizārī Ismāʿīlī Tradition,* 50.

11. Jan Vansina, *Oral Tradition as History* (Madison: The Unversity of Wisconsin Press, 1985), 24.

12. Ivanow notes they are about eighty miles apart. Ivanow, "Some Muhammadan," 6.

13. Ibid., 3.

14. Zawahir Noorally, "Hazrat Pir Shamsuddin Sabzawari Multani," *Great Ismaili Heroes,* (Karachi: Ismailia Association for Pakistan, 1973), 84.

15. Chunara, 326.

16. Ivanow, "Some Muhammadan," 3; also see Wladimir Ivanow, "Shams Tabriz of Multan," *Professor Shafi Presentation Volume,* ed. S. M. Abdullah (Lahore: Majlis-e-Armughan-e-Ilmi, 1955), 110.

17. Nanji, *The Nizārī Ismāʿīlī Tradition,* 66.

18. Personal communication from Vernon Schubel, who did fieldwork on Muslim saints and Shīʿī piety in Multān. See Vernon J. Schubel, *Religious Performance in Contemporary Islam: Shīʿī Devotional Rituals in South Asia* (Columbia: University of South Carolina Press, 1994).

19. R. A. Nicholson, *Selected Poems from the Dīvān-i-Shams-i-Tabrīz* (Cambridge: Cambridge University Press, 1898), xviii.

20. Hodgson, *Venture of Islam,* vol. 2, 245.

21. Ahmad Akhtar, "Shams Tabrīzī—Was He Ismāilīan?" *Islamic Culture,* 10 (1930): 131.

22. Ivanow, "Some Muhammadan," 5.

23. Ibid., 6.

24. Ivanow, "Satpanth," 13.

25. Ivanow, "Some Muhammadan," 6.

26. Hodgson, *Venture of Islam,* vol. 2, 245.

27. Nanji, *The Nizārī Ismāʿīlī Tradition,* 63.

28. Akhtar, 135.

29. Quoted by Akhtar: ibid.

30. Ibid., 136.

31. Mumtaz Sadikali, "Imam Shamsud-din Muhammad," *Ilm,* vol. 6, no. 4 (1981): 30.

32. Hodgson, *Order of Assassins,* 270; for the Juvaini reference, see tr. by J. A. Boyle, *Tarikh-i Jhangusha by Ata Malik Juvaini,* a Persian text of Mirza Mohammed Qazvini, vol. 2 (Manchester: 1958), 724–5.

33. Sadikali, 36.

34. Wladimir Ivanow, "A Forgotten Branch of Ismailis," *Journal of the Royal Asiatic Society,* (1938): 69.

35. Sadikali, 29. Unfortunately, he does not make explicit which manuscripts mention this.

36. Ibid., 30.

37. Ibid., 32; also Nanji, *The Nizārī Ismāʿīlī Tradition,* 64. See *Khiṭābāt-i ʿĀliya* (Supreme Admonitions), ed. Hushang Ojaqi (Tehran: 1963), 42.

38. For a discussion of this split, see Ivanow, "The Sect of the Imam Shah," 19–70.

39. Nanji, *The Nizārī Ismāʿīlī Tradition,* 63.

40. Ivanow, "The Sect of the Imam Shah," 24.

41. Ibid., 29.

42. Ibid., 31–33; also see Nanji, *The Nizārī Ismāʿīlī Tradition,* 63–64.

43. Nanji, *The Nizārī Ismāʿīlī Tradition,* 66.

44. Ivanow, "Some Muhammadan," 6.

45. Ivanow, "The Sect of the Imam Shah," 28.

46. Ibid.

47. Vansina, 24.

48. Ivanow, "The Sect of the Imam Shah," 28.

49. For the genealogies of the Nizārī Ismāʿīlī *pīrs* in the *Mirʾāt-i Aḥmadī,* see Misra, 54–55.

50. Ivanow, "The Sect of the Imam Shah," 31.

51. Ibid., 31–32.

52. Ivanow, "Satpanth," 14–15.

53. Misra, 54.

54. Ibid., 55.

55. Nanji, *The Nizārī Ismāʿīlī Tradition,* 157, note 88. See A. Semenov. "An Ismaili Ode containing the *Qasida-i- Dhurriyya* by Raqqami Khurasani, and a list of Imams given by an Iranian Ismaili of the 17th century," (in Russian) *Iran II* (1928):1–24. Nanji himself offers a list of *pīrs* (including variants) preserved among the Ismāʿīlīs. His list is based on the following sources: two of the oldest copied lists available in Khojki manuscripts dated s. 1813/1756 C.E. and s. 1793/1736 C.E.; a list found in the old *duʿā* in a mss. dated s. 1893/1836 C.E.; and for purposes of comparison, the genealogy of Imām Shāh given in *Mirʾāt-i Aḥmadī,* as well as the list of *pīrs* preserved among the Nizārī Ismāʿīlī of Iran given in Ivanow's *Ismailitica.* See Nanji, Appendix A, 139–142.

56. Ibid., 61.

57. Ibid., also see 164, note 132.

58. Ibid., 140; Khakee, 9; Misra, 54. The manuscripts used by Nanji were dated 1756 C.E. and 1736 C.E. These are the same dates as the ones cited in the manuscripts used by Khakee. It is not clear, however, whether they were, in fact, the same manuscripts.

59. Ivanow, "Some Muhammadan," 5.

60. Ali S. Asani, "The Ginān Literature of the Ismailis of Indo-Pakistan: Its Origins, Characteristics, and Themes," *Devotion Divine,* ed. D. Eck & F. Mallison, Gröningen Oriental Series, vol. 8 (Gröningen & Paris: Egbert Forsten and École Française d'Extrême-Orient, 1991), 2.

61. Ivanow, "Satpanth," 4.

62. Ibid., 3–4.

63. Ibid., 12.

64. Among others, see Claude Levi-Strauss, *Myth and Meaning* (Toronto: University of Toronto Press, 1978); Jack Goody, *The Interface between the Written and the Oral* (New York: Cambridge University Press: 1987); Bruno Bettelheim, *The Uses of Enchantment* (New York: Vintage Books, 1976); Cornelius Loew, *Myth, Sacred History, and Philosophy* (New York: Harcourt, Brace & World, Inc., 1967); Ruth Finnegan, *Oral Poetry: Its Nature, Significance and Social Context* (Cambridge: Cambridge University Press, 1977); and Alan Dundes, *The Study of Folklore* (Englewood Cliffs: Prentice-Hall, Inc., 1977).

65. Vansina, 13.

66. Ivanow, "Satpanth," 2.

67. Nanji, *The Nizārī Ismāʿīlī Tradition,* 9–14.

68. Asani, *The Harvard Collection,* 7.

69. Ibid.

70. Nanji, *The Nizārī Ismāʿīlī Tradition,* 10.

71. Annemarie Schimmel, *Sindhi Literature* (Wiesbaden: Otto Harrassowitz: 1974), 4.

72. For instance, both *ginān*s *Brahma Prakāśa* and *Garbīs* traditionally ascribed to Pīr Shams contain references to historical persons who lived much later than his period.

73. Ali S. Asani, "The Ismāʿīlī Ginān*s*: Reflections on Authority and Authorship," *Essays in Ismāʿīlī Thought and History,* ed. Farhad Daftary (London: Cambridge University Press, 1995). It is not clear whether Asani is thus apt to question or reconsider his conclusion that the *ginān Būjh Nirañjan* is

not an Ismāʿīlī poem, a conclusion which he arrived at using the canons of textual criticism.

74. Nanji, *The Nizārī Ismāʿīlī Tradition,* 17.

75. This review was undertaken in the summer of 1985 at the Institute of Ismaili Studies in London, England. At that time, Zawahir Moir [Noorally] was still in the process of preparing a catalogue of the Khojkī manuscripts at the IIS which was completed a couple of years later. (The only copy of her catalogue which she left at the Institute has since been "misplaced.") At that time, the Institute had a collection of about 130 Khojkī manuscripts, the bulk of which had been received from the Ismailia Association of Pakistan in a badly refurbished state. Without a catalogue, and given the fairly damaged and disorderly physical condition of the manuscripts, it was evident that little attempt could be made to trace the recensions of individual *ginān*s. Nonetheless, I searched the entire collection for the *ginān*s of Pīr Shams found in the Gujarati edition. Although I was able to locate several, it should be noted that most of the manuscripts consulted belonged to the nineteenth century. Of the whole collection, only fifteen manuscripts were dated between 1750 and 1850 C.E. The IIS has reportedly microfilmed its collection of Khojkī manuscripts, which are now kept in storage. Without a catalogue, however, it is difficult to envision how these microfilms, if they are accessible for research, can profitably be used.

76. Vansina, 13–14.

77. These interpretations are regularly offered in sermons made in the *jamāʿat khānah.*

78. Nanji, *The Nizārī Ismāʿīlī Tradition,* 17.

79. The likelihood of mistakes going unobserved is much higher in the West, where a growing segment of the Ismāʿīlī *jamāʿat* is unfamiliar with the languages of the tradition. However, elderly members will frequently come up to reciters to point out mistakes made during recitation.

80. Vansina, 46.

81. Ibid., 95.

82. Nanji, *The Nizārī Ismāʿīlī Tradition,* 9.

83. Asani, "The Khojkī Script," 443.

84. Ibid.

85. Nanji, *The Nizārī Ismāʿīlī Tradition,* 50.

86. Vansina, 92.

87. Ivanow, "Satpanth," 14, note 2.

88. Nanji, *The Nizārī Ismāʿīlī Tradition,* 165, note 134. Noorally gives dates as s. 1174/1117 C.E. See Noorally, "Shamsudd in Sabzawari," 84.

89. Noorally, "Shamsuddin Sabzawari," 84.

90. Ibid.; also Jamani, 24 and Nanji, *The Nizārī Ismāʿīlī Tradition,* 165, note 134.

91. Three other towns called Godī Vilod̤, Bhoṭnagar, and Analvād̤ form the context of different and lengthy narratives, but, with the exception of Analvād, which may, in fact, refer to Anhilwād̤ Pāṭan of Siddharāj Jaisingh's fame, the geographic location of the other two places has not been found.

92. Ginān 10 makes an implicit identification between Multān and Cīnab.

93. They are ginān: 8; 10; 39; 47; 55; 65; and 2; 10; 14; 22; 25; 28.

94. Ginān 14:9; 14:11.

95. For a discussion of this metaphor, cf. Katherine K. Young, "Tīrtha and the Metaphor of Crossing Over," *Studies in Religion,* vol. 9, no. 1 (1980): 61–68.

96. The specific name of the *imām* given in this *ginān* is Islām Shāh.

97. Ginān 2; 4:2, 3; 10:14; 22:11.

98. Both Hinduism and Islam have traditions that valorize the warrior who dies in battle for his faith and who is thus assured a place in heaven. For instance, in India a warrior or servant who pledged to follow his master to death and literally dedicated his life to serving his master was called *veḷe-vāḷi.* I would like to thank Katherine Young for pointing my attention to this Indian practice of self-willed death. For more details, see S. Settar and M. M. Kalaburgi, "The Hero Cult," *Memorial Stones,* eds. S. Settar & G. D. Sontheimer (Delhi: Manipal Power Press, 1982), 17–36.

99. Ginān 17:5; 41:35; 41:39; 39:12; 47:2.

100. Kassam, "Syncretism on the Model of Figure-ground" and "Syncretism or Synthesis."

101. For example, see Christopher Schackle & Zawahir Moir, *Ismaili Hymns from South Asia* (London: School of Oriental and African Studies, 1992) 6ff.

102. Jūzjānī, 450–451, note 3.

103. Ibid.

104. Ginān 74–77.

105. Ginān 28.

106. Nanji, *The Nizārī Ismāʿīlī Tradition,* 68.

107. Schackle & Moir, 6.

108. Ginān 79–106.

109. Ginān 83:17; 90:13; 92:7; 95:1; 96:11; 105:4.

110. Ginān 92:9.

111. Ginān 89:12; 91:11; 99:13.

112. Ginān 91:12; 99:13.

113. Ginān 82:14.

114. See Young, "Tīrtha and the Metaphor."

115. Noorally, "Shamsuddin Sabzawari," 84.

116. The skirmish is believed to have been an Ismāʿīlī attempt at gaining power in Delhi. Some scholars have identified this Nūr Turk with the Ismāʿīlī Pīr Nūr al-Dīn or Satgūr Nūr as he is popularly known among the Khojah Ismāʿīlīs, but this is uncertain.

117. Ginān 14:4, 14; 17:10; 45:1.

118. Ginān 14:4; 17:10.

119. Ginān 26; 64; 95.

120. Ginān 95.

121. Quote of Ansar Khan in Zahid, 41.

Conclusion

1. See Chapter 1, p. 1.

2. See analysis of the *garbīs* in Chapter 4. See also Kassam, "Syncretism on the Model of Figure-ground."

3. Khakee, 3.

4. Cantwell Smith, *The Faith of Other Men* (New York: New American Library, 1963).

5. Geertz, 18–19.

PART II

Translator's Preface

Over the course of history, translation styles have oscillated between the extremes of strict literalism and free expression. Renaissance Italian writers contended that translations were homely when faithful and unfaithful when lovely,[1] epitomizing a timeworn controversy over the merits of literal versus free translation. Proponents of strictly literal translation have been criticized for tolerating awkward, stiff, and unintelligible renderings while supporters of the free style have been reproached for promoting translations which are excessively florid, exotic, and unfaithful to the original. Commenting early this century on this division, T. F. Higham wrote incisively:

> The one sect aims at transporting us back to the poetry of Greece, and the other at bringing Greek poetry closer to our own. The former aim is deserving of respect. . . . On the other hand, it is evident that such translators are praised more often than read.[2]

This debate as to whether the letter or the spirit is more important in translation may be better understood in relation to the different purposes intended for a translation. The biblical scholar and linguist Eugene Nida insists that the principal purpose of a translation is to evoke from the present reader the same response that the message elicited in its original context. Based on the principle of achieving equivalent effect, he recommends that the form of the translation be shaped by the semantics and gestalt of the target and not the source language. Nida calls this type of translation "dynamic equivalence:"

> A translation of dynamic equivalence aims at complete naturalness of expression, and tries to relate the receptor to

> modes of behavior relevant within the context of his own culture; it does not insist that he understand the cultural patterns of the source-language context in order to comprehend the message.[3]

This orientation is in direct conflict with translations of "formal equivalence" whose principal aim is to permit the reader to comprehend as fully as possible the historical context of the original receptors. Translations guided by formal equivalence pay closer attention both to form and content and attempt thoroughly to expose the structural, syntactic, and idiomatic characteristics of the original. This orientation is preferred in academic scholarship where scholars must regularly consult authoritative translations of primary texts to pursue critical, textual and historical analysis.

Unlike theological or literary translations, which are deliberately intended to evoke from the current reader a response parallel to that of the original recipient, scholarly translations of texts are meant to provide a sound and accurate basis upon which the thought and culture of a group represented in their primary sources may be examined in detail. Thus, whereas dynamic or free translations may entertain alterations and adjustments to the original in order to make its message more meaningful to current readers, such a liberty would not be permissible in formal equivalence where accuracy is judged on the basis of a translation's closeness or fidelity to the original.

At the outset, it should be made clear that the purpose of the translations in this collection are intended neither for literary effect nor theological service. That is, these translations have not been crafted to evoke a response (literary, theological, or any other kind) from the reader. The basic aim of the *ginān*s attributed to Pīr Shams is didactic and theological. To attempt to evoke the same response that the works of Pīr Shams may have elicited from the original audience would require the translator to identify with and reenact the author's mission. Such a goal does not fall within the scope of scholarly translations. Rather, the prime objective of the translations given here has been to achieve the closest formal equivalence to the original as possible and, thus, to allow for critical and precise textual analysis.

Since textual analysis involves the systematic study of technical terms, consistent and exact translation is of great importance. Furthermore, to examine a work for what it may reveal about itself, its own context, and its own users, the least amount of intrusion of the translator's own interpretation of the text is desirable. Such intrusions, moreover, are more likely to occur when translations aim to have a literary or theological effect upon the modern reader. For, in the case of translations meant for literary and theological purposes, it is desirable to close the cultural gap between the receivers of the original text and current readers by eliminating unknown allusions and traces of foreign setting. Such an approach, however, would seriously hamper a reconstruction of the historical and cultural milieu of users of the original text. In order to examine the meaning of the message in its original context, the greater the retention of cultural, linguistic, and idiomatic expressions of the original, the better. To paraphrase Higham, the purpose here is to take the reader back to the poetry of Pīr Shams and not to bring his poetry closer to modern verse. It should be stressed, therefore, that the following translations fall under the category of formal–literal and not dynamic–free, and no attempt has been made to make the *ginān*s of Pīr Shams relevant to a modern context.

It is appropriate at this point to describe briefly the procedure followed while translating the *ginān*s of Pīr Shams. Essentially, my translations were guided by the principle that any reader familiar with the language of the *ginān*s should readily be able to trace the rendering back to its original. That is, the translations were to be firmly rooted in the wording of the original text and not in any general impression of their meaning.

The first stage of translations consisted of an interlineal translation of each *ginān* in this Anthology. That is, every verse was written out, followed by a word-for-word identification in Gujarati and its meaning in English, and then by an English translation. Especially problematic at this stage of the translation was the identification of those word formations in the text of the *ginān*s which were impossible to trace in standard Gujarati dictionaries. Some of these were recognized to be linguistic characteristics common to medieval Gujarati and Hindi literature, while others appeared to be linguistic peculiarities specific to the *ginān*s.

In addition to a word-for-word identification, the *ginān*s of Pīr Shams were also paraphrased into Gujarati, a procedure that proved to be extremely beneficial on several counts.[4] Firstly, immersion in the idiom and style of the language helped bring to life the religious and cultural tone and nuances of the literature that were otherwise inert in the initial interlineal English translation. Secondly, and more specifically, since the syntax of the *ginān*s was in many instances too vague to ascertain the exact subject, object, or voice, paraphrasing *ginān*s in Gujarati clarified these decisions. Paraphrasing *ginān*s into modern Gujarati also made it possible to determine, in the case of archaism, idioms, and unfamiliar forms, the conventional Gujarati wording that would suit the context. For example, the first verse of Ginān 84 in the Anthology reads:

> māṅpe   varase   amarata   nūra   ke

The first word, *māṅpe*, can easily be misconstrued as *māṅ* (mother) *pe* or *para* (on). In fact, however, it is more likely to be *māthuṅ* (head) and, if inflected, would read in modern Gujarati as *māthāpara* (on the head of). The word *amarata* is *amṛta* or ambrosia, although it may be confused for *amara* or *amratya* (immortal). Word for word, the line means: on head—falls—nectar—light—of/that. Paraphrased as a full sentence in modern Gujarati, it would read, *[tamārā] māthāpara [khudāi]-nūra [rūpī] amṛta varase [che]:* Divine Light, which is in the form of nectar, rains upon your head. In the case of this phrase, three questions were resolved through the Gujarati paraphrase: firstly, that the word *māṅpe* is most likely the word *māthuṅ* (head), which in the *ginān* has lost the syllable *tha*. Secondly, as is common with many other words in the *ginān*s, the consonant cluster *mṛta* has been broken down to full syllables *marata*. And finally, the verb *varasavuṅ* (to fall, to rain) is to be construed in the present tense *varase che*, it is raining, and not as *varase ke*, in which case, it would indicate a conditional: if it rains.

These word-for-word interlineal translations, as well as the literal English translations based on the Gujarati paraphrases, represented the first stage of work. While the vocabulary of my translations was English, their syntax and grammatical structures closely imitated those of the Gujarati text. The primary purpose was to determine, as far as possible, the exact meaning of each word, to take note of forms that could not be identified, and to become versed in the style and syntax of the *ginān*s.

The next stage involved the identification of terms and passages whose meanings remained obscure. These terms fell into three categories: ones that belonged to other regional lexicons such as Punjabi, Sindhi, and Multānī; ones which appeared to be specific to a Satpanth Ismāʿīlī lexicon; and ones whose morphology remained obscure and difficult to reconstruct. Also included among these were familiar Gujarati or Hindi terms that, however, had meanings and usages not shared by the larger linguistic region. A fitting example is the very word *ginān*, which is derived from the Skt. *jñāna* (knowledge). In Satpanth Ismāʿīlī usage, it is also synonymous with the word *bhajan*. That is, not only does *ginān* refer to sacred teaching or knowledge, but it also refers to a literary form, a religious or devotional song that is full of wisdom—hence, *ginān*.[5]

To gain further insight into these specific usages and other obscure words, particularly those that were peculiar to the Satpanth Ismāʿīlīs, interviews were conducted with various Wāʿiẓīn, traditional preachers and religious specialists, in the community both in India and Canada. Some of these traditional specialists have had professional language training, but many depend on long years of oral teachings and familiarity with the dialects of the *ginān* for their knowledge of its language and idiom. It is not uncommon for religious preachers in the subcontinent to be bilingual or even trilingual—most can comfortably give sermons in Gujarati, Kutchi, Punjabi, Hindi, or Urdu, and even English. Unfortunately, on the level of linguistic analysis, these discussions did not always yield results; however, they were instructive on the significance of the *ginān* tradition to the Satpanthī Ismāʿīlīs.[6]

At the end of the second stage, the translations of the entire collection of the 106 *ginān*s of Pīr Shams were revised. In working with the collection as a whole, the meaning of several terms or phrases that had been obscure in some poems became clarified through other poems where their significance was evident from the context. Thus, by reviewing the translations several times as a whole, previously ambiguous verses became more intelligible, as one *ginān* helped elucidate another. In his translation of Rūmī's *Mathnawī*, Reynold Nicholson says in his introduction:

> When our author gives no sign whether he is speaking in his own person or by the voice of one of his innumerable puppets—celestial, infernal, human or animal—who talk just like himself; when he mingles his comments with their discourse and glides imperceptibly from the narrative into the exposition; when he leaves us in doubt as to whom he is addressing or what he is describing—the translator is driven to conjecture, and on occasion must leap in the dark.[7]

A similar problem obtains in the *ginān*s, but during this stage of revision and rereading conversations began to take definite shape, places where pauses would be most appropriate became evident, and natural breaks in otherwise seemingly continuous lines of poetry surfaced.

The initial and middle stages of translation were focused exclusively on the original text: whether or not the translation was accurate, which verses remained difficult and obscure, what were the problems of syntax, and so forth. The final stage of translation, however, was preoccupied with a different set of concerns. By this stage, it was possible to identify those terms that appeared to play a technical role in the collection as a whole. In order to conduct critical textual analysis, it was vital to ensure that such technical terms were translated consistently and in a systematic manner. Therefore, at this stage, the translations were carefully checked for consistency in their rendering of technical terms (which have been retained in parenthesis in the translations) and to confirm that the weight these terms held in the original was preserved. For instance, four words are frequently used in this collection of *ginãns* to denote heaven: *vaikuṇṭha, svarga, amarāpūri,* and *bahiśta.* If one wished systematically to examine the nuances of each in the Anthology, it would be ineffective to translate them arbitrarily as heaven or paradise. Thus, *vaikuṇṭha* and *svarga* have been consistently translated as Heaven, *bahiśta* as Paradise, and *amarāpūri* as City of Immortality.

Another concern at this stage that was deliberately ignored in the previous stages involved polishing the language of the poems. The translations were read independently of the Gujarati text and sparingly revised so that the grammar, style, and choice of vocabulary was in tune with English expression. Excessively stiff and awkward literal translations were refined, repetitious phrases which suited the original but were redundant in translation were reduced, and other grammatical and stylistic problems were addressed. Literary flourishes were avoided, and any touches that were added were kept to a bare minimum.

Finally, decisions had to be made on the form of presentation: whether or not technical terms, place names, character names be retained as they appeared in the *ginãns* or in their Gujarati, Sanskrit, or Arabo–Persian forms; whether or not annotations should appear at the foot of the poems or separately; and whether to document linguistic problems. In the case of technical terms and names, retaining the forms found in the *ginãns* would have been confusing because, as mentioned previously, the language of the *ginãns* is polyglottic, and its vocabulary often contains corruptions or variations. Thus, there is considerable inconsistency in spelling in that one word may occur with different spellings. For instance, the term for deed or act, *kriyā,* appears variously as *kiriyā, kriyā,* and *kiryā.* Similarly, the name of Pīr Shams appears as *śamaśa, śamsa,* or *śamasa.*

Thus, rather than citing technical terms with the spellings that appear in the Gujarati edition of the Anthology, they have been shown in modern standard Gujarati forms as given in Pandurang G. Deshpande's *Gujerati–English Dictionary* or L. R. Gala's *Viśāl Śabdakoś*.[8] Terms in the *gināns* that do not appear in these dictionaries are considered loan-words and transliterated in their proper Hindi, Punjabi, Persian, or Arabic forms as these appear in the standard dictionaries of these respective languages.[9] It should further be noted that there are many Arabic and Persian words that have become part of the Gujarati and Hindi lexicon, for example, *kāfar* (infidel), *mahobat* (love), *bahiśta* (paradise) and so on. These terms have been cited in their Gujarati form and not in their original Persian or Arabic form, with some exceptions, for instance, words such as *ʿishq* (love) and *qāḍi* (judge).

The following rules have been observed for names. All names of Hindu mythological figures are given in their Sanskrit form in the text of the translations so that they may easily be recognized by scholars familiar with the Indian tradition. The variants of these names in the *gināns* are indicated in the annotations. Names of figures who have been historically identified are given in their conventional spelling: Arabic or Persian for Muslim names, Sanskrit, Hindi, or Gujarati for Indian names. Names of characters who are local to a region and whose identity is known only through their action and description in the *gināns* are given as they appear in the *ginān* text.

Annotations of terms and names have been given separately in an Appendix rather than at the foot of each translation to avoid needless repetition as well as to facilitate quicker reference. The annotations of character names fall into three groups: mythological, historical, and local. Mythological names include descriptions of those characters who appear in Hindu mythology; historical names describe those individuals who are known to have existed and concerning whom some historical record is available; and finally, local names constitute figures who play a role in the *ginān* narratives but about whom we have no external evidence or historical information. Frequently occurring epithets have also been annotated. All personal names, titles, and epithets are capitalized. A map indicating the location of identifiable place names has been included in the front matter.

Finally, a few points should be made about the format of the translations. A technical term that appears several times in the same *ginān* is given in parenthesis and italics only in its first appearance. However, it is consistently translated by the same English word every time it reappears in the poem. The notes at the foot of the poems are reserved for clarification of an idiom or unusual phrase in the translation and for indicating alternative translations and obscure words or verses. The order of the translations and the numeration of verses at the right of the translations correspond to the Gujarati printed edition of the *ginān*s of Pīr Shams entitled, *Mahān Īsmāīlī Saṅta Pīr Shams Racīt Gīnānono Saṅgraha.* Following the traditional practice of identifying individual *ginān*s by their first line, I have included a transliteration of the incipit before the translation of each *ginān* in the Anthology. To make it easier to locate the translation of a particular *ginān,* an index of incipits with the page number of the translation is included as Appendix A for readers familiar with the Gujarati edition. Finally, in keeping with the teachings of Satpanth Ismāʿīlism which does not discriminate between men and women devotees as regards religious duty and salvation, I have endeavored to make the translations gender-inclusive. Thus, a singular may be changed to a plural to avoid use of the pronoun "he" as a generic category. Names or nouns following the vocative "O" have been capitalized.

Introduction to the Anthology

Arrangement

The translations in this section are based on the first Gujarati edition of an Anthology of *gināns* attributed to Pīr Shams published by the Ismailia Association of India in 1952. The preface of the Anthology identifies it as the second in a series of Gujarati books intended for the *jamā*ʿ*at* (community) containing the collected works of different Ismāʿīlī *pīrs*. It notes further that the *gināns* in the Anthology were compiled from various manuscripts *(pothī)* and notebooks *(copaḍī)* that contained not only *gināns* of Ismāʿīlī *pīrs* but other miscellaneous religious writings.[1]

The system of classification of *gināns* in the manuscript tradition appears to have varied over time. The earliest extant manuscripts classify *gināns* according to their ritual use and ceremonial context indicating that many "*gināns* were composed for the purpose of relating ritual to the new set of doctrines adopted by the recent converts."[2] The close linkage between *ginān* recitation and the performance of Satpanth rituals has been noted earlier. Another loose method followed for the arrangement of *gināns* in manuscripts was by length: longer *gināns* were frequently compiled in one volume and shorter ones in another. This practice continued through to the lithographed and printed editions of the *gināns*. Occasionally, *gināns* were also arranged by their tunes *(rāg)*.

Interestingly, *gināns* have rarely been arranged by the *pīr* who composed them, nor does there appear to have been any effort in the manuscripts to organize *gināns* by their subject or theme. In general, extant *ginān* manuscripts contain a selection of *gināns* by various *pīrs*, and the composer is determined by reference to the signature line *(bhaṇitā)*. Sometimes, a *ginān* manuscript contains a *tafsilo* or list of *ginān* incipits given in seriatim order which is placed either in the middle or at the end of the volume. Without this aid, however, since shorter *ginān*s are unmarked by titles, locating any particular *ginān* can be extremely difficult.[3] Zawahir Moir has explained the somewhat idiosyncratic nature of *ginān* manuscripts in terms of their usage. Individual manuscripts and handbooks of *ginān*s belonged to specific families or were held in trust by the *mukhīs* (chiefs) of a particular *jamāʿat khānah,* and they essentially contained "ginās of their choice and collection."[4] Thus, if an unfamiliar *ginān* was heard in another home or *jamāʿat khānah,* it was duly recorded and brought back to one's own family collection and congregation. The frequent appearance of certain *ginān*s in several manuscripts may suggest that they were quite popular and were recited regularly.

Except for the fact that it compiles the various compositions of *ginān*s attributed to Pīr Shams in alphabetical order, the Gujarati edition of the Anthology of the 106 *ginān*s is not arranged by any special criteria: not by subject, by ritual, nor by length. The table of contents functions like a *tafsilo* and lists, according to the Gujarati alphabet, the incipit, that is, the first line of each *ginān.* In practice, short *ginān*s are known or tagged by their first line; thus, a reciter may be requested to sing the *ginān, Dhana dhana ājano* or *Gat māhe āvīne.* This approach, while suitable in practice, has had a curious outcome in the arrangement of the Anthology of Pīr Shams. To illustrate, instead of being listed under one title and arranged in consecutive order, the twenty-eight individual compositions in the cycle of *Garbīs* attributed to Pīr Shams are arranged alphabetically by their incipits as single poems. It seems that, over time, as longer works were sung less frequently in one sitting, individual compositions such as those in the *Garbīs* came to be treated as individual *ginān*s.

The table of contents of the Anthology is basically an index of incipits. This organization is a telling expression of the actual function of the *ginān* collection for its users. Lacking any organization by theme or subject, the Anthology of Pīr Shams underscores the point made earlier, namely, that the *ginān*s were less commonly read and studied as literature *per se;* rather, they were sung and celebrated as an oral teaching and a form of worship. From the point of view of the compiler of the Gujarati edition, the main purpose of providing indexed incipits as the table of contents was to help direct the reciter to the specific page of the *ginān* the reciter had in mind. The Anthology is thus organized like a song book, and its indexed table of contents quickly refers the singer to the approproate page.

Language

Ivanow's characterization of the *ginān* literature as "polyglottic" also applies to the Anthology of *gināns* of Pīr Shams. The Satpanth corpus as a whole includes *gināns* composed in different Indian languages and dialects including Punjabi, Sindhi, Multāni (or Saraiki, a mixture of Sindhi and Punjabi), Hindi (or Sādhukaḍī Bolī), Kutchi, and Gujarati. Individual *gināns* are also permeated with loan words and vocabulary drawn from the languages of Arabic and Persian. Except for a few *gināns* in Punjabi, Sindhi, and Hindi, most of the *gināns* in the Anthology of Pīr Shams are in Gujarati. Regardless of their language or dialect, however, a notable characteristic of the *gināns* in the Anthology is the consistent appearance of certain key Arabic and Persian terms such as *shāh, khudāwand, pīr, nūr,* and *Qur'ān.*

Various explanations have been advanced to account for the polyglottic nature of the *gināns.* In what we may call the "manuscript-locale theory," Nanji speculates that "the languages in which the ginans exist reflect the areas from which the manuscripts originate,"[5] namely, Sind, Punjab, Multān, or Gujarat. G. Allana advances a "travel theory," namely, that the Ismā'īlī pīrs composed in different languages because "they did not have a fixed abode in one city or village. They wandered all over Sindh, Punjab, Gujarat, Kathiawar, Cutch, spreading the message of Islam," and as they travelled through different regions, they incorporated or modified their compositions to fit the linguistic needs of their specific milieu.[6] The third explanation is the "translation theory." It is given by Ivanow who argues that *gināns* must have been originally composed either in Sindhi or Multāni, "but, while spreading to other provinces, these became translated into local dialects."[7] Ivanow felt that "in the case of those [*gināns*] in Gujarati and Marāthi, there can be little doubt that they are fairly modern renderings of the earlier ones."[8] To these there might be added the "transcription theory." Asani notes that when printed versions of *gināns* were transcribed from the Khojki into the Gujarati script during the last century, "many *gināns* seem to have incorporated elements from Gujarati—the language spoken by a substantial segment of the community."[9]

As noted earlier, most of the *gināns* in the Anthology of Pīr Shams are in Gujarati or in a "gujaratified" Hindi. If the compositions did originate from the activities and preaching of Pīr Shams who operated mainly in the regions of Sind and Multān, then the translation theory may help to explain why many of his compositions now exist in Gujarati or Hindi. Unless earlier manuscripts closer to the time of Pīr Shams are found, we will be unable to ascertain the proximity of the Gujarati *gināns* to their prototype. Nonetheless, as argued before, it is likely that, in practice, the tradition has been more rather than less conservative in the transmission and preservation of the *gināns*. What all of the above theories commonly point to is the linguistic complexity of the *ginān* tradition and the difficulties that face the textual scholar.

Poetry

In common with traditional regional forms of Indian verse, *gināns* generally take the form of *dohās* (couplets) or *caupāīs* (quatrains). Typically, the *dohā* is a two-line verse consisting of twenty-four *mātrās* (accents), and the *caupāī* consists of four lines with sixteen *mātrās* each. Longer *gināns* often have both *dohās* and *caupāīs*, as well as *ślokas*, two-line verses of sixteen *mātrās*.[10] A scansion of the *gināns* in the Anthology reveals quickly their highly irregular nature. Both Nanji and Asani attribute this imprecision to "negligence in transmission and linguistic acculturation."[11] However, the translation and transliteration theories described above may also account for the linguistic and prosodic inconsistencies found in the *gināns*.

Although the metrical and prosodic features of the *gināns* in the Anthology are irregular, the *gināns* nevertheless preserve a strong semblance to verse and song. Most verses in the *gināns* regularly end in rhyme or have a refrain (*varaṇī, tek*) that is poetic in effect. For instance, the verses of many *gināns* end simply in a consonant followed by a long "ā" *(liyā/dharīyā/paḍīyā/gatīyā)* or followed by "oī" or "ohī" *(koi koi/sohī sohī/dhoī dhoī/roī roī/hoi hoi)*. Often, endings are appended onto the final word of verses in order to create the rhyme (using suffixes such as "re" or "jī" which may have no intrinsic meaning, but rather, an exclamatory effect: *kājare/pārare/dāsare/deśare/pāyare)*.[12] A fruitful line of inquiry would be to analyze the poetic and prosodic features of the *gināns* and assess how their linguistic features are utilized to create poetry and rhythm and to compare and contrast these stylistic features to other similar devotional poetic forms such as the Indian *gīt* and *bhajan*.

The *ginān* corpus contains works that range from short hymns of four to five verses in length to poems that are over one thousand verses long. As noted, short *gināns* are rarely titled; they are customarily identified by their first lines or incipits. More frequently, the longer compositions called *granths* have titles, for example, *Brahma Prakāśa, Das Avatār* or *Būjh Nirañjan.* The Anthology of Pīr Shams contains two long compositions: the *Garbīs,* a sequence of twenty-eight songs meant to accompany a circle dance of the same name; and a *ginān* (with no title) which starts with the line *prema pāṭaṇa rājā* and is ninety-nine verses long. It also contains a category of *gināns* known as *joḍilo* (linked, appended). These are typically *gināns* that are strung together on the basis of a common author, theme, or narrative sequence. The Anthology contains one such set of eighteen *joḍilos.* Often, long *gināns* will have two versions (sometimes dissimilar in content), called the major (*moṭo* or *vaḍho*) and minor (*nāno* or *nindho*). This Anthology contains a *ginān* titled *Nāno Das Avatār* which describes the ten *avatārs* (forms) of Viṣṇu in ten verses. Although short *gināns* rarely have titles, three in the Anthology have the following: *Popaṭ ane Surjā Rāṇīnī Vāt* (Conversation between the Parrot and Queen Surjā); *Janājo* (The Burial or the Bier); and *Caūd Ratna* (Fourteen Jewels).

Content and Themes

The tone of the *gināns* in the Anthology of Pīr Shams ranges from prosaic preaching to fervent devotion, and the style of the poems is primarily didactic. G. Allana categorizes *gināns* as a whole into two groups: *gināns* that seem to be directed to a Hindu audience, and whose purpose is conversion; and *gināns* composed for the newly converted, whose purpose is to teach them the rudiments of their new faith.[13] This is generally true of the *gināns* in the Anthology and parallels Nanji's broad characterization of the two phases of the tradition as a whole: emergence and consolidation. The analysis of the *gināns* presented in this study indicates, however, that at the stage of emergence the meaning of conversion had both political and religious connotations. At this nascent stage, conversion in the sense of political alliance may well have preceded conversion in the sense of religious affiliation. With the stage of consolidation, however, conversion to Satpanth would have lost its early political implications and denoted primarily religious initiation and transformation.

Asani has classified the *gināns* of the Satpanth tradition into five major themes "according to the theme of greatest importance": Conversion; Eschatology; Moral Conduct; Mysticism; and Festivals or Special Rituals.[14] While Asani's five major categories are present in the Anthology of *gināns* attributed to Pīr Shams, it is often impossible to designate precisely the subject or topic of specific *ginān*s under the heading of conversion, or moral instruction, or eschatology, because often an individual *ginān* will contain several topics. For example, Ginān 26 in this Anthology may be classified both under conversion and moral instruction. Many *ginān*s that may be categorized under conversion also deal at length with moral instruction, ritual performances, eschatology, and the *avatār* theory, as for instance, in the *Garbīs*.

A wide range of topics, motifs, and symbols permeate the *ginān*s in the Anthology. Longer compositions such as the *Brahma Prakāśa* or the *Das Avatār* are more focused on one theme, but not the shorter *ginān*s. Rather, the latter appear to have a kind of interdependency, amplifying and completing each other. The more *ginān*s one examines, the clearer the meaning of individual poems becomes. It is within this interconnected corpus of poems that the matrix of Satpanth religious ideas is sustained. A study that examines how various themes in individual *ginān*s are linked and how *ginān*s define and modify one another would help to bring to the fore the key structures and constituent elements of Satpanth Ismāʿīlism.

The *ginān*s in the Anthology of Pīr Shams may be classified into two literary genres, narrative and non-narrative. The category of narrative includes *ginān*s whose content is sacred tradition (myth, legend, or tale), parables, prophecy, and politics. The non-narrative genre includes *ginān*s with didactic, devotional, moral, prescriptive, and doctrinal themes. This study has concentrated primarily upon the category of narrative *ginān*s in the Anthology which has provided important clues regarding the historical basis of Satpanth. The narrative *ginān*s attributed to Pīr Shams encompass stories, traditions, and recollections which are pregnant with allusions to the foundational period and political underpinnings of Satpanth Ismāʿīlism in Western India. Devoted mainly to the travels of Pīr Shams and his conflicts, miracles, and conversions, the narratives allude to political tensions in forecasts of battles to be won by the distant Shāh, persecutions suffered by the Pīr's devotees, and victories over enemies.

The non-narrative category of *ginān*s, on the other hand, reveals important information about Satpanth practices and beliefs. Under religious practices, one finds in the Anthology of *ginān*s attributed to Pīr Shams references to the following topics: paying the tithe *(dasond)*; performing the *ghaṭpāṭ* ceremony (installation of holy water); following the instructions of the *pīr;* service *(sevā)*; charity *(sakhāvat; dāna)*; meditation *(smaraṇa, dhyāna)*; keeping vows *(vrata)*; moral conduct *(dharma),* for instance, overcoming greed, lust, lassitude, and so forth. The subject of belief includes topics such as the True Guru *(satguru)*; the Last Age *(kalyug)*; the Day of Judgment *(mahādin)*; the Tenth Avatār *(das avatār)*; and release from the cycle of death and rebirth *(āvāgamaṇa*—lit., coming and going; *caurāsī ferā*—lit., eighty-four turns or revolutions).

A careful and systematic study of these topics and their connections would shed light on the rich and intricate lattice of religious ideas and practices found in Satpanth Ismāʿīlism. While it is true that the *avatār* theory is a central concept in Satpanth Ismāʿīlism, of equal importance and interest are the other, less-explored elements in its complex system of religious, ritual, and social connections that helped anchor the Satpanth Ismāʿīlīs as a faith and a community. A detailed analysis of the religious worldview and practices of Satpanth Ismāʿīlism as revealed in the *ginān*s has yet to be undertaken and would offer promising insights into the religious fabric of this tradition.

Notes

Translator's Preface

1. Eugene A. Nida, *Towards a Science of Translating* (Leiden: E. J. Brill, 1964), 2.

2. Ibid., 25.

3. Ibid., 159.

4. I owe this helpful advice to Prof. Bhupendra Trivedi, a specialist in medieval Gujarati and Hindi religious literature in Bombay, India, with whom I addressed the many idiosyncracies in the text of Pīr Shams.

5. It is interesting to note that when I left the word *ginān* in my Gujarāti paraphrase of such a line as "and Pīr Shams sang sweet *gināns*," Prof. Trivedi replaced the word *ginān* with *bhajan*. This confirms that, while the word has the extended meaning of hymn to the insider, Trivedi's use of the word *ginān* was restricted to its primary Sanskrit meaning of knowledge or wisdom.

6. The traditional specialists were often unable to shed light on obscure terms or corruptions. They more readily entered a philosophical discussion on the "essence" of a verse or *ginān* as a whole. This is understandable since, as preachers, their interest in *gināns* was theological and devotional. For homiletic purposes, they were interested in *gināns* as proof texts for their sermons.

7. Reynold A. Nicholson, ed. & trans., *The Mathnawī of Jalālu'ddin Rūmī* (London: Luzac & Co., 1977), xvi.

8. Deshpande, Pandurang, *Gujerati–English Dictionary* (Ahmedabad: University Book Production Board, 1978); L. R. Gala, *Viśāl Śabdakoś: Gujarātī–Gujarātī–Angrejī Koś* (Ahmedabad: Gala Publishers, n.d.).

9. For these languages, the following dictionaries were consulted: Brij

Mohan & Badrinath Kapoor, eds., *Meenakshi Hindi–English Dictionary* (New Delhi: Meenakshi Prakashan, 1980); Maya Singh, compiler, *The Punjabi Dictionary* (Lahore: Vanguard Books, 1st ed. 1895; repr. 1983); F. Steingass, *A Comprehensive Persian–English Dictionary* (New Delhi: Oriental Books, 1973); J. M. Cowan, ed. *Arabic–English Dictionary* (New York: Spoken Language Services, Inc., 1976 3rd ed.).

Introduction to the Anthology

1. For a description of the types of materials found in *ginān* manuscripts, see Asani's *The Harvard Collection,* 3–22.

2. Nanji, *The Nizārī Ismāʿīlī Tradition,* 15.

3. In this respect, Asani's detailed catalogue of the Satpanth manuscripts in the Harvard Collection is of immeasurable value to the *ginān* scholar.

4. Zawahir Noorally, "Khojki Manuscripts" (Karachi: Manpower Training Project, n.d.), 1.

5. Nanji, *The Nizārī Ismāʿīlī Tradition,* 9.

6. Allana, 44.

7. Ivanow, "Satpanth," 40.

8. Ibid.

9. Asani, "The Ginān Literature of the Ismailis of Indo-Pakistan," 8.

10. Ibid., 9, n. 25.

11. Ibid., 9; Nanji, *The Nizārī Ismāʿīlī Tradition,* 20.

12. Ginān 6, 12, 14 and 29, respectively.

13. Allana, 39.

14. Ali. S. Asani, "Ginān," *Encyclopedia of Religion,* ed. Mircea Eliade, vol. 5 (New York: Macmillan, 1986), 561.

Translations of
Mahān Īsmāīlī Sañta Pīr Shams Racīt Gīnānono Saṅgraha
(An Anthology of Gināns composed by the Great Ismāʿīlī Saint, Pīr Shams)

1

tāre puthīaḍe che pāñcha sācalo samara lejo sātha

O Trader! The five[1] are in pursuit of you!
So take along provisions of truth *(sat)*. 1

O Trader! Gain plentiful profit in this world!
For up ahead the Swāmī Rājā will take stock. 2

O Trader! This chest of a skeleton is full of fuel!
Five bullocks keep stuffing it with wood. 3

O Trader! Take with you then a pot of water!
For up ahead no one will fetch you any. 4

O Trader! Carry with you a basket of rations!
For yonder there is neither store nor merchant. 5

O Trader! [Here] family and friends have fed you!
But up ahead there are no kith nor kin. 6

O Trader! She too is a traitor, the wife in your house!
Seeing you off [to the grave] she will herself return.[2] 7

O Trader! Pīr Shams, the famous, has spoken this wisdom *(ginān)*!
Take along with you the provisions of truth. 8

1. Possibly an allusion to the five evils of desire *(kāma)*, anger *(krodha)*, greed *(moha)*, lust *(mada)*, and delusion *(māyā)*.
2. That is, his wife does not accompany him on his journey beyond death.

2

candrabhāṇa surbhāṇa be bandhavā gura shamasa nā celā

Two brothers Candrabhāṇ and Surbhāṇ
were the disciples *(celā)* of Pīr Shams;
Of a common ancestor, they are the Devotees *(bhagat)*
of the present age *(kalyug)*.

In the city of Delhi,[1] Sāheb the King *(rājā)*
will capture the fort and rule;
When the Sāheb arrives, the wicked will flee,
and he will let the pious rule. 1

The Shāh will come to Multān in Jambudvīpa[2]
with the five Pāṇḍavas;
Attacking the wicked, the Sāheb will expel them,
and the Shāh himself will rule. 2

The good and the wicked began to argue,
and the wicked feared in their hearts:
"This Shāh will rid the earth of us and grant
dominion to the pious *(rīkhīsar)*!"[3] 3

Pīr Shams, the Satgur said,
"O Believers *(mu'min)*, be vigilant!"
Three ages have passed away,
and now is the turn of the fourth *(kalyug)*. 4

---

1. *diladi:* may be *dil* (heart) or *Dilli/Dilhi* (Delhi).
2. *Jampudīpa:* The Indian peninsula, lit. the land surrounded by water.
3. *rikhīyā:* der. Skt. *ṛṣi*–seer, holy man; pious, righteous, good; also occurs as *rīkhīsar*.

3

bhāī tame sufala falo morā bhāī

O Brother! Be prosperous *(sufala)* my brother!
O Brother! Be affectionate towards each other.
O Brother! Such affection is dear to the Sāheb.
O Brother! Such affection is dear to other brothers.
Indeed, be wise in your dealings!

O Brother! Purchase the pearl of Immortality *(amṛta)*!
The man who awakens, he alone will procure it. 1

O Brother! Select the pearl of the Guru,
Lest without the Guru, you go astray. 2

O Brother! He whose mind lusts for the other woman,
That creature is devoid of honorable deed. 3

O Brother! Who comes not into my Sāheb's temple,
That person will turn into a ghost or spirit. 4

Pīr Shams, the Generous *(dātār)*, pleads:
"O Swāmī, release me from the cycle of rebirth *(āvāgamaṇa)*."[1] 5

1. *āvāgamaṇa:* lit. coming and going.

4

shāhanī sevāye tame jāgajo āvīyā te kolane karārīyā

Rouse yourselves in the service *(sevā)* of the Shāh!
He, the one who made a promise *(kol)*, has come. 1

Naklaṅkī, the bearer [of Light], has become manifest!
He, the Shāh, rides on the mount Duldul. 2

As pledged, the Shāh will bring justice *(adal)*:
His hands will seize that three-edged sword.[1] 3

The Shāh will twirl it in all four directions,
And he will attack the rogues and the infidels *(kāfar)*! 4

Counting them infidels, he will strike down corrupt judges *(qāḍi)*!
In Allah's [court], Muḥammed is the chief minister *(vazīr)*. 5

Neither the ranks of Khān nor Malik[2] exist up there;
Paupers and kings stand on equal ground. 6

Dispel your heedlessness and awaken!
All who slumber are condemned to rebirth *(saṃsār)*. 7

For our Sāheb is all our fervor and zeal!
So said Pīr Shams, the Generous *(dātār)*. 8

---

1. *khaḍaṅga tradhārīyā:* Guj. *traṇa* (three) *dhāranī* (edged) *khaḍaṅga* (sword). An allusion to ʿAlī's sword, Ḍhulfikār; may also allude to Śiva's *triṣūla* (trident).
2. That is, the aristocrats, royalty.

5

jīrevīrā mīṭhaḍuṅ āṅ(h)ī bolo vīrā namī khamī ho yāra cālo

O Brother! Come here and speak amicably!
Friend! Walk humbly and be patient!
Never forsake the love of True Religion *(sat dharma)*. 1

O Brother! That bile of hatred within you;
Friend! Get rid of that bitter fluid!
Thus will Sāheb's heart be highly pleased and much endeared. 2

O Brother! This body *(kāyā)*, so raw and imperfect!
Friend! Be not proud of it!
Today or tomorrow, surely its form will go limp. 3

O Brother! This flesh which is but clay;
Friend! It will get mixed into the earth!
The body will turn sallow as the rusty-hued *kuṃkuṃ*.[1] 4

O Brother! The soul *(jīv)* is spiritual,[2]
But alas it is fond of its body!
Lotuslike, the attachment lasts but two days. 5

O Brother! True believers *(mu'min)* are they,
Friend, who have their selves under firm control!
How then, O Brothers, can anyone else constrain you? 6

O Brother! True believers are they,
Friend, who mend their own faults!
Their souls will surely go to heaven *(svarga)*. 7

---

1. Saffron or yellow color typically used to mark the forehead with a circular dot.
2. *ākāśī:* of the heavens/ether, celestial, ethereal, spiritual.

O Brother! Auspicious are followers of the True Path *(satpanth)*!
Friend! Whoever unveils their curtain [of secrecy],
That soul will surely go to hell *(narak)*.

O Brother! Those who make pious offerings *(prasād)*,
Pīr Shams said: Friend!
How could their souls have any desire for the body?

6

gaṭa gurujī gaṭa gurujī dharama sañca rahyā

The heart of the Guru, yes, his heart
    is filled with religion[1] *(dharma).*
In the True Faith *(dīn)*, indeed,
    in the True Faith, he was born. 2
Fair-complexioned, yes, well-disposed,
    the Guru held a cup before his face.
He placed his hand, indeed,
    he laid his hand on top of my head. 4
Then the Sāheb placed the tithe *(dasond)*, yes,
    the tithe on the head.
Give it to the Sāheb, indeed, give!
    For the servant who gives not falls into greed. 6
If [the tithe] is incorrect, yes, if it falls short,
    the mind will become defective.
Afterward do not wring your hands, indeed,
    do not get torn with remorse. 8
Make ten portions, yes, divide [your earning]
    into ten equal measures of weight.
Dare not be negligent, indeed, delinquent!
    Be wary, be conscientious. 10
Else it will turn into a heavy burden, yes,
    a terrible affliction upon you.
Your life, indeed, the whole of it will be worthless,
    it will be wasted. 12
The soul *(jīv)* scorched and your body crushed,
    you will repent, yes, bemoan.
Pīr Shams said: If you want release,
    know your religion *(dharma)*, yes, realize it! 14

1. In the original, the second phrase of all the verses is repeated.

7

sāheba deākuṅ de gusāṅhīyā moro tuṅ bhīde

O Sāheb! Be compassionate! My Master! Bestow mercy!
Brothers! Say not to one another, "Mine, all this is mine." 1

Keep your minds so stainless that He
Who created us, O Brother, will raise us. 2

Blessed that moment when Sāheb showers
Light upon Light *(nūr)*!
When the nectar cup of Immortality *(amṛta)*
is filled to the brim. 3

O Brothers! The earth asks the sky,
"Those two sages who just went by, who were they?" 4

[The sky replied:]
"They have been blessed by a vision *(dīdār)* of my Shāh;
Indeed, Brother! Those two sages
have left for Heaven *(vaikuṇṭha)*." 5

Said Pīr Shams: The heart of the Shāh is an ocean.
O Shāh! Benign King *(rājā)* of great and small,
have mercy upon the world! 6

8

kīrīyā kāraṇa ahonīśa jāgo te mana cevā khelo

Waken day and night to perform meritorious deeds *(kriyā)*!
Then play to your heart's content.
O Brother, so be it. 1

With unbending trust, take refuge *(śaraṇa)* in the Shāh;
Traversing the three paths, he has given blessings.
O Brother, so be it. 2

Thirty-three crore[1] gods *(sur)* enjoyed that lasting pleasure;
Then man *(puruṣa)* was created.
O Brother, so be it. 3

The gods contemplated upon Gurunātha;[2]
And behold! This world was born.
O Brother, so be it. 4

He [the Lord] struck down Śaṅkhāsura and rescued the Vedas;
As Matsya, he took birth in the waters.
O Brother, so be it. 5

The foolish demons Maḍhu, Kaiṭabha, and Mura;
They made him furious and were utterly destroyed.
O Brother, so be it. 6

The man Narasiṃha was the Supreme Swāmī;
He slaughtered the demon Hiraṇyakaśipu.
O Brother, so be it. 7

King Bali was so vain and foolish in his action;
He had to bear Viṣṇu's feet upon his head.
O Brother, so be it. 8

---

1. One crore is the equivalent of ten million.
2. *nātha:* Master, Lord, Beloved.

Facing King Sahasrārjuna, [Rāvaṇa] did not recognize his might;
Overconfident, he was easily destroyed.
O Brother, so be it.

Not recognizing the man was Swāmī, the Lord Nārāyaṇa;
He foolishly let his feet into the cage.
O Brother, so be it.

Lord Rāma, Swāmī, the Bow-Wielder;
He dwells in many places around the world.[3]
O Brother, so be it.

The ten-faced demon Daśāsana roared in vainglory;
He transformed himself into a golden-hued deer.
O Brother, so be it.

To rescue Sītā, the Shāh raided Laṅkā;
He gave Mandodari the following boon.
O Brother, so be it.

Mandodari got for a husband, Prince Vibhiṣaṇa and his mansion
To him was given the castle of Laṅkā.
O Brother, so be it.

Rāvaṇa suffered destruction [at the hands of] Swāmī Uparājana;
The blessed Nirguṇa took his form.
O Brother, so be it.

The Infant-Lord was surrounded by 160 damsels *(gopīs)*;
He was Kṛṣṇa, ferocious Lord of the three worlds.
O Brother, so be it.

Keśava destroyed Cāṇūra, [accomplice of King] Kaṃsa;
He spun him around with the snake Vāsuki.
O Brother, so be it.

Nārāyaṇa assumed the form of Buddha,
When the turn came for the second age *(yuga)*.
O Brother, so be it.

The saint-seer Nārada invoked the name of Viṣṇu;
Duryodhana was then summoned.
O Brother, so be it.

---

3. *nava khaṇḍa:* lit. nine sections, continents.

The war-drums were beaten and the bugles were blown;
Prince Duryodhana had arrived.
O Brother, so be it. 20

Wearing his bow, Arjuna sat in his chariot,
Duryodhana had brought (his, too).
O Brother, so be it. 21

Wielder of the mace Bhīma thundered across the sky;
His menacing threats froze the army.
O Brother, so be it. 22

Dhamalā, on whose head rested the earth, trembled;
Nakula endured great suffering.
O Brother, so be it. 23

Arjuna and Karṇa met, enemy facing enemy;
Whereupon night cloaked the sun.
O Brother, so be it. 24

The Kauravas were beaten and the Pāṇḍavas victorious;
For the Swāmī had sent an army.
O Brother, so be it. 25

The Kauravas were beaten and the Pāṇḍavas victorious;
That deed was recorded forever.
O Brother, so be it. 26

The five, they were the Pāṇḍavas, the sixth was Nārāyaṇa;
From their midst came the great faith *(dīn)*.
O Brother, so be it. 27

The Kauravas were beaten and the righteous *(rīkhīsar)*
attained success;
Along with Arjuna, countless were honored.
O Brother, so be it. 28

At Cīnab, yes at Cīnab, you can hear the tenth demon;
Surjā's husband did not return.
O Brother, so be it. 29

A man prostrated at the feet of Nizār with an offering *(prasād)*;
He praised the name of Śrī Islām Shāh.
O Brother, so be it. 30

So said Pīr Shams who came to the Shāh to seek refuge *(śaraṇa)*;
He praised the name of Śrī Islām Shāh before the Shāh. 31

9

prema pāṭaṇa rājā manasudha tīsa ghara radīyāde rāṇī

In the city of love was King Manaśudha;[1]
In his palace was Queen Radīyā.[2] 1

The King and the Queen relaxed in their palace;
While five ministers governed the kingdom. 2

Then once, O Brother, a summons *(hukam)* came
from the Guru;
Now how could they leave it unheeded? 3

The summons had come for only two persons;
How possibly could they take a third along? 4

So the chaste *(satī)* Queen put her child into a cradle to sleep;
Then the two proceeded towards the Lord's *(deva)* portal. 5

When the King reached halfway,
He came upon a deer suckling her fawn. 6

On seeing the babe, [the Queen's] breasts swelled with milk[3];
So pained was she by her longing for her child that she died. 7

O Brother, a summons had come from the Guru;
Now how could it be left unheeded? 8

A summons had come for two;
How could he, the King go there all alone? 9

---

1. lit. one of pure mind.
2. Possible connection to Queen Raḍiyya who ruled Delhi in the twelth century?
3. Guj. *pāno caḍhavuṅ*—when the mother's breasts fill with milk, and she has a desire to feed her young; to feel affection for a lost child. There is a folk belief that, if a mother's milk is left in the breast, it turns into poison and kills her.

So [the King] bundled her up in a sheet and tied a knot;
He lifted her and proceeded towards the Lord's presence. 10

Soon enough golden lights glittered ahead of him;
In their midst was seated Śyāma,
Master of the three worlds *(tribhovar)*. 11

"Rise Queen Radīyā and drink this divine nectar
of Immortality *(amṛta)*![4]
Lift your child onto your lap and nurse it!" [said the Lord]. 12

Pīr Shams, the Defender *(ghāzī)*, said:
Listen carefully, O you gathered ones *(gat jamāʿat)*! 13

---

4. This term often appears as *amī* or *amījala*, lit. water of Immortality.

10

surbhāṇane sāhebe mokalīyā surajāde rāṇīne pāsa

The Sāheb has sent Surbhāṇ
To go visit Queen Surjā.
"In the demon's home is a lady," he said.
"She is my Devotee *(dāsī)*." 1

Surbhāṇ spoke these words to her.
"Listen, O Queen Surjā!
The Guru out of his love for you,
Has sent [me here] to this demon's *(daitya)* land." 2

Upon hearing this, Queen Surjā stood up
And she came out of her retreat;
Letting go her *chedo,*[1] she prostrated at the Guru's feet.
"Indeed, Swāmī has done us a favor!" 3

[Surbhāṇ] related to her the Guru's wisdom *(ginān)*,
And they meditated on its teaching *(veda)*.
"We will impart to you the principles of religion *(dharma)*,
But lady, you are mistress in a demon's house!" 4

Thereupon Queen Surjādevī said this:
"Standing on my feet, I, the Queen, plead!
O Swāmī, have mercy upon us!
Carry us safely across to the other shore *(pahele pār)*." 5

"If you [promise to] recollect Shāh Pīr, [replied Surbhāṇ]
We will assure you and give you our word of honor *(kol)*;
But Queen Surjādevī, surely if you remain righteous *(sat)*,
You will attain the other shore." 6

---

1. The border of the *sāri* or delicate cloth typically draped around Indian women. The border is often worn as a scarf to cover the head as a sign of modesty or respect.

Saying this much, he made ready to leave.
But standing up, the Queen begged:
"O Swāmī! Please return to us and grace our home
Once more by your presence." 7

Then Kamalā and Dhamalā appeared;
They too prostrated at his feet.
Ajīyā and Vajīyā also emerged,
And then came brother Robaḍa. 8

Then Kamalā's son came out;
He too paid his respects.
They all stood with hands clasped
Whereupon Locanā too arrived. 9

[They said:] "O Swāmī! Please visit our home again
And impart to us the sacred knowledge *(veda)*!
O Swāmī, have mercy upon us!
And ferry us across to the other shore." 10

He gave assurance to the pious servants *(sevak)*,
And then the respected Kamalā spoke:
"O Swāmī, have mercy upon us!
Deliver us to the other shore!" 11

Then Vimras spoke these words
Concerning the Guru's wisdom *(ginān)*:
"If you remember Shāh Pīr,
You will attain the supreme boon of Heaven *(vaikuṇṭha)*." 12

"You will attain the supreme boon of Heaven,
You will enter that glorious City of Immortality *(amarāpurī)*."
Surbhāṇ read aloud from the scriptures *(śāstra)*
That Pīr Shams had made the [following] promise *(kol)*. 13

"Pīr Shams and Śrī Islām Shāh,
They, too, will come to the fort in Multān.
Whoever will bring to them the exact tithe *(dasond)*,
Will attain the station of the City of Immortality. 14

If you enter the City of Immortality and then, too,
By the very path shown to you by the Guru,
As a result of your success, boons will be given
To seven and a half crore others. 15

These seven and a half crore will be chosen
From among the citizens of Cīnab town.
So keep in your hearts the wisdom *(ginān)* of the Guru
And do service *(sevā)* at the feet of Pīr Shams." 16

11

ajaba śahera mede khālaka sīrajyā śahera samāyā nāma

My Creator *(khaliq)* built a wondrous city;
In the city, he established the Name *(nām)*, O Sir![1] 1

Spontaneously the Sāheb brought forth salt and water;
Similarly, he created grain, O Sir! 2

A rampart whose foundation measured seventy yards;[2]
Such a fortress did he construct, O Sir! 3

When man and woman united face to face,
All waters were sanctified, O Sir! 4

When the woman gave birth to a son,
She did not inform the stepmother, O Sir![3] 5

When the son grew old enough to wear a coat,
He followed the commands *(farmān)* of faith *(dīn)*, O Sir! 6

Whenever his coat became soiled,
He washed the coat in fire, O Sir! 7

At every courtyard were two springs;
Know they were fresh and sparkling, O Sir! 8

Each received two loaves of bread and one chicken;
And water sweet as sugar, O Sir! 9

A canister would descend from the Lord *(ḥaḍrat)*;
One ate to one's heart's content, O Sir! 10

---

1. *ejī:* this vocative usually appears at the beginning of the verse in most *gināns;* here it appears both at the beginning and end of the verse.
2. *gaja:* Guj. measure of length equal roughly to a yard.
3. Perhaps this refers to the other wife (or wives) of the husband.

Pīr Shams beholds the lamp plainly;
The Light *(nūr)* glows like the moon, O Sir! 11

Water-laden clouds go there and descend,
Where there are mountains and fields, O Sir! 12

Snakes nor scorpions can be found up there;
Nor tigers nor any lions, O Sir! 13

There are no dumb nor deaf up there;
Nor are there any lame or crippled, O Sir! 14

Behind each home are two bountiful gardens;
One eats the fruits of one's heart's desire, O Sir! 15

When the Creator sent forth the Prophet *(nabī)*[4] of Light *(nūr)*,
The people *(ummat)* did not believe him, O Sir! 16

They did not believe the Pīr nor did they recognize the Shāh;
No, they stuck stubbornly to their old positions, O Sir! 17

But they reaped what they had sown:
Their city caused its own destruction, O Sir! 18

The soul *(jīv)* which rejects this religious knowledge *(ʿilm)*,
Will get drowned in wickedness, O Sir! 19

The Shāh has sent us a message *(farmān)*;
He has captured the fort and razed it to the ground, O Sir! 20

In our town those alone will we accommodate
Who believe in my Sāheb, O Sir! 21

Whoever is sheltered by the Sāheb,
How can such a devout servant *(bando)* drown, O Sir! 22

But of the wicked, their trustworthiness
And their faith are lost, O Sir! 23

Pīr Shams said the lamp would be cloaked;
They would be left in profound darkness, O Sir! 24

The Prophet of Light *(nūr)* ascended the mountain;
Water rose above the temple, O Sir! 25

Pīr Shams, the Guru, has related this wisdom *(ginān)*;
O Believers, *(mu'min)* recite and dwell upon it, O Sir! 26

4. *jabī:* typographical error; should be *nabī.*

12

kāyama dāyama tuṅ moro sāmī tere nāme bī koī koī

You are my Swāmī, O Everlasting *(qā'im)* and Eternal *(dā'im)*!
But only a few, yes, only a few,
know your Name *(nām)*. 1

Indeed the promise *(kol)* of the trustworthy one is certain;
The true servant *(bando)* was Muḥammed himself,
yes, Muḥammed himself. 2

The Pīr will take reckoning of the servant;
So follow humbly, yes, follow humbly,
the sayings of the Guru. 3

Keeping company of the pious *(sādhu)*,
the servant becomes pure;
Whereas the heedless one *(gāfal)* sits there
weeping, yes, weeping. 4

Life is but a hundred odd years long;
O Devotee! Finally death too comes,
yes, it comes. 5

Pīr Shams, the ocean-hearted and moonlike, said:
What the Creator *(kirtār)* intends,
that occurs, yes, it occurs. 6

13

tīratha vedhaḍā pīra shamasa gāzī sadhaṇā

Go on the pilgrimage *(tīrtha)*!
Pīr Shams, the defender *(ghāzī)* has gone;
O Brother, go [to the sacred waters]
to bathe, to bathe, to bathe! 1

Washed and bathed, those souls who follow
the Guru's orders *(farmān)*
They will bathe nowhere else,
no they will bathe nowhere else! 2

Walk on the straight path *(rāh)*, ask the Pīr,
and then walk on that path;
Do not let your feet stray upon barren land,
no do not go astray! 3

Pīr Shams gives the best instruction for all souls;[1]
Even hard-hearted souls can he convince, yes he can convince. 4

My Sāheb has graciously opened a door—it is like a
Needle's eye through which the elephant-self[2] must pass. 5

Pīr Shams, the defender [of the faith], said:
True friends and believers *(mu'min)* will reap the fruits! 6

---

1. *arvāh:* Ar. bkn. pl. of *ruh*—soul, spirit, breath.
2. *hasatī:* Urd. *hastī*—elephant; one's being, individuality, personality, self. Based on a proverb that says the ego is as huge as an elephant, and it must be shrunk (humbled) to pass through the eye of a needle.

14

jīva tuṅ jāvāde ene saṃsārano savāda

O Soul *(jīv)*! Cast off your attraction
 for this world *(saṃsār)*!
If you worship the Primordial *(ādi)* Brahman,
 your efforts will triumph. 1

Primordial Brahman has come
 in the form *(avatār)* of Pīr Shams.
If you recognise him,
 you will attain the other shore. 2

Hari came to the province of Daylamān
 and then stayed in Multān;
Vimras, Hari's devotee, recited *ginānS*
 in honor of the Guru. 3

Then Shāh Shams arrived and travelled
 in the dress of a *faqīr;*
Taking along two youths,
 he came to the province of Ghazni. 4

He reached Emnābāī's house and approached
 a water-well;
Chaste Emnābāī prostrated at Guru Shams' feet
 and begged for protection. 5

"How fortunate you have come Gurujī!
 Great indeed is my fortune!
O Swāmī, please enter my house today
 and thus fulfill my heart's desire." 6

He accompanied the chaste woman *(satī)*
 and entered her quarters;

For showing his devotee *(dāsī)* this kindness,
she bowed down again. 7

"O Hari, please agree to dine at my house
at least this once.
Be kind and stay, O Swāmī, deliver me
to the other shore *(pahele pār)*!" 8

Chandrabhāṇ reflected a moment
and then said to the lady:
"You, O Lady, are chaste; you have a mission
to perform for the people." 9

Emnābāī replied: "O Swāmī, I am under
your protection *(śaraṇa)*.
You are the child of Brahma!
I prostrate at your feet." 10

Surbhāṇ then said to the chaste woman,
"Your name is Emnābāī.
Guru Shams has accepted your invitation,
and you are a true devotee." 11

"Go fetch an unbaked pot from the potter
and then fill it with water!
If you do this before preparing dinner,
only then will Pīr Shams dine." 12

The chaste Emnābāī left and returned
with an unbaked pot full of water;
Very pleased were her three guests,
Pīr Shams and the two youths then ate. 13

Her sister-in-law Nānābāī said:
"Sister! What are you doing!
Who are these guests you have just fed?
Where do they live?" 14

"They are staying in the town Godī Viloḍa
with my father.
He is my Guru, O Sister,
and I am his devotee." 15

Nānābāī replied:
"But they are dressed in Muslim clothing!

Our house has been defiled!
    O Sister, what remains of your customs?"[1] 16

Chaste Emnābāī knelt down and pleaded:
    "O Sister, I have a diamond.
I will give you the diamond but please
    do not tell father-in-law." 17

"Keep your diamond to yourself!
    Now I know your whole secret!
I will surely inform my mother.
    Why should I spare you from misery?" 18

Lovely Hemābāī smiled at her husband, Master Śāmdās.
"That girl left her parents' home and came to ours!"[2] . . . 19

. . . the daughter told her father.
    "What is the matter?" asked the mother.
"Call everyone together!
    Daughter-in-law has defiled our house." 20

Sneering, Hemābāī said spitefully to her husband:
"We can do without daughter-in-law.
    Send her back to her father's place!" 21

Soon, everybody in the city was gossiping
    and poking fun at Emnābāī;
But the chaste lady's *(satī)* deeds were noble,
    and she attained the other shore. 22

Candrabhāṇ said: "O my Sāheb, have mercy upon her!"
Guru Shams was merciful and sent her
    to her home in Heaven *(vaikuṇṭha)*. 23

A carrier descended from Heaven
    and she boarded the craft;
The chaste lady had served Pīr Shams
    and was delivered to the other shore. 24

Vimras uttered these words:
    "Listen together carefully, all of you!
Whoever serves Guru Shams
    will also be borne to Heaven." 25

---

1. lit. what remains of your country *(deś)*.
2. Thus, she must submit to the rules of her in-laws' household.

15

popaṭa ane surjā rāṇīṇī vāta

Conversation between Queen Surjā and the Parrot

Queen Surjā said:
"Tell me about the two travellers *(musāfar)*.
O Swāmī, how will they come to us
and what is their caste *(jāt)?*" 1

In the form of a parrot, Pīr Shams replied:
"O Queen, both of them live with me.
They will come reciting the *gināns* of the Guru;
their caste is that of worshipper."[1] 2

Queen Surjā asked:
"What kind of dwelling do they inhabit?
Tell us something about them,
these two disciples *(dāsa)* of yours." 3

Pīr Shams in his parrot form said:
"Listen, O Queen, I will disclose all!
First let me teach you about the *avatār;*
get your group together and sit!" 4

Queen Surjā said:
"Our gathering is composed of eight souls *(jīv)*.
All of them will attend;
please inform them about everything." 5

1. *dāsapaṇā:* lit. having the quality of a *dāsa* or "devotee-hood." In translation, while *dāsa* and *dāsī* both mean devotee, when *dāsa* refers to the two male devotees who accompanied Pīr Shams during his travels, it is consistently translated as "disciple."

Pīr Shams in his parrot form said:
"Listen, O Queen, to all the Names *(nām)*!
Once, when there was neither earth nor sky,
we all lived together." 6

Queen Surjā asked:
"What is the secret to that place, O Swāmī?
Reveal to us some sign *(niśān)*,
some name by which to realize it." 7

Pīr Shams in his parrot form said:
"Long ago there was a barren land;
But in the waters where the Master *(nāth)* slept,
we enjoyed great happiness." 8

Queen Surjā asked:
"O Swāmī, how many days did he sleep?
From there, where did you go, O Guru,
you who are a wealth of blessings?" 9

Pīr Shams in his parrot form replied:
"Thereafter, we lived upon land.
They[2] recognized who we were, and so we went
and stayed at their place." 10

Queen Surjā said: "O Swāmī, you have lived
both in water and on land!
Reveal to us the method by which
your disciples recognized you?" 11

Pīr Shams in his parrot form said:
"I took birth in my mother's home.
Thus did I assume human form *(avatār)*.
Then I was met by my two disciples." 12

Queen Surjā asked:
"When will they come to us?
Will they come to show us [the path],
O Swāmī, they who are your disciples?" 13

Pīr Shams in his parrot form replied:
"Queen Surjā, hear this wisdom *(ginān)*!
The names of the two travellers who will come
are Vimras and Surbhāṇ." 14

2. His two disciples or followers. See next verse.

16

jīrebhāī antara jāmī antara sāmī īsa dunīyāme kucha nāhī

O Brother! In your heart is God *(antaryāmī)*,
in your heart is the Master *(swāmī)*;
But within this world *(duniyā)*, there is nothing at all! 1

O Brother! Indeed the sky
extends well beyond your reach;
In its midst burns the thousand-rayed sun. 2

O Brother! The *jogī* is one
who practices discipline *(yoga)*;
And the *bhogī* is one who remains enticed by the world. 3

O Brother! Formidable is the hour when
the Great Day *(mahādin)*[1] arrives!
On that day, one will be subject to severe punishment. 4

O Brother! Surjā said,
"Listen, my son Kamalā!
When sacred knowledge *(āgama)* comes, go acquire it." 5

O Brother! If you are sincere
before the Gurunara;
You will truly attain the vision *(dīdār)* of Paradise *(bahiśta)*. 6

O Brother! "Prince Kamalā, listen to this talk
about the Great Day!"
"Let us go then, Surjā, to the *jogī*." 7

O Brother! The earth will smolder
and appear copper-colored;
The keeper of books will appear at the end of time. 8

---

1. That is, the Day of Judgment.

O Brother! The *jogī* is he
who practices discipline;
Of what use is it merely to don earrings? 9

O Brother! Nor is anyone a *jogī*
who wears ochre robes;
No indeed, we cannot truly call that person a *jogī.* 10

O Brother! To the one who loves truth
and keeps virtuous company;
A hundred, nay, a thousand cheers are due! 11

O Brother! Upon hearing this talk,
Prince Kamalā departed;
He, too, became Immortal *(amar).* 12

O Brother! Then Prince Kamalā's father, the King,
came to the *jogī;*
[Thinking] "Let me listen to the *jogī's* talk." 13

O Brother! The vision of Paradise awaits one
who conquers the world;
Listen to what the *jogī* has to say. 14

O Brother! Hell *(dozaḳh)* awaits
one who goes astray;
And one who does not believe in what the Guru says. 15

O Brother! If one is from the same ancestor,
one is no stranger;
But if one joins the company of strangers, one will go astray. 16

O Brother! Pīr Shams has spoken
this sacred speech *(āgama vāṇī)*:
"I am your servant *(bando),* I entreat you [O Lord]!" 17

O Brother! Those who do not follow
what has been inscribed on paper;
They will surely beat their breasts in remorse. 18

17

satagura shamasa ema bolīyā āja che daśamo avatāra

Satgur Shams said:
    This is the time of the tenth *avatār;*
His ninth form *(rūpa)* has been changed,
    and he now resides in the West *(paścim).* 1

If you recognize that form,
    it will be to your benefit;
The gods *(devatā)* of this fourth age *(kalyug)*
    have known this. 2

Kṛṣṇa took form as the Buddha *avatār*
    and came to the Pāṇḍavas;
Draupadī recognized him and delivered him
    into the hands of King Yudhiṣṭhira. 3

He rescued Prahlād, and the labors of Kamalā's husband
    were successful;
He who rescued the fort in Rāma's form,
    that person has arrived today. 4

The *avatār* of this fourth age is Nakalaṅka[1];
    know that he is a Muslim;
He who was wrathful with the infidels *(kāfir),*
    indeed, he has come. 5

He has taken form *(avatār)* as the man Islām Shāh;
    know that he is the Satgur!
Pīr Shams says:
    O pious ones, listen to this wisdom *(ginān)*! 6

---

1. *nakalaṅkī:* Guj. *niṣkalaṅka*—the one without blemish, the immaculate one; reference to Kālkī, the tenth *avatār.*

Then Makaḍa Bhudara demanded:
    "Show him to us!"
Shams revealed the Shāh's form,
    and they beheld the four-armed Swāmī. 7

Thereupon all were filled with faith *(imān)*
    and gave the Guru great respect;
They said: "All our hopes have been fulfilled
    for we saw Kṛṣṇa himself!" 8

The Satgur then disclosed the rules
    and prescriptions *(vrata)* of religion *(dharma)*;
"Pray together on Friday of the new moon,
    and you will reach the other shore." 9

He made them recite the word *(japa)* Pīr Shāh,
    name of the Gurunara;
Then Pīr Shams left
    and proceeded to the town of Ghazni. 10

18

guranarathī bhulā tāsuṅ vāda na kījejī

Do not make the mistake of
disputing with the Gurunara,
For he can imbalance the minds of strangers. 1

Those who make this mistake
are labeled great sinners *(pāpī)*;
Without the Guru, the soul *(jīv)* cannot be freed. 2

The demon *(daitya)* will seat himself
in a cross-legged posture;
He will make the entire earth prostrate before him. 3

The devil Kaliṅga
has forty-thousand demon attendants;
Each one of whom will bring about great strife. 4

Reciting magic spells *(mantra)* over sand,
they will produce grain;
Thus will they run canteens which provide free food. 5

Reciting magic spells over water,
the demons will make butter;
Thus will they run canteens which provide free butterfat. 6

Reciting magic spells over dust,
the demons will produce sugar;
Thus will they run canteens which provide free sugar. 7

Reciting magic spells over their wings,
the demons will train parrots;
Thus will they teach them to chant the name of Kaliṅga. 8

The demons will make wooden horses
appear to be eating food;
Indeed, they will promote such sorry spectacles. 9

The devil Kaliṅga
    will bring dead men back to life;
In this fourth age he will show people their [dead] parents. 10

The demons will raise an umbrella
    beneath an overcast sky;
They will let the rain lightly drizzle with a cool breeze. 11

The devil Kaliṅga will sell bread
    in exchange for copper coins;
But my Swāmī Rājā can turn those into gold. 12

In times of such adversity,
    the heart will find no peace;
But the Swāmī Rājā will protect it and preserve it. 13

Pīr Shams recites this wisdom *(ginān)*
    so full of great significance;
Beware, for the demons will engineer such kinds of trickery. 14

19

dasa bandhī yārā sīra bandhī nara kāyamashāha nī pujā

Sacrifice a tenth,[1] O Friend, and surrender your life
in worship of Nara, the Qā'im, the Shāh!
Inevitably upon your head will descend
The Day of Judgment *(qiyāmat)*.
Indeed, that day draws close! 1

The Eternal Śyāma has himself taught
that the path is thus[2];
Pīr Kabīr al-Dīn says Pīr Ṣadr al-Dīn said:
"As you sow, so shall you reap." 2

Pīr Shams says, O Friends! So long as you live,
you can achieve [results].
After death, what can be done?
But the negligent *(gāfal)* waste their lives.
Brother, how can they attain freedom *(mokṣa)?* 3

Pīr Shams says, O Friends!
If you are negligent, you will lose.
Rather, O Brother, be vigilant day in and day out!
And join the company of the thirty-three crore deities,
so said Pīr Shams. 4

Pīr Shams says, O Friends!
This fourth age *(kalyug)* is full of treachery.
O Brother, I have observed this even between friends;
The shoulder is offered in embrace but the hand
twisted around [the waist].[3] 5

---

1. That is, of one's earnings; a reference to the tithe.
2. Verse is obscure.
3. Allusion to a technique of combat: the unsuspecting "friend" is hugged with one hand and knived with the other!

Pīr Shams says, O Friends!
    If you strain too hard, [the cord] will snap;
Leave things be, do not hanker after them so;
Just as a spring flows naturally, so what you desire
    will come to you. 6

Pīr Shams says, O Friends!
    As a sword is sharpened by whetstone
And as clothing is washed with water;
So is the believer purified by wisdom *(ginān)*!
    So said Pīr Shams. 7

Pīr Shams says, the fool who weeds not his soil
    cannot grow greens.
Likewise, unless the coward shoots off his arrow,
Brother, he will have no flesh to pack beneath his skin.[4] 8

Pīr Shams says, O Friends!
    That which is born must also die.
Do not count upon the body!
See, a blade of grass breaks and falls down.
    Brother, every moment something perishes. 9

Pīr Shams visited four countries [and prayed:]
O Swāmī, upon you is our reliance!
Fulfill our unfulfilled hopes,
O Swāmī, deliver us all to the other shore *(pahele pār)*. 10

4. A reference to hunting, that is, he will have no food.

20

satagura bheṭayā kema jāṇīye e mana parakhīne joya

How does one recognize the Satgur when one meets him?
Only that mind that knows the test can see.
O Brother, he dwells in sandal woods
and fresh-scented lime. 1

In the sandalwood forest,
there lives our Beloved *(piyuṅ)*;
Come, O Friend *(sakhī)*! Let's go to that forest
to find joy for our souls *(jīv)*. 2

In the mind *(man)* are the divisions "you" and "I";
leave these thoughts behind!
A mere curtain separates "you" and "I";
if you forget this, you are the fool! 3

"You" and "I" are bonded in love;
"you" and "I" speak words to each other.
"You" and "I" are both one with the Lord;
O Brother, dispel this curtain! 4

"You" and "I" should not be arrogant,
for pride destroys all;
If "you" and "I" killed our pride,
we would attain our heart's desire. 5

"You" and "I" passed the night together,[1]
do not forget that dear sir!
"You" and "I" bathed in the moonlight;
so bring a mind filled with affection *(heta)*. 6

---

1. That is, endured fear, hardship, and danger together.

"You" and "I" crossed the ocean even as the waves
rose up high above us;
"You" and "I" crossed the river,
and Satgur Sahadeva[2] showered us with Light *(nūr)*. 7

Satgur's Light is concealed within;
recognize the divine *(deva)* in the Guru;
What will you give to satisfy the Guru,
and what should be your service *(seva)*? 8

If you serve him with sincere mind,
indeed, no gift is necessary;
Give the mind and heart full of love *(sneha)*,
and let the love greatly increase! 9

When the heart *(dil)* is given, all is given.
Stay awake night and day, O my Brother!
Pīr Shams said: Go join the ranks
of the thirty-three crore deities! 10

---

2. This may be a reference to Pīr Ṣadr al-Dīn who occasionally used this pen name.

21

sacā merā khālaka sarajaṇahāra āpe upāyā shāha dhandhukāra

True is my Maker *(ḳhāliq)*, Creator of the world *(sirjaṇahār)*;
The Shāh created [the world] from utter darkness. 1

Prophet *(nabī)* Muḥammed was God's *(ḳhudā)* chosen one;
To the Prophet came a summons from Him. 2

In the summons, God made a command *(farmān)*;
Lo! From mere mud, a body took shape. 3

After creating the soul *(ruh)*, He breathed life into it;
Indeed, but for the soul, the body is an empty cage. 4

Strive to earn your goal, O Brother!
Believe me, my Creator is trustworthy. 5

True is my Creator in whose grip
 is the prize of Paradise *(bahiśta)*;
This wisdom *(ginān)* of supreme essence
 is the word of Pīr Shams. 6

22

e sabhāgā hara puja nita nīravāṇa pañjetana

O Lucky Ones *(subhāgī)*! Worship
the five holy ones[1] *(panj tan)* day in day out;
Let your concentration *(dhyāna)* rest upon the Guru's crown. 1

O Lucky Ones! Submit the tithe *(dasond)*
and live according to the Guru;
Stop chattering about worldly things. 2

O Lucky Ones! Life is momentary,
so keep some water with you;
Purify the water and then drink it. 3

O Lucky Ones! All that you eat
and drink will vanish;
Only that which you give away remains secure. 4

O Lucky Ones! What you give to the Shāh
increases 150,000 fold;
The record-keeper *(dīwān)* is at each person's doorstep. 5

O Lucky One! The hammer
strikes the anvil;
Thus is the iron beaten and molded into shape. 6

O Lucky Ones! When all is devastated,
the Lord *(rabb)* will take account;
So keep company with those who are resolute. 7

O Lucky Ones! The Shāh is the expert *(mullah)*,
the Shāh is the judge *(qāḍi)*;
He himself is the Veda and the Qur'ān. 8

---

1. Prophet Muḥammad, his daughter Fāṭimah, his son-in-law and cousin ʿAlī, and his two grandsons, Ḥasan and Ḥusayn.

O Lucky Ones! Station by station,
    the Sāheb will cross Sind;
He will soon come to visit Multān. 9

O Lucky Ones! At the crossroad
    facing the four directions;
He will come there at the main square of Multān. 10

O Lucky Ones! Pīr Shams has spoken
    this essence-filled wisdom *(ginān)*;
The faithful will get across to the other shore *(pahele pār)*. 11

23

e sabhāgā īsa dunīyādhe vīca kīyā gīna āve

O Lucky Ones *(subhāgī)*! What did you bring with you
into the world?
What are you going to take back with you? 1

O Lucky Ones! You were born naked
and naked will you die!
So be scrupulous in your trade and dealings. 2

O Lucky Ones! Bare were you born
and bare-skinned will you die!
You will take nothing along with you. 3

O Lucky Ones! When you lie on the stretcher
with feet extended,
Your family will neither keep you nor come with you. 4

O Lucky Ones! They will cover you with earth
after the funeral rites;
Thus will you be bundled off to the Lord *(hari)*. 5

O Lucky Ones! Your body will crumble
and turn into clay;
Ants and worms will feast upon your flesh. 6

O Lucky Ones! Grass will take root over the top
of your body;
Cows will come and graze on this grass. 7

O Lucky Ones! That for which you have
earned demerit;
It will not endure nor abide with you. 8

O Lucky Ones! When the red-hot iron
strikes your throat,
You will scream and cry out to no avail. 9

O Lucky Ones! When the Swāmī Rājā
asks for an account,
Those who have toiled will be amply rewarded. 10

O Lucky Ones! Pīr Shams recited this wisdom *(ginān)*
in essence supreme;
Those who are faithful will attain the other shore *(pahele pār)*. 11

24

aba terī mahobata lāgī dīla mere mahobata lāgī

Alas, I have been struck by love *(mahobat)* for you!
O my beloved Sāheb! My heart has been swept away by love!
Permit our eyes to meet, O my precious Sāheb! 1

Part the curtains and look at me face-to-face;
Let me see your smiling countenance, O my precious Sāheb! 2

Pīr Shams yearns for your countenance *(sūrat)*;
Bless me with a vision *(dīdār)* of you, O my precious Sāheb! 3

O Beloved One, be not displeased with me;
Take me along with you, O my precious Sāheb! 4

The ardor of youth does not last long;
Like river waters, it rushes away, O my precious Sāheb! 5

All your lovers will come with you;
Be tender to me in your heart, O my precious Sāheb! 6

Listen, O Enchanting Chabīlā,* the Lord who bewitches!
Be compassionate towards me, O my precious Sāheb! 7

O Proud Jobana,* whose gait is full of mischief!
Bear love for me in your heart, O my precious Sāheb! 8

O Beloved *(pīyā)*, your mystery has driven me crazy!
Let ardor *(ʿishq)* consume my mind, O my precious Sāheb! 9

When I beheld your face *(mukh)*, my mind became ecstatic;
Singing, Pīr Shams has made you hear, O my precious Sāheb! 10

* Epithets of Kṛṣṇa.

25

faramāna karī narajī bolīyā tame sāmbhaḷo pīra shamasa vāta

The Coffin (Janājo)

Giving an order *(farmān)*, the Lord said:
"Listen, Pīr Shams!
Go amidst the following *(jamāʿat)* today
and administer a test of faith *(imān)*." 1

Pīr Shams replied:
"Listen, O Shāh!
I will demand from the gathering *(gat)*
whatsoever it is you wish." 2

"Ask for bread made of *kāṭhā*[1] flour
and order human flesh;
Whoever submits flesh will attain
the abode of Heaven *(vaikuṇṭha)*." 3

Then Pīr Shams departed
and arrived at Uchh in Multān;
All followers assembled and prostrated:
"O Gurujī, your wish is our command!" 4

"Offer only what is within your means
and be of steadfast mind;
But if you prepare some food for me,
I will bestow heartfelt blessings *(āśiṣa)*." 5

Pīr Shams then said:
"Listen, O Gathering of followers *(gat jamāʿat)*!
I require of you only this for which
I shall bestow heartfelt blessings!" 6

---

1. A kind of hard reddish wheat.

"Bring to me some bread made of *kāṭhā* flour
and fetch me some human flesh;
The one who gives this flesh will attain
a dwelling in Heaven." 7

Stunned, the gathering discussed this:
"Who will give up their own flesh?
Pīr Shams will save the resolute, but who, indeed,
dares to go near the Pīr?" 8

Pīr Shams sat down with a rosary to pray:
"O Sāheb, preserve my honor *(lāj)*!"
For seven days he kept fast *(rozā)*, and nobody
dared to go near the Pīr. 9

Then a blind mendicant arrived
and promptly sat down in the prayer-house;
"Take your gold dagger in your hand
and feast upon my flesh!" 10

"Your offer has satisfied me.
Auspicious *(dhanya)* that moment, blessed that night!
That day when you were born!
Great, indeed, shall be your fortune!" 11

Then Qāsim Shāh himself appeared
and began the rite of Holy Water *(ghaṭpāṭ)*;
He brought a cupful of Light *(nūr)*,
and Pīr Shams accompanied him. 12

Pīr Shams said:
"Listen, O my Lord!
In the prayer-house is a blind sage;
deliver him into Divine Light *(nūr ilāhī)*!" 13

[The Shāh gave the blind mendicant the cup][2];
He drank the cupful of Light *(nūr)*
and lo! he witnessed the entire universe! 14

Then Pīr Shams said:
"O Blind Ascetic, listen!
Go and join the congregation for it is now time
for us to depart." 15

---

2. The first line of this verse is missing in the Gujarati text.

The blind mendicant stood up,
and he came amidst the following;
"Now fetch the cases and prepare,
for time has come for the Pīr to depart!" 16

The gathering asked the blind man:
"Did you sacrifice yourself to the Pīr?
Only yesterday, you bumped into walls
but now you walk tall!" 17

"Yes, I sacrificed myself to the Pīr
and thus drank of Divine Light;
Had he not promised a place in Heaven
to the sacrificer of one's flesh?" 18

The assembly pondered over his words
and then approached the Pīr;
"Take the gold dagger in your hand
and feast upon our flesh." 19

"That opportunity has passed!
Indeed, who can consume human flesh?"
"Now fetch the cases and prepare,
for the time has come for the Pīr to depart!" 20

The whole gathering began to weep;
men and women both wept!
"If the Pīr departs from here upset,
wretched will be our fate!" 21

Pīr Shams said:
"Listen, O following!
I will give the final verdict at my own place;
now it is time to depart." 22

On Thursday, the seventeenth day
of the month Vaiśākha,[3]
On that day the Pīr travelled all the way
to Ucch in Multān. 23

Seventeen-hundred people followed the Pīr
to his own place;
Placing their cases there, they said:
"Pīr give us your last decree." 24

3. Seventh month of the Vikram year.

Pīr Shams said:
"Listen, O gathering! Every twelve months
Keep a fast *(rozā)* on this day,
and you will attain Heaven *(vaikuṇṭha)*." 25

"All men and women must observe this fast,
even little children;
If every twelve months you keep the fast,
you will attain Heaven." 26

Pīr Shams spoke his wisdom *(ginān)* firmly:
"Listen, O Followers!
Only thus will my curse not strike you,
and you will attain Heaven." 27

26

sāmī tamārī vāḍī māṅhe gura bhīramā sīñcaṇahāra

O Swāmī, in your meadow,
you are Guru Brahmā, the Gardener!
In the nine continents [of the world] you scatter seeds,
The Swāmī scattered countless seeds. 1

In a marsh, you planted two seeds,
one green, the other parched!
The one deprived of the Guru did not find a way out;
O Brother, dry was the one lacking the truth *(sat)*. 2

Tear out the roots of sin *(pāp)*, O Brother,
and the soul *(jīv)* will stay green!
Sever your head and submit it willingly to the Guru;
Then, the Gurunara will become your Helper *(belī)*. 3

Simple is the path of the Gurunara, the Helper,
infallible is his word *(śabda)*!
The deeds by which the soul will be released,
Such deeds should you devotedly perform. 4

O Devotees *(dāsa)*, bear your faults humbly
and be patient!
Entreat the Helper for his mercy!
Single and fast is the color of the Master *(pati)*, easy is his path. 5

O Pious ones *(rīkhīsar)*, meet and form a gathering
for the sake of your souls!
Wear the four precious jewels on your forehead;
Brother, gain mastery over the five elements. 6

Discharge your debts quickly
and profit from the Guru's wisdom *(ginān)*;
By the grace of the Lord *(nara)*, Pīr Shams has spoken:
Adore the true Swāmī! 7

27

seje poḍhayā sahastra varaṇā hajī te navaśā bāḷā

Thousands of husbands sleep easy, but this groom is still a child[1];
Day and night, O Brother, the water wheel turns.
Swāmī is the Gardener. 1

He has planted many fresh seeds; Swāmī is himself the Caretaker!
He tends the garden himself, he nourishes the garden himself!
The flowers and leaves yield fruits,
  and the Swāmī enjoys their fragrance:
The heart of the Gardener is contented. 2

From five buds came fifty blossoms all full-blown and beautiful;
A strong wind brought showers of Light *(nūr)*.
Indeed, the Eternal *(qā'im)* King made a wonderful garden.
But then the Swāmī increased it in creepers—
So beware, my pious Brothers *(munivar)*! 3

Meditate on religion *(dharma)*, keep your word *(vāc)*,
  and perform your duties!
Else you will repent when Yama comes today or tomorrow
  with his summons. 4

Beware! Keep your vows *(vrata)* and earn your merit
  in this fourth age *(kalyug)*;
By the grace of the Lord *(nara)*, Pīr Shams says:
"The tenth [*avatār*] is the Shāh! He has kindled the Light *(jyota)*,
  and made the Invisible *(alakha)* manifest." 5

---

1. The meaning of this line is obscure.

28

prema pāṭaṇa rājā mana sudha tīsa ghare radeyāde rāṇī

In the city of love *(prem pāṭan)* lived King *(rājā)* Manaśudha;
At his palace was his wife, Queen *(rāṇī)* Radīyā. 1

Five prime ministers came to stay there;
They engaged the King in discussion. 2

The King and Queen lived in contemplation *(dhyāna)*;
They were devoted to the Swāmī. 3

The ministers inspected the city;
Then they engaged the King in discussion. 4

The King and Queen remained in the palace;
They unceasingly performed holy rites *(kriyā)*. 5

Joining their two minds together,
They strengthened their love *(pyār)* for Pīr Shams. 6

Of no other desire did they speak;
Their utter concentration was on the Lord *(hari)*. 7

The townsfolk, all of them used to say:
The King's nature is full of devotion *(bhakti)*. 8

The five prime ministers lived there;
They kept the city in its place. 9

The King and the Queen lived in the palace;
The ministers administered all. 10

They lived in the city in such a manner,
That no one could censure them. 11

Pīr Shams, the Defender of the faith *(ghāzī)*, said:
"They received only praise from the townsfolk." 12

The city of love was a town;
Nay, it should be called a city. 13

Its foundations were broad and strong;
Encircling it was a fortress of Light *(prakāś)*. 14

Its new gates were truly attractive;
What exquisite skill had gone into their decoration! 15

Ornate with rich and delicate designs,
At the summit [of the fortress] was an open court. 16

Composed of seventy-two chambers;
Its bricks were laid in countless patterns. 17

Four vazīrs stood at its gates;
Lofty indeed was their abode. 18

It went beyond one's eyesight, so high it was;
Supreme was this fortress of Light. 19

It had sixty-four squares and sixteen junctions;
It had three hundred and sixty bazaars. 20

Lovely indeed was this city,
It were as if created on Mount Kailāsa. 21

A mighty army lived in its square;
Nearby was the guesthouse for visitors. 22

The river bank flowed abundantly;
Its sweet, unending waters sparkled. 23

In such a way did the King and Queen live;
Their kingdom was filled with Light. 24

Listen, O pious ones *(rīkhīsar)* to all of them,
Who lived with the King and Queen. 25

Kamalā was the King's attendant;
Listen to his thoughts! 26

Broad and strong were its foundations;
Inside the city was the imperial palace. 27

The King and Queen sat in the palace;
They sat forlorn all eight quarters of the day. 28

Diamonds and gems sparkled and shone,
Bright as the light of the sun. 29

(Change tune)

Then the King had a thought: "Let me go to the Guru!
Let me submit a plea standing on top of the palace. 30

Let me have quiet converse night and day with the Gurunara!"
Having thus entreated him, the Guru heard his plea. 31

Awakening at midnight, he thought about him;
When the sun rose at dawn, Pīr Shams arrived. 32

Pīr Shams made a speech and [the King said]:
"Come visit our home."
[He replied] "Make the preparations—
we will return in six months." 33

(Change tune)

The King and Queen remained standing,
but seated the Pīr on a dais. 34

Lovingly they washed his feet making many a plea. 35

"Profound is our reverence for you;
you have fulfilled our request. 36

Indeed, Gurujī has been gracious for he has come to visit us! 37

Be merciful, dear Lord and lead us to the divine vision *(dīdār)*!" 38

The King and Queen said: "Be merciful, be kind!" 39

"Great is the reward for paying the tithe *(dasond)*, so deliver us! 40

Bring to us the eternal reward that we may attain
the other shore *(pahele pār)*." 41

They entertained the Guru fondly
and rendered him much service *(sevā)*. 42

(Change tune)

Day and night they had conversations with the Gurunara;
Having occupied himself thus,
the King became elated. 43

The King said: "Listen to me, O Queen,
about the chaste ones *(satī)*:
Single-minded should be our attention on the Gurunara!" 44

The Queen replied: "Listen King, this is a matter of secrecy!
Let us pay our respects to the Gurunara
and become his followers. 45

Mercifully he granted us divine vision
and our deeds are redeemed;
He will certainly keep his promise *(kol)* and accomplish our task." 46

The King's heart rejoiced
when the Gurujī spoke his wisdom *(ginān)*;
The King listened attentively, and the Queen came nearby. 47

(Change tune)

There the Gurujī spoke his wisdom *(ginān)*;
"Listen to the essence, O pious ones! 48

Who acts upon the teachings of the Gurunara,
That one reaches the other shore *(pahele pār)*. 49

You have arrived at the site of the sixty-fourth pilgrimage *(tīrtha)*[1];
Know that it is at the feet of the Guru. 50

For millions of aeons and ages the Gurujī has come;
Infinite is his artistry and perpetual. 51

God *(devatā)* in his tenth manifestation *(avatār)*,
Assumed a form *(rūpa)* and became visible. 52

The Supreme King first came in the form of a Fish *(Matsya)*;
He was the support for the seer Mugḍala. 53

In his form as Tortoise *(Kūrma)*, he churned the ocean;
The fourteen jewels were thus recovered. 54

He came to the aid of King Ambarīśa;
Thus the King reached the other shore. 55

In the form of the Boar *(Varāha)*, he seized the universe;
He clenched the whole of it with his great teeth. 56

Nārāyaṇa then descended as the Lion *(Narasiṃha)*;
Prahlād fell prostrate and begged at his feet. 57

In the form of the Dwarf *(Vāmana)*, he spoke;
He delivered Kamalā, the fortunate. 58

---

1. *aḍasaṭha tīratha:* the last of the sixty-four pilgrimages to be performed by the *brahmin.*

Parṣurāma twirled his axe around six times;
He grabbed Kamalā's husband in his hand. 59

In the form of Rāma, he killed Rāvaṇa;
He took a hold of Hariścandra's hand. 60

He saved Hariścandra's son, Rohita
As well as his wife, Queen Tārāmatī. 61

Luckily, he came as Kṛṣṇa!
He protected Draupadī[2] with reams of cloth. 62

In this fourth age *(kalyug)*, he has become manifest;
He is ʿAlī, mighty comrade of Muḥammad. 63

Whoever worships him single-mindedly,
That man or woman will be delivered." 64

Thus did Pīr Shams, the Defender of faith *(ghāzī)*, speak
To the King and his Queen. 65

(Change tune)

Hearing the Guru's wisdom *(ginān)*,
the King's heart was convinced!
"We entreat you Pīr Shams,
we prostrate at the Guru's feet. 66

Hearing the Guru's wisdom *(ginān)*
has given assurance to our hearts;
The Lord who has been so merciful
will take us to the Eternal abode *(amar vās)*." 67

"Come to Multān both of you, O King and Queen!
I will send you two messengers after six months have passed." 68

So saying, Pīr Shams arose from there to depart;
"Listen to my words and hasten to visit me!" 69

(Change tune)

The King's heart was enraptured,
and he said to the Queen: 70

"Gurujī has been merciful!
He has come again and again." 71

---

2. *pañcāvalī: Pañcālī:* the princess of Pañcala, namely, Draupadī.

The pious *(satī)* remained standing
and talked about religion *(dharma).* 72

They followed the True Path *(satpanth)*
and recalled the unutterable word *(jāp).*[3] 73

Then the Gurunara dispatched a disciple
to deliver a summons *(hukam).*[4] 74

A summons had come from the Guru;
how could it be neglected? 75

The summons had come for two people;
how could a third be taken along? 76

The summons had come now, but they had a child;
should it be taken along? 77

The Queen asked the King:
"How can we go?" 78

Queen Radīyā said:
"O King, think! What are we to do?" 79

King Manaśudha replied:
"We will go to the Lord *(deva)* [alone]." 80

The child was laid down to sleep,
and the two prepared to leave. 81

Thinking of the Gurujī, they departed
and came past the guesthouse. 82

The road bruised their bare feet,
but they both kept walking on. 83

When the King reached halfway,
a deer was feeding its young. 84

Sighting the fawn, on the spot the Queen
became distressed with pain. 85

So severe was her pain, she instantly died,
and the King had to think. 86

"The command has come for two;
Now what can be done?" 87

---

3. *ajampīyā jāpa:* lit. the sacred word which is not to be uttered; the *mantra.*
4. Note the resemblance between the following verses and Ginān 9.

Covering her in a sheet, he tied a knot
    and started towards the Lord. 88

When at last he arrived at his entrance,
    he prostrated himself at the Guru's feet. 89

Golden lights sparkled, and there sat
    the Lord of three worlds *(tribhovar)*, Śyāma. 90

"Rise, Queen Raḍīyā! Drink the Immortal nectar *(amṛta)*
    and feed your child!" 91

Abiding by the Gurunara's words,
    they had come to the Lord's porch. 92

Worship with single mind and concentrate *(dhyāna)*
    upon the Gurunara! 93

Remain in the refuge of the Gurunara,
    and you will attain the other shore. 94

The King and the Queen were both delivered
    together with their child. 95

The Guru said: "Listen, O pious ones, to the story
    about the King and Queen!" 96

Pīr Shams recited this wisdom *(ginān)*,
    "Listen O Congregation *(gat jamāʿat)*!" 97

(Change tune)

Pīr Shams, the Defender of faith,
    recited this wisdom *(ginān)* at that time;
"He who believes the Gurunara to be true
    will reach the other shore. 98

Think about this wisdom *(ginān)*, O pious Brothers!
    Do not talk about other things!
Serve *(sevā)* your Shāh single-mindedly,
    and you will attain Heaven *(vaikuṇṭha)*." 99

29

e vīrābhāī eka dhandhukāra farī dujā hovegā

O Brothers! Darkness will follow upon darkness;
So will it be on the Day of Judgment *(qiyāmah)*! 1

O Brothers! Fifty-thousand will remain unconscious;
There will be rainfalls of fire! 2

O Brothers! Titanic mountains will come smashing down;
Waterfalls will be ablaze with flames! 3

O Brothers! Mt. Meru will tremble and its boulders fracture;
The earth will be engulfed in water! 4

O Brothers! So fitfully will the sky shake,
The land will be sick with calamity! 5

O Brothers! The color of the earth will change;
It will turn into the reds of copper! 6

O Brothers! Ḳhudāvand himself will sit to take account;
He will demand the price of each and every grain! 7

O Brothers! The thirty-five crore strands of hair
  will harden into iron;
Time and again, they will prick the body! 8

O Brothers! Neither wares nor wealth will be of any use;
Only your earnings of meritorious deeds! 9

O Brothers! In forty-eight hours such a hurricane will blast,
Rocks and stones will fly in all directions! 10

O Brothers! The earth will be utterly demolished;
In accordance with God's *(ilāhī)* decree *(farmān)*! 11

O Brothers! Calling Indra, Ḳhudāvand will give blessing *(duʿa)*
To him who brings forth rain and storm! 12

O Brothers! Twelve types of rain will begin to pour,
When God's command *(hukam)* arrives! 13

O Brothers! Water will cascade in such proportions,
Even the resolute North Star *(Dhruva)* will shudder! 14

O Brothers! The waters will seethe to such a degree,
Nothing can be said to describe it! 15

O Brothers! Then what will all you pious ones *(rīkhīsar)* do?
It will be impossible for you to swim! 16

O Brothers! The Pīr reports what is in
the scriptures *(āgama, veda)*;
Listen, O my dear believers *(mu'min)*! 17

O Brothers! Take care and preserve your life!
Pīr Shams has said this. 18

O Brothers! Pīr Shams Qalandar said:
O Ḳhudāvand! Who can attain the limits
of your infinite Self! 19

30

e vīrābhāī cāra ghaḍīkā cāra jugaja kīdhā

O Brother! He turned four moments
into four ages *(yug)*,
Ḳhudāvand told this to the sea. 1

O Brother! In the first three ages,
religion *(dharma)* prevailed;
But this fourth age of Kalyug will be precarious. 2

O Brother! Father and son
will battle with one another;
Such awful scenes will you witness. 3

O Brother! The wife will demand expenses
from her mother-in-law;
Listen, O my Brother believers *(mu'min)*! 4

O Brother! Both the sky and the earth
will roar with laughter;
An amazing God *(ilāhi)* indeed is Ḳhudāvand! 5

O Brother! The pious ones *(rīkhīsar)*
will have fear in their hearts;
Listen, O my Brother believers! 6

O Brother! Imagine
what will be their condition,
Those who have misused their authority. 7

O Brother! This raw body
will be useless there;
For it has been made of mere clay. 8

O Brother! Indeed, of what use
will be your pride in it?
Listen, O my Brother believers! 9

O Brother! In a split second
you will rise and depart;
The world will just sit back and watch. 10

O Brother! Further on,
Ḳhudāvand will ask you,
"What good deeds have you brought along?" 11

O Brother! Then my pious ones,
what will you do?
At that instant, nothing can be done. 12

O Brother! All your wealth and possessions
will be in vain;
For you can take nothing along with you. 13

O Brother! Merit *(puṇya)* and sin *(pāp)*,
these alone will you take;
On that occasion, drums will be beaten. 14

O Brother! Pīr Shams Qalandar has said this;
O Ḳhudāvand! Who can attain
the limits of your infinite Self! 15

31

jīyā e yārā je karīyo se āpa murāda

O Friend! Whatever you do,
do it of your own will;
For the world will be of no help. 1

O Friend! If you succeed, indeed,
you will attain the divine vision *(dīdār)*;
But you must overcome your worldly cravings. 2

O Friend! Pay the tithe *(dasond)*
and take refuge in truth;
The mother [of truth] will raise you to the other shore *(pār)*. 3

O Friend! Lost fools they are
who lack in good deeds *(kriyā)*;
They will remain upon this shore. 4

O Friend! Word by word
I have revealed this to you;
So Brother, worship *(ārādhanā)* in the correct manner. 5

O Friend! By the Pīr's words
you can be saved;
Where the Pīr puts you, settle yourself there. 6

O Friend! I am the master,
and I am the servant;
My name is Fortunate One *(subhāgī)*. 7

O Friend! I did not strike a deal
anywhere else;
Rather, I sold my goods only to the Shāh. 8

O Friend! The lightest weight
cannot measure a grain of flour;
Humble yourself into such a tiny grain. 9

O Friend! Without merit,
no one can be saved;
How will you easily save yourselves? 10

O Friend! King Prahlād
delivered fifty million [souls];
Hariścandra delivered seventy million. 11

O Friend! In the second age,
the five Pāṇḍavas arrived;
They granted success to the works of the pious. 12

O Friend! King Yudhiṣṭhira
saved ninety-million;
All twelve attained Ḳhudāvand. 13

O Friend! Serve *(sevā)* firmly,
says Pīr Shams;
O Brother believers *(mu'min)*, pay the tithe! 14

32

ketare calatre shāha deva murāra

Abridged[1] *Das Avatār (Nāno Daśa Avatāra)*

Know what marvels the Shāh,
  the lord *(deva)* Murārī has executed!
Swāmī descended into the ocean
  in the form *(rūpa)* of the Fish *(Matsya)*;
The Shāh slew the demon Śaṅkha;
  ʿAlī made the Invisible *(alakha)* manifest.
Listen gathering *(gat)*, be attentive!
  Now the Lord Murārī is the Shāh.
Listen gathering, bring hither a firm mind!
  The Shāh resides in Kahak.
Listen gathering, bring hither a firm mind!
  The Pīr lives with the Shāh.
Listen gathering, bring hither a firm mind!
  The Eternal *(qā'im)* is All-Forgiving. 1

The second time the Swāmī descended
  as the Tortoise *(Kaurabha) avatār*;
Scorching their backs, the Shāh killed the demons
  Madhu and Kaiṭabha. 2

Swāmī's third descent was as the Boar *(Varāha)*
  whom none could cheat;
Thus he slew Mura, for the Shāh knew
  the demon's intentions. 3

1. *nāno:* lit. small, little, tiny.

Swāmī's fourth form was that of the Man-Lion *(Narasiṃha)*,
King of Kashmir;
With his nails, the Shāh tore apart Hiraṇyakaśipu
at a place midway. 4

In the third age, the Shāh's fifth form
was the brahmin Dwarf *(Vāmana)*;
For failing to recognize him, the Swāmī
sacked the demon Bali who lost all. 5

His sixth form was as Parśurām,
and he gave the army *(kṣatriya)* weapons;
The Shāh threw Sahasrārjuna into a cage;
each time he performed newer feats. 6

Swāmī's seventh descent was as Rāma
who triumphed over Kumbha in Laṅkā;
He slew Mandodari's husband,
the ten-headed demon Rāvaṇa. 7

The eighth form was the child Govinda
who was called Kṛṣṇa;
He killed Kaṃsa and Cāṇūra.
Indeed, we, too, are lucky to have the Shāh. 8

In the ninth form as Buddha,
he sat in deep concentration *(dhyāna)*;
The Shāh destroyed all the Kauravas and killed Duryodhana,
and the Pāṇḍavas attained freedom *(mokṣa)*. 9

Verily, his tenth form is right before you—
the Shāh rides upon a chariot!
He who has impurities in his heart,
how will he get across?
Leave the sixty-three rebirths,[2]
and seek the thirty-three [million gods]!
The promise-keeper has come at the last juncture[3];
Know him, recognize him, for now
the promised one has arrived;
Pīr Shams says, Listen O gathering of believers *(mu'min)*:
Be true in conduct! 10

---

2. *varaṇa:* Skt. *varṇa*—lit. color; social division, caste.
3. That is, the fourth age, *kalyug*.

33

eka śabda suṇo mere bhāī maṅya āvī sughaḍa panthamāṅ

Listen to a tale,[1] O my Brothers!
I have entered a clear path *(panth)*. 1

"Whose daughter are you, who is your brother-in-law?"
[They asked me], "In which man's house are you wife?" 2

"I am daughter of the truth *(sat)*, sister-in-law
of satisfaction *(santoṣ)*;
My husband is a resolute man. 3

I deserted my steadfast husband while he was asleep;
I left my dear child swinging in its cradle. 4

I removed some milk from my breast and left it in the oven;
Then I departed for the portal of my Lord *(deva)*. 5

For the sake of my Lord, I have given up everything;
I have no desire to go to any other place. 6

I have thoughts of nothing else;
My only concern now is for my soul *(jīv)*. 7

For the sake of my soul, I have relinquished all;
I have come to take refuge *(śaraṇa)* in you." 8

In the skirt of truth are the strings of contentment;
I weave it with the knots of concentration *(dhyān)*. 9

In the vessel of truth is the tap of satisfaction;
I sprinkle [the waters] of religion *(dharma)* in all directions. 10

Pir Shams says, Listen, O my Brothers!
I have come as I had promised *(kol)*. 11

---

1. *śabda:* lit. word.

34

suno suno momano sunī mana lāvanā sunane sarīkhī bātīyājī

Give ear, O Mu'mins, be attentive and listen!
Listen to this precious message:
Fear the Day of Judgment *(qiyāmah)*!
Yes, let your hearts be filled with fear!
The Prophet Muḥammad asked Gabriel:
"How many times must you come back?
How many times will you have to return
to this world after me?"
Gabriel replied: "Listen, O Prophet Muḥammad!
I must return ten times." 1

O Muḥammad! The first time that I must return,
That first time I will come to take away good fortune *(barakat)*.
I will take away fortune from the world,
and nothing of it will remain. 2

O Muḥammad! The second time that I must return,
That second time I will come to take away love *(mahobat)*.
I will take away love from the world,
and all will be empty of love. 3

O Muḥammad! The third time that I must return,
That third time I will come to take away mercy *(rahemat)*.
I will take away mercy from the world,
and only a few crops will ripen. 4

O Muḥammad! The fourth time that I must return,
That fourth time I will come to take away honor *(śaram)*.[1]
I will take the wife's regard for her husband,
and all will behave like beasts. 5

---

1. lit. shame, self-respect.

O Muḥammad! The fifth time that I must return,
That fifth time I will come to take away charity *(sakhāvat).*
I will take away good will from the rich,
    and nothing of it will remain. 6

O Muḥammad! The sixth time that I must return,
That sixth time I will come to take away faith *(imān).*
Only a few will be faithful,
    and the rest will be traitors. 7

O Muḥammad! The seventh time that I must return,
That seventh time I will come to take away the word of honor *(kol).*
The ruler himself will be dishonest,
    and will not keep his promise. 8

O Muḥammad! The eighth time that I must return,
That eighth time I will come to take away justice *(adal).*
I will take away fairness from kings,
    and everywhere there will be treachery. 9

O Muḥammad! The ninth time that I must return,
That ninth time I will come to take away forbearance *(sabūr).*
I will take away patience from the world,
    and all will be restless. 10

O Muḥammad! The tenth time that I must return,
That tenth time I will come to take away the Qur'ān.
I will take away the Qur'ān from the world,
    and nothing will remain. 11

No one in the universe will realize,
    all will be lost in ignorance *(jāhil)*;
No one will attain knowledge *(ʿilm),*
    all will perceive only the outer clothing;
Indeed, they will take as Lord *(ḵhudā)*
    those who wear saffron robes!
Know that these ten will come true in good time,
    and thus beware, O Brother!
When abundance, love, honor—these ten things—
    leave the world,
Recognize it to be an omen
    of the Day of Judgment *(qiyāmah).*
Pīr Shams Qalandar says:
    The turn of Qā'im Shāh[2] has come. 12

---

2. The king of Resurrection.

35

navarojanā dīna sohāmaṇā śrī harī kāyama śīkāra ramavā vana gayā

On the beautiful day of the New Year *(navroz)*,
The venerable Lord *(śrī hari)* Qā'im went to the forest to hunt.
The minds of his servants became forlorn
For their spirits lay at the Lord's *(hari)* feet. 1

Having bound our minds with love *(prīta)* to Śrī Qā'im,
For love of our Lord *(nara)*, we, too, proceeded to the forest.
In the forest, made beautiful by his presence,
we saw the venerable Sāheb.
Submitting our hearts *(to him)*, we stayed with our Lord *(deva)*. 2

Fortunate it was that our thoughts of the Sāheb were so strong,
For when we went to the forest to hunt
with the venerable Lord *(hari)* Qā'im,
He fulfilled all our countless wishes!
Our hearts were filled with love for our Lord *(deva)*. 3

Bind yourselves to the Lord *(hari)* with joyful love;
Soak yourselves in the steadfast dye [of love] for the Sāheb!
So bound were our thoughts to Lord *(nara)* Qā'im
He filled our laps with pearls and the treasures of truth *(sat)*. 4

We went on a merry picnic with our Sāheb,
And thus we gained great prosperity.
One who listens attentively to this wisdom *(ginān)*
That soul *(jīv)*, it will be saved. 5

When the soul attains ultimate union *(yukti)*
The spirit will sport on its own.
From love will rise the tasteful aroma of sandalwood,
And like a swan in a lake, [the soul] will frolic in ecstacy. 6

Shāh Ḳhalīl Allāh dwells there in the fort where he reigns;
Showing mercy upon me, he summoned
    myself, Fateh ʿAli Shāh, there.
Then he fulfilled all our countless hopes!
The Lord *(hari)* eternally manifests his Light *(nūr)*. 7

O Brother believers *(muʾmin)*, worship devotedly!
Shams says, listen, O you pious ones *(ṛṣi)*!
He who never forgets the virtues of the Sāheb,
His spirit will never suffer. 8

36

hamadīla khālaka allāha sohī vasejī jeṇe kāyama kudarata calāī

The universe is in my heart, and Allah resides within it;
It is He who eternally sustains nature.
Indeed, He is Allah! 1

Listen, O Scholar *(mullah)*! Listen, O Judge *(qāḍī)*!
It is He who gave rise to creation.
Indeed, He is Allah! 2

From this very clay, He fashioned the entire world!
So how do you tell the Muslim apart from the Hindu?
Indeed, He is Allah! 3

The Hindu is the one who goes on sixty-four pilgrimages;
The Muslim is the one who goes to the mosque.
Indeed, he is Allah! 4

But neither of them, Hindu nor Muslim, knows of my Shāh;
The Shāh sits within—he is the Immaculate *(nirañjan)*.
Indeed, he is Allah! 5

My heart is my prayer-mat, and Allah is my judge;
My body is my mosque.
Indeed, He is Allah! 6

Within myself, I sit and submit my prayers *(namāz)*;
What can a fool know of my worship *(tāʿat)*.
Indeed, He is Allah! 7

If [food] comes my way, I feast—if not, I fast;
Thus my mind remains fixed on my Sāheb.
Indeed, he is Allah! 8

A believer *(mu'min)* is he who comes to know all the secrets;
He walks upon the path of knowledge *('ilm)*.
Indeed, He is Allah! 9

Through study *(gyān)* and meditation *(dhyān)*
he comes to realize all things;
Searching and penetrating, he discovers all.
Indeed, He is Allah! 10

Says Pīr Shams, Listen, O my Brothers!
How can you cross to the other shore without the Pīr?
Indeed, He is Allah! 11

37

jaṇone bujo aṅ(h)ī pātra pīchāṇo guranara īyuṅ faramāyājī

Know! Realize! Recognize the one who has authority!
Thus commands *(farmān)* the Gurunara. 1

Nārāyaṇa assumed the form of ʿAlī;
Brother, his turn came along, too. 2

ʿAlī exists and has always existed;
This creation is his masterpiece. 3

In this day and age, serve Shāh Mahdī;
Do not be forgetful, O my Brother! 4

By virtue of King Prahlād, fifty million [were saved];
They profited by following the Guru's advice. 5

Seventy million [were saved] by King Hariścandra;
They attained a home in the City of Immortality *(amarāpurī)*. 6

Ninety million [were saved] by King Yudhiṣṭhira;
They remained ever close to the Eternal *(qāʾim)*. 7

One hundred and twenty million [were saved]
by Pīr Ṣadr al-Dīn;
The entire *jamāʿat* went with him. 8

Come together and contemplate the true Shāh;
Dispel all doubts from your mind! 9

Indeed, draw from this wisdom *(ginān)*
the essence of Immortality *(amṛta)*!
Pīr Shams has recited and conveyed it to you. 10

38

achaḍā khojo āṅhī achaḍā khojo lāgo te satake dhāgejī

Search for goodness here, search for goodness!
Attach yourself to the rope of truth *(sat)*. 1

Cleanse yourselves here, be pure in conduct!
Do not let dirt smear your soul. 2

As gold is tested by rubbing it against a touchstone,
So be sure to put your own self to the test. 3

As colorfast dye is applied to cloth,
So set your own hue from within yourself. 4

If you want to meet, then meet in secret[1];
But outside, perform sacrifice *(yajña)*. 5

The one whose cup the Guru fills,
That disciple drinks and drinks in ecstacy. 6

Pīr Shams, the Generous, recites this wisdom *(ginān)*;
Destroy the five[2] and hold steadfast to prayer. 7

---

1. lit. between the curtains.
2. That is, the five senses or the five evils of greed, lust, etc. See 1:1.

39

apanuṅ antara maya suṇīo re bande maya suṇīo

O Devotee! I heard this in a dream,
O yes, I heard it!
You cannot attain [liberation] whilst living in the world. 1

O Brother! Do trade and earn an honest living,
O yes, earn it!
For you will not return to this world again. 2

O Devotee! Give charity with your own hands,
O yes, your own!
Then you will not have to chew on your own fingers.[1] 3

O Devotee! Control your five,
O yes, your five [evils];
Then certainly you will attain the City of Immortality *(amarāpurī)*. 4

O Devotee! In the fifth month, the soul was cast forth,
O yes, it was cast;
In the sixth, it was enkindled with Light *(prakāś)*. 5

O Devotee! In the seventh, fire awakened the body,
O yes, awakened it;
In the eighth, the eyes witnessed the Lord *(ḳhudāvand)*. 6

O Devotee! In the ninth, the Satgur sent it on earth,
O yes, he sent it;
He took from it the promise *(kol)* to give tithe *(dasond)*. 7

O Devotee! Twelve years [the soul] lived as a child,
O yes, as a child;
At the age of twenty, it became a youth. 8

---

1. That is, you will never go hungry.

O Devotee! For forty years it did not pray
nor practice austerities;
Dealing in foolish things, it lost all. 9

Developing a taste [for pleasure],
it forgot the Swāmī;
In its greed, the foolish soul forgot its Mawlā. 10

The Satgur dyed a cloth
with colored dots;
He dyed it with many colors. 11

From the West, Mawlā will come, O yes,
the Beloved will come;
He, the true Lord *(ḳhudāvand)* will certainly come. 12

The fort at Cīnab is crooked,
O yes, it is crooked;
Know that a demon dwells in Yodhā. 13

Kaliṅga will be beheaded,
O yes, beheaded;
He will be spun into the middle of the sea. 14

O Devotee! Make your body a boat,
O yes, a boat;
Do business with it for the sake of the Shāh. 15

O Devotee! You will rise up to the thirty-three [gods],
O yes, rise up;
Once you have mastered the five [evils]. 16

Pīr Shams, the Defender of faith *(ghāzī)*,
has spoken and told;
Pīr Shams has recited this and made you listen. 17

40

pahelī prīta sāhebajīsuṅ kījīye evo amulakha ratana sambhārīne lījīye

The Fourteen Jewels (Cauda Ratna)

The first jewel is to love *(prīta)* the Sāheb;
Take such a priceless jewel and safeguard it. 1

The second jewel is to know the Guru's wisdom *(ginān)*
in one's heart;
O Brother, realize the true vision *(darśan)*
of your Shāh Pīr! 2

The third jewel is to think hard about
the spirit of religion *(dharma)*;
O Pious Ones *(munivar)*! Practice the precepts
of the True Faith *(sat dharma)*. 3

The fourth jewel is to be humble, patient,
and kindhearted;
Then, indeed, will you realize your Gurunara
as the true and just. 4

The fifth jewel is to serve *(sevā)* the Guru
as if he were your guest;
Felicitations to him who satisfies
the Guru's heart! 5

The sixth jewel is to serve one's mother and father
with great devotion;
O Brother, hold fast to such a priceless jewel
in the heart! 6

The seventh jewel is to heed the words of the ascetic
at your doorstep;
A believer *(mu'min)* listens to him and does not
turn him away empty-handed. 7

The eighth jewel is to make haste in helping
the poor and suffering;
Lovingly feed them grain and water,
and you will surely go to the Immortal City. 8

The ninth jewel is to keep pure one's trust
in Muḥammad and Allah;
Be firm and steadfast in faith *(imān)*,
and you will receive divine blessings. 9

The tenth jewel is not to miss
the three times of prayer *(duʿā)* , O believer!
Then alone will the Sāheb accept
your tithe *(dasond)* as legitimate. 10

The eleventh jewel is to place one's hopes in Allah,
to think before you speak and ask the Shāh for truth *(sat)*!
Injure none with words nor be greedy, for greed is hell's abyss!
Always beg the Shāh for goodness. 11

The twelfth jewel is never to afflict children with pain,
for surely God *(brahma)* comes in their form!
Nor be needlessly ferocious towards ant or beast!
As the moth extinguishes itself in flame,
so kill your ego while alive. 12

The thirteenth jewel, for one who has attained
the True Path *(sat mārga)*,
Is to deliver the body into flames for the sake of the soul;
Just as King Hariścandra, Queen Tārā,
Prince Locana, and Rohidās
Gave themselves up for the sake of truth. 13

The fourteenth jewel is to be constantly vigilant,
O Saintly Ones *(munivar)*!
Those who, in the name of Allah, perform virtues
and give with satisfaction,
Ahead, such pious ones will reap abundant fruit
and enjoy immensely.
These fourteen jewels Pīr Shams has made manifest
by relating them to you. 14

41

tyāṅ duladula ghoḍe sāmī rājo caḍaśe momanakī dīla purī

Yes sir! There the Swāmī Rājā mounts the horse Duldul;
He grants the believer *(mu'min)* his heart's desire. 1

Yes sir! There he refreshes the horses of the army
With the full waters of the Ganges. 2

Yes sir! There a nightingale sings, and a hammock swings;
The [army] rides before the wind. 3

Yes sir! There he shakes up seven lakes;
The ground cannot support his weight. 4

Yes sir! There in Yodhā is the brave bowholder Bhīma;
Fearless, all treasures are his. 5

Yes sir! There three hundred and thirty bowmen climb;
Arjuna's army is endless. 6

Yes sir! There Sahadeva and Nakula are truly praiseworthy;
They destroy the mountain with their weapons. 7

Yes sir! There King Prahlād delivered fifty million;
Hariścandra delivered seventy [million]. 8

Yes sir! There King Yudhiṣṭhira delivered ninety million;
He also rescued the five Pāṇḍavas. 9

Yes sir! There King Yudhiṣṭhira delivered ninety million;
Twelve [million] attained the Lord *(ḳhudāvand)*. 10

Yes sir! There a countless million march in the Shāh's army;
Their endless limits cannot be fathomed. 11

Yes sir! There five hundred thousand came
with Lord *(īśvar)* Gorakha;
They all came blowing trumpets. 12

Yes sir! There seventy-thousand mounted with Ḥusayn;
The entire world was shaken with rumbling noise. 13

Yes sir! There about nine hundred million and fifty-six
Of the castes of Medhā and Ḍamara found salvation. 14

Yes sir! There thirty-two million of the Kīnara caste ascended;
They all attained the shining Lord *(nara)*. 15

Yes sir! There twenty-five million blow horns for the Shāh;
Nine [million] are descendents of the Nāgas. 16

Yes sir! There former armies walk around the Shāh;
Six hundred and forty thousand attain union. 17

Yes sir! There the Shāh advances four arm-lengths
on his wooden slippers;
He slays the demon Kaliṅga. 18

Yes sir! There Queen Surjā warns, "Listen, Kāliṅga!
ʿAlī has come with a great army." 19

Yes sir! There comes ʿAlī from the West to the East;
And Yodhā meets its end. 20

Yes sir! There the Shāh as Fish *(Matsya)* dried up the ocean;
He killed the demon Śaṅkhā. 21

Yes sir! There the Shāh twisted the devil Śaṅkhā's head;
He prevented him from stealing the Veda. 22

Yes sir! There as Tortoise *(Kaurabha)* he slew
Madhu and Kaiṭabha;
He set them on fire from behind. 23

Yes sir! There the Shāh churned the seven lakes;
With his own eyes, he used snakes to churn them. 24

Yes sir! There the Shāh took form as the Boar *(Varāha)*;
The Shāh killed the demon Muḍa. 25

Yes sir! There he rescued King Prahlād who saved fifty million;
He destroyed the demon Hiraṇyakaśipu. 26

Yes sir! There the many colored Shāh sat
as the Dwarf *(Vāmana)*;
Stepping on King Bali's head, he banished him to hell. 27

Yes sir! There the Shāh prisoned Sahasrārjuna in a cage;
He, the Lord, was known as Parśurām. 28

Yes sir! There in the form of Rāma, the Shāh recovered Sītā;
He killed the ten-headed demon Rāvaṇa. 29

Yes sir! There the Shāh slew the ten-headed Rāvaṇa;
He gave sovereignty to Vibhiśaṇa. 30

Yes sir! There as Kṛṣṇa, the Shāh slew the serpent;
He relieved the weight on the lotuses. 31

Yes sir! There his eighth form was the child Nanda Govinda;
He killed the demon Kaṃsa. 32

Yes sir! There the Shāh became manifest
in the form of Buddha;
He saved the five Pāṇḍavas. 33

Yes sir! There he rescued King Yudhiṣṭhira
who saved ninety million;
He slew the demon Duryodhana. 34

Yes sir! There the Shāh has now become manifest
in his tenth form;
He is known by the name and form *(rūpa)* of ʿAlī. 35

Yes sir! There he rides on Duldul,
and the trumpets are blown;
By a mere puff, he can cause a mountain to crumble. 36

Yes sir! There before the world is the Shāh's sword Ḍhulfikār;
So brightly does the Light *(teja)* of ʿAlī shine forth. 37

Yes sir! There six thousand instruments will play for the Shāh;
ʿAlī will come on to the field. 38

Yes sir! There ʿAlī will come with Ḍhulfikār from the West;
No one will dare challenge him face to face. 39

Yes sir! There his horse Duldul will gallop,
and the earth will shake;
When ʿAlī will come on to the field. 40

Yes sir! There the serpent Vāsukī will tremble
in the seventh hell;
The ground cannot support his weight. 41

Yes sir! There when he sees the mustache-faced devil *(dāṇav)*;
Yodhā will have an earthquake. 42

Yes sir! There the Shāh's weapons will move
faster than the wind;
They will tear asunder the heads of the demons *(daitya)*. 43

Yes sir! There, Pīr Shams says,
"Listen O Gathering of believers *(mu'min)*!
You will have a vision *(dīdār)* of the Shāh." 44

Yes sir! There Pīr Shams, the Qalandar of ʿAlī, says:
The sky will thunder with the Shāh's countless[1] weapons!
The Sāheb of innumerable wanderers will mount his horse,
And nothing will be able to arrest his speed. 45

1. lit. sixty-four times eighty-six pairs of weapons.

42

dhana dhana sāmī rājā tuṅ sīrajaṇahāra sāṅhījī

Blessed *(dhanya)*, indeed, are you,
O Swāmī Rājā, O Beloved Creator *(sirjaṇahār)*!
From utter darkness, my Shāh has created the world. 1

Prophet Muḥammad was beloved to my Shāh;
He went to reside in Heaven *(svarga)* with the Lord. 2

From his sweat, my Beloved Lord *(saiyāṅ)*
brought forth four angels *(firastā)*;
Upon his command, they brought clay,
and he fashioned the figure of man. 3

Beholding the angels, the clay began to tremble;
Indeed, O Beloved Lord! The clay began to weep! 4

My Beloved Lord, the Shāh, commanded:
"Weep not, O Clay!"
Water was brought, and the Beloved Lord
kneaded [the clay] with yeast. 5

Having kneaded it with yeast, the Beloved Lord
made the body of man;
Then, from the seventh heaven
he ordered a soul *(ruh)* for it. 6

Infusing the soul into the body,
the Beloved Lord said: "This is your dwelling!"
The soul looked up,
and it saw only darkness ahead. 7

"No, my Beloved Lord,
    I do not want to go in there!"
The Beloved Lord said:
    "As I have confined you, so I can set you free." 8

The soul then made this promise
    to the King *(rājā)*;
Give the tithe *(dasond)*, O Brother—
    religion *(dharma)* will rescue you. 9

When the man was born into the world, he became neglectful;
Thus, whatever he earned in the world was surely a waste. 10

Gaining only limited merit, the man's time was up;
Like the lamp whose wick goes out, so did the man's life. 11

His brothers came together and built him a case;
They fetched some water and sprinkled it on the man's body. 12

They draped the man's limbs in the finest of garments;
Having thus covered him, they returned to their homes. 13

They brought the man his favorite foods;
His maternal family came and began to strap the man's thighs. 14

The angels took account of all the good deeds of the man;
The dwelling of the Sāheb was in a land far off. 15

Swāmī Rājā bestows blissful Paradise *(bahiśta)*
    to all the true ones;
This essence-filled wisdom *(ginān)*
    has been recited by Pīr Shams. 16

43

suno suno bhāīve momano esā kalajuga, esā kalajuga āyā

Listen, O Brothers, O Believers *(mu'min)*!
The final age of *kalyug* has come. 1

We have sat around for many days—
now the last ones have arrived. 2

If you can think, reflect upon this,
O Brothers, O Believers! 3

Be steadfast in religious practices *(niyam)*
and earn abundant profits. 4

The turn of ʿAlī Shāh has come
in whose religion *(dīn)* there are multitudes. 5

The Swāmī Rājā will demand an account,
so keep your mind *(jīv)* resolute. 6

Without the Pīr, there is no heaven *(bahiśta)*—
know this for sure, O Brother! 7

Listen to what the Pīr says, O Brothers,
and always bear it in mind. 8

Night and day, O Brothers, recite the *japa*
and realize the Creator's word *(śabda)*. 9

On clear ground, sit all of you in union
and together dwell upon it. 10

ʿAlī Shāh's boat is, indeed, blessed
and has unlimited places in it. 11

Whoever clambers into this boat,
he too becomes one of us. 12

When the vision *(darśan)* of ʿAlī Shāh is attained,
the mind will frolic in joy. 13

A believer of the True Path *(satpanth)*
knows the religious precepts *(ācār)*. 14

One whose heart has no religion *(dharma)*,
surely that one is a fake. 15

Pīr Shams relates the facts as they are—
know that they are the truth *(sāc)*! 16

44

uñcathī āyo bande nīca kīyuṅ dhīyāve

O Brother! You came from a place on high,
why dwell upon the low?
O Comrade! Your stay is but four days long,
why accumulate untruth?
What kind of fruit can sin yield,
yes indeed, what type of fruit?

Refrain:
O Fellow, let your arrogance not delude you—
walk humbly and die!
Beg for the Messenger's *(rasūl)* intercession,
for the Prophet's *(nabī)* mercy!
O Brother, fear evil, yes indeed,
be fearful of falsehood!
Let your arrogance not lead you astray—
walk humbly and die! 1

You came [into the world] naked, you will go back under covers!
What you gain in one moment, why must you lose it in the next?
Why commit sin and depart from True Religion *(satdharma)*? 2
[Refrain]

Those who discard religion*(dīn)* and engage in disputes;
Those who shun the path and stand with the sinners *(pāpī)*;
By their own doing, their souls have fallen into hell *(dozaḳh)*. 3
[Refrain]

Only those brave few will persist in fulfilling this path *(panth)*;
Prophet Muḥammed related what he himself had witnessed;
Pīr Shams preaches the true knowledge *(ʿilm)*. 4
[Refrain]

45

āyelo āyelo pīrala āyelo hāre allāha analathe śahera gazanīyāre

The Pīr came, yes he came, hay Allah, he came!
From Anala he came to the city of Ghazni, O Allah! 1

Strolling, he wandered about the city, hay Allah, he wandered!
Emnā invited him to rest at her home, O Allah! 2

We will fetch different kinds of grapes [for you], hay Allah!
And thrash pippal leaves near the water-well, O Allah! 3

The earthen pot was raw and so was its string, hay Allah!
Yet she went to the well to fetch some water, O Allah! 4

My pot did not burst nor did my string break, hay Allah!
Pīr Shams is in my house as my guest, O Allah! 5

My pot did not burst nor did my string break, hay Allah!
Emnā, that is due to your faith *(dharma)*, O Allah! 6

Listen, O Sister-in-law, please listen my Sister-in-law, hay Allah!
I will give you the two gold bangles on my wrist, O Allah! 7

To hell with your gold-minted bracelets, hay Allah!
My little tongue twitches with intrigue, O Allah! 8

Listen, O Mother! You my dear Mother, listen to me, hay Allah!
Emnā has brought impurity upon our house, O Allah! 9

Listen, O son Hariścandra! Listen son Hariścandra, hay Allah!
Throw Emnā out, [yes, throw her out], O Allah! 10

With Huramal in her arms and Kuramal[1] at her side, hay Allah!
Emnā was driven out, [yes, she was thrown out], O Allah! 11

---

1. Her two children.

With a bit of corn in the fold of her *sāri*, a mere handful, hay Allah!
She left along with her roasting oven, O Allah! 12

Baking and roasting, the corn began to jump and pop, hay Allah!
O Emnā, this is due to the strength of your faith, O Allah! 13

The dry lake swelled up, splashing waves of water, hay Allah!
When her lovely children cried out in thirst, O Allah! 14

The dry lake swelled up, splashing waves of water, hay Allah!
O Emnā, that was due to your [steadfast] faith, O Allah! 15

Pīr Shams said, "Listen, O Believers *(mu'min)*, hay Allah!
Emnā was thus triumphant over Kulicanda, O Allah!" 16

46

lahāvo to āṅhī loṇīyo e suṇo bhāīyamajī ho yārājī

Hear, O Brother! Listen, O Friend!
    If you want profit, gain it here!
O Friend, give your heart some wisdom,
    yes [enlighten] yourself. 1

Hear, O Brother! Listen, O Friend!
    Give up your heart here sincerely;
O Friend, be like the firebird[1] that attained
    the greatest heights. 2

Hear, O Brother! Listen, O Friend!
    Spread religion *(dīn)* while you are here;
O Friend, be like Vimras, yes, your brother
    believer *(mu'min)* Vimras. 3

Hear, O Brother! Listen, O Friend!
    What did he do for his own sake!
O Friend, he cut off his head and sacrificed it,
    yes, he chopped his head off. 4

Hear, O Brother! Listen, O Friend!
    Crush all the mind's desires here.
O Friend, then you will attain the Immortal City *(amarāpurī)*,
    yes, the Immortal City. 5

Hear, O Brother! Listen, O Friend!
    This body is but a stranger;
O Friend, you will leave it in a couple of days,
    yes, in a couple of days. 6

---

1. *anaḷa paṅkhī:* Allusion to an imaginary bird that caught fire as it approached heaven and from whose ashes a new bird was born.

Hear, O Brother! Listen, O Friend!
Put your foot here and follow [me]!
O Friend, be like the camel who obeys the string,
yes, that tugs at its nose-ring. 7

Hear, O Brother! Listen, O Friend!
Fall into line here and walk!
O Friend, walk along the path on which
the Guru leads the believers, yes, walk. 8

Hear, O Brother! Listen, O Friend!
Pay heed to these words *(śabda)* in this lifetime!
O Friend, Pīr Shams recites a prayer *(vinantī)*,
yes O Believers, a supplication! 9

47

jāke pāchama dīśe me khaṇḍa īrākamāṅhe sentara dīpa mīṅjāra

Westward in the land of Irāq in the peninsula of Svetadvīpa
A decorated home welcomes you with many colorful delights!
That is where my dear Master *(dhaṇī)* reigns.

Refrain:
Flee! Flee, O demon Kaliṅga!
My Master *(dhaṇī)* is coming from the West *(paścim)*.
Ninety battalions will be crushed just under his horse's shoe!
Alas! When your army is conquered
before your very own face,
Who will rescue you then, I do not know. 1

From the West will beat the claps of many drums—
They will beat to signal the thunders of war!
My Shāh will cry out his orders
across the three worlds *(tribhovan)*;
They will instantly herald him as the Sultān. 2
[Refrain]

Harken! Horses vigorous in step and chariots the speed of wind!
And elephants all beautifully decked out for the Shāh.
Wielding thirty-six weapons, the man who is Nakalaṅkī,
will mount,
And in fourteen worlds will resound the hail: Victory! Victory! 3
[Refrain]

Witness the nine Nāths, the eighty-four Siddhas,
And the different types of Jogīs. They will all cry, Bravo! Bravo!
Ajīyā and Vajīyā will wave the great leather fans,
And Prince Kamalā will wear the crown on his head. 4
[Refrain]

The trumpets and conch shells will blow many a sound,
And the nine continents will fall into destruction.
A hundred thousand braves will march on the path
of my Shāh.
In this manner will they forge ahead. 5
[Refrain]

O Queen! I have three times as many forts all
in splendid shape!
Indeed, within their walls the gods *(devatā)* earn their living.
The god of torrential rain clouds replenishes my water-well,
And the sun-god fuels the cooking pots in my kitchen. 6
[Refrain]

O King! What! Are you going to contest and challenge Him?
Him, the Protector *(dātār)* of the souls *(jīv)* of three worlds?
Him, the Master *(swāmī)* of the fourteen realms?
Better that you serve *(sevā)* Him and gain [salvation]! 7
[Refrain]

O Queen! I, who can revive the dead and who reveres
our ancestors *(pitṛ)*!
I, who can feed straw to wooden horses! [I should serve Him?]
My army has more than a million strong,
nay infinite is its number.
By contrast, a trifle, indeed, is the army of your Shāh! 8
[Refrain]

O King! So you can revive the dead, and you revere
the ancestors!
But your battalions—they are naive, inexperienced!
When my Shāh mounts before their eyes
and performs the awesome,
The true and pure amongst them will stand transfixed. 9
[Refrain]

O Queen! You eat, drink, and make merry at the expense
of my wealth.
And then you dare to swear,
"My Shāh is this, and my Shāh is that!"
Oh! Is there such a one here in this city of Cīnab
Who can bring my Queen Surjādevī back to her senses? 10
[Refrain]

O King! For ages and ages I have kept on telling you
That you, O Kaliṅga, have been performing evil deeds!
You paid no heed in the three ages that have passed;
But now, in this fourth one, the Sāheb will take account. 11
[Refrain]

O Queen! Go tell this talk of yours to your dear Lord *(deva)*!
Listen to me, O Queen Surjādevī!
You live and reside in my city—
Yet you dare to speak to me about some foreigner? 12
[Refrain]

The demon *(daitya)* climbed his mount and his troops
fell into sequence
There in the city of Cīnab.
Then, the Lord Brahma descended;
Presently, He is the tenth *avatār*. 13
[Refrain]

O King! My Shāh will take account of each and every grain,
And upon it the Satgur will put his seal!
By the grace of the Lord *(nara)*, Pīr Shams said,
The Shāh will give sovereignty to the pious *(rīkhīsar)*. 14
[Refrain]

48

hathī hathī parabata tolande bande samudra ghuṇṭa bhare

One who can cradle mountains in a hand
and swallow the sea in a gulp;
O Brother, even one as powerful as this returns to clay—
So of what use is your arrogance?

Refrain:
O negligent Brother! Each moment do worship,
for this world will pass!
O miserly Brother! Each moment do worship,
for this world will pass! 1

O Brother! Beware not to put off till tomorrow
what must be done today!
[For, when death strikes], not even an eye can blink—
And the morsel of food, it remains uneaten in the mouth. 2
[Refrain]

O Brother! Those in whose company you merrily talked,
[when death came]
Not a moment longer did you let them linger;
On your shoulders you carried them.
O Brother, you buried them and turned them over to the grave. 3
[Refrain]

O Brother! Queen Tārā had all her heart's desire;
Indeed, she displayed around her neck
jewels worth nine million! But alas!
In the town square of Kāśī, King Hariścandra
had to sell his own wife. 4
[Refrain]

Pīr Shams, the Generous Guru, uttered this wisdom *(ginān)*!
O Shāh! Ferry all those [present] to the other shore *(pār)*.
O Believers *(mu'min)*, if you give the tithe *(dasond)*,
you will attain the other shore.
[Refrain]

49

pīra shamasa kahe suno bhāī momano ane kahuṅ āda uṇādakī vāṇī

Pīr Shams says, Listen, O Brothers! Listen, O Believers!
I am telling a tale concerning beginningless beginnings!
Thirty-six ages *(yug)* of eighty-four times four,
Fourteen years of eighteen hours, [this long time ago]—
My Shāh exclaimed the sacred syllable "aum!"
Lo! The dark depths of the sky bear witness to this. 1

Countless aeons had already gone by before that,
Aeons whose magnitude no one can fathom.
Then, the Unique Nirañjan was totally alone,
And there were no sacred words of the Vedas. 2

When God *(ḳhudāvand)* cried out, "So be it!"
He summoned the Pīr close to Him.
O Brothers, O Believers *(mu'min)*, listen to this account!
I tell only what I have experienced firsthand. 3

In the seventeenth age at the twenty-fourth hour,
The Shāh lifted an egg and held it.
My Sāheb exclaimed: "See how I create!" 4

Whereupon he burst the egg and made earth and sky!
Next he fashioned wind and water;
In a wink, he created in pairs, eighty-four lakh souls *(jīv)*!
Such is the majesty of my Sāheb. 5

He gave birth to the speech of sixteen castes;
Sāheb guided each and every soul to our path.
The Lord *(ḳhudāvand)* gave four messages,
Listen, O you pious *(munivar)* Brothers! 6

The earth and sky heard the first message
And thus earth and sky became fixed.
The seven domes readily lifted up into place,
Just with a single glance from my Sāheb. 7

When the Sāheb turned his sight towards the earth and sky,
He derived satisfaction from His creation.
The second message was heard by the earth;
It came into the hands of the Hindus. 8

The Hindus worshipped *(pūjā)* stones and made offerings
to them;
They fashioned idols *(mūrti)* and established them.
They heard the message but fathomed not its secret;
And thus lost the profits of this life. 9

Worshipping stones has no meaning, no value.
Listen to me, O my pious Brothers!
The secret *(bhed)* of the third message became manifest;
That magic appeared in the Qur'ān. 10

They read the Qur'ān, but they did not comprehend it;
They did not realize its inner secrets.
What the Veda says is all true,
But to abide by it is a difficult task. 11

The Lord *(khudāvand)* then gave the fourth message,
This time it was sent through the Pīr's, the Guru's mouth.
The Atharva Veda became manifest through him,
Listen all of you, O my pious Brothers! 12

The fourth age *(kalyug)* will turn out to be rough times;
Those who lie are celebrated and glorified,
While there is no place for the modest!
Alas! the ignoble stand at the entrances of power. 13

Donkeys will bear burdens meant for elephants,
Pīr Shams, the Satgur, predicts this very thing.
You will encounter much slander and backbiting,
People will come together just to boast. 14

The upright will be called wicked,
And the wicked will be paid great respect.
But ultimately, truth will be victorious,
So Pīr Shams has said. 15

Indeed, [severe] punishment awaits the deceivers,
When the end of time *(ākhira)* arrives.
Sāheb will shout to the sun,
And it will begin to approach, O Brother. 16

You will see it then, the hundred-eyed sun,
Once Allah has issued His command *(farmān)*.
Those creatures who were up to playing their tricks,
They will stand up and weep. 17

The Shāh who is Mawlā will himself be the judge *(qāḍī)*;
He is the Sāheb who sustains the nine continents by his glance.
They will plead to him, "O our Shāh, O our Shāh!"
But he will hear no one, says Pīr Shams. 18

The Pīrs and Messengers *(paygambar)* will stand trembling,
No plea at all may they put before the Sāheb.
The Sāheb's robes will begin to shine with a dazzling Light *(jyoti)*,
Thus relates Pīr Shams. 19

When the Sāheb examines their sins and their merits,
The earth and the sky will begin to shake, O Brother!
God will ask for an accounting of each and every particle,
Listen to me, O you my pious Brothers! 20

He will set the evildoers apart,
Yielding the faithful under the care of my ʿAlī.
Pīr Shams Qalandar said this:
O God! None can comprehend your infinitude. 21

Blessed souls will indeed live in Paradise *(bahiśta)* itself,
That is, those who win the favor of Pīr Shams.
Pīr Shams says, listen, O Brothers, O Believers!
I have told you a tale about beginningless beginnings. 22

50

ajaba jamānā suṇo momana bhāījī kalajuga āyā khoṭā jire

O Brother Believers *(mu'min)*! Listen to a story of bizarre times!
Kalyug, the age of iniquity, has come. 1

Disciples *(murīd)* will fight with their spiritual masters *(pīr)*,
Sons will beat up their fathers. 2

Be intelligent and clever, O Brother Believers, beware!
The last [moment] comes close. 3

The times of the last age *(kalyug)* are troublesome, my brothers;
Those who tell lies gain in popularity. 4

Thus, the honest, too, will abandon truth;
Ripened fruits will get parched and dry up. 5

No rainwater will fall from the sky;
No crops will flourish upon the earth. 6

Mother and daughter will quarrel together;
Each will swear that the other is a step-wife. 7

Though they eat, drink, and sleep together,
Friends will turn into each others' foes. 8

The mother-in-law will rise to fetch drinking water,
While the daughter-in-law sits and eats her meal. 9

The master will be oppressed by his servant;
Old man, times such as these will come! 10

Two brothers will fight one another,
They will tear each other apart. 11

Wives will batter their husbands,
Old man, see the spectacle before your very own eyes! 12

Hindus and Muslims will meet each other,
They will sit and eat their meals together. 13

Mullahs and Brahmins will join to slaughter cows;
At every turn they will fight and quarrel. 14

Calamity will befall the heads of the destitute,
Yet [the rich] will clutch at their own wealth. 15

Know this is *Kalyug*, such are the times;
Old man, such [terrible] times have arrived. 16

Rare indeed will be that pious ascetic,
Who leaves home when there is a squabble. 17

Alas! There will be no place for the virtuous,
And the corrupt will have positions in government. 18

When all is ablaze the rains will pour,
Water will flood the earth everywhere. 19

One day, a cyclone of great force will burst forth,
Mountains and hills will fly asunder. 20

Upon the head of the world will be sin,
Old man, accordingly, it will be judged. 21

These quarrelsome people have no idea
What kind of judgment this will be. 22

Waters of the seven seas will drain away;
And all water-life will perish. 23

Sun and moon, both will be hidden;
There will be utter and complete darkness. 24

Forts will shake, and their towers will topple over;
The whole earth will be immersed in water. 25

In between the distance of two furlongs,
Only one light will burn. 26

The entire world will be destroyed,
No one will remain upon it. 27

Only the people of Allah will remain;
There will be only one God. 28

As near as the span of a hand
Is the kingdom of our Sāheb. 29

Pīr Shams Qalandar related all this
About the amazing powers of our Sāheb. 30

51

haka tuṅ pāka tuṅ bādaśāha maherabāna bī alī tuṅhī tuṅ

You are the Truth *(haqq)*, you the Holy *(pāk)*, the King *(bādshāh)*!
O ʿAlī! Indeed, you alone are the Benevolent *(meharbān)*! 1

You are the Lord *(rabb)*! You are the Merciful *(rehmān)*!
O ʿAlī! Indeed, you alone are the first and final Judge *(qāḍī)*! 2

You orginated, and you brought forth!
O ʿAlī! Indeed, you alone are the Creator *(sirjaṇhār)*! 3

Maker of water and earth, the roots of Creation,
O ʿAlī! Indeed, yours alone is the [final] command *(hukam)*! 4

Pīr Shams speaks out love for you;
O ʿAlī! Indeed! I am your devoted servant *(bando)*! 5

52

veda vacana guru taṇā te samajo sācā soya

Understand as truth *(sāc)* the sacred speech *(veda-vacan)*
of the Guru!
Without the truth, he will not come,
but the wicked do not understand him. 1

The wicked do not find the Shāh,
whereas the upright recognize the Satgur;
Keep the sacred speech of the Satgur
fixed firmly in the heart. 2

They heed not what the Guru says
nor believe anybody else's word;
They will remain alone and abandoned,
deprived of the Guru's company. 3

The assembly *(jamāʿat)* sets up the water-pot *(ghaṭ)*,
and numerous folk congregate;
Only a few recognize the Lord *(nara)*—
the rest are engrossed in worldly affairs. 4

All meet their family and friends
remaining oblivious to matters concerning Truth *(sat)*;
All drink holy water *(pāval)*,
but none realize the Guru's essence *(ḍhāt)*. 5

Few understand the *ghaṭ* ceremony
and the stature of the water-pot;
The virgin of the universe[1] will drink it
and wed Śyāma, Lord of the three worlds. 6

---

1. *viśva-kuṃvārī:* lit. virgin of the universe.

She is called Bībī Fāṭimah—
know that she is the virgin of the universe;
Pīr Shams says: the *ghaṭ* was established
by the order *(farmān)* of the Shāh. 7

53

jyāṅ ghaṭa thāpanā dharama taṇī ane bījānuṅ nahīṅ haśe nāma

When the *ghaṭ* is established according to religion *(dharma)*,
and no other name is taken;
The world will then fill with Light and [you will] attain
the ranks of the immortal. 1

[1]For the sake of the True Religion *(sat dharma)*,
Draupadī endured suffering;
She did not surrender her chastity,
and thus she acquired every happiness *(sukha)*. 2

The *satī* did not forsake her purity,
and her hero came to meet her;
She fixed her concentration [upon him]
when the devil tried to disrobe her. 3

None is superior to Draupadī upon whom posterity
may shower such great praise;
But today whoever performs the *ghaṭ* ceremony,
know that one to be a *satī*. 4

Various gods *(deva)* and spirits *(yakśa)* preside—
Vimras and Surbhāṇ, too, are present;
Such times have come to pass today,
but no one knows it. 5

The *Medha* deities await him
whose stay is in *Kalyug*;
In that pot *(kumbha)* is the holy water *(pāval)*[2]—
we brought it one night. 6

---

1. Note vs. 2–7 are repeated in Ginān 65.
2. Note that the holy water is either called *niyam* or *pāval*. *Nīyam* may be

Twenty-three million *Kinnar* deities come
to practice the religion *(dharma)*;
They, too, come with this intention,[3]
says Pīr Shams. 7

related to Guj. *nīm*—a religious vow, custom, or rule or Per. *niʿmah* and Hin. *niyāmat*—blessing, boon, bounty; also see Hin. *niyam*—rule, law. *pāval* may be connected with the Guj. verb *pāvuṅ*—to drink or cause to drink; Guj. *pāvan*—pure, sacred, or sanctifying; or to the Guj. *pāvalī*—old silver coin (coins are offered during the *ghaṭ* ceremony); or perhaps to the Guj. *pyālī*—a small cup (in which the holy water is served).

3. That is, to partake in the *ghaṭ* ceremony.

54

shāha vīśava kuṅvārī paraṇaśe paraṇe trībhovara nātha

Shāh, the Lord of the three worlds *(tribhovar)*,
    will marry the virgin of the universe;
On that day will the *ghaṭ* be established,
    and the deceitful will not come near. 1

Concentrate upon the Omniscient!
    Our dwelling is in this world *(saṃsār)*;
Recognize Vimras and Surbhāṇ—
    they are our disciples *(dāsa)*. 2

Our disciples have been with us,
    indeed, since time immemorial;
These devotees *(bhakta)* will come to the world in *Kalyug*—
    know this for certain. 3

Where the *ghaṭ* ceremony takes place,
    incense will be passed around;
Many lamps will be lit,
    and there we will make our dwelling. 4

In *Kalyug* many will perform the rite
    of the holy water *(amṛta)* in the pot *(kumbha)*;
But only where my devotees *(bhakta)* are present
    will it be fully established. 5

Where such a *ghaṭ* is established,
    and devotees perform their devotions,
Pīr Shams says, there they will attain
    the abode of heaven *(vaikuṇṭha)*. 6

55[1]

veda māṅhe ema lakhīyā cīṇaba nagarīmāṅ jāṇa

In the scripture *(veda)*, it is written thus:
Know that in the city of Cīnab!
Everybody lives there and so, indeed,
does Queen Surjādevī. 1

Queen Surjādevī practices recollection *(smaraṇa)*,
and serves at the Guru's feet;
Everyone performs the *ghaṭ* ceremony,
and all go to drink holy water *(pāval)*. 2

Thirty-three million gods *(devatā)*
dwell in this world of rebirth *(saṃsār)*;
Among them are Vimras and Surbhāṇ,
but no one recognizes them. 3

All of them, both the gods *(deva)* and
the devils *(dāṇava)* inhabit human bodies;
Just as you recognize the worldly,
[try to] distinguish them from the crowd. 4

Call those souls *(jīv)* true
in whom there is no impurity;
They who live reflecting upon the Guru's wisdom *(ginān)*
will see the sham. 5

In this world of rebirth *(saṃsār)*,
they construct games from which there is no refuge;
They speak and act one thing
and then go and commit evil deeds. 6

---

1. See *Joḍilo* 6, Ginān 65, vss. 7–13.

Those who behold our scripture *(veda)*
    and step with the right foot;
They will attain the company of the Guru,
    so says Pīr Shams. 7

56[1]

dunīyā prīta na kījīye ane rākho dīnasuṅ neha

Do not cherish the world;
    instead, foster love for religion *(dīn)*;
The world lasts but four days
    so why not surrender oneself to religion? 1

In this world of rebirth *(saṃsār)*,
    be single-minded and be not deceived;
Perform the true *japa* and austerities *(tapa)*,
    and you will join the Sāheb. 2

Realize the temple is in the mind, and, indeed,
    in the mind is the Lord *(deva)*;
Perform the rite of *kumbha*[2] in the mind,
    and surely you will meet the Satgur. 3

Construct a plain tent
    and make your dwelling within it;
There the pure and chaste *(satī)* should congregate
    and fulfill their heart's desire. 4

They are the pure and noble
    whose concentration *(dhyāna)* is fixed on the Sāheb;
They are the truly pure *(satī)*
    whose minds and hearts are blissful. 5

All their hopes are fulfilled,
    and the Guru's words *(vāc)* come true;
Their desires come to pass—
    they are living proofs for the world. 6

---

1. See *Joḍilo* 7, Ginān 66, vss. 1–7.
2. lit. the vessel; that is, the *ghaṭ* ceremony.

Man and woman are one and the same
  though their bodies are distinct;
All walk and talk alike;
  those on the path of religion *(dharma)* are equal. 7

Attain the permanent kingdom *(rāj)*
  by repeating the *japa* with single mind;
Then ahead will you gain kingship *(bādshāhī)*,
  Guru Shams says so himself. 8

57

satapantha voharī vīrā alagā na rahīye

O Brother! The True Path *(satpanth)* that you have taken—
stray not from it;
Take in the Light *(nūr)* and speak no falsehood
with your mouth. 1

He who created [all things]
and He who brought them forth;
Alas, not for even a moment have you paid heed
to that Sāheb. 2

Forever saying, "Mine, it is mine,"
you have squandered away your life;
This priceless[1] form of humankind,
you have debased it. 3

Come hither, O my merchants
of pearls!
Trading in pearls, yet you have missed
the most precious thing. 4

The world is mistaken,
it knows not the real essence;
It recognizes not the Imām,
the matchless Nirañjan. 5

Pīr Shams' advice is:
Conduct yourselves carefully!
For when you are reborn again,
you may not gain the human form. 6

1. lit. a form that is as precious as a gem.

This body of yours
    is like a bouquet of flowers;
There is no way
    to save it [from withering away]. 7

Having seen the true authority,
    give charity *(dāna)* and do good deeds *(puṇya)*!
O Brother! Reap the fruits of worship *(pūjā)*
    [whilst you can]. 8

O Brother! Give charity and do good
    with your own hands;
At the end of time *(antakāla)*,
    this [merit] will accompany your soul *(jīv)*. 9

Pīr Shams has spoken
    such wisdom *(ginān)*;
Identifying the pious ones *(rīkhīsar)*,
    the Sāheb withdrew the curtain. 10

With curtains withdrawn,
    their eyes met those of the Sāheb;
Whereupon their eighty-four lakh[2] cycles
    of rebirth *(ferā)* dissolved! 11

---

2. One lakh is one hundred thousand.

58[1]

abadhu jugata jola santoṣa pātra karo ane ḍaṇḍā karo vīcāra

O Ascetic![2] Make the world your sack,
 satisfaction your bowl!
Let discernment be your rod!
Don the earrings of humility and kindness!
Let wisdom *(ginān)* be your sustenance.

 Refrain:
 O Ascetic! He in this world is a *jogī*
 In whose mind is no other [save God]. 1

O Ascetic! Knowledge *(ginān)* is my Guru,
Renounce the senses and apply ash![3]
Believing in its truth *(sat),*
 meditate on the True Religion *(sat dharma)*!
Then ascetic you are a real *jogī.* 2
[Refrain]

O Ascetic! With concentration as your rod,
Still the mind and arrest the moon and sun![4]
Then will the *suṣumaṇā* string begin to play,
Such a mystery is the portion of but a few. 3
[Refrain]

---

1. See Ginān 78 which is identical. Perhaps a printing error.
2. *abadhu:* Guj. *avadhūta*—ascetic, renunciate.
3. *bhabhūtā:* Guj. *bhabhūtī*—sacred ash, ash from sacrificial fire; cf. Hin. *vibhūti.*
4. Symbols in Tantric meditation and Kuṇḍalinī yoga.

O Ascetic! Abandon all your sins—
Bathe in the crossing of the three rivers *(triveṇi)*
And strike up the unstruck sound *(anāhata nāda)*;
Pīr Shams says: Die when still alive,
    and you will not be reborn. 4

[Refrain]

59

kesarī sīṅha sarūpa bhulāyo ajā kere saṅge ajā hoī rahyo

The golden-maned lion forgot his own true form;
Keeping the company of sheep, he became as a lamb.
Under such a delusion, he left behind his own life.
O Brother! Banish all your delusions and repeat, "ʿAlī, ʿAlī."

Refrain:
ʿAlī is present, and ʿAlī will always be!
Hold fast to this assurance in your heart.
Yes indeed! Hold fast to this pledge in your heart!
O Brother! Banish all your delusions and repeat, "ʿAlī, ʿAlī." 1

If he crushed his illusion, the lion would come to his senses;
His heart would be rid of its sheeplike qualities,
And never again would he slumber under such an illusion.
O Brother! Banish all your delusions and repeat, "ʿAlī, ʿAlī." 2
[Refrain]

All souls *(jīv)* have come and fallen into ignorance *(avidyā)*;
In their egoism, they have lost the Beloved by their own doing;
They came [into the world] by accident, yet they act arrogantly.
O Brother! Banish all your delusions and repeat, "ʿAlī, ʿAlī." 3
[Refrain]

If you keep the company of the Perfect Man *(murshid al-kāmil)*,
When ignorance approaches, it will be dispelled;
Then will you realize matters concerning the heart.
O Brother! Banish all your delusions and repeat, "ʿAlī, ʿAlī." 4
[Refrain]

If you conquer delusion you will recognize the Beloved *(saiyāṅ)*;
O Believer *(muʾmin)*, recognize your true self by yourself!
Pīr Shams says you should practice this.
O Brother! Banish all your delusions and repeat, "ʿAlī, ʿAlī."
[Refrain]

60

mālā līje manamāṅ ane vaḷī pīra shāhanuṅ jāpa
(*Joḍīlo 1*)

Take the rosary in your hand
and [repeat] the *japa* of Pīr Shāh;
If you truly realize both the Guru and Nara,
you will attain Heaven *(vaikuṇṭha)*. 1

Do not chatter at the place of prayer,
and be upright in your conduct;
Keep such piety and calm that the world *(saṃsār)*
does not notice you. 2

Live purely in the world,
and harbor affection *(sneha)* for the Satgur;
Consider yourself to be nothing,
and you will attain the highest form. 3

Never depart from your affection—
love *(prīta)* the Satgur profusely;
Gossip not in the congregation *(gat)*,
and reach the supreme station. 4

Ponder upon the Guru's wisdom *(ginān)*,
and you will gain understanding *(bodha)*;
The soul that keeps its promise *(kol)*
will reach the other shore *(pahele pār)*. 5

Establish the rite of *ghaṭpāṭ*
where thirty-three million deities *(devatā)* will attend;
Practice religion *(dharma)* purely,
and you will attain the Immortal City *(amarāpurī)*. 6

Distribute holy water *(niyam)* to the gathering,
  and converse together quietly;
If you let doubts enter the mind,
  you will not attain the Eternal *(ananta)*. 7

The water symbolizes Light *(nūr)*;
  at every chance take the food-offering *(sukrita)*[1]
Drinking holy water purges impurity—
  else there is no release *(mokṣa)* at death. 8

The water in the vessel *(kumbha)* is from Light
  and brings forth more Light *(nūr)*;
Fools do not know this secret—
  they remain engulfed in the world of rebirth. 9

When in the gathering the *ghaṭ* is established
  by invoking the Guru's name,
Whoever drinks this *niyam* with love
  will attain the place of Immortality. 10

In Light *(nūr)* resides Light,
  and only the Satgur has knowledge of it;
Chaste *(satī)* Ansūyā clasped her hands
  whereupon Devadutta was born. 11

Pīr Shams said, "Whoever performs
  the ceremony of *ghaṭpāṭ*,
Whoever establishes the pot *(ghaṭ)*
  is indeed a true believer *(mu'min)*." 12

---

1. *sukarīta:* a term used for the *prasāda* or food offering made of wheat flour, ghee, sugar, milk, and holy water served at the end of this ceremony to symbolize the doing of good deeds, that is, *su-krita*.

61

nītonīta ghaṭa pujā kījīye ane rākhīye vīrata sāra
(Joḍīlo 2)

Perform daily the worship (*pūjā*) of *ghaṭ*
and keep all the vows (*vrata*);
He who drinks *pāval* invoking the Guru's name
will reach the other shore. 1

Observe the vow of *bīj*[1] and this, too,
when it is a Friday;
Bring along some *sukrita*[2]
and perform the religious ceremonies. 2

The *ghaṭ* should be set up by one
whose vision is pure;
All will be absolved of sin (*pāp*),
and all will witness the Immortal (*amar*) home. 3

Whoever concentrates on religion (*dharma*)
will attain the boon of Immortality;
At home is your other half—
regard all others as your brother or sister. 4

Whoever walks on the True Path (*satmārga*)
and recoils from backbiters;
Whoever treats others with humility
is indeed our devotee (*dāsa*). 5

---

1. A fast to be observed on the second day of the new moon called *cāndrāt*.
2. See Ginān 60, note 1.

Whoever remains absorbed in truth (*sat*)
and gossips not about others;
Whoever walks firm on one's own path
will enter our company. 6

Wherever our Light (*nūr*) is spread
and we are known with true faith (*viśvās*);
Make there a quiet gathering (*gat*)
and converse about the Satgur. 7

Whoever listens to our teaching (*veda*)
and understands all that is said;
Whoever practices self-restraint—
that one is in our company. 8

Offer a coin or two and submit it
into the hands of the gathering;
With hands clasped,
stand before the congregation (*gat jamāʿat*). 9

The gathering will offer blessings (*āśiṣa*)
so stand in its midst;
To be relieved of tribulations,
submit yourselves as sincere devotees. 10

If you follow our orders (*farmān*),
you will attain the Immortal City (*amarāpurī*);
There you will gain endless happiness
and the protection of the Lord (*nara*). 11

Pīr Shams says:
"Know this to be the real truth!
Be certain that thus will you attain
the rank of Immortality." 12

62

satane mārage cāliye to bheda pāmīye sāra
(*Joḍīlo 3*)

If you walk on the True Path (*satmārga*),
    you will attain the secret essence (*sār*);
If you study[1] the Guru's wisdom (*ginān*),
    understanding will deliver you. 1

Those who observe not our advice (*farmān*),
    who believe not in our words;
They will attain a place nowhere
    nor will they attain the Gurunara's support. 2

Those lacking understanding are like stones—
    do not grieve[2] after them;
Those who follow not the Satgur's words,
    how will they become immortal (*amar*)? 3

Keep a stone in water
    and let a whole year pass by,
Yet when you [finally] remove it,
    it will still not be moist within. 4

Those whose hearts remain untouched[3]
    by the Guru's wisdom (*ginān*) and who grasp it not;
Even if you had taught them for six months,
    know them to be like stones. 5

---

1. *vāñcīye:* Guj. *vāñcvuṅ*—to read.
2. lit. beat one's chest.
3. lit. moistened, made wet.

For ten months when they were in the womb,
    they rendered much service (*sevā*);
But once born, they became greedy,
    and none reached the other shore (*pār*). 6

These words of wisdom (*ginān*) are from us—
    whoever bears their essence in the heart,
Know that one is our devotee (*bhakta*)!
    Such wise ones (*gyānī*) reach the other shore. 7

The pearl is brought forth from a mere shell
    yet, indeed, it is a priceless gem;
Know that the devotees are as precious [as pearls]—
    and none can equal their worth. 8

Who knows well the Guru's wisdom (*ginān*)
    and keeps the self steadfast;
The Lord (*deva*) dwells in such persons,
    and their bodies become Immortal. 9

Keeping in heart the Guru's wisdom,
    the devotee (*dāsa*) contemplates the Name (*nām*);
Wherever s/he comes and goes,
    there the Gurunara is nearby. 10

Vimras and Surbhāṇ became manifest;
    and they came into the fourth age of *Kali*;
Pīr Shams the Satgur says that they entered
    the world of rebirth (*saṃsār*). 11

63

evā avatāre avatāra avatarīyā ane bhagata rūpa paramāṇa (*Joḍīlo 4*)

Birth after birth they became manifest
in the form of true devotees (*bhakta*);
Assuming human form (*rūpa*),
they went on to dwell in Heaven (*vaikuṇṭha*). 1

Whoever keeps the mind fixed on the Guru's words
and becomes truly devoted,
Know for sure—among humankind,
such a person is indeed divine (*devatā*). 2

Thus is a devotee (*bhakta*) born, that is,
when one has understood the teachings (*veda*);
Without the sanction of the Satgur,
whoever speaks is a deceiver. 3

Only that minted gold coin is authentic
which complies with the scripture (*śāstra*);
Without the seal of the Satgur,
realize that all else is a forgery. 4

Know as truth these teachings (*veda*)
and reflect upon the Guru's knowledge (*ʿilm*);
If like a *satpanthī*[1] you walk upon the True Path,
you will reach the other shore. 5

This knowledge and scripture come from the Guru[2]—
he utters this wisdom (*ginān*);
Whoever believes in it as the truth (*sat*),
that person's endeavors will be fulfilled. 6

1. Follower of the true path.
2. lit. the Guru's face.

Those who remain firm on the path of truth
    and keep a watch on their intentions;
For them the Satgur is ever-present—
    they surely reach the Immortal City (*amarāpurī*). 7

The hidden religion (*gupta dharma*) is very difficult—
    indeed, none knows its secrets,
Vimras and Surbhāṇ are devotees—
    the teachings (*veda*) declare their seal of authority. 8

These words of teachings (*veda vacan*) are from the Guru—
    recognize them as the truth;
Without truth, [salvation] will not come;
    certainly no evildoer will attain it. 9

The evildoer will not attain the Shāh—
    know that the latter is, in fact, the Satgur;
Keep these words of teaching,
    which are from the Guru, fixed in your heart. 10

Those who believe not what the Guru says
    nor accept the message in his teachings,
Ultimately they will remain apart
    and will not attain the Guru's company. 11

I, Pīr Shams, have arrived
    and am going to Ucch in Multān;
Pīr Shams himself says: "Follow all of you
    the wisdom (*ginān*) of the Guru!" 12

64

tyānthī ame āvīyā uñcamāṅ ane vaḷī karī fakīrī sāra
(*Joḍīlo 5*)

From there we came to Ucch, and, indeed,
    we looked like poor mendicants (*faqīr*);
But Satgur came later on,
    and he stayed outside [the city] of Multān. 1

We came into Ucch,
    and there we settled down;
Since the Satgur left,
    two hundred and fifty years have passed. 2

His devotees (*bhakta*) were Vimras and Surbhāṇ—
    they too came here;
They came to meet the Guru
    and fell prostrate at his feet. 3

Where the assembly (*jamāʿat*) performs the *ghaṭ*,
    many will attain the essence (*sār*);
But just a few will know the Light (*nūr*)—
    the rest are lost in worldly affairs. 4

Meeting family and friends,
    they remain ignorant of matters concerning truth (*sat*);
All alike drink the holy water (*pāval*),
    but none realize the Guru's being (*ḍhāt*). 5

Whatever we tell about religion (*dharma*)
    is a revelation of truth;
Many pious ones (*satī*) have come to us,
    and we have forgiven them. 6

Only the brave will know about the rite of *ghaṭ*
named after the water-pot (*kumbha jal*);
The virgin of the universe drinks it
and weds Śyām, Lord of the three worlds. 7

She is called Bībī Fāṭimah—
know that she is the virgin of the universe;
Says Pīr Shams with certitude:
"Establish the *ghaṭ* in this world of rebirth (*saṃsār*)!" 8

65

e dharamane kāraṇe ane dropadīe sahyā dukha
(*Joḍilo 6*)

[1]For the sake of religion (*dharma*),
Draupadī endured great suffering;
She did not give up her chastity
and thus sacrificed all happiness.[2] 1

The chaste lady (*satī*) yielded not her purity,
and her hero came to meet her;
She held her concentration fixed [upon him]
when the devil tried to disrobe her. 2

None is superior to Draupadī whose virtues
we can extol [in equal measure];
But today whoever performs the *ghaṭ* ceremony,
know that one to be a *satī*. 3

Various gods (*deva*) and spirits (*yakṣa*) preside—
Vimras and Surbhāṇ too are present;
Such times have come to pass today,
but no one knows it. 4

The *Medha* deities await him
whose dwelling is in *Kalyug*;
In that pot (*kumbha*) is the holy water (*pāval*)—
bring it to us one night.[3] 5

---

1. Cf. Ginān 53:2–7.
2. Ginān 53:2 is translated "acquired every happiness": the difference is due to a mere vowel in Gujerati, *maliyā* (to get) rather than *meliyā* (to leave).
3. Cf. Ginān 53:6 "we brought it . . .": *ame ālo* (we brought) versus *amne ālo* (bring to us).

With twenty-three million *Kinnar* deities
we spoke about religious practices[4];
They, too, come and attend time and again
for this very purpose.[5] 6

[6]All this is written in the scripture (*veda*):
Know that they reside in Cīnab city!
All of them are [his] servants,
and certainly they all dwell there. 7

Queen Surjādevī practices recollection (*smaraṇa*)
and serves at the Gurunara's feet;
She established this *ghaṭ*, and all went
to drink the holy water (*pāval*). 8

Thirty-three million gods (*devatā*) dwell
in this world of rebirth (*saṃsār*);
Among them are Vimras and Surbhāṇ,
but no one recognizes them. 9

Everything dwells in the human body
including both the gods and the devils;
Follow the True Religion (*satdharma*),
and you will reach the other shore (*pahele pār*). 10

Call those souls (*jīv*) true
in whom there is no impurity;
They who live reflecting upon the Guru's wisdom (*ginān*)
will see the sham. 11

In this world of rebirth, they construct games
from which there is no refuge;
They speak and act one way
and then go and commit evil deeds. 12

Those who behold our scripture (*veda*)
and step with the right foot;
Pīr Shams says they will be reunited
and join Vimras and Surbhāṇ. 13

---

4. Cf. Ginān 53:7 "come to practice . . ." *kare* (do, perform) versus *kahiye* (we tell, relate).
5. That is, to partake in the *ghaṭ* ceremony.
6. Cf. Ginān 55:1–7.

66

dunīyā prīta na kījīye ane rākho dīnasuṅ neha
(*Joḍilo* 7)[1]

Do not cherish the world;
instead, foster love for religion (*dīn*);
The world lasts but four days
so why not surrender oneself to religion? 1

In this world of rebirth (*saṃsār*),
be single-minded and be not deceived;
Perform the *japa* and austerities (*tapa*) of truth (*sat*),
and you will join the Sāheb. 2

[2]Fashion a temple (*mandir*) in your mind (*mana*)[3]
and realize all things within it;
Turn the beads of the mind's rosary,
for mental worship is sublime. 3

Realize the temple is in the mind
and, indeed, in the mind is the *ghaṭ*[4];
Perform the rite of *kumbha* in the mind,
and surely you will meet the Satgur. 4

Construct a visible tent
but let your [true] dwelling be the mind[5];
The pure and chaste (*satī*) will come together
and fulfill their hearts' desire. 5

1. Cf. Ginān 56:1–8; similar except for some variation in vocabulary.
2. This verse is not in Ginān 56.
3. Often synomymous with heart.
4. Cf. Ginān 56:3, the word is *deva*.
5. Cf. Ginān 56:4, the word *mana* is absent and significantly alters the sentence.

They are the pure and chaste
whose concentration is fixed on the Sāheb;
They are the truly chaste (*satī*)
whose minds and hearts are blissful. 6

All their hopes are fulfilled,
and the Guru's words come true;
Their desires come to pass—
they are living proofs for the world. 7

Man and woman are one and the same
although their bodies are different;
All are equal on the path of religion (*dharma*)
and walk and talk alike. 8

[6]Walk all on the True Path (*satmārga*)!
Pīr Shams speaks with the stamp of authority;
Submit the gift of tithe (*dasond dān*) to the Guru
and receive millions in return. 9

6. This verse is completely different from the last verse of Ginān 56.

67

pīra shamasa sadhāvīyā ane vāṭe saṅgha tīrathe jāya
(*Joḍilo 8*)

Pīr Shams left.
On the way, a group was making a pilgrimage (*tīrtha*);
Three of them came to the Guru
and prostrated themselves at his feet. 1

The first was a *banyā*[1] called Saṅgjī,
the second a *brahmin* called Devrām;
The third was a *golārāṇā*[2] Devcand;
they all converged on the town Godī Vīloḍ. 2

They came to a halt at the outskirts
and proceeded to wash themselves;
Soon the two devotees (*bhakta*) Vimras
and Surbhāṇ also arrived there. 3

As the devotees pumped up some water,
a few drops splashed on Devrām;
[He exclaimed:] "I am a *brahmin*,
and you two are Muslims. You have defiled me!" 4

Devrām went into the town [distraught],
and many people gathered around him;
All were Hindus—not a single one who lived there
had a Muslim name. 5

All the people came together and said:
"We will beat up the [two] Muslims!
How dare they splash water on you!"
The whole town had assembled there. 6

1. Caste name particularly associated with trade; from Guj. *vāṇiyo*—trader.
2. Probably from the *śūdra* caste.

A man was sent to call for them and ask,
"In whose company are you?"
All agreed that they should be questioned once.
"Let us hear their reply!" 7

The two children (*bālaka*) replied:
"There is a Pīr who accompanies us.
We just came to wash up, and a few drops of water
were accidentally splashed." 8

So the people gathered together
and went over to the Pīr;
"These children splashed water on our *brahmin*!
What is their caste (*jāti*)?" 9

Satgur Shams replied:
"They are our devotees (*dāsa*)!
So some drops splashed while they were washing.
Why kick up such a fuss?" 10

68

vaḷatā brāhmaṇa bolīyā ane tame cho moṭā pīra
(*Joḍilo 9*)

In reply, the *brahmin* challenged:
    "So you are supposed to be a great Pīr?
I will be purified only once I wash
    with water from the Ganges!" 1

Satgur Shams stood up
    and went to the outskirts [of the town];
From the earth, water sprang forth—
    water from the Ganges overflowed. 2

[The townfolk] bathed in it
    and came to prostrate at the feet of the Pīr;
They went towards the Pīr's place
    and then came and sat in his house. 3

They sat in his house and said:
    "Swāmī, give us your word (*kol*).
You are our Master (*prabhu*)!
    You are the Satgur!" 4

Devrām [the *brahmin*] came hurriedly:
    "O Guru! Please put your hand on my head!
[Bless me] that I may follow your words!
    I am your servant (*dāsa*)." 5

The *banyā* Sangjī came [and pleaded]:
    "O Swāmī, listen!
O Swāmī, deliver us!
    We are at your mercy." 6

The *rāṇogolo*[1] came,
    he whose name was Devcand;
Bowing, he fell prostrate and said:
    "O Gurujī, please fulfill our tasks." 7

All the pilgrims bathed together
    in the water of the Ganges;
Then all the townsfolk went
    to bathe in it, too. 8

After bathing, they all returned
    and sat in the town square [saying]:
"To perform such a pilgrimage (*tīrtha*)
    would have cost us thousands." 9

They all bowed at the Guru's feet
    and confessed everything to him;
"Show us, O Swāmī,
    all about the fellowship of truth (*satsaṅga*)." 10

"Our devotees (*bhakta*) are models of wisdom (*ginān*)—
    they will teach you;
They are Vimras and Surbhāṇ;
    they will give you the fellowship of truth." 11

Satgur Shams said:
    "Know that they are our devotees (*bhakta*);
They will preach to you the wisdom (*ginān*).
    Keep its meaning within!" 12

1. Golārāṇā in the previous *ginān*.

69

bhagata pāse āvīyā sahue āvī karīyo vīcāra
(*Jodilo 10*)

They went to the devotees (*bhakta*),
and they all began to ask questions:
"O Bhaktas! Teach us how we can free our souls
from the perplexities of life." 1

The devotees recited *gināns*,
and they all heard about the True Path (*satpanth*);
They became happy and said:
"Please hold more meetings (*saṅgat*) with us." 2

They all assembled together
and resolved to begin the *ghaṭ* ceremony;
They established the water-pot (*kaḷaśa*),
and all of them drank the holy water (*niyam*). 3

Vimras instructed them on precepts and vows (*vrata*);
Surbhāṇ read the scriptures (*śāstra*);
Guru Shams fastened the bracelet,[1]
and all were assured of liberation (*nirvāṇa*). 4

Shams spoke these words: "Give tithe (*dasond*)
and the gift of charity (*dān*);
You will attain Heaven (*vaikuṇṭha*)
and be honored in the Immortal City (*amarāpurī*)." 5

1. *kāṅkaṇa:* lit. bangle, bracelet; like the thread-tying (*gaṇḍā bandhan*) ceremony between a *guru* and the *śiṣya* (disciple) when a vow of allegiance and loyalty to the guru is taken. The bracelet symbolizes that one is bound to the guru.

Promising this, the Guru left.
    Faith (*imān*) filled [the hearts of] the gathering;
Pīr Shams departed in haste
    and returned to his place in the jungle. 6

70

tyāṅ gure gīnānā karīyā ane kabutara kare bahu koḍa
(*Joḍilo 11*)

There the Guru imparted wisdom (*ginān*),
and the pigeons pleaded profusely:
"O Guru! Show us how the soul (*jīv*)
can be enlightened." 1

Pīr Shams the Satgur is Light (*nūr*);
he made them drink holy water (*niyam*)[1];
The pigeons prostrated themselves at his feet
and made many a supplication (*ardās*). 2

They stood there on one foot—
what a huge flock had gathered!
Blessing (*āśiṣa*) them,
the Guru showed them the way. 3

Fixing his sack on his back,
the Guru told them the secret (*bhed*):
"Give the gift (*dān*) of the tithe (*dasond*),
and your sins will be erased." 4

"Nine parts are your share,
but the tenth portion[2] is ours;
Keep it aside,
that portion which is our right." 5

The tiny souls (*jīv*) were grateful,
and again he lifted his sack on his back;
"Go submit it (*dasond*) at the time [of sunset]
when the evening falls." 6

---

1. *nīm:* cf. Note 2, Ginān 53.
2. Namely, of what you own or earn.

When the Pīr gave this order (*farmān*),
Vimras and Surbhāṇ were with him;
The Pīr then departed and from there
proceeded along a barren path. 7

He entered Mālwā, a region where beasts and tigers
lived and roamed;
Intercepting his path, a tiger snarled a command:
"Give us your flesh!" 8

Satgur Shams replied:
"O you, king of the jungle!
Leave me be on my own path
and return to your forest." 9

At that moment, a cow came
and stood next to the Pīr;
The lion[3] said: "I will take pity on you.
Instead, I will eat the cow's flesh." 10

Satgur Shams said: "Dare not take the name of one
who stands besides me;
She is now under my protection (*śaraṇa*),
and you may not feast upon her." 11

The devotees (*bhakta*) began to recite wisdom (*ginān*),
and the tiger listened quietly;
Faith (*imān*) penetrated his heart,
and he gave up his claim on the cow. 12

Resolving to give the tithe (*dasond*),
the lion ceased to frequent [a part of] the jungle;
"We will not go hunting
in [that part of] the forest for our prey." 13

Realization filled the beast,
for he had paid heed to the Guru's wisdom (*ginān*);
He attained Heaven (*vaikuṇṭha*)
for making his offering (*dān*) before the Guru. 14

Satgur Shams said:
"Learn [a lesson] from such birds and beasts!
Whoever follows the Guru's words (*vacan*) today
will truly be liberated (*nirvāṇa*)." 15

---

3. The words tiger and lion are used interchangeably.

71

gura vacane cālīyā te potā vaikuṇṭha vāsa
(*Joḍīlo 12*)

Those who followed the Guru's words
attained Heaven (*vaikuṇṭha*);
Recognize our devotees (*bhakta*)
for they are our servants (*dāsa*). 1

Fill the heart with submission (*dāsapaṇa*)
and have full confidence (*viśvās*);
Wherever you look you will see
Pīr Shams coming beside you. 2

Cultivate this kind of devotion (*bhakti*)
and perform your duties quietly;
Perform the rite of *ghaṭ*
and submit the offering (*dān*) to the Guru. 3

Vimras and Surbhāṇ performed the worship (*pūjā*)—
they set up the *ghaṭ* stand;
"What offering (*dān*) you wish to make,
give it to these devotees (*bhakta*)." 4

Devotees have come since time immemorial
to impart the Guru's wisdom (*ginān*);
Today in *Kalyug* they have descended again
to relate the Guru's wisdom. 5

Those who follow the Guru's wisdom (*ginān*)
will come towards us;
Their descendants[1] will go to Heaven (*svarga*)
and attain the Immortal City (*amarāpurī*). 6

---

1. lit. seventy-one generations of descendants.

Shams spoke these words:
  "Listen to the essence (*sār*), O my Devotees!
We have roamed through foreign lands
  and twenty-four kingdoms." 7

The devotees listened and then
  prostrated themselves before the Guru:
"Your speech (*vāc*) is the truth (*sāc*);
  immutable (*avical*) is your name (*nām*)." 8

"For aeons (*kalpa*) you sported,
  and today you have become manifest (*avatār*);
Now, O Guru, show us all [that exists]
  in the twenty-four kingdoms!" 9

"O Guru! You played a trick
  and dressed up as a poor mendicant (*faqīr*);
You stood up from there[2]
  and began to roam through foreign lands." 10

"You performed many a feat,
  and you, O Guru, recited wisdom (*ginān*);
You set up countless[3] tents
  where God's (*hari*) name was chanted." 11

"You gave religion (*dharma*) to many[4] castes,
  and your devotees set up the *ghaṭ* stand;
You kept Vimras and Surbhāṇ with you—
  they are the true servants of Guru Shams." 12

---

2. Not clear from where.
3. lit. seven and a half hundred thousand.
4. lit. eighteen.

72

baṅgalā deśamāṅ āvīyā atīta verāgī ne bhaṇḍāra
(Joḍilo 14)

They entered the country Bengāl[1]
where there was a feast of ascetics (*vairāgī*);
They came and met Pīr Shams,
and the Guru began to recite verses. 1

Pīr Shams then paid a gracious visit
and joined in the feasting;
Vimras and Surbhāṇ were with him,
and all three sat together. 2

The devotees traced a square with colored powders
while the Guru sat in the house;
They performed the rite (*pūjā*) of *ghaṭ*
and made all drink the holy water (*nīm*). 3

They taught the True Path (*satpanth*)
to everyone and chanted the Guru's name;
In [the languages of] Keśavpūrī and Multānī
were the words (*japa*) of their chant. 4

Then the Guru gave up his own seat
to a man by the name of Vasto;
He made him responsible
for all matters to do with Bengāl. 5

The traveller [Shams] appointed [Vasto]
the chief (*mukhī*) of the assembly (*jamā'at*);
"Only when Vasto takes his seat
may the ceremony of *ghaṭpāt* be performed." 6

---

1. *bangālādeśa:* the region of Bengal in India?

They offered a coin or two to the Pīr
and held their feast there;
All the pious ones gathered together
and held a quiet meeting. 7

Vimras and Surbhāṇ taught them
all the religious vows (*vrata*);
The pious ones (*rīkhīsar*) were all content
and joined with conviction. 8

The Bengālis took on the religion (*dharma*)—
they were ascetics of various types[2];
They embraced the religion
but kept it completely secret (*gupta*). 9

Satgur Shams uttered these words:
"Listen, O brave mendicants!
Entrust all to Vasto,
for he is our deputy." 10

2. *jogī sanyāsī atīta verāgī.*

73

satagura shamasa vācā ocarīyā ane karīyā saravanā kāja (*Joḍilo 14*)

Satgur Shams uttered this speech
and fulfilled the tasks of all;
His devotees (*bhakta*) Vimras and Candrabhāṇ
tied the bracelets [of loyalty]. 1

The devotees Vimras and Surbhāṇ
said to Guru Shams:
"O Guru! Give us your orders (*farmān*);
we are your servants (*dāsa*)." 2

Pīr Shams said: "O Devotees!
Learn about the primordial times;
That ancient worship (*pūjā*) is with you—
make it your emancipation (*nirvāṇa*)!" 3

Satgur Shams said: "O Devotees!
Keep your minds steadfast!
Establish [the *ghaṭ*], and we will make you drink
the holy water (*nīrmala nīr*)." 4

Satgur Shams gave the following instruction—
"Listen well, all of you!
Form a gathering (*gat*) and especially on Fridays,
observe this vow (*vrata*)." 5

Pīr Shams talked, and he conveyed
the essence of wisdom (*ginān*);
"Whoever has faith (*imān*) and worships the Guru
will attain the other shore." 6

Then he divulged the secret wisdom (*ginān*)
    and revealed the word (*śabda*);
Those who believe it as truth (*sat*),
    their dwelling will be in Heaven (*vaikuṇṭha*). 7

Pīr Shams the Guru recited wisdom (*ginān*),
    and all in the gathering listened;
Whoever follows his wisdom will attain Immortality (*amar*)
    and the divine vision (*dīdār*). 8

74

satagura shamasa cālīyā āvīyā bhoṭa nagara māṅhe
(*Joḍilo 15*)

Satgur Shams then departed
    and came to the town of Bhoṭ;
Only Hindus were to be seen—
    no one there would ever offer water to a Muslim. 1

He went and sat on the west side;
    a throng of Hindus soon approached him.
"Get away from here!
    We can smell your odor inside [our homes]!" 2

Satgur Shams said:
    "Show us a place [to sit];
We are travellers from a foreign land
    and would like to rest awhile." 3

Satgur Shams stood up,
    and the Hindus sent two men along with him;
They led him out of the town
    to a terribly desolate and barren wasteland. 4

"You can rest here!
    Don't come back into the town!
Else we will beat you up;
    only Hindus may live there." 5

Satgur Shams replied:
    "Go back and stay in that town of yours!
Rest assured that we will sit right here;
    go back to your own homes!" 6

The two men went back into the town [thinking],
"What will this achieve?
The town outskirts are extremely dry;
what will they eat sitting out there?" 7

[Meanwhile] Satgur Shams had settled down
and was quietly resting;
There were two children (*bālak*) beside him—
Vimras and Surbhāṇ. 8

The two devotees (*bhakta*) said:
"May we go to the town [gates]?"
These were their thoughts:
"We will fetch some food and water." 9

Satgur Shams said:
"[Yes], go to the ascetic's hut and call out to him;
[Tell him] to take our money and obtain water for us,
for you are of Hindu born." 10

75

vimarasa surabhāṇa bolīyā hīndu dayāvanta sāra
(*Joḍilo 16*)

Vimras and Surbhāṇ said:
"O Hindu! You are truly merciful.
We are Muslims and are very hungry
but must remain outside [the town]." 1

So the ascetic came before the entrance
of the town Bhoṭ and cried:
"Why have you locked the gates?
These poor *faqīrs* are very hungry." 2

The townsfolk replied:
"After we locked up all the gates,
The keys suddenly fell into pieces.
The ironsmiths have all gathered." 3

The ascetic replied: "What! Why have you committed
such an awful deed?
Despite their garb you left them to starve?"
He exclaimed, "O Rāma! O Rāma!" 4

"Lord Nārāyaṇa's fury is now upon you!
The gates will never be opened.
Not even if the whole world gathers.
They are merely the ironsmiths of the town!" 5

He rushed to the king's palace shouting;
the guard stood up and called out:
"Three *faqīrs* are dying of hunger,
and tonight they must stay outside [the town]." 6

"Let in the ascetic and then go
    and proclaim that there will be a hearing;
Who threw them out of the town
    and with whom did they fight?" 7

The guard replied: "The *faqīr* is still
    in the barren outskirts [of the town].
Standing out here is an ascetic;
    it is he who has brought this news." 8

The king said, "Send the ascetic to go
    and hail [this message] to the *faqīr*.
Tell him King Rāmsaṅgaji has invited him.
    Why do you pick this fight for nothing!" 9

He went to the ascetic and said:
    "The king orders that you go to the *faqīr*.
Fetch him and bring him here.
    [Say to him:] Come and stay in the town." 10

So the ascetic Śivbhaṭ
    returned to his own hut;
He went and sat where
    Vimras and Surbhāṇ were standing. 11

Satgur Shams said:
    "This happened in that town of Bhoṭ;
Vimras and Surbhāṇ are my devotees (*bhakta*);
    they are my servants (*dāsa*)." 12

76

tamane rājāe bolāvīyā gāmamāṅ che utapāta
(Joḍilo 17)

"The king has summoned you;
the town is in utter chaos—
Its gates cannot be opened.
[The king] calls for you." 1

The devotees (*bhakta*) replied:
"We will not enter the king's town;
We will meet him in the wilderness.
I am Surbhāṇ, [born of] a Hindu." 2

Then Śivbhaṭ asked:
"Who showed you to that place?"
"Two men came with us
and ordered us to stay there!" 3

"We had stopped outside the town
in front of that gate over there;
The Hindus came rushing up to us saying:
'Get up from here at once!'" 4

"Our Pīr stood up, left the town limits
and went into the wasteland."
Śivbhaṭ promptly stood up
and went to the king. 5

"Listen, O King Rāmsaṅgadev!
That *faqīr* is none other than a Pīr!
He was sent off to the wasteland;
his body will remain starved and thirsty!" 6

The king asked:
"Who has inflicted this suffering upon him?"
He sent a man at once
to bring [the Pīr] to his home. 7

Well until after noon,
the gates of the fort remained locked;
"Go fetch the people
who have caused all this trouble!" 8

The people were summoned
and brought before the king;
"We know nothing except that the dwellers
on the west side troubled him." 9

Folks of the west end were summoned
and brought before the king;
"What kind of odor did you smell
that you banished the *faqīr*?" 10

"Now you have sealed the city's gates
of which five are on the west side;
Go and have them opened or else
I will decide your fate this evening!" 11

The dwellers of the west end came
and sat in the king's court;
"We have failed to undo the locks;
you must fetch the Pīr at once." 12

Outside sat the ascetic
whose name was Śivbhaṭ;
The king called out to him and said:
"O sage, do this job for us!" 13

"Go fall at the Pīr's feet
and convey to him our respects (*praṇām*); [Tell him:]
The king prostrates himself at your feet
and entreats you to unfasten the town gates." 14

Śivbhaṭ left from there
and went over to the Pīr;
He stood saying: "You are Nārāyaṇa!
O Swāmī, I am your servant (*dāsa*)." 15

Satgur Shams looked at him:
"Dear old man! What brings you to this place?"
"King Rāmsaṅgadev says our town gates are sealed—
[please set them free]." 16

77

ame na āvīye gāmamāṅ ane rahīye eṇe ṭhāma
(*Joḍilo No. 18*)

"We will not come to the town
    but will remain right here;
Repeat our name in front of one gate,
    and it will open." 1

The ascetic rushed back quickly
    and conveyed his reply to the king:
"Repeat our name in front of one gate,
    and it will open." 2

The king immediately stood up
    and went before the gate;
Humbly,[1] he pleaded and invoked the name
    of the *faqīr* who was, indeed, a Pīr. 3

The king walked ahead and with him
    were a hundred-thousand strong;
All came to the parched wilderness
    and stood before the Pīr. 4

The king prostrated himself at his feet
    and then standing up, pleaded:
"O Swāmī! Please come to our town
    and make your dwelling there." 5

Pīr Shams replied:
    "We will sit right here in this barren place.
It is your own people
    who made us sit here in the wilderness." 6

---

1. lit. standing, as a sign of respect.

The king fell prostrate again
    at the feet of Satgur Shams and entreated him:
"O Pīr! Please come."
    Just then, a cow descended from heaven (*svarga*). 7

Satgur Shams said:
    "Listen, O my brave Devotees (*bhakta*)!
Go fetch a bowl of water
    and wash the cow's feet!" 8

Obeying his order (*farmān*),
    the devotees of Satgur Shams fetched water;
With [this] water from the Ganges
    they sprinkled [the cow], the body of all creation. 9

Vimras brought out a cup
    and went near the cow;
He milked her and placed the cup [of milk]
    in the hands of Pīr Shams. 10

Satgur Shams said:
    "King, take this cup in your hand.
Give some milk to all
    those who came along with you!" 11

The king said:
    "No one must go back to Bhoṭnagar!
First drink this milk from the Pīr;
    only then may you all return." 12

The king gave a portion of milk to everyone,
    and he marveled at the cup;
Though all drank to their satisfaction,
    the cup was not drained. 13

King Devsaṅga[2] called for his Queen,
    and she came to the town outskirts;
Releasing her *cheḍo*,[3] she prostrated herself
    and touched the Pīr's feet. 14

Blessing her (*āśiṣa*), Satgur Shams said:
    "O Lady, may you go to Heaven (*vaikuṇṭha*)!"

---

2. Note the king's name changes from Rāmsaṅga to Devsaṅga.
3. Portion of the *sāri* which is used to cover the head like a scarf.

The Queen's name was Śīlvantī Sadā,[4]
and she went and stood by the king. 15

King Rāmsaṅgadev
and Queen Śīlvantī Sadā,
The two of them remained standing
and made plea after plea (*vinantī*). 16

"Now go back to your own place;
our dwelling is right here!"
Standing next to the Pīr
were his servants Vimras and Surbhāṇ. 17

The king wept and wept,
and the queen begged the Pīr:
"O Satgur! Indeed, you are so great.
O Swāmī, will you not save us?" 18

The queen counselled the king:
"Let us fall prostrate at the Pīr's feet;
Once we submit to him,[5]
we can return to our homes." 19

The king said again and again:
"O Swāmī, purify us!
Accept us as your own;
only then shall we partake of food." 20

Satgur Shams said:
"We had stopped [to rest] on that side;
Then some of your people shouted,
'How dare a Muslim sit up here!'" 21

A *banyo* from the west side
whose name was Rugjī Raṇachoḍ,
And another called Trikam came forward—
the whole town had gathered. 22

"O Master (*prabhu*)! [Forgive us!]
We did not know that you were a great sage;
Now we will ever remain your servants (*sevak*)—
indeed, you are kind and merciful." 23

---

4. lit. the eternally pure, pious, patient.
5. lit. become his, belong to him.

"O King! Take charge of your kingdom
and insure our protection!
The day has come to an end
and dusk set in." 24

In the year *Samvaṭ* 1178
on the last day of the month of *Kartik*,
The Guru established a place [for himself],
and the day was a Tuesday. 25

He taught the religious vows (*vrata*),
and he installed the *ghaṭpāṭ* ceremony;
The whole town drank the holy water (*niyam*)—
what a huge crowd had formed. 26

Seventy rounds of food were cooked
and 360 ascetics were fed;
The gathering (*gat*) assembled together
and came to the king's palace. 27

Satgur Shams taught them religion (*dharma*)—
Vimras and Surbhāṇ were his devotees;
The Guru spoke wisdom (*ginān*),
and the king listened to his teachings. 28

"Submit in the hands of the collector[6]
the Pīr's portion of tithe (*dasond*)!
Whatever it is, be it one coin or two,
O King, keep that aside!" 29

"Keep aside in your palace that portion of income
which belongs to the Pīr;
Put it together in a bundle and make sure
it reaches us at our place." 30

The assembly (*gat*) gathered at the west gate,
Rugjī Raṇachoḍ and Trikam, too;
They all came to visit the Guru
at his own place. 31

The three hundred and sixty ascetics
also came there in a group;

6. *musāfar:* lit. traveller, courier: traditionally, the tithe was collected by someone appointed by the Imām or Pīr who travelled from place to place.

Having performed his religious vows,
Śivbhaṭ went to the treasury. 32

Śivbhaṭ came to king Devsaṅga
who was from the Gaekvāḍ caste;
He would explain to all of them
the meaning of the Guru's wisdom (*ginān*). 33

He imparted the principles of religion,
and the Guru revealed the word (*japa*);
Then the Satgur assured them all:
"We are always with you." 34

Seating his disciples (*bhakta*) at the table,
he made them repeat the Guru's name;
The hearts of all were delighted,
and they all came near the Guru. 35

The king and queen said:
"O Guru! Please visit our house.
Once you depart, O Guru,
what will be our condition?!" 36

Satgur Shams replied:
"We will come back to see you again.
Pray with a single mind,
and you will surely attain Heaven (*vaikuṇṭha*)." 37

Satgur Shams then said:
"We will now proceed to Jambudvīpa;
We have established our center there—
make a note of this." 38

Satgur Shams rose to leave
and told the king one more thing:
"Recommend all to repeat
the voiceless word (*ajampiyā japa*)." 39

Satgur Shams said:
"O King, have faith (*viśvās*)!
We have two devotees (*bhakta*);
they are our servants (*dāsa*)." 40

78

abadhu jugata jola santośa pātra karo ane daṇḍā karo vīcāra
(*The Ascetic's Wisdom*)[1]

O Ascetic![2] Make the world your sack,
satisfaction your bowl!
Let discernment be your rod!
Don the earrings of humility and kindness!
Let wisdom (*ginān*) be your sustenance.

Refrain:
O Ascetic! He in this world is a *jogī*
In whose mind is no other [save God]. 1

O Ascetic! Knowledge (*ginān*) is my Guru,
Renounce the senses and apply ash![3]
Believing in its truth (*sat*),
meditate on the True Religion (*sat-dharma*)!
Then ascetic you are a real *jogī*. 2
[Refrain]

O Ascetic! With concentration as your rod,
Still the mind and arrest the moon and sun![4]
Then will the *suṣumaṇā* string begin to play,
Such a mystery is the portion of but a few. 3
[Refrain]

---

1. *gīnān abadhu*: Guj. *avadhūta*—ascetic, renunciate; cf. Ginān 58 is identical but does not have this title.
2. *abadhu:* Guj. *avadhūta*—ascetic, renunciate.
3. *bhabhūtā:* Guj. *bhabhūtī*—sacred ash, ash from sacrificial fire; cf. Hin. *vibhūti.*
4. Symbols in Tantric meditation and Kuṇḍalinī yoga.

O Ascetic! Abandon all your sins—
Bathe in the crossing of the three rivers (*triveṇi*)
And strike up the the unstruck sound (*anāhata nāda*);
Pīr Shams says: Die when still alive,
and you will not be reborn. 4

[Refrain]

79

āda guru shamasa munnavara jāṇa te to farīyā bahu juga pramāṇa (Garbī 1)

O Austere Ones (*munivar*)!
Know that Shams is the primordial Guru;
Indeed, he has roamed through many an age (*yuga*). 1

[One day] he went to a village called Analvāḍ
Where countless numbers of Hindus lived. 2

The village was full of shrines and temples
Dedicated to their dear [goddess] *Mātā Bhavānī.* 3

It was *Navrātrī,*[1] and everyone was dancing the *garbī*[2];
To such a place Guru Shams went. 4

It was the first night of the month *āso śuddha*[3];
Everyone had come together to dance the first *garbī.* 5

Thirty-six *paṇḍits* were telling tales of lore (*kathā*),
With five hundred actors enacting them as drama. 6

The Guru went and stood beside them;
He listened to the entire recital of the Hindus. 7

They danced fervently and sang with intensity;
They dearly worshipped their stone idols. 8

---

1. *noratā:* i.e., *navrātrī*—festival held during the first nine days of *Aṣvin* in honor of the goddess Durgā.
2. A circular pot-dance in which the rhythm is kept by clapping the hands and feet. *Garbī* also refers to the songs sung during the dance. Derived from *garbha*—a holed pot used as the deity's receptacle. The women generally carry earthen pots with lamps on their heads as they dance.
3. *Āso* or *Aṣvin* is the twelvth or last month of the Hindu calender; *śuddha* refers to the bright half of the lunar month held sacred to Durgā.

All this aroused anger in Pīr Shams;
He went and joined the dancers in their dance. 9

Then the Guru began to sing his songs of wisdom (*ginān*);
The ignorant Hindus [were startled] and listened to them. 10

80

āja ānanda pāmyā mana ke satagura sevīyāre lola
(Garbī 2)

Today this mind has attained bliss (*ānanda*)
By serving (*sevā*) the Satgur. 1

Do not be deceived, O you foolish people!
Hold the essence in your hearts. 2

Those idols in the temple are but stones!
Why dance around them in circles? 3

Serve the Light (*nūr*) of Satgur!
The Guru who is the master of Divine Light. 4

Be loyal in giving the offering (*dāna*) of tithe (*dasond*)!
Then you will reap success. 5

Those who walk on the True Path (*satpanth*)—
These pious ones (*rīkhīsar*) will reign. 6

Keep on dancing, all of you, night and day!
But alas, you will attain nothing! 7

All those idols are mere stones!
They cannot even utter a single word. 8

Why are you deceived by such fake idols?
They are just man-made toys. 9

It is a lie that a god (*deva*) is in this *garbī*!
Where is [this Goddess] Bhavānī? 10

The creative powers of Guru Brahmā are abundant.
All existence is within it. 11

Regard the whole world (*saṃsār*) as false!
Know this from Yama.[1] 12

Believe in the manifestation (*avatār*) of ʿAlī!
Then you will reap fruit. 13

You will thus be absolved of sin and regret
And attain an elevated rank. 14

In this manner, the Satgur explained the truth (*sāc*),
But they did not understand. 15

All the people listened to him
And then said: 16

"Come back on the second night,
And we will dance together." 17

Pīr Shams the Guru said:
"Be heedful of your conduct!" 18

1. The god of death.

81

gurū āvyā bījī rāta ke āvīne nācīyāre lola
(*Garbī 3*)

The Guru came the second night;
he came, and he danced. 1

He uttered sweet words (*bol*);
his words were like nectar (*amṛta*). 2

Listen together all of you:
be mindful of your conduct! 3

All this is nothing but a sham;
know this for sure! 4

Think about it yourselves:
what is a stone [after all, but a stone]? 5

Rather serve Sāheb, the Creator (*sirjaṇhār*),
with a firm faith (*viśvās*). 6

He who created four types of creatures[1]
and infused them with life. 7

He who came age after age
to fulfill the tasks of his devotees (*bhakta*). 8

He who rescued the sage Ṛṣi Mugat
by relieving him of his vows. 9

He who protected Gautam's honor
by reviving his sunken wife. 10

---

1. *cāra khāṇa:* perhaps a reference to the four modes of genesis of all creatures, viz., through 1) egg, 2) sprout, 3) perspiration, and 4) womb.

He who secured an invincible rule for Dhruva
who thus attained the zenith. 11

He who came bursting through the pillar
and saved the life of Prahlād. 12

He who mercilessly slew Hiraṇyakaśipu
and tore him to pieces with his nails. 13

He who held the hand of [King] Hariścandra
and rescued him [from death]. 14

He who was supreme in the second age (*dvāpur*)
and saved the Pāṇḍavas. 15

He who in this age of *Kalyug*
saved twelve crore devout followers (*satī*) with truth. 16

He who in this last phase [of *Kalyug*]
will save countless austere ones (*munivar*). 17

Guru Shams the Pīr said:
"Attain purity (*śuddha*) through truth (*sat*)." 18

82

gura āvatā sarave rāta ke gīnāna suṇāvatāre lola
(*Garbī 4*)

The Guru came every night
  and made them listen to wisdom (*ginān*). 1

But the ignorant fools did not hear,
  for their ears were deaf. 2

The Guru uttered sweet words (*bol*);
  listen to them attentively! 3

Why do you perform such false drama?
  Why not realize their deceit? 4

You should worship the true name,
  that of the Lord Naklaṅkī. 5

He who established the heavenly throne[1]
  and who gave rise to all things. 6

He who created the moon and the sun,
  the wind, and the water. 7

Perform good deeds
  to secure the purity of your self. 8

None of you knows the True Path (*satpanth*);
  your hearts are full of falsehood. 9

Purge yourselves of evil and deceit,
  and preserve your self-worth! 10

---

1. *arasa kurśa:* Ar. *al-arsh wa al-kursī*; Qur'ānic reference to Allah's divine platform or throne.

Meditate upon the precepts (*ācār*) of religion (*dharma*)
revealed by Guru Brahmā. 11

The name of the final Prophet was Muḥammad—
[bearer of] Divine Light (*nūr*). 12

Recall and meditate upon his essence
and believe in Mawlānā ʿAlī. 13

Who now holds the mantle [of authority]?
We disclose his name—it is Shāh Nizār. 14

The Imāms are from Light;
they are ever-present (*qā'im*) in the world. 15

Listen to this true wisdom (*jñāna*) and serve [them]. 16

Then you will reach the other shore (*pahele pār*)
and attain Heaven (*svarga*). 17

Guru Shams the Pīr spoke thus:
"Be honest in giving your tithe (*dasond*)." 18

83

ke tame amirasa pījo dīna ne rāta ke nura nurānīyāre lol
(*Garbī 5*)

Drink nectar (*amīras*) day and night
and thus be filled with Light upon Light (*nūr*)! 1

Your sins and regrets will vanish,
and your mind will be cleansed. 2

Listen carefully to this sacred speech (*āgama*)
and believe it in your hearts. 3

Reflect upon this wisdom (*ginān*) and then act,
else you will go astray. 4

Those who did not listen carefully to this wisdom
they have gone astray. 5

Do not let this human life slip away from your hands;
you will not have it again. 6

Meditate on the precepts (*ācār*) of religion (*dharma*);
the faithless have gone astray. 7

Perform righteous deeds,
and you will attain Heaven (*vaikuṇṭha*). 8

Know the straight path of truth (*sat*)!
The dishonest have departed from it. 9

Those who realize the whole essence,
they alone attain the fruits. 10

Listen carefully to such wisdom (*ginān*),
for it is a priceless gem. 11

Lest you go astray again and again,
be mindful of your conduct! 12

Keep the company of truth
    and purify your minds. 13

Expel evil and deceit,
    and you will reap the fruits. 14

Perform good and excellent deeds
    and harbor affection in the heart. 15

Hold pious gatherings (*satsaṅga*) properly
    and keep true to your religion (*dharma*). 16

Serve (*sevā*) sincerely the Light of the Satgur;
    know he is Lord (*nara*) Qāsim Shāh. 17

Thus spoke Guru Shams the Pīr:
    "[Do this and] you will reap the fruit." 18

84

maṅpe varase amarata nura ke kudaratī khelajore lola
(Garbī 6)

Lo! The nectar (*amṛta*) of Divine Light (*nūr*) rains on us,
and we take delight in Nature! 1

Keep on each side four lively oxen
and hold their reins firmly. 2

All is in the hands of the Guru;
into yours take the remembrance (*smaraṇa*) [of God]. 3

Plough your field with good deeds
and plant in it the seeds of vows (*vrata*). 4

Cast away your crust of sins
and let your mind beware. 5

Tear away at the roots of evil deeds
and make your minds pure. 6

Daily uproot the weeds [of evil]
and furrow the sad path of separation. 7

If the lion of truth (*sat*) is left outside [to guard the crop],
what can the crows do? 8

Love the company of virtue
and in your hearts cultivate devotion for God (*hari*). 9

You will see your land yield abundant crops
and heap upon heap [of harvest]. 10

Reap it [while you can] and be fruitful in your farming!
Keep vigil day and night! 11

Take care when you remove the husk!
Thrash both sides [of the grain]. 12

Work as if you were the oxen of religion (*dharma*);
thus attain the eternal [reward]. 13

Fill your carts with the Guru's wisdom (*ginān*)
and carry it within yourself. 14

Do not willfully cheat in your minds:
give the tithe (*dasond*) [faithfully]. 15

In this manner, if you dance day and night,
you will abide in bliss. 16

Perform your works with devotion (*bhakti*) and ardor,
and you will attain the fruit. 17

Thus spoke Guru Shams, the Pīr:
"Believe in this with all your heart!" 18

85

tame ramajo dīna ne rāta ke rāja rūḍā karore lola
(*Garbī* 7)

Dance in this manner night and day
and enjoy the reign of bliss. 1

The Creator (*kirtār*) stamps
his peacock seal[1] age after age. 2

Reap your harvest in this world itself
and enjoy the reign of bliss. 3

Heaven-bound, Divine Light (*nūr*)
will shower upon you at the fixed entrance. 4

Hold the Guru's wisdom (*ginān*) with the right hand
and follow the book (*pustak*). 5

Grasp the reins of intellect
and use them to control your mind. 6

If you are well-trained in self-sacrifice,
what [fear] can the sword inspire? 7

Why return to be born in this world again,
why take the rounds of rebirth (*ferā*)? 8

Ultimately what aid will the world give you
that [you covet it like an] ardent prince? 9

Without a Master (*prabhu*), you read scripture (*purāṇ*)—
without a seed, you try to sow! 10

In [such a land], only embers of fire come forth,
only poisoned grass and weeds. 11

---

1. *mora chāpa:* allusion not known.

Without the Guru, these people are frauds, deceivers!
Why remain with them? 12

The scriptures (*veda purāṇ*) are the Guru's throne!
Why be foolish, misguided? 13

The Swāmī will come to Jambudvīpa,
for it is virgin land. 14

Over and over you slander and gossip!
Hence you go astray in the journey. 15

All are ravaged who go astray;
their business and livelihood crumble to dust. 16

The True Path (*satpanth*) is like a sword's edge—
so be engrossed in wisdom (*ginān*). 17

Keep pondering over the Guru's teachings
and have supreme faith (*viśvās*). 18

Thus spoke Guru Shams the Pīr:
"Believe this in your hearts." 19

86

tame japajo dīna rāta ke mandīra maṅhe mahālajore lola
(*Garbī 8*)

Repeat the word (*japa*) day and night
and rejoice in the [inner] temple (*mandir*). 1

When concentration (*surti*) is fixed between the brows,
rejoice in Immortality (*amar*). 2

The concentration should be like the string
which remains intact when stretched. 3

Then the unstruck sound will play
and the even breathing of "I am He" sets in. 4

When you thus sit absorbed in concentration,
how can the wicked distract you? 5

When concentration is fixed between the brows,
you will bathe in the Light (*nūr*). 6

They read the scripture (*purāṇ*) but realize not
its secret (*bhed*)—what to expect of fools? 7

Come and recognize that All-Knowing!
Be mindful and vigilant! 8

Focus between the brows where the sun is ablaze,
and take the universe in hand. 9

If you must give up your head to acquire it,
know this is still a good bargain. 10

Indeed, only with the refinement of previous births
will you attain success. 11

Be brave and fight face-to-face!
Be willing to sacrifice your head and return. 12

In your hearts you must harbor
affection for the Guru. 13

Then the [soul's] immortal field will yield ripe fruit,
and happily you will pick it. 14

Acquire the gem in your hand, O Believer (*mu'min*)!
Why go on the rounds of rebirths? 15

Watch [yourselves] carefully and be fully devoted;
then you will reap success. 16

O Brother, do not steal in secret!
Give your tithe (*dasond*) [faithfully]. 17

Know how to act in the world—
abide by the book (*pustak*). 18

O Pious! Be careful in your minds,
and you will rejoice in freedom (*mukti*). 19

Pay attention to the Guru's wisdom (*ginān*)!
Why wander in aimless circles? 20

Those who have followed the Guru's wisdom (*ginān*)
they have become Immortal (*amar*). 21

Thus spoke Guru Shams the Pīr:
"Believe this in your heart and thoughts!" 22

87

bhulo bhulo te bhulo bhamarahore lola
(*Garbī 9*)

Dazed! Dazed like that stunned wasp!
O my Soul![1] Why are you lost too?
In the fires of sacrifice, awaken the body.
That soul that errs now, surely it will lose out.
Once before, others went safely across [the ocean of] life.
How will you go across to the other shore?[2]
Ahead of you there will be no raft nor boat.
There will be no weights nor scales.
With truth (*sat*) [alone] you must go across to the other shore.
Religion (*dharma*) will take you across to the other shore.
Brother, the Guru will accompany you as your guarantor.
In this way will you go across to the other shore.
Whoever stepped lightly, O Brother, was saved.
Those who carried baggage on their heads drowned.
There will be no shops, no traders before you.
There will be no business, no merchants.
Ahead of you will be no brother, no sister.
There will be no father, no mother.

---

1. *prāṇa:* lit. breath.
2. *pāḷīyā:* Guj. *pāḷa*—barricade, barrier, wall; but also *pāra*—bank, shore.

Brother, alone you will get up and go. 19

So take religion (*dharma*) along with you. 20

Guru Shams has spoken this wisdom (*ginān*). 21

Friends! Perform some good deeds for religion (*dharma*). 22

88

sata māraga shamasa pīra dekhāḍīyā garabīere lola (*Garbī 10*)

Pīr Shams has shown the True Path (*satmārga*)
through the *garbī*. 1

Those who contemplated the eternal name (*nām*)
themselves became Immortal (*amar*). 2

Word by word, the Guru has imparted knowledge
and disclosed it to all. 3

He explained the scriptures (*veda purāṇ*)
and told the stories from memory. 4

The Guru danced in the *garbī*,
and he recited the *Qur'ān*. 5

Speaking priceless words,
he himself acted out a drama. 6

First he described the four cycles (*kalpa*)
and the creation of the universe. 7

Guru Brahmā played the role
of creating the ages of time (*yuga*). 8

From Viṣṇu's yawn came forth
[creation] due to his Light (*teja*). 9

Brahmā's creations were innumerable,
some eight hundred thousand. 10

Then Māyā wove her web of worldly delusion
by which all were bewitched. 11

Into delusion she threw [the world]
and troubled the saints (*ṛṣi*) [with temptation]. 12

Also in this age of *Kalyug*, she entices the world (*saṃsār*),
and the ignorant go astray. 13

Once the first cycle was spread far and wide,
the Yakṣas were created. 14

Since then has He, the Lord (*nara*) himself,
established the religion of *Satpanth*. 15

Guru Shams was present on that occasion;
in truth, he was Brahmā. 16

He took the holy water (*pāval*) and made the saints drink—
thus did he purify them. 17

Guru Shams the Pīr said:
"Drink the holy water (*pāval*) with sincerity." 18

89

sate pāvala pīyo dīna ne rāta ke to faḷa pāmaśore lola
(Garbī 11)

Drink the holy water (*pāval*) sincerely day and night,
and you will reap fruit. 1

Just as ninety crore Yakṣas[1] were successful
and became Immortal (*amar*). 2

Similarly the Meghas, fifty-six crores of them,
were successful. 3

Likewise the Kinnar deities, thirty-two crores of them,
were successful. 4

And among the Devas, thirty-three crore
were successful and attained fruit. 5

Then in four moments of the last cycle (*kalpa*)
numerous souls (*jīv*) were saved. 6

Five crore [were saved] by King Prahlād
who recited the name of Narsiṃha. 7

Seven crore [were saved] by King Hariścandra
who was saved by Śrī Rāma. 8

Nine crore [were saved] by the Pāṇḍava princes
who were saved by Śrī Buddha. 9

Under Prince Yudhiṣṭhira, the heir to the throne,
every one of them was saved. 10

Twelve crore pious (*satī*) [were saved]
by truth (*sat*) in this age of *Kalyug*. 11

---

1. A species of semidivine beings.

Their rescuer was Pīr Ṣadr al-Dīn;
he saved them all by himself. 12

They meditated on the name of Muḥammad
and the manifestation (*avatār*) of ʿAlī. 13

In this last phase, all will be saved
who follow the True Path (*satpanth*). 14

That austere one (*munivar*) who drinks the holy water
and submits the tithe (*dasond*); 15

That person who performs his forty rites,
he will enter the Infinite (*ananta*). 16

He will be welcomed into Heaven (*svarga*),
and he will reap the fruit of Immortality. 17

His mother and father and their ancestors,
seventy-one of them. 18

They will all accompany him,
they too will attain Heaven (*vaikuṇṭha*). 19

[But] those who worship (*pūjā*) false deities of stone,
they will go to hell (*dozaḳh*). 20

Thus spoke Guru Shams the Pīr:
"Dance in the company of truth (*satsaṅga*)!" 21

90

ceto ceto te cañcala cetīyāre lola
(*Garbī 12*)

Beware! Beware that wavering mind, O wary ones! 1
Dance! Play with colorful delight, O pious ones! 2
Give up foolishness, greed, and falsehood! 3
Remember that Wielder of the bow, [Viṣṇu]! 4
You believe lovingly in stones; 5
[But] you will not thereby attain Brahmā. 6
These *garbīs* for [the goddess] Bhavānī are all a sham. 7
These lamps (*jyoti*) are but a fistful of deceptions. 8
What will dancing achieve? Lack of breath and tiredness! 9
Do not color your hearts with such false merriment! 10
You have united together merely to enjoy the food! 11
Earnings from such deception and fraud are counterfeit. 12
Serve the Lord (*nara*) whose name is Qāsim Shāh. 13
Then you will attain the place of Heaven (*vaikuṇṭha*). 14
Concentrate upon religion (*dharma*), the path of *Satpanth*. 15
Powerful is the true Sāheb—[serve him]! 16
Thus spoke Guru Shams the Pīr. 17
He unlocked [the hearts] of all the dancers. 18

91

gurajī āvyā sātamī rātake nāce bahu raṅgare lola
(Garbī 13)

The Guru came on the seventh night
and danced with great delight. 1

All the people of the city were gathered there,
and they danced with the Guru. 2

Guru Shams recited wisdom (*ginān*)
with intense fervor and feeling. 3

He described the spread of *Ratnayug*[1];
"Listen carefully, all of you!" 4

Ninety-nine [crore] Yakṣas will come together there
with as many Medhas. 5

Thirty-two crore Kinnars will come together there
and they will rejoice. 6

Thirty-three crore Devas will worshipfully
welcome the Gurunara. 7

Five crore will come with King Prahlād
and meet all the gods. 8

Then King Hariścandra will make a plea
on behalf of his gathering (*jamāʿat*). 9

Nine crore will come with the Pāṇḍava princes
and enjoy supreme happiness (*sukha*). 10

Numerous will come together with Pīr Ṣadr al-Dīn,
some twelve crore. 11

---

1. *ratenayuga:* lit. the age of *ratna*, the jewel; reference unknown.

Countless crore will come with Guru Ḥasan Shāh[2]
who upheld the *Vedas*. 12

All the divine Prophets (*pegambar*) will meet there,
124,000 of them. 13

Ḥusayn's followers will be present,
and Light (*nūr*) will shower upon them. 14

When the dancers heard about the glorious *Ratnayug*,
they were awe-struck. 15

But they could not grasp the Guru's art
and remained selfish and ignorant. 16

From amidst the *garbī* crowd rose hails
and cries of rejoicing: "*Jai jai! Jai jai!*" 17

The whole night passed thus in bliss (*ānanda*),
and no one withdrew till dawn. 18

This became the talk of the town,
and everybody wanted to see for themselves. 19

Thus spoke Guru Shams the Pīr;
he had delivered a [great] performance. 20

2. Pīr Hasan Kabīr al-Dīn.

92

satagura shamasa ema kahere gāfalo kema utaraśo pāra
(*Garbī 14*)

Satgur Shams says: O Careless Ones (*gāfal*)!
How will you go across to the other shore (*pār*)? 1

O Careless Ones! You adorn these stone idols with colors!
But this will not earn you the Creator (*sirjaṇhār*). 2

O Careless Ones! Why go round and round in circles?
Concentrate on the religion (*dharma*) of *Satpanth*! 3

O Careless Ones! Discard your idols of stones!
Free yourselves from past deeds (*karma*) with the truth (*sat*). 4

O Careless Ones! Cast off [the goddess] Mātā Bhavānī!
Serve (*sevā*) instead the manifestation (*avatār*) of ʿAlī. 5

O Careless Ones! Drink the holy water (*pāval*)!
Dwell on the precepts (*ācār*) of religion (*dharma*). 6

O Careless Ones! Believe in the Light (*nūr*) of Qāsim Shāh!
He is the legitimate heir, the true Imām[1] in this age of *Kalyug*. 7

O Careless Ones! Release the padlocks on your hearts!
Witness that place of liberation (*mukti*)! 8

O Careless Ones! The Divine Light shines in Śrī Islām Shāh!
Recognize the Lord (*nara*) when you see him! 9

O Careless Ones! By his magic I have come here;
Indeed, I am Pīr Shams. 10

---

1. *āla imām:* Per. *ahl-e-imām:* family of the *imām*, descendants in the line of imāmate.

O Careless Ones! I have come to take a pledge (*kol*);
Today, give me your word (*vāc*)! 11

O Careless Ones! Those who act paying heed to our teachings,
They will enjoy that immovable reign [of bliss]. 12

O Careless Ones! This is the age (*yuga*) of the last battlefield;
O my Brothers, be vigilant! 13

O Careless Ones! Believe in the religion (*dharma*) of *Satpanth*!
Hold fast to the resolve in your hearts. 14

O Careless Ones! You will not be saved by false practices!
I am revealing to you words of truth (*sat*). 15

O Careless Ones! This is the final stage of *Kalyug*, so beware!
Remember the Wielder of the bow [Viṣṇu]. 16

O Careless Ones! Take care, thoughtful ones, take care!
Drink the pure water (*nirmala nīr*). 17

O Careless Ones! Composing this [*garbī*], the Guru declared it;
Thus spoke Shams, the Pīr. 18

93

gura kahere gāfalo sāmbhaḷore lola
(*Garbī 15*)

The Guru says: Listen, O Careless Ones (*gāfal*)! 1
Why go round and round in the vain circles [of rebirth]? 2
There will not be an eleventh form (*rūpa*). 3
There will be no fifth age after this [last age] of *Kalyug*. 4
Today the Gurunara has arrived and become manifest. 5
He has revealed himself in human form. 6
Recognize the essence (*sār*) of that true receptacle. 7
Else you will fall apart from him, the Creator (*sirjaṇhār*). 8
Then truly will you regret your foolishness, 9
When every one of you faces the [final] trial. 10
The Guru said repeatedly to the dancers: 11
Why dance this way in vain? You are foolish! 12
If you apprehend the Guru, you will attain [salvation]. 13
You will gain immortality in the Immortal City (*amarāpurī*). 14
Now we have fulfilled our promise (*kol*). 15
The final message has been made plain and evident. 16
Guru Shams has kept the promise that he gave. 17
He appeared in this age of *Kalyug* and roamed. 18

94

tītha āṭhamī āvyā gāmanā loka jue sarave sārathīre lola
(*Garbī 16*)

On the eighth night the townsfolk came;
they watched everything attentively. 1

Guru Shams sang sweet words (*bol*),
and all of them listened together. 2

The Guru recited nectarlike wisdom (*ginān*)
about primordial beginnings. 3

[About the times] when earth and sky,
wind and water were created. 4

Then four kinds of beings were brought forth
and eighteen types of vegetation. 5

His ancestor was the Master (*īśvar*) Adam
who was created from Light (*nūr*). 6

First the Holy Five[1] were created;
they [too] were created from Light. 7

Those who know the secret know
that the religion (*dīn*) *Satpanth* was created that day. 8

Those who obey the chief (*mukhī*) of the assembly (*jamā'at*)
will be freed of past deeds. 9

The gathering (*gat*) is filled with infinite enchantment:
all [who join] are filled by it. 10

---

1. *panjatan pāka* lit. the five pure ones. A reference to Muḥammed, 'Alī, Fāṭimah, Ḥasan, and Ḥusayn.

The gathering is filled with Yakṣas, Medhas, Kinnars,
and thirty-three crore [deities]. 11

The gathering is filled with the saints (*awliyā*)
who all bear Divine Light (*teja*). 12

The gathering radiates with the Gurunara
who is also full of Divine Light. 13

In the gathering is the Creator himself
who is forever [resplendent]. 14

In the gathering is the path to freedom (*mukti*)—
those who understand will have it. 15

Alas, those in this foolish world who remain in error—
they will not understand! 16

Such a secret (*bhed*) the Guru has disclosed himself:
Do not be foolish and go astray! 17

Thus spoke Guru Shams the Pīr;
the Guru has narrated this wisdom (*ginān*). 18

95

nara kāsama shāhanā faramānathī gura shamasa pīra ramavā nīsarīya
(*Garbī 17*)

Upon the order (*farmān*) of Lord Qāsim Shāh
Guru Shams, the Pīr, went to roam. 1

Refrain:
O Mother, he left to roam!

He travelled through twenty-four kingdoms.[1] 2

First he went to the city of Cīnab
where he enlightened the lady Surjādevī. 3

Then at Meru, he witnessed many wonders
that were endless in number. 4

Then, he who belonged to the family of the Prophet,
came to the city of Ucch. 5

Here he exposed Bahā' al-Dīn's wickedness,
cursing him with a pair of horns. 6

Then the Guru revived a corpse
and performed countless [other] feats. 7

The whole world watched as the Satgur
bade the sun [to descend]. 8

The Guru performed such miracles for,
verily, he was as Kṛṣṇa[2] himself. 9

---

1. *srī vara mīr:* this phrase which forms the rest of the sentence is obscure.
2. *murārī:* lit. slayer of demons; epithet of Kṛṣṇa.

From there he came to Analvāḍ
where he danced in the *garbī* dance. 10

Fools did not grasp the essence and,
circling round and round, went astray. 11

Reciting wisdom (*ginān*), the Guru said this
to the endless in number. 12

While narrating the four scriptures (*veda*),
he revealed the four books (*kitāb*). 13

To all he imparted the true teaching—
the path of the religion (*dharma*) of *Satpanth*. 14

In many talks the Guru explained
that the last scripture (*veda*) was the *Qur'ān*. 15

Whoever understood must surely have been
meritorious in their past deeds. 16

For, the Guru said they became Immortal (*amar*).
Beware, this age of *Kalyug* is the last. 17

This is what Guru Shams said;
indeed, this wisdom (*ginān*) reveals the truth (*sāc*)! 18

96

bhulā ma bhule bhamajore hīndu juo cho śuṅ marama
(Garbī 18)

O Hindus! Stop going aimlessly in circles!
What meaning do you see in this? 1

O Hindus! What will you gain by stone-worship
except to accumulate *karma*? 2

O Hindus! You adorn stones with garlands:
do not be foolish, do not go astray! 3

O Hindus! He who errs loses the essence (*sār*);
he will find a place nowhere. 4

O Hindus! Those who dwell on the three *Vedas*!
Know that their time is over. 5

O Hindus! Gone are the nine saviors (*avatār*)
upon whom you meditate! 6

O Hindus! Gone is Brahmā of the *brahmins*!
He has become the Ḥusaynī *imām*. 7

O Hindus! Gone are the [times of] cow-worship!
Now worship ʿAlī's name (*nām*). 8

O Hindus! Gone are the sixty-eight pilgrimages (*tīrtha*)
[once] so full of Brahmā's feats. 9

O Hindus! On and on why wander in circles?
Drink in the pure Light (*nūr*)![1] 10

O Hindus! Why bow your heads before stone?
Know that the *avatār* is Qāsim Shāh. 11

---

1. *niramala nūra:* in other cases, *niramala nīra*, that is, holy or pure water.

O Hindus! He who lives in Kahak city is the Sāheb—
he is the giver of boons! 12

O Hindus! Worshipping him, you will be freed—
today I have revealed the truth (*sāc*). 13

O Hindus! Attaining Heaven (*vaikuṇṭha*),
you will reign in ceaseless bliss. 14

O Hindus! You will gain fifty damsels
if you accept the religion (*dharma*) of *Satpanth*. 15

O Hindus! Give up your sins in the gathering,
and all your deeds (*karma*) will dissolve. 16

O Hindus! Pīr Shams said this:
I am revealing to you the final message. 17

O Hindus! Do not be fools and go astray;
serve the Bow-Wielder [Viṣṇu]! 18

97

tītha navamī āvyā gurujī āpa rame sarave sārathīre lola (*Garbī 19*)

On the ninth night the Guru himself came,
and everyone danced with joy. 1

He danced with a purpose
and imparted many teachings. 2

He praised the *Panjtan Pāk*
who were born of Divine Light (*nūr*). 3

From the Light (*nūr*) of the *Panjtan Pāk*,
[Pole Star] Dhruva was created. 4

It took him 70,000 years to ascend,
and it will take him the same to descend. 5

Prophet (*nabī*) Muḥammed is the name of that star,
and ʿAlī is [his] crown. 6

Around his beautiful neck flashes
the brilliant Light (*nūr*) of Fāṭimah. 7

Bathed in Light (*teja*) between his two ears
are the Imāms Ḥasan and Ḥusayn. 8

From Light (*nūr*), he created the sky
and the seven subregions of the earth. 9

He himself made the Divine Seat and Throne[1]
and created the Pen and Tablet.[2] 10

---

1. *arasa kurṣa:* Ar. *al-arsh wa-l kursī.*
2. *loha kalama:* Ar. *al-lawh wa-l kalām.*

Then with the Pen he wrote upon the Tablet
the names of the holy saints. 11

Holding it carefully, he inscribed on it
those who accepted the religion of *Satpanth*. 12

It was then that the debt of tithe (*dasond*) began,
the payment of which brings freedom. 13

Make that offering (*dān*) from the fruits of your own labors—
such is the true tithe. 14

Near and dear to the Lord (*nara*) is such a one
who toils hard [and then gives tithe]. 15

The Gurunara has shown you the best sacrifice—
perform it, O Pious Ones (*munivar*)! 16

Then you will attain the other shore (*pahele pār*)
and reign in eternal bliss. 17

Thus spoke Guru Shams the Pīr:
"All your works will be fulfilled." 18

98

pīra nācīne kathe ginānare mā ema samajāvīne
(*Garbī 20*)

The Pīr dances and recites wisdom (*ginān*)! 1

Refrain:
O Mother, the Guru explains things thus:

Try and understand the signs of truth (*sat*)! 2

Why have you adopted such false practices! 3

The Guru repeats over and over: 4

Why are all of you being deceived? 5

The Pīr has come to hold your hand. 6

Probe deep for the essence of scripture (*veda*). 7

Why do you forget this, O Careless Ones! 8

The Pīr is performing a feat today. 9

What is the use if you remain ignorant? 10

O People, serve (*sevā*) the True Path of *Satpanth*! 11

Keep your mind firm and steadfast! 12

Abandon that fake idol of yours! 13

Grasp this knowledge this instant! 14

The holy water (*pāval*) will purify you. 15

You will promptly go to Heaven (*vaikuṇṭha*). 16

Thus did Guru Shams, the Pīr, speak: 17

Remain steadfast in your hearts. 18

99

sata māraga satavantīyā sambhaḷo sarave jana
(Garbī 21)

Listen all you people, followers of the True Path (*satmārga*)! 1

Refrain:
O Mother, Guru Shams is saying this:

Search the essence of scripture (*purāṇ*),
and your mind will be purified. 2

Today you have made merriment with the *garbī*,
but do not be fooled. 3

The gods (*deva*) and goddesses (*devī*) entered
the True Path—you can verify this! 4

The Yakṣas, Medhas, Kinnars,
and thirty-three crore deities all attained salvation. 5

That person witnesses them clearly
whose mind and deed are pure. 6

Prahlād, Hariścandra, and the Pāṇḍavas
are all in the True Religion (*satdharma*). 7

Whose mind is pure and whose heart steadfast
such a one can witness them. 8

Those pious ones (*rīkhīsar*) who are staunch in faith (*viśvās*),
they attained salvation. 9

They are all present at the site of the Ganges[1]
in the pious gathering (*gat*). 10

---

1. That is, in the water of the *ghaṭ* ceremony.

Know also that Pīr Ṣadr al-Dīn
    took twelve crore with him [to Heaven]. 11

Those who purify the mind and clasp our hand
    will witness them. 12

In this last phase, countless
    will draw strength from Pīr Ḥasan Shāh's name. 13

Pervading the gathering of the Ganges,
    they fill it night and day with Light. 14

Whoever enters the religion of *Satpanth*
    attains freedom and Divine vision (*dīdār*). 15

That man or woman will be saved
    whose former deeds (*pūnya*) were pure. 16

The Guru sang this *garbī* with full voice
    and made [the truth] manifest. 17

Whoever enters the religion of *Satpanth*
    is a servant of God (*hari*). 18

100

gura vādīyā daśamī rāta ke āvīyā garabīere lola
(Garbī 22)

The Guru came to the *garbī* dance
on the tenth night and spoke. 1

He danced untiringly,
and everybody had a great time. 2

But then one *brahmin* whose name was Śaṅkar
quit the *garbī* dance. 3

He did not comprehend the Guru's secret (*bhed*)—
that all this was a miracle. 4

Surely mean was his merit of former deeds,
for he had thus abandoned Brahmā. 5

Being poor in true merit,
what could he realize of [the Guru's] powers! 6

But all the other people of the city came together,
and they listened. 7

They all knew the Guru's secret—
that, in fact, this man was a holy man (*devatā*). 8

The thirty-five remaining *paṇḍits* who
were reading the scripture (*purāṇ*) recognized him. 9

They discarded the *Purāṇas* to hear
the words uttered by the Guru himself. 10

They understood his words of truth (*sat*)
and lodged them firmly in their hearts. 11

The minds of all the *paṇḍits* were reformed,
and they whirled in ecstacy. 12

They had understood the various aspects [of truth]
described by the Guru. 13

They beat seven drums, blew trumpets,
and repeated the Guru's speech. 14

Hailing the Guru, they beat their drums
over and over again. 15

They hailed him and cried *jay! jay!*
whilst the people looked on. 16

Everybody there was astonished,
and they all listened very intently indeed. 17

Pīr Shams the Guru said:
"Listen carefully, all of you!" 18

101

gura kahe che mīṭhī vāṇe ke sahu sāmbhaḷatāre
(*Garbī 23*)

The Guru spoke his sweet words,
and everybody listened. 1

Remember the Bow-Wielder
lest your souls (*jīv*) go astray! 2

All of you, men and women,
be attentive and listen! 3

Seize upon the religion (*dharma*) of *Satpanth*
[which is] for the whole world. 4

Be honest in your business dealings,
and your trade will flourish. 5

Absorb this wisdom (*ginān*) and bear
the religion of *Satpanth* in your hearts. 6

Understand that subtle secret
and drink the holy water (*pāval*). 7

Give tithe (*dasond*) and you will be relieved
of your accumulated deeds (*karma*). 8

But give it from the labor of your own bodies,
O Followers of *Satpanth*! 9

If you practice such religion in your veins,
you will become powerful. 10

Do not go astray over and over again;
know the [true] path (*mārga*)! 11

We have come up to your door;
[now] recognize us! 12

We have kept our word (*vāc*);
[now] what have you to say? 13

Countless souls have not yet been saved;
why remain with them? 14

Come join those innumerable
who have concentrated on religion (*dharma*). 15

If you earn the truth (*haqq*),
you will attain the abode of Heaven (*vaikuṇṭha*). 16

Thus has Pīr Shams spoken:
"Conduct yourselves with care! 17

Keep firm and steadfast in your heart
and give the tithe (*dasond*)." 18

102

tāre vāgā te gīnānanā vājāre mā khela kīdhā te gura shamasare mā (*Garbī 24*)

Then he played the melody of that *ginān*! 1

Refrain:
Yes, O Mother, Guru Shams performed such a spectacle!

All the pious ones came and stood there. 2

Then the instruments of religion (*dharma*) began to play. 3

The shackles of all former deeds (*karma*) were released. 4

The great kings, too, came to join in the dance. 5

Leaving behind their lands, they came and stood. 6

Everywhere there was great bliss and rejoicing. 7

In the city, there lived a king. 8

He came to know about the *garbī* dance. 9

[He heard] that the Bow-Wielder himself was at the *garbī*. 10

So the king also came to the scene. 11

He was accompanied by an escort of ministers. 12

They all witnessed the art and marvels of the Guru. 13

The residents of the entire city had come and gathered. 14

They were all struck with utter amazement. 15

They came before the Guru and prostrated at his feet. 16

Thus has Pīr Shams spoken: 17

O Brothers, be devoted to the True Path (*satpanth*)! 18

103

jyāre āvī che chellī rāta ke malyā sarave sārathīre lola
(*Garbī 25*)

When the last night arrived,
all were gathered in great delight. 1

The Guru had performed endless miracles,
and all the pious (*ṛṣi*) were present. 2

The king and his subjects were present,
and all prostrated themselves at the Guru's feet. 3

They went near Guru Shams
and implored him with this request (*vinantī*). 4

They all said: "Impart to us
your religion (*dharma*), O Guru! 5

So that truth (*sat*) may release us
from our past deeds (*karma*)." 6

The *brahmins* discarded their *Purāṇas*
and fell prostrate at the Guru's feet. 7

They said: "Guru, show us your religion,
and we all will follow it. 8

We shall give up all this falsehood and sham
for your sake, O Satgur! 9

Now that the three *Vedas* are of no further use to us,
you protect us. 10

You, O Guru, are a true Muslim;
show us the religion (*dīn*). 11

We Hindus relinquish our false gods (*deva*);
we worship the religion (*dīn*). 12

If we plant seeds of goodness in our fields,
    we will be able to reap the fruit. 13

Give to us your religion (*dharma*),
    and we shall preserve it in our hearts. 14

We have cast away these false scriptures (*śāstras*);
    show us the *Qur'ān*. 15

You have brought to us the pure religion
    and revealed to us its value." 16

Humbly, the *brahmins* said:
    "The Guru has indeed shown us great mercy!" 17

Pīr Shams then uttered these enduring words—
    the Guru spoke them himself. 18

104

gure bhulyāne māraga batāvīyāre lola
(*Garbī 26*)

The Guru revealed the path (*mārga*) to the astray. 1

He brought religion (*dharma*) to all the *brahmins*. 2

Thus the king and queen adopted the religion. 3

[So did] all the citizens and creatures of the city. 4

The ascetics (*jātīs* and *jogīs*) abandoned their *yoga*. 5

They yoked their hearts to the True Religion (*satdharma*). 6

Similarly, the renunciates (*sannyāsin*) left their asceticism (*sannyāsa*). 7

They led their hearts into the path of the True Path (*satpanth*). 8

The recluses (*vairāgī*) left their renunciation (*vairāgya*). 9

They fixed their minds on the path of *Satpanth*. 10

All the worshippers (*pūjārī*) set aside their worship (*pūjā*). 11

They delighted in the bliss of the path (*mārga*) of religion. 12

[Sacred] threads of one and a quarter mounds were broken. 13

In the hearts of all, Light (*nūr*) began to shine. 14

They threw every one of the *garbī* [pots] into the sea. 15

Then they took instruction in the path of *Satpanth*. 16

Guru Shams showed mercy and preached. 17

He unlocked the hearts of the wicked and unbelievers alike. 18

105

gure kāḍhī che pāvala nāthe amījala bharīyāre
(*Garbī 27*)

The Guru himself brought
the [cups filled with the] holy water (*pāval*). 1

He made sure one and all drank from it;
indeed, the Pīr was merciful. 2

By drinking this nectar (*amīras*),
they were all purified by the True Path (*satpanth*). 3

The Lord (*nara*) Qāsim Shāh himself came
and gave his beneficient Vision (*dīdār*). 4

In the city there was great rejoicing,
and everybody sang [the Guru's] *gināns*. 5

He appointed the head (*mukhī*) of the gathering (*gat*),
and all gave offerings (*dān*). 6

All gave the exact offering of tithe (*dasond*)
and became purified and pious (*munivar*). 7

"O Guru, you have been truly merciful!
You led countless of us to [salvation]." 8

All those who lived in that city,
their works were successful. 9

O Brother, they will enjoy the reign of eternal bliss
in the City of Immortality. 10

Those who having known and witnessed this
and yet err, they will not attain that state. 11

Errant, such are denied liberation (*mukti*),
and they meander from house to house. 12

And those who accept the religion (*dharma*) of *Satpanth*
but still do not practice it— 13

On their heads befall a heavy load of *karma*;
they will be dumped in hell. 14

O my Brother, be devoted to the religion
so you may attain the other shore (*pahele pār*). 15

If your earnings are honest and pure,
you will enter the gates of Heaven (*svarga*). 16

Such a *garbī* [song] Pīr Shams,
the Guru, himself has sung. 17

O Believers (*mu'min*), attain the Divine Vision (*dīdār*),
and your sins will vanish! 18

106

evī garabī saṃpūrṇa sāra gura shamasa bolyā vīcāra
(*Garbī 28*)

This *garbī* completes the cycle of *garbīs*—
Guru Shams has spoken his thoughts. 1

Who listens to them with single mind
will gain a thousandfold merit (*puṇya*). 2

Man or woman, whoever sings them
will attain the other shore (*pahele pār*). 3

Whoever sings the garbīs of *Satpanth*
will be relieved of all repentance. 4

Listen truly, O Man and Woman!
Such false festivity has been costly for you. 5

You will attain Heaven (*vaikuṇṭha*) only if
you sing the *garbīs* steadfastly. 6

Singing *garbīs* and cherishing the religion (*dharma*)
will free you of ages of sin. 7

Seventy-one ancestors of those will be saved
who hear the *garbīs* of *Satpanth*. 8

One who has kept steadfast faith (*viśvās*)
will indeed be a true devotee (*dās*) of ʿAlī. 9

Those devotees of ʿAlī who sing [*garbīs*]
will attain the abode of Heaven (*vaikuṇṭha*). 10

Whoever recites them on a Friday night
will gain the state of Immortality (*amar*). 11

Be honest and sincere in purpose, O Brother,
and your earnings will be true. 12

O Pious (*rīkhīsar*)! Be patient and steadfast in your hearts,
so said Guru Shams, the Pīr. 13

The Pīr had made a promise (*kol*), and he came—
see how he showed them the path! 14

After gaining such understanding,
if you lose enthusiasm do not blame the Pīr. 15

The Pīr has explained this word by word
to those who accepted *Satpanth*. 16

They were saved, man and woman,
when Pīr Shams uttered his thoughts. 17

This *garbī* [cycle] is now complete;
verily, it is the true speech (*vāc*) of the Guru! 18

Appendix A: Incipits

Appendix B: Translation of "A Short Life-History of Our Twenty-Third Pīr—Ḥaḍrat Pīr Shams al-Dīn Sabzawārī"[1] in the Anthology

Ḥaḍrat Pīr Shams al-Dīn was born in the town of Sabzawār. His father's name was Ḥaḍrat Pīr Ṣalāḥ al-Dīn, and his mother's name was Fāṭimah bin Sayyid Abd al-Hādī.

Our twenty-ninth Imām, Ḥaḍrat Mawlānā Imām Shāh Qāsim Shāh, appointed Pīr Shams al-Dīn as *pīr* and ordered him to preach wisdom and spread the Ismāʿīlī faith in lands outside Iran. Kissing the hand of the Imām, he left with his blessings and arrived at Badakhshān where he began his duty to preach. Revealing the Imām of the time *(zamānā nā imām)* to the people, he accepted their allegiance to Ḥaḍrat Mawlānā Imām Shāh Qāsim Shāh on his behalf and initiated them into the religion of Ismāʿīlism.

From Badakhshān he passed through Ghazni, Cīnab, and other towns, and, trekking through the Hindukush and Pāmir mountain ranges, he reached Kashmir. At every town that he passed through, he kept up his duty of preaching. During his journey, he endured many troubles and afflictions. Suffering hunger and thirst, he arrived in India (Hindustān) where, in order to teach and preach, he had to learn and master many different Indian dialects.

One day, he came to a town called Anal where he found Hindus singing *garbīs* on the occasion of Daserā. Pīr Shams al-Dīn mixed in

1. This is a translation of the introduction to Pīr Shams that is given in the Gujarati edition of the Anthology. The title of the Gujarati version is *āpaṇā trevīsamā pīr hazarat pīr shamsudīn sabzawārīnuṅ ṭuṅk jīvan vṛattāṅt.* The author of this piece is not stated in the *Saṅgraha.* The translation given here is mine.

with them and began to sing his own *garbīs*. These *garbīs* were filled to the brim with the philosophy of Ismāʿīlism and the revelation of the Imām of the time. Over ten days, he sang twenty-eight *garbīs*. Their effect was so profound that the local *paṇḍits* hurriedly wrote them down, and countless Hindus discarded their sacred threads *(janoi)* which piled up into a huge mound at the feet of Pīr Shams al-Dīn. [Then], accepting the faith of Islam, they all gave allegiance to the Imām of the time, Imām Qāsim Shāh.

In the same village, there lived a pious woman by the name of Emnābāī. She, too, was inspired with feelings of devotion for the *pīr* and invited him to dine at her home. The master, Pīr Shams al-Dīn, accepted her request and entered her house to eat. When the meal was laid before Pīr Shams al-Dīn, however, he refused to eat the food. To test Emnābāī, he said, "We do not want this cooking! We shall eat only if you cook a meal with water that has been fetched in an unbaked pot drawn up from the water-well with a rope made of raw cotton." Emnābāī was faithful *(imānī)*, and she followed Pīr Shams al-Dīn's instructions. She fetched water from the well and then cooked and fed him. Pīr Shams al-Dīn was greatly pleased with this [proof of] devotion and gave Emnābāī many blessings. Thus, Emnābāī passed the test.

In the year 715 A.H., Pīr Shams al-Dīn went to the delightful land of Kashmir to preach when a band of ruffians belonging to a tribe called Caṅgaḍ captured him with ropes (made of cactus). Pīr Shams al-Dīn, however, showed no fear toward these people and prayed before the presence of God Almighty. Immediately, a change came over them, and they all sought Pīr Shams al-Dīn's protection. The Caṅgaḍ tribe numbered some two lakh strong, and they all became followers of Pīr Shams al-Dīn. Thereafter, other citizens of Kashmir also became followers in great numbers, among whom could also be found [some of] its kings.

In this way, Pīr Shams al-Dīn spread the teachings of the *daʿwah* in Tibet, Kashmir, Gilān, Yārkand, Askard, Punjab, Multān, and other countries and showed the people the true path of the Ismāʿīlī faith; to a few special individuals, he also gave guidance about the "divine secret" or the "divine essence."

However, the major portion of Pīr Shams al-Dīn's followers were the Hindus, especially the people known as Cakkas who were famous for their heroism and splendor, and whose chiefs had reigned over Kashmir and the Punjab for about 280 years.

In those times, as a result of the king's oppressive orders to his provincial governors, Pīr Shams al-Dīn and his Ismāʿīlī followers suffered endless hardships. To safeguard their lives and possessions, Pīr Shams al-Dīn had to change his method of spreading the *daʿwah* and, instead, preached his message in disguise. The Hindus called this path the Shamsi sect *(śamsī mat)*, and its followers believed Ḥaḍrat ʿAlī to be the epiphany *(maẓhar)* of God Almighty.

Giving [religious] guidance to this region in such manner, Pīr Shams al-Dīn eventually reached Karachi, and from there he proceeded to Multān.

In Multān, he took up residence in an ancient mosque where a group of people had gathered to pray. He joined the group for prayer, and the *imām* leading the prayer began. In the middle of the prayer, Pīr Shams al-Dīn suddenly sat down. Once the prayer was over, people rushed to the Pīr demanding an explanation for his irreverent attitude. Pīr Shams al-Dīn gestured to them to sit down and said that, "As long as the *imām* who led the prayer was remembering Allah, I performed the prayer with him, but I sat down in the middle of the prayer when his attention strayed from Allah's recollection and idly wandered to other places." Everyone was astonished by this answer. They urged him, "Please stand forward as the *imām* who leads the prayer and make us pray." The Pīr consented to their request. As the prayer commenced, lights came alive in all their hearts, and, when those in prayer bowed, the minarets of the mosque began to bow, too. Witnessing this, the people became frightened and midway through the prayer fled outside the mosque. When Pīr Shams al-Dīn completed his prayer and came out, the people asked, "What happened?" In reply, Pīr Shams al-Dīn recited the following verse of a *ginān*:

> My mind is the prayer mat and the judge;
>   and my body is my mosque;
> Sitting in it, I perform the *namāz*;
>   indeed, [is there one] who knows my submission?

After hearing the above words, their hearts became filled with respect for Pīr Shams al-Dīn. But when the Ṣūfī of Multān, Bahā' al-Dīn Zakariyya, heard about this incident, he began to fear for his fame. Thus, he ordered his staunch disciple Khān Muḥammad Seyyid Hākīm Shahīd to make sure that Pīr Shams al-Dīn would not be able to enter Multān by hauling in all the rafts and boats onto the city's shore. And thus it was done. When Pīr Shams al-Dīn arrived at the river bank and did not see any boats, he constructed one from a piece of paper. Sitting in it, he asked his companions to hold on to his fingers, and the boat began to move; but it unsteadily lurched to and fro. Seeing this, he asked: "Is there anyone who carries material possessions?" Shāhzādah Muḥammad presented him his mother's jewelry which she had given him for his journey. The Pīr threw it into the water, and the boat began to glide forward smoothly. Bahā' al-Dīn Zakariyya was sitting in the balcony of his palace when his eyes fell upon a boat that was halfway across the river. He promptly swore for it to stop dead in its tracks, and the boat abruptly came to a halt. Pīr Shams al-Dīn peered in all four directions to search for the cause of this event, and then he saw Bahā' al-Dīn Zakariyya sitting in his balcony. Immediately, he understood the gist of the situation and cast a glance towards Bahā' al-Dīn. When this divine glance fell upon him, two horns burst forth from Bahā' al-Dīn Zakariyya's temple, and his head got stuck in the balcony. The boat began to move forward at full speed. Bahā' al-Dīn was petrified by this miraculous feat and dispatched his sons Ṣadr al-Dīn and Shaykh al-Dīn to Pīr Shams al-Dīn to ask for forgiveness. Pīr Shams al-Dīn arrived at the ancient mosque before the two got there. They prostrated at his feet and pleaded for mercy. Accepting their imploring pleas, Pīr Shams al-Dīn recited a prayer on behalf of their father, and the horns on Bahā' al-Dīn Zakariyya's head disappeared. However, the marks left by the horns have remained imprinted upon the foreheads of his progeny. The balcony where Bahā' al-Dīn sat still exists in Multān.

During the time that Pīr Shams al-Dīn resided in Multān, it so happened that, one by one, the sons of its ruler began to die. The king could not control his grief. He summoned all the saints, *ṣūfīs,* and learned men, and said: "It is your calling that you are close to God Almighty, and thus have I showered you with many priceless favors and gifts. So today, in return I wish you to revive my son. If you are truly near God, you will be able to accomplish this task. If you fail in it, surely I will crush you up in the oil-mill."

Hearing this, they could not contain their fears, and they rushed to Pīr Shams al-Dīn, pleading him to rescue them from the jaw of death. Pīr Shams al-Dīn felt pity on them and, consenting to their request, arrived by the side of the dead prince. Gazing at the corpse, he said: "*kum be-iḍhan allāh!*" which means "By the command of Allah, Rise!" But this had no effect, so the Pīr said again, "*kum be-iḍhanī!*" which means "Rise by my command!" Immediately the prince came alive.

The king was supremely delighted by this miracle. However, since the learned men had been forced to look down in shame, they issued an order *(fatwā)* charging that Pīr Shams al-Dīn was sinful for having accomplished this feat by his own command and not by the will of God. They decreed that by religious law, the punishment for this sin was to be as follows: to strip off the Pīr's skin while he was still alive. This injunction turned the people against the Pīr, but, as Pīr Shams al-Dīn was a divine personage capable of miracles, he promptly covered his body with a black blanket and, by his own hand, peeled the skin off his body and threw it before the learned men. Seeing this, everyone was stunned and began to tremble. Yet, even after this scene, since he had been branded a sinner by the *fatwā,* and due to the religious command against having any relations or contact with him, people did not associate with the Pīr.

After a great deal of time had elapsed, Pīr Shams al-Dīn, suffering from hunger, begged the people for some food. However, nobody paid any attention to him. A butcher took heart and gave him a piece of meat. Pīr Shams al-Dīn began to ponder on how he would cook the meat. Taking it along with him, he went outside the city of Multān and, by his own powers, brought the sun down to cook it. The people of Multān began to sizzle under the sun's unbearable heat, and many of them scurried to the Pīr, fell at his feet, and begged for forgiveness. The Pīr was merciful, and, since by this time the piece of meat had been cooked, he ordered the sun to go back to its original place, which it did. The site at which the sun descended was henceforth called Suryakand. It exists even now, and each year a huge festival is celebrated there.

Pīr Shams al-Dīn then arrived in Kashmir where there was a large sect that worshipped the sun. As long as the sun shone, they were absorbed in prayer and other religious ceremonies, but, once the sun had set, they were not afraid of committing sinful deeds. For, these people believed that, when it was dark, the sun was asleep and could not see their sins, and, therefore, sins committed in darkness were not to be counted as sins. The Pīr enlightened these deluded people and showed them the true path of the Ismāʿīlī faith. They came to be known as the Shamsīs.

At present, the Shamsīs in the Punjab, who are very great in number, [are descendants of those who] were originally enlightened by Pīr Shams al-Dīn, and [now] they openly practice the Ismāʿīlī faith. In order to spread the Ismāʿīlī faith, the master, Pīr Shams al-Dīn, endured all kinds of obstacles. In India, wherever he went to give wisdom, he composed *gināns* and *garbīs* in beautiful language to disclose the true religion, thus winning many followers.

Pīr Shams al-Dīn was married to Bibi Ḥāfizah Jamāl, the daughter of his uncle, Sayyid Jalāl al-Dīn. She bore him two sons: Ḥaḍrat Naṣīr al-Dīn and Ḥaḍrat Sayyid Aḥmad Zindāpīr. When Pīr Shams al-Dīn departed this temporal world, the Imām of the time entrusted the title and position of *pīr* upon his son, Naṣīr al-Dīn, who is our twenty-fourth *pīr*. His name is cited in the genealogy of the *pīrs* as Pīr Naṣīr al-Dīn.

During his service of Ḥaḍrat Mawlānā Imām Shāh Qāsim Shāh, Pīr Shams al-Dīn lived for a long time in the town called Tabrīz. This is why he is often known as Pīr Shams al-Dīn Tabrīzī. Moreover, as he was born in the town Sabzawār, he is also known as Pīr Shams al-Dīn Sabzawārī. The people of Egypt and Syria know him as Shams Maghrībī. After he had lived in Kashmir, he was also called Shams al-Dīn Irāqī. In the *duʿā,* he is addressed as Pīr Shams Coṭa.

Here, it is extremely important to clarify that the great Ṣūfī saint Ḥaḍrat Shams Tabrīzī who was Jalāl al-Dīn Rūmī's spiritual guide, and who lived during the time of our twenty-eighth Imām, Ḥaḍrat Mawlānā Imām Shāh Shams al-Dīn Muḥammad, was not the same person who was our twenty-third *pīr,* Pīr Shams al-Dīn Sabzawārī, who was also called Pīr Shams Tabrīzī. These were two different individuals. Pīr Shams al-Dīn died in Multān in the year 757 A.H.

Even today, we still sing the *ginans* and *garbīs* composed by Pīr Shams al-Dīn with great devotional fervor. In addition to their insightful verses and their lofty philosophy of the Ismāʿīlī faith, these *ginans* and *garbīs* are saturated with the complete and clear-cut teachings on the obedience to and recognition of the Imām of the time. After reading this short life-history of Pīr Shams al-Dīn and studying his *ginans,* it is essential that the teachings expressed in them be put into practice in life so that our faith remains strong and firm. [We pray] that we should be able to gain a true understanding of the Ismāʿīlī faith; that we should have no hesitation in obeying the orders of the Imām of the time; and that the living Imām, Mawlānā Ṣulṭān Muḥammad Shāh Dātār, should perpetually keep alive in each one of us feelings of loyalty. May Mawlā bless every Ismāʿīlī with true guidance. Āmīn. Ṣalawāt.

Appendix C: Notes on Names and Epithets in the Anthology[1]

Mythological Figures

Ambarīśa: A king of Ayodhyā who visited the sage Tricitmuni. The sage insisted on using the king's son, Suse, as the sacrificial animal. However, the sacrifice was interrupted by Indra who rescued the sacrificial victim, who had extolled Indra and Viṣṇu at the stake. Suse had learned Vedic hymns from his uncle, Viśvamitra. Also, an appellation of Śiva; the name of one of eighteen hells.

Arjuna: Third of the Pāṇḍava* princes. Son of Indra and Droṇa's favorite pupil. Earned Draupadī as his wife when he won the contest of strength in her *swayamvara* (a public event where a princess chooses her husband from an assembly of suitors). It was to Arjuna that Kṛṣṇa, his charioteer, related the *Bhagavad Gītā* at the battle-scene with the Kauravas* in Kurukṣetra.

Asura: Antagonists of the Suras.* Consist of several classes of which the most frequently mentioned are *daitya,* dānava,* dāsyu, nāga,* and *rākṣasa.** Asuras dwell in mountain caves and in Pātāla, the lower depths of the earth. Skilled in sorcery and magic, they transform themselves into any form and terrify humans with their awful roaring.

1. The annotation of Personal Names has been divided into three groups a) mythological, b) historical, or c) local names. Names and terms are listed in their Sanskritic or Arabic forms or as they appear in the translations.

* Terms marked with an asterisk have an entry in the appendix.

Avatāra: "descent": incarnation or appearance of a deity; associated especially with Viṣṇu. The capacity of divine beings to manifest themselves by virtue of their creative power, *māyā.** Viṣṇu incarnates in order to preserve righteousness. Thus, when the earth is overwhelmed with evil and suffering, his salvific power manifests itself in *avatāras.* In *Bhagavad Gītā* IV:7–8, Viṣṇu promises to come forth from age to age to protect the good and destroy evil when *dharma** declines.

Bali/Balirājā: Descendant of the demon Hiraṇyakaśipu.* A *daitya** king who defeated Indra through penance and thus won rule over three worlds. The gods were mortified and appealed to Viṣṇu who came to their rescue as Vāmana,* the dwarf *avatāra.* Begging the proud king to grant him a mere three steps of land, which boon the king carelessly gave, Viṣṇu then assumed his real stature and stepped over the heaven and earth in two strides; Bali had to take the third step on his head and, hence, descended into the infernal region of hell, Pātāla, where he was allowed to rule out of respect due to his virtuous ancestor, Prahlāda.*

Bhavānī (mātā): "mother goddess"; one of Śiva's consorts; his female energy, *śakti,* which consists in two opposite natures, mild and ferocious. The female principle is worshipped especially under the ferocious form as Durgā, "inaccessible," Kālī, "black," and Bhairavī, "terrible, fearful." The Tāntrikas, in particular, celebrate her powers and seek her favors. She is also known as *kanyā-kuṁvārī,** "youthful virgin," and *satī,** "pure, virtuous."

Bhīma/Bhīma Sena: "the terrible"; second of the five Pāṇḍava* princes and son of Vāyu, God of Wind. A man colossal in size, of daunting strength and voracious appetite. Brave, crude in manners, and fierce-tempered as a foe, Bhīma's favorite weapon was the club. He played a prominent role in the battle of Kurukṣetra where he avenged Draupadī* by slaying Duḥśāsana who had insulted her and on the last day of battle, unfairly defeated the chief of the Kauravas,* Duryodhana.*

Brahmā: Creator; first god of the Hindu triad manifesting the impersonal Brahman's three aspects: Brahmā (creator), Viṣṇu,* (preserver) and Śiva (destroyer). An epithet of Brahmā is *adikartār,* "fashioner of all things." He is also referred to as Mānasa or Puruṣa, the Primeval Man. In many instances, Brahmā is confused with Brahman, the Universal Principle.

Buddha: "enlightened, awakened"; a title or honorific meaning wise or learned man, sage, one who is fully enlightened and has achieved perfection or truth. Applied specifically to a *kṣatriya* prince in Northern India called Siddhārata, son of King Śuddhodhana of the Gautama clan, who became known as the sage of the Śākyas, *śākyamuni,* and founded a religion (that was later called Buddhism) around the sixth century B.C.E. The central teaching of the Buddha, captured in his Four Noble Truths, is that all life is suffering and there is no permanent self. He prescribed a way out of suffering through The Eightfold Path.

Cānūra: A wrestler and demon friend of King Kaṃsa* who was killed by Kṛṣṇa.* Kṛṣṇa whirled him around a hundred times till he choked and then dashed him against the ground so violently that his body was smashed into a hundred pieces.

Daitya/Dāṇava: A class or race of Asuras*: demons, giants, monsters, and ogres. They dwell in cavernous regions of the earth, are skilled in sorcery and magic, and enjoy interfering with sacrifices and warring with the Devas.*

Das Avatāra: "ten descents"; by the eleventh century C.E., the typical list of Viṣṇu's manifestations in Vaiṣṇavism were the ten *avatāras* as follows: Matsya* (fish), Kūrma* (Tortoise), Varāha* (boar), Narasiṃha* (man-lion), Vāmana* (dwarf), Paraśurāma* (axe-wielding Rāma), Rāma* (hero of the Rāmāyana), Kṛṣṇa* (beloved of gopīs), Buddha* (founder of the "false" religion of Buddhism), and Kalki* (last incarnation expected at the end of *Kalyug**).

Daśāsana: Name of Rāvaṇa* the twenty-armed and ten-faced demon king of Laṅkā who abducted Sītā,* Rāma's wife.

Deva: Gods, deities, divine celestial beings, spoken of as thirty-three crore in number, eleven crore for each realm; also applied as an epithet to pious, righteous, godly men.

Devadutta: Name of Indra's* trumpet, *śaṅkha.*

Dharma/Dharmarāja: Yama,* god who ministers justice to the dead. An epithet of Yudhiṣṭhira,* eldest of the Pāṇḍava brothers and mythical son of Dharma, god of Justice.

Dhruva: "immovable, firm, fixed." Though a *kṣatriya,* Dhruva renounced the world because of the tauntings of his stepmother, Suruci, and, through his penance and steadfast will, became a great *ṛṣi* who obtained from Viṣṇu* the boon of immortality. Viṣṇu elevated him to the skies immortalizing him as the Pole Star. His epithet is *grahadhāra,* "pivot of the planets."

Draupadī: Daughter of Draupada, King of Pañcāla. Wife of the five Pāṇḍava* princes won by Arjuna* during her *svayamvara.* While Arjuna was her favorite, it was to Bhīma* that she turned for help when the Pāṇḍu brothers lost her and their kingdom in a game of dice with the Kauravas.* Duḥśāsana mocked her as their slave and, dragging her by her hair, tore off her *sari* while Duryodhana taunted her to sit on his thigh. Showing mercy on her, Kṛṣṇa restored her garment as soon as it was ripped off, thus preserving her dignity. Bhīma swore he would avenge her, and Draupadī vowed not to tie her hair until Bhīma had wet it with Duḥśāsana's blood. She accompanied her husband, during their thirteen years of exile during which time she bore untold suffering and humiliation on their behalf.

Duryodhana: Eldest son of Dhṛtarāśtra, uncle of the Pāṇḍavas*; head of the Kauravas,* he was intensely jealous of his cousins, the five Pāṇḍava brothers and thus plotted to destroy them through a game of dice. The Pāṇḍavas were defeated and lost all their wealth and kingdom, including their wife, Draupadī.* However, at the battle of Kurukṣetra, Bhīma* killed Duryodhana,* and the Pāṇḍavas regained the sovereignty of which the Kauravas had cheated them.

Gautama: The Buddha* is often called by his *gotra* name, Gautama. Name of a great *ṛṣi* Śaradvata whose beautiful wife, Ahalyā, was seduced by Indra*; the god assumed Gautama's form when the latter was away from his hermitage and seduced his wife. Gautama discovered her infidelity and expelled her from his dwelling, depriving her as well of her handsome form.

Govinda: "cowherd"; epithet of Kṛṣṇa from his times among the herdsmen and *gopīs* in Vṛndāvana.

Hariścandra. An imperial sage, the son of Triśaṅku, virtuous king of the Solar dynasty, Hariścandra was the embodiment of truth, justice, and steadfastness of word. There are several legends about him, the most famous of which relates the terrible suffering and humiliations he endured at the hands of the sage Viśvamitra who demanded from him his country, son, wife, and his own life as sacrificial gift to atone for disturbing Viśvamitra during an experiment with the Sciences. Hariścandra, destitute and shorn of all possessions, attempted to escape to Benares, but his relentless oppressor was there waiting for the rest of his gift. His wife and child were sold to a *caṇḍāla* and he himself was assigned the lowly duty of stealing grave-cloths from the cemetery. Ultimately, the gods took pity on him and raised him to heaven where Hariścandra insisted on taking along his faithful subjects. However, prompted by the sage Nāradā to boast of his merits, he and his people were expelled from there. He immediately repented, and his fall was arrested in mid-air, where he and his subjects dwell to this day.

Hiraṇyakaśipu: "golden-robed"; a demon king, son of Diṭi and Kaśyapa, of immense wealth and power, who through his penance obtained from Śiva sovereignty over the three worlds for a million years. He was assured by Brahmā* that no man, animal, or created being could kill him, and thus took every chance to increase his wealth and power, finally usurping Indra's* throne. He resented his son, Prahlād,* for worshipping Viṣṇu* and cruelly persecuted him. To rescue Prahlād from his father's persecutions, Viṣṇu assumed his form as the Man-lion *avatāra* Narasiṁha* and mercilessly tore Hiraṇyakaśipu to pieces.

Indra: God of the firmament and guardian of the eastern quarter who rides the Golden Chariot and whose weapon is the thunderbolt *(vajra)*. Chief of the gods in the Vedas to whom many hymns are addressed. Reigning over Svarga* and its capital, Amarāvati, heavenly dwelling of gods and celestial being, he is also the god of the weather and fertility.

Kaiṭabha: One of the two demons who issued forth from the root of Viṣṇu's* ear while he was asleep. With the other demon,

Madhu,* Kaiṭabha planned to kill Brahmā* who was seated on a lotus on Viṣṇu's navel. Viṣṇu awoke in time to save Brahmā and destroy them. Another story in the *Mahābhārata* relates that the two demons stole the Vedas from Brahmā who appealed to Viṣṇu for help. Viṣṇu manifested himself as Hayaśirṣa, the horse-headed *avatāra,* and killed the two demons after retrieving the Vedas from the bottom of the sea where they had hidden them. Hence, Viṣṇu is also called Madhusūdana and Kaiṭabhyajīta.

Kālī: "black." Hideous in appearance, fang-toothed, emaciated, skulls in hand, Kālī is the goddess of time, fierce and bloody consort of Śiva, personification of his female energy *śakti.* She is also named Durgā, Mātā Bhavānī, etc., and, in the mystical Tāntric tradition, she represents the supreme realization of truth. As symbol of eternal time, she is both the giver and taker of life.

Kaliṅga: Name of a kingdom on the east coast of India north of Madras derived from the monarchy that ruled it. The Kaliṅgas were descendants of Anu and constituted one of several classes of Asuras* or demons.

Kalki: The tenth and final *avatāra* of Viṣṇu* which will become manifest at the end of *Kalyug,** the last age of darkness, strife, and untruth. Mounted on a white horse, he wields a drawn, razor-edged sword as the destroyer of evil. Appearing at the end of the fourth age, he will punish the wicked, comfort the virtuous, reestablish the golden age of righteousness, and then bring the world to an end.

Kāmadhenu: Mythical cow who grants every wish belonging to the sage Vaśiṣṭha. She was produced when the gods churned the ocean in search for *amṛta,* the nectar of Immortality. The cow of plenty, she stands for abundance, prosperity, motherhood, nature, and regeneration.

Kaṃsa: Eldest son of Ugrasena, tyrannical King of Mathura, stepbrother of Kṛṣṇa's mother, Devakī, and incarnation of the demon Kālenemi. When astrologers forecast that Kaṃsa would be killed by Devakī's son, he imprisoned her and her husband, Vasudeva, killing their first six children. The seventh child, Baladeva, was miraculously transferred from Devakī's womb to that of Rohini, and when the eighth child Kṛṣṇa* was born, they were all secretly smuggled out to Gokula. Kaṃsa ordered all male infants to be massacred, but Kṛṣṇa escaped. He persecuted Kṛṣṇa at every turn but was finally killed by Kṛṣṇa in a contest staged by him to destroy Kṛṣṇa.

Karṇa: Illegitimate son of Kuntī by the sun god, Sūrya, whom she abandoned on Yamunā to escape social stigma before her marriage to Pāṇḍu. Karṇa was brought up by a poor childless couple and became a skilled bowman and charioteer equal to none other than his rival and half brother, Arjuna.* However, since he was ostensibly of lowly origin and not of noble lineage, his participation at Draupadī's *svayamvara* was disqualified, although he was able to take up and bend the bow that no other warrior had been able to draw save Arjuna. When Arjuna was thus declared the winner of the *svayamvara,* Karṇa joined ranks with the Kauravas. Knowing he would be a valuable ally in their conflict with the Pāṇḍavas,* Duryodhana* made him King of Aṅga, but in the end he was killed by Arjuna in the battle of Kurukṣetra.

Kaurava: Patronymic name of the descendants of Kuru. Specifically refers to the hundred sons of Dhṛtarāśtra, blind brother of Pāṇḍu who was ruler and father of the five Pāṇḍava* princes. When Pāṇḍu died, Dhṛtarāśtra ascended the throne and took the latter's sons under his care, ensuring that they along with his own sons received training in the art of warfare under the supervision of the *brahmin ācāryas* Bhīśma and Droṇa. The *Mahābhārata* narrates the story of the enmity and war among the jealous sons of Dhṛtarāśtra led by his eldest son, Duryodhana,* and their cousins, the five Pāṇḍava brothers, which culminates in the battle of Kurukṣetra.

Keśava: Name of Kṛṣṇa* or Viṣṇu.* Various interpretations have been suggested for this name: "long-haired"; slayer of demon Keśin; "radiant" from Skt. *keśa*—light.

Kṛṣṇa: "black; dark-complexioned." The eighth of Viṣṇu's* *avatāras* considered to be the direct and full manifestation of Viṣṇu himself, Kṛṣṇa is the most celebrated, important, and beloved of Indian deities. A Yādava prince, son of Devakī and

Vasudeva, his life-story is variously told in the *Mahābhārata,* the *Bhāgavata Purāṇa* and *Harivamsa.* Favorite of the *gopīs* of Gokula, slayer of his uncle Kaṃsa,* charioteer of Arjuna* at the battle of Kurukṣetra, the figure of Kṛṣṇa forms the subject of a vast number of vivid legends and myths.

Kinnar: Celestial musicians who dwell in Kuvera's heaven, these mythical beings have the form of a man and the head of a horse. Together with the Gandharvas (celestial singers) and Apsaras (celestial nymphs), they provide entertainment at the banquets of the gods.

Kumbhakarṇa: lit. "pot-eared." A Rākṣasa and the monstrous brother of the demon king Rāvaṇa* who was cursed by Brahmā* to sleep for six months and awaken for a single day only to slumber again. This turned out to be a boon for the *ṛṣis* and *apsaras,* the food which Kumbha gorged himself on when he awoke. He was beheaded by Rāma.*

Kūrma: "tortoise." Form assumed by Viṣṇu* during Satyuga,* the first age, to help recover the precious *amṛta,* elixir of Immortality that was lost in a deluge. Placing himself at the bottom of the sea of milk, the gods used him as the base on which to pivot Mt. Mandara around which they twisted the serpent Vāsuki and churned the ocean until it yielded the cherished object.

Madhu: q.v. Kaiṭabha

Mandodarī: "narrow-waisted." Beautiful daughter of Māyā, architect of Asuras.* Rāvaṇa's favorite wife who bore him a son, Indrajīt. Considered to be one of the five *satīs.**

Matsya: "fish." In one telling of the myth, Viṣṇu* incarnated himself as a fish to save Vaivasvata, the seventh Manu and patriarch of the human race, from an impending deluge that would destroy the world. In the *Bhāgavata Purāṇa,* Viṣṇu takes the form of a fish to rescue the *Vedas* from Hayagrīva, a horse-necked demon who stole them from the mouth of Brahmā while the latter was asleep. When Brahmā finally awoke, Viṣṇu restored them to him and killed Hayagrīva.

Māyā: "illusion, deception, magic, supernatural power." Personified as the goddess who beguiles beings with her enchanting powers. Durgā is sometimes identified as the goddess of spells who personifies the unreality of created things.

Medhā: "intelligence, wisdom." Personified as wife of Dharma and daughter of Dakṣa.

Mugḍala: A Vedic *ṛṣi* who lived a life of piety, poverty, and restraint. Noted for generously offering hospitality to thousands of *brahmins*, his meager resource of grain never diminished when required. The sage, Durvāsas, was so impressed that he gave Mugḍala the chance to enter heaven in bodily form, but the *ṛṣi* declined, preferring instead to devote himself to practicing austerities and the ascetic virtues of indifference and fixed concentration by which he ultimately gained his aim, the state of supreme perfection *(nirvāṇa)*.

Mura: A great demon with 7,000 sons. He assisted Naraka, ruler of Prāg-jyoṭiṣa, in defending his city against Kṛṣṇa who chopped off his head and burnt his 7,000 sons with the flame blazing at the edge of his discus. Hence, Kṛṣṇa is also called Murārī—slayer of Mura.

Murārī: Epithet of Kṛṣṇa.

Nāga: "snake, serpent"; also called *sarpa*. Semi-divine beings, mythical serpents who are guardians of the wealth in the depths of the earth. Viṣṇu's favorite symbol, his couch is the serpent Ananta, also called Śeṣa and Vāsuki. The Nāgas reign in Pātāla, the region below the earth, where they flourish in great number.

Nakalaṅkī: q. v. Kalki*

Nakula: Son of Mādrī, mythical son of Aśvin, second wife of King Pāṇḍu, youngest of the five Pāṇḍava brothers and twin brother of Sahadeva* who became a skilled and acclaimed horse trainer.

Narasiṃha: "man-lion." Fourth incarnation of Viṣṇu* as half-man, half-lion who slew the demon Hiraṇyakaśipu,* who by

Brahmā's* favor was invulnerable to god, man, or beast and who could not be killed by day or night, indoors or outdoors. Incensed by his son Prahlāda's* worship of Viṣṇu, Hiranya relentlessly persecuted him and even tried to kill him. Taunting his son's belief in Viṣṇu's omnipotence and omnipresence, he once struck a stone pillar in his hall and demanded to see Viṣṇu. To avenge Prahlāda and vindicate his own majesty, Viṣṇu came forth from the pillar and tore the arrogant demon to pieces.

Nārada: Name of a mythical *ṛṣi* to whom a few hymns of the *Ṛg Veda* are ascribed. Inspirer of poets, counsellor of kings, and messenger between men and gods, he is the patron of music and inventor of the stringed musical instrument called *vīna*. He is the priest and seer who forewarned the demon Kaṃsa* of his death by his sister's son Kṛṣṇa.*

Pāṇḍava: The five sons of King Pāṇḍu called Yudhiṣṭhira,* Bhīma,* Arjuna* (by his first wife, Kuntī), and twins Nakula* and Sahadeva* (by his second wife, Mādrī), the chief protagonists in the *Mahābhārata* which describes the battle between the Pāṇḍava brothers and their first cousins, the Kauravas.* King Pāṇḍu, the son of the sage Vyāsa, King of Hastināpūra and brother of blind Dhṛtarāṣṭra, was cursed by a sage that he would die during intercourse. Hence, he gave himself up to religious austerities and practiced strict continence, urging his wives to conceive his children through adulterous union with other gods. Thus, Dhṛtarāṣṭra's sons taunted the Pāṇḍava brothers for being illegitimate sons of Pāṇḍu, and this marked the beginning of their life-long conflict.

Paraśurāma: "Rāma of the Axe." Sixth incarnation of Viṣṇu,* *brahmin* son of sage Jamadagni and his wife, Renukā, whose steadfast worship of Śiva earned from him the reward of the magic battle axe, *paraśu*. Once, when his father was away, the thousand-armed king of Haihayas, Kārtavīrya, paid a visit to his hermitage where he was respectfully received by the sage's wife. However, Kārtavīrya's intentions were evil, and after abducting her and Kāmadhenu,* Jamadagni's sacred cow acquired through great penance, he desecrated the hermitage. Paraśurāma was furious and pursued the king, slaughtered him like an animal, and cleared the earth of his Kṣatriya race twenty-one times.

Prahlāda. Son of *daitya* king Hiraṇyakaśipu, father of the arrogant king Bali,* and pious devotee of Viṣṇu who was incarnated as Narasiṃha to save Prahlāda from his cruel father. Despite his father's terrifying attempts to destroy Prahlāda, the latter's devotion to Viṣṇu remained singular and unyielding, and his earnest worship of Viṣṇu obtained him ultimate release.

Rākṣasa: Hideous, bloodthirsty, and repellent demons and fiends who haunt cemeteries, animate the dead, devour human flesh, interrupt sacrifices or place obstacles to prevent offerings to the gods, harass the devout and pious, and vex humans in every possible way. Their king is Rāvaṇa.*

Rāma: Rāmacandra: "moon among men." The eldest son of Daśāratha, King of Kosala, who ruled from his capital Ayodhyā, Rāma is the hero of the *Rāmāyaṇa* composed by the sage Vālmiki, which recounts the story of his unfair exile orchestrated by his stepmother, Kaikeyī, and the trials and tribulations he suffered in the Daṇḍaka forest with his loyal wife, Sītā.* It describes his war with the demon king Rāvaṇa* of Laṅkā who abducted Sītā and his ascension to the throne after rescuing her. While in Vālmiki, Rāma is portrayed as the epitome of a brave and righteous prince, by the time of the *Purāṇas* and later rescensions, he has been raised to the status of an *avatāra* of Viṣṇu,* second only to Kṛṣṇa in importance.

Rāvaṇa: Demon king of Laṅkā, half-brother of Kuvera whom he expelled. Described as Daśāsana,* "ten-faced," he had twenty arms, and his physical appearance alone inspired intense terror. King of the class of frightful and malignant demons called Rākṣasas,* Rāvaṇa was the embodiment of all evil and wickedness. With his cannibal Rākṣasas, he attacked the Devas* and Dāityas* from whose loud wails and lamentations *(rāvayān āsa)* he is named. By his penance and devotion to Brahmā,* he was made invulnerable to demon or god and could assume any form he pleased; his doom lay in the hands of a woman. Viṣṇu became incarnate as Rāmacandra to destroy him. Rāvaṇa, disguised in the form of a pious mendicant, visited Rāma's dwelling in the forest while the latter was out to hunt and abducted Sītā* carrying her off to Laṅkā. The *Rāmāyaṇa* describes the war Rāma waged against Rāvaṇa at Laṅkā to rescue Sītā.

Rohiṭa: Son of King Hariścandra.*

Sahadeva: Son of Mādrī, mythical son of Aśvin, second wife of King Pāṇḍu, youngest of the five Pāṇḍava brothers, twin of Nakula* who was an accomplished swordsman and skilled in astronomy. Sahadeva was also considered to be the ideal in masculine beauty.

Sahasrārjuna: "thousand-armed Arjuna." Real name and epithet of the Kṣatriya king of Haihayas, best known by his patronymic, Kārtavīrya. Winning a boon through his worship of the saint Dattātreya, he aquired one thousand arms, the power to rule through justice, and sovereignty over the seven continents of the world. Extolled for his sacrifices, liberal ways, austerities, courtesy, and self-restraint, his righteous rule of 85,000 years had an unfortunate ending. For, it was he who abducted the sage Jamadagni's wife, Renukā, and stole the latter's sacred cow, Kāmadhenu, for which he was mercilessly slaughtered by Paraśurāma,* Viṣṇu's sixth *avatāra.*

Sītā: Daughter of King Janaka of Videha and wife of Rāmacandra.* Embodiment of purity, steadfastness, and fidelity, Sītā accompanied Rāma in his exile and quietly endured with him the harshness of life in the forest. The demon Rāvaṇa, who was impassioned by Sītā, kidnapped her to his palace in Laṅka where he made many attempts to ravish her and convince her to marry him, but she stood firm against all persuasion, enticements, and threats. When Rāma destroyed Rāvaṇa and rescued Sītā, however, he received her coldly, doubting her honor and chastity. Though she proved her purity by the ordeal of fire, which she endured unscathed, Rāma remained unconvinced of her innocence. Encouraged by the criticism of his subjects for retaining her as Queen when he became King of Ayodhyā, he banished her to the hermitage of the sage Vālmīki where she bore his twin sons. Many years later, Rāma recalled Sītā, repenting his distrust of her innocence, but she invoked the mother earth to attest to her purity which it did by drawing her back into itself.

Śaṅkha: Name of an Asura* who conquered the gods, stole the *Vedas*, and carried them off to the bottom of the sea whence they were rescued by Viṣṇu in his *avatāra* as Matsya.*

Śārṅgadhārī: "bow-wielder." Epithet of Viṣṇu.

Siddha: Semidivine beings of great purity said to be 88,000 in number who dwell in the region between the earth and the sun.

Sura: God, deity; also called *deva*—the shining ones, and *amara*—the immortal. The Suras dwell high above the earth in *svarga*, Indra's heaven. They descend onto Mt. Meru which is their pleasure ground and meeting place. The summit of Mt. Meru is resplendent as the morning sun and is the favorite spot of the Apsaras, Devas, Asuras, and the heavenly musicians, the Kinnaras and Ghandharvas.

Tārāmatī/Tārā: Wife of King Hariścandra.*

Uparājana: Rāvaṇa's* deputy.

Vāmana: The fifth incarnation of Viṣṇu as the dwarf son of the *brahmin* couple Kaśyapa and Aditi who humbled the demon king Bali.* Bali had acquired dominion over the three worlds by his devotions and patience. However, he abused this power by troubling both humans and gods who entreated Viṣṇu to come to their aid and restore their dignity. As small-framed Vāmana, Viṣṇu begged Bali for a mere three steps of land. Bali granted his wish. Assuming his true form, Viṣṇu strode over heaven and earth in two steps, placing the third on Bali's head who sank into the infernal regions where he was allowed to reign.

Varāha: "boar." Viṣṇu's fourth incarnation as the Boar. To recover the earth, which the demon Hiraṇyakaśipu had dragged to the bottom of the sea, Viṣṇu was incarnated as the Boar. After a contest that lasted a thousand years, he finally overcame the demon and raised up the earth again.

Vāsuki: King of serpents (Nāgas*) in the underworld whom the gods used as a rope which they twisted around Mt. Mandara to churn the ocean and obtain *amṛta*, the nectar of Immortality.

Also called Śeṣa, the serpent-king has a thousand heads and serves as Viṣṇu's couch and canopy when the latter sleeps during the intervals of creation. As symbol of eternity, another one of his names is Ananta, "the endless."

Vibhiśaṇa: "terrible." Rāvaṇa's younger brother who, like his brother, worshipped Brahmā and obtained a boon that he should never commit an unworthy act even when under great distress. He was opposed to the ways of the Rākṣasas and tried to convince Rāvaṇa not to wage war with Rāma. Furious, Rāvaṇa persecuted him. Vibhiśaṇa joined forces with Rāma, and, after Rāvaṇa's defeat, Rāma raised him to the throne of Laṅka, and he was given the boon of Immortality.

Viṣṇu: Preserver, second god of the Hindu triad, Viṣṇu occupies a predominant place in the Hindu pantheon. To his worshippers, he is the Supreme Being from which all creation emanates. He is frequently referred to as Nārāyaṇa, the all-pervading, and Hari, the resplendent. As preserver and restorer, later tradition assigned to him the function of redeemer, and he is best known and worshipped through his savior forms or *avatāras.* Amongst them, the most widely known and accepted are his *dasāvatāra* or ten incarnations: Matsya,* Kūrma,* Varāha,* Narasiṃha,* Vāmana,* Paraśurāma,* Rāma,* Kṛṣṇa,* Buddha,* and Kalki.* His celestial dwelling is the heavenly city of Vaikuṇṭha where he resides with his consort Lakṣmī or Śrī, Goddess of Wealth. He wields a bow called Śārṅga.*

Yama: "restrainer." Ruler and judge of the dead, god of the dead with whom the spirits of the departed reside. Held by some to be the progenitor of the human race and thus the first man to die, Yama conducts the dead to the realm of the ancestors *(pitṛs).* He seizes his victims by his noose and punishes them with his mace.

Yakṣa: Although frequently mentioned with the Rākṣasas, the Yakṣas are a different class of Asuras who seceded from the former with Kubera as their king. Unlike the Rākṣasas of Rāvaṇa, these demons are inoffensive and benign, and their principal role is to protect Kubera, God of Wealth, whose heaven is on Mt. Meru.

Yudhiṣṭhira: Eldest of the Pāṇḍava brothers, mythical son of Dharma, God of Justice. Praised for his calm, fair, and dispassionate judgment, he was renowned as a just ruler but known to be inept at war and politics. Thus, when his wicked cousin Duryodhana challenged him to a game of dice, Yudhiṣṭhira, foolishly expecting fair play, lost everything including his kingdom, wealth, brothers, and wife, all of whom were reduced with him to the status of slaves and sent into exile for thirteen years.

Historical Figures

Adam: father of humanity *(abu'l-bashar);* primordial man, first human created by Allah. In the Qur'ān, after Allah had created the heavens and the earth, He decided to create man and place him on earth as his *khalīfah* or deputy. He taught Adam the names of all things (II:28–32) which even the angels knew not and then commanded the angels to bow before him. All prostrated before Adam save Iblis, who, unlike Adam, was created from fire not clay (II:33; VII:12f; XV:26–36). Iblis or Satan was expelled from the Garden. God then asked who would bear His trust *(amānah),* and all in His creation shied away, whereas Adam accepted the burden. When Adam repented after he was banished to earth for eating of the forbidden fruit, God promised him His guidance (III:36–37; VII:24–26) and reminded Adam of the covenant he had forgotten (XX:115) not to serve Satan (XXXVI:60). In Ṣūfism and Shī'ism, Adam is *al-insān al-kāmil*—the perfect man in whom Muḥammad's Light *(nūr)* is manifest, hence, the first of the prophets sent to mankind.

ʿAlī: ʿAlī b. Abī Ṭālib, d. 661 C.E., cousin and son-in-law of Prophet Muḥammad; fourth Caliph in Sunni Islam; after Khadīja, the first male to accept the Prophet's message and mission; facilitated Muḥammad's escape from Mecca to Medina. According to Shīʿites, ʿAlī is *walī allāh*—friend of Allah who, after the Prophet, inherited both the spiritual and the political leadership *(imāmah)* of the Muslim community. ʿAlī married the Prophet's daughter Fāṭimah who bore him two sons, Ḥasan and Ḥusayn; the five constitute the *ahl al-bayt,* lit. family of the [prophet's] house, to whose lineage belong the authority of *imāmah.*

Bahā' al-Dīn Zakariyya: d. 1227 C.E., a saint of the Suhrawardī order who was born near Multān in 1182 to 1183 C.E. On the order of his mentor, Shaykh Shihāb al-Dīn Suhrawardī of Baghdad, Bahā' al-Dīn founded the Suhrawardī order in India. He set up a *khanaqāh* in Multān which became a famous center of mystical discipline in medieval India. The order flourished in Sind and Punjab. Zakariyya lived in an aristocratic manner and kept close contact with the ruling class; he rejected itinerant and ascetic mystics such as the Qalandars and did not approve of severe fasts and other austere practices; nor did he approve of the religious use of music, *samā'*, as a means to mystical experience. He played a key role in helping Iltūtmish gain control over Multān in 1210 to 1235 C.E. The *gināns* preserve a story about the confrontation between Pīr Shams and Bahā' al-Dīn.

Duldul: Name of the Prophet's white horse that he rode on his campaigns; she survived him, and according to Shī'ah tradition, 'Alī inherited her and rode her in the Battles of the Camel and Ṣiffin.

Gorakh: Gorakhnāth c. 1120 C.E., founder of the order of the Kānphaṭa Yogis in northern India, named thus because the ears of disciples were split to insert enormous earrings during their initiation ceremony (*kān-phaṭa* lit. means split-earred). A vast legendary folklore surrounds the figure of Gorakhnāth and his followers who were notorious for their utter disregard of custom and their perverse rites and practices. Poetry attributed to Gorakh survives in Panjabi; his followers have composed several writings on magic and alchemy.

Ḥasan Kabīr al-Dīn: Ismā'īlī Pīr, son of Pīr Ṣadr al-Dīn, born in Ucch c. 1329 C.E. and died c. 1470 C.E. His shrine lies outside Ucch and is locally known as Ḥasan Daryā. Credited with the conversion of many Hindus to Satpanth Ismā'īlism; also may have had ties with the Suhrawardī order.

Ḥusayn: Ḥusayn b. 'Alī b. Abī Ṭālib, grandson of the Prophet Muḥammad, son of Fāṭimah and 'Alī who came to a tragic end at Karbalā' in 680 C.E. After 'Alī's rival Mu'āwiya died, the Kūfans—many of whom had Shī'ite sympathies—invited Ḥusayn to their town. Led to Kūfa by false assurances of his popularity there, when he approached Kūfa he was met instead by enemies. Refusing to fight, he encamped at a place nearby called Karbalā', but an army from Kūfa under ʿUmar b. Saʿd surrounded him and eventually massacred Ḥusayn, his family, and his small circle of supporters.

Islām Shāh: Thirtieth Nizārī Ismāʿīlī Imām d. 1423 C.E. His name is associated in the *ginān*s with three Ismāʿīlī Pīrs: Pīr Shams, Pīr Ṣadr al-Dīn, and Pīr Ḥasan Kabīr al-Dīn. The surname Islām Shāh may have been used to identify either of the two Imāms, Islām Shāh or Muḥammad b. Islām Shāh, who lived in Anjudān in the fifteenth century.

Ḳhalīl Allah: Ḳhalīl Allah ʿAlī I, thirty-ninth Nizārī Ismāʿīlī Imām d. 1585 C.E.; Ḳhalīl Allah ʿAlī II, forty-fifth Nizārī Ismāʿīlī Imām d. 1817 C.E. The latter Imām was assassinated by members of the Qājār court in Yazd. Fearing this would create trouble, the Shāh of Iran granted his son and successor, Imām Ḥasan ʿAlī Shāh, the districts of Qumm and Mahallāt as well as conferred on him the title of Āghā Khān. However, since Ḥasan ʿAlī Shāh continued to receive hostile treatment from certain court members, he migrated in 1848 C.E. to India where he settled in Bombay.

Mahdī: al-Mahdī ʿUbayd Allah c. 874–934 C.E. was the first of the open or manifest (*ẓāhir*) Ismāʿīlī *imāms*. He was declared the first caliph of the Fāṭimid dynasty in Egypt in 910 C.E., twelve years after he became the eleventh Ismāʿīlī Imām. Under him, the *daʿwah* or religious mission of the Ismāʿīlīs emerged from its period of secrecy (*satr*) and flourished in the Maghrib and the East. While al-Mahdī was not particularly successful in his ambition to conquer North Africa, he laid firm political foundations for over a century of Fāṭimid rule. Mahdī also means "the rightly guided one," the title of the expected messiah who will restore justice and religion before the world ends. From the Ar. *h-d-y* meaning divine guidance, the Mahdī is he who will return Islām to its original perfection and bring an end to all oppression. In the Shīʿite tradition, the Mahdī must be from among the *ahl al-bayt*.

Nizār: Nineteenth Ismāʿīlī Imām who died in 1095 C.E. The previous Imām Mustanṣīr bi'llāh had two sons, Nizār and Mustaʿli. The

Fāṭimid line split when, following Mustanṣīr's death, the elder son and designated heir Nizār was hailed Imām in Iran and Syria, whereas in Egypt, Yemen, and Sind, his younger brother al-Mustaʿli succeeded in claiming this position with the help of his military commander, al-Afdal. The focal point of the Nizāri Ismāʿīlīs henceforth centered around the fortress of Alamūt in the Rūdbār district of the Alburz mountain ranges in the northern frontiers of modern Iran just south of the Caspian Sea. This fortress was captured by Ḥasan-i-Ṣabbaḥ in 1090 C.E. a few years before the Nizārī–Mustaʿlian schism took place. Note also that Nizār was the name of the thirty-third Nizārī Ismāʿīlī Imām who died in 1628 C.E. and whose tomb resides in Kahak.

Qāsim Shāh: Qāsim ʿAlī Shāh d. c. 1369 C.E., twenty-ninth Nizārī Ismāʿīlī Imām, grandson of Imām Rukn al-Dīn Khūrshāh who in 1256 C.E. had to surrender the Ismāʿīlī fortress of Alamūt to the ruthless Mongol, Hülagü Khān, and witness the mass destruction and massacre of his followers at this and other Ismāʿīlī strongholds. Moving westward, Qāsim Shāh settled in Ādharbayjān. By the sixteenth century, later Imāms had proceeded from there to Farāhan, Mahallāt, and finally Anjudān, where under the Shīʿite dynasty of the Safavids, they experienced more tolerable conditions.

Ṣadr al-Dīn: c. 1350–1420 C.E., the third major Ismāʿīlī Pīr after Satgur Nūr and Pīr Shams who is credited with the consolidation of Satpanth Ismāʿīlism in the Indian subcontinent. Traditional sources attribute the establishment of Ismāʿīlī places of prayer *(jamāʿat ḳhānah)* to Pīr Ṣadr al-Dīn and suggest that he named his Hindu converts *ḳhwājah*—lords; the name stuck to the community who became commonly known as the Khojahs.

Local Characters

Note: Characters appearing in the *ginān* narratives have not been listed below in alphabetical order. Rather, they are presented in sets as the *dramatis personnae* of a particular story or of linked incidents and episodes. I have titled these stories for ease of reference. The stories are given in the sequence that they appear in the translations. Details of identity, role, and attributes of specific characters have been drawn from the various *ginān*s in which they appear. Together, these details give a fuller portrayal of each character. While individuals in the *ginān* narratives for whom there is no historical evidence have been styled here as "local," it is possible that these characters were, in fact, historical persons. This question, however, may never be resolved, since, apart from the *ginān*s, all traces of them have been lost.

The Story of King Manaśuddha

Manaśudha Rājā; Radīyā (*devī*) Rāṇī: King Manaśudha (lit. pure of mind); king of Prempāṭan (lit. city of love) whose wife is Queen Radīyāde (lit. *hṛdaya+devī* goddess of the heart) [9:1; 28:1]; the rule of their kingdom is entrusted to five ministers [9:2; 28:2]; they are pious devotees of Pīr Shams [28:6]; they have a child [9:5; 28:77]; they are summoned by the Guru [9:4; 28:75] and undergo a trial at the end of which they attain the vision of Śyāma [9:11; 28:90] and Immortality [9:12; 28:91].

The Story of Queen Surjā(devī)

Surjā; Ajīyā; Vajīyā; Kamalā; Dhamalā; Robaḍa; Locana: Circle of eight followers in the city of Cīnab [15:5] led by Queen Surjā who beseeched Surbhāṇ for religious knowledge and enlightenment [10:8–11].

Kamalā: Queen Surjā's son [16:5] who becomes immortal after hearing the Guru [16:12]; name of King Manaśudha's attendant [28:26]; Viṣṇu as Vāmana saved the sacred cow called Kāmadhenu [28:58]; name of wife of a demon slain by Paraśurām (*kamalā:* lotus; name of Lakṣmī and typical name of women).

Surjā (*devī*) Rāṇī: Queen Surjā, wife of the tenth demon king of Cīṇab [8:29]; a servant (*dāsi*) of the Sāheb to whom his disciple Surbhāṇ was sent [10:1]; mistress of a demon [10:4]; she has a pious gathering of eight [15:5] all who desire religious knowledge and salvation [10:8] including her son Kamalā [16:5]; her demon husband is king of Yodhā [39:13] and is called Kalinga [39:14]; she warns him that Yodhā will meet its end at the hands of ʿAlī's army [41:20] and counsels him to flee [47:1]; he criticizes her for extolling another in his own city of Cīnab [47:10]; she is a devotee of the Guru whom she recollects and serves [55:1]; she dutifully practices divine recollection and drinks holy water [65:7].

The Story of Emnābāī

Nānābāī: Emnābāī's spiteful Hindu sister-in-law who discloses the latter's secret service of the Guru, thus causing Emnābāī's expulsion from her in-laws' home [14:14–16].

Hemābāī: Nānābāī's mother, Emnābāī's mother-in-law, Śyāmdās's wife [14:19]; condemns Emnābāī and advises her husband to banish her and send her back to her father's home [14:21].

Śyāmdās: Hemābāī's husband and Emnābāī's father-in-law [14:19].

Hariścandra: Hemābāī's son: either Emnābāī's brother-in-law or husband [45:10].

Kulicanda: Possibly the name of Emnābāī's husband over whom she triumphs by attaining heaven [45:16].

Huramala and Kuramala: Emnābāī's two children who are expelled with their mother from their grandparents' house [45:11].

Emnābāī: A secret follower of Pīr Shams who lives with her Hindu in-laws in the town of Ghazni [14:4]; her father lives in Godi Vilod̤ [14:15]; she invites Pīr Shams to her place [14:5; 45:1–2]; a *satī,* she passes a test to prove her steadfast faith [14:7–13; 45:3]; she begs her sister-in-law not to disclose her secret [14:17; 45:7]; she endures humiliation at the hands of her in-laws and townsfolk for serving him [14:22] but escapes her persecutors when a palanquin specially sent for her transports her to heaven [14:24]; she is expelled with her two children by Hariścandra [45:10–11]; but she is miraculously able to feed her hungry and thirsty children popped corn and water [45:13–14].

The Story of Godi Vilod̤

Devcand; Devrām; Saṅgjī: Hindu pilgrims who stop to wash at the outskirts of town Godi Vilod̤ (where Emnābāī's father lives

[67:2]); Sangjī is from the Banyā caste (*vaiśya* or merchant class), Devrām is a *brahmin*, and Devcand is from the Golārāṇā caste (*śudra* or untouchable class). Devrām, the *brahmin*, causes a ruckus when drops of water accidentally splash on him [62:4] and challenges Pīr Shams to produce water from the Ganges to purify him of this defilement caused by his two disciples [68:1]; eventually, all three beg the Pīr for forgiveness [68:5–7].

The Story of Banglādeśa

Vasto: Name of the *mukhī* or chief of a following in Bengal or Bangladesh appointed by Pīr Shams [72:5–6]; Vasto was to oversee religious ceremonies and collect the tithe [72:10].

The Story of Bhoṭnagar

Śivbhaṭ: An ascetic living just outside the town of Bhoṭnagar to whom the disciples of Pīr Shams go for help in getting food [75:11]; he informs the King of Bhoṭnagar of the injustice done to the Pīr [76:3] and acts as the King's messenger. Declaring himself the Pīr's follower, he begs the latter to open up the city gates [76:16]; later, he goes to King Devsangjī's treasury; he also preaches the new religion to his circle [77:33].

Rugjī Raṇachoḍ & Trikam: Two residents of Bhoṭnagar from the Banyā caste who pledge themselves to the Pīr and ask him to forgive them [77:22–23]; possibly the very characters who first cast the Pīr out of the town.

Rāmsaṅgji or Devsaṅgjī; Śīlvantī Sadā: King of Bhoṭnagar who was upset about the infraction against the Pīr by his subjects [75:9] and asks for an inquiry to seek out the offenders [76:6–7]; of the Gaekwāḍ caste [77:33]; he goes before the Pīr after the city gates open when the latter's name was invoked and begs him to visit his palace [77:4–5]; the Pīr declines but performs a miracle, and the King is told to make sure that all residents of Bhoṭnagar drink milk from a cow that descended from heaven [77:11]; the King and his Queen, Śīlvantī Sadā, entreat the Pīr to visit their palace and to save them [77:18].

The Story of Navrātrī

Śaṅkar: A *brahmin paṇḍit* who in rejection of the Guru's teaching quit the *garbī* dance [100:3], for he was inferior in understanding and merit [10:5].

The Disciples of Pīr Shams

Candrabhāṇ: A disciple *(celā)* of Pīr Shams and brother of Surbhāṇ [2:1]; one of the two youths who visits Emnābāī [14:9]; the child of Brahma (i.e., Pīr Shams) [14:10] who pleads for Emnābāī's release [14:23].

Surbhāṇ: A disciple *(celā)* of Pīr Shams and brother of Candrabhāṇ [2:1]; sent to visit Queen Surjā at Cīnab [10:1]; a messenger of the Guru's *gināns* who teaches her the principles of religion [10:4]; one of the two youths who visits Emnābāī [14:11].

Vimras: Most likely another name of the disciple Candrabhāṇ; the names of the two "brothers," namely, Vimras and Surbhāṇ, appear together consistently after Ginān 10.

Vimras and Surbhāṇ: They impart religious knowledge to Queen Surjā [10:4,12]; the names of the two youths who accompany Pīr Shams to Ghazni to visit Emnābāī [14:4; 15:1; 15:14], to Banglādeśa [72:2], to Godi Vilod̤ [67:3], and to Bhoṭnagar [74:8]. Vimras is Hari's devotee and recites *gināns* in honor of the Guru [14:3]; a model of self-sacrifice, he cut off his head and submitted it to the Guru [46:4]; though unrecognized, both Vimras and Surbhāṇ are present with the gods at the *ghaṭ* ceremony [53:5; 65:9]. Since time immemorial, they have been servants *(dāsa)* of Pīr Shams, and they will become manifest in *Kalyug* [54:5; 62:11]; they are devotees *(bhakta)* of Guru Shams of Multān [64:3; 77:28]; to join their company is to attain release [65:13]; they are two Muslim devotees *(bhakta)* [67:4; 68:11; 75:1] (Surbhāṇ calls himself a Hindu once [76:2]) who are the disciples *(dāsa)* of Pīr Shams [67:10; 71:12; 73:2; 77:40]; Pīr Shams declares they will transmit the teachings of the True Path *(satpanth)* [68:11]; they impart religious knowledge through *gināns* and give instructions on how to perform rituals [69:2,4; 70:12; 72:8]; they perform the *ghaṭ* ceremony and collect the tithe *(dasond)* [71:4], and they tie the bracelet of allegiance on new devotees [73:1]; the two disciples went in search of help when their Guru was denied passage in Godi Viloḍ [75:1]; Vimras fetched a cup and milked the cow that descended from heaven [77:10].

Obscure Characters

Ansūyā: Another name of Sitā whose piety and devotion won her the vision of Devadutta (Indra) [60:11].

Makaḍa Bhudara: Character who challenged Pīr Shams to reveal the *avatāra* of whom he spoke [17:7].

Epithets and Titles

Alakha: Skt. *alakṣaṇa.* Without attribute; epithet for the Supreme who is beyond the particularity of attributes and whose nature cannot be summed up by a specific quality.

Brahman: Skt. The Impersonal, All-Pervading, Eternal, Self-Existing Being from which all existence has sprung; the essential Cosmic Principle of the universe.

Coṭa: Hin./Guj. Famous, well-known; certain, sure; aim, blow.

Daryā: Per./Hin. Ocean, sea; *daryā-dil*—ocean-hearted, bountiful as the sea, generous.

Dātār: Hin./Guj. Generous, kind, forgiving; *dhātar* (Skt. *dhātṛ*—creator, supporter) Creator, Preserver, Sustainer.

Dāyam: Per. *dā'im.* Permanent, Eternal, Perpetual.

Ġhāzī: Per./Guj. One who participates in a raid (Ar. *ghazwa*) against infidels; title of honor for one who fought or died for his religion; Muslim crusader; common title of Muslim princes; itinerant soldier of fortune.

Guru: Skt./Hin. Lit. dispeller of darkness; religious guide, master, teacher who initiates disciples in the spiritual quest; possessor of the esoteric secrets of truth and self-realization, traditionally, the spiritual preceptor receives pupils at his hermitage teaching them as if they were his own sons while they serve him in total obedience and submission; the living guru is often regarded as the embodiment of deity whose spiritual lineage traces back to the *ādiguru,* the founding guru of a religious group.

Hari: Hin./Guj. Lit. red, pale, yellow; lord, god, deity; applied to fire *(Agni),* sun *(Viṣṇu)* and lightning *(Indra)* in Vedic usage, the epithet *hari* is frequently used for Viṣṇu.

Hazrat: Ar. *ḥaḍrat.* Presence, majesty, dominion; epithet joined to the name of a venerated saint, scholar, religious figure; title of address for royalty and great persons, such as His Majesty, Lordship, Highness.

Imām: Ar. Lit. leader of prayer; in Shīʿism, successor designated by the Prophet to assume leadership of the Muslim community after him; possessor of the esoteric meaning *(bāṭin)* of the exoteric *(ẓāhir)* form of the Divine Revelation brought by Muḥammad, hence, its legitimate interpreter; revealer of esoteric truths, spiritual rebirth must be sought through recognition of his divine essence or light *(nūr).*

Kirtār: Hin. Creator, Maker, Originator.

Ḳhāliq: Per. Creator, God; *ḳhalq*—created things, creatures.

Ḳhudāvand: Per. *ḳhudā*—God, Master, Owner; *ḳhudāvand*—title of address: Lord, King, Prince, Sir, Your Majesty.

Murshid al-Kāmil: Ar. Lit. the Perfect Master; *al-insān al-kāmil*— the Perfect Man, the archetype of humanity whose spiritual and physical potential is perfected or realized; in Islamic mysticism, he is mirror of all the Names of God, manifesting all divine attributes; through God's light *(nūr)* which shines in him, the believer's heart finds perfection.

Nara: Guj. Man, husband, master, person.

Nārāyaṇa: Skt. Lit. he whose place of motion is the waters; epithet of Viṣṇu; the Supreme Being, God, Creator.

Nirañjana: Skt. Faultless, without blemish, spotless; the Supreme Being, God.

Nirguṇa: Skt. Without qualities or attributes; epithet of God, Brahman.

Panj tan pāk: Per. Lit. the five holy ones, namely, Prophet Muḥammad, his daughter Fāṭimah, his cousin and son-in-law ʿAlī, and his two grandsons Ḥasan and Ḥusayn.

Pīr: Per. Lit. aged, old; Ṣūfī master, spiritual guide, Muslim teacher, also called *murshid* who is qualified to lead disciples along the mystical path.

Qā'im: Ar. Upright, firm, just; resolute, steadfast, perpetual; also al-Qā'im is the "riser"; the eschatological messiah or Mahdī.

Qalandar: Per. Wandering Muslim *darwish* or mystic who has relinquished his family and possessions and set out in search of spiritual enlightenment; represents the antinomian *ṣūfī* who defies conventional piety.

Sāheb Rājā: Per. *ṣāhib*—lit. possessor of; king, master, lord; honorific for sir, lord; also friend, companion; Guj. *rājā*—king, ruler.

Sarjaṇahār: Hin. Creator, Maker, God.

Satgur: Hin. *sadguru*—the worthy preceptor, the True Guru.

Shāh: Per. King, sovereign, prince of noble lineage, excellent in any degree; Lord, King, Ruler.

Śrī: Skt. Honorific sir, lord, majesty, blessed or auspicious one; prefixed to name of great men, gods, sacred or celebrated works.

Swāmī Rājā: Hin. Lit. Master–King; lord and spiritual guide, spiritual master.

Bibliography

Primary Sources: Ginān̄s

Brahma Prakāśa (with explanation in Gujerati). Bombay: Lalji Devraj, 1921.

Garbī in *Mahān Ismāīlī Santa Pīr Shams Racit Gīnānono Saṅgraha.* Bombay: Ismailia Association for India, 1952.

Ginan-e Sharif: Our Wonderful Tradition. Vancouver: Ismailia Association for Canada, n.d.

Mahān Īsmāīlī Santa Pīr Shams Racīt Gīnānono Saṅgraha (English title: Collection of Ginans Composed by the Great Ismaili Saint Pīr Shams). Bombay: Ismailia Association for India, 1952. 106 pages. Reprint by N. G. Dareḍiyā.

Satvarṇi Vaḍi. Bombay: Lalji Devraj, 1926.

Surbhāṇaji Vel and *Candrabhaṇaji Vel* in *Gīnāna Grantha Pīr Shamas.* Bombay: Ghulam Husain, 1907.

Secondary Sources

Ahmed, Aziz. *Islamic Culture in an Indian Environment.* London: Oxford University Press, 1964.

———. *An Intellectual History of Islam in India.* Edinburgh: Edinburgh University Press, 1969.

Ahmed, Imtiaz, ed. *Ritual and Religion among Muslims in India.* New Delhi: Manohar, 1984.

Akhtar, Ahmad. "Shams Tabrīzī—Was He Ismāilīan?" *Islamic Culture,* 10 (1930): 131–136.

ʿAlī Muḥammad Khān. *Khātima Mirʾāt-i Aḥmadī,* ed. by S. Nawab Ali. Baroda: Oriental Institute, 1928. Transl. by M. F. Lokhandwala. Baroda: Oriental Institute, 1965.

Ali, Syed Mujtaba. *The Origin of the Khojāhs and Their Religious Life Today.* Wurzburg: Buchdruckerei Richard Mayr, 1936.

Allana, G. *Ginans of Ismaili Pirs: Rendered into English Verse.* Karachi: Ismailia Association for Pakistan, 1984.

Alston, A. J. *The Devotional Poems of Mīrābāī.* Delhi: Motilal Banarasidass, 1980.

Asani, Ali S. "The Khojahs of Indo-Pakistan: The Quest for an Islamic Identity." *Journal of the Institute of Muslim Minority Affairs,* vol. 8, no. 1 (1983): 31–41.

———. "The *Būjh Nirañjan:* A Critical Edition of a Mystical Poem in Medieval Hindustani with its Khojkī and Gujarati Recensions." Harvard University: Ph.D. dissertation, 1984.

———. "Ginān." *Encyclopedia of Religion,* vol. 5, ed. Mircea Eliade. New York: MacMillan, 1986.

———. "The Khojkī Script: A Legacy of Ismaili Islam in the Indo-Pakistan Subcontinent." *Journal of the American Oriental Society,* 107, no. 1 (1987): 439–449.

———. *The Būjh Nirañjan: An Ismaili Mystical Poem.* Cambridge: Harvard Center for Middle Eastern Studies, 1991.

———. "The Ginān Literature of the Ismailis of Indo-Pakistan: Its Origins, Characteristics, and Themes." *Folk Sources of the Bhakti Tradition,* ed. D. Eck & F. Mallison. Gröningen & Paris: Egbert Forsten and École Française d'Extrême-Orient, 1991, 1–18.

———. *The Harvard Collection of Ismaili Literature in Indic Languages: A Descriptive Catalog and Finding Aid.* Boston: G. K. Hall & Co., 1992.

———. "The Ismaili Ginans as Devotional Literature." *Devotional Literature in South Asia: Current Research 1985–8,* ed. R. S. McGregor. Cambridge: Cambridge University Press, 1992, 101–112.

———. "The Ismāʿīlī Ginān: Reflections on Authority and Authorship." *Essays in Ismāʿīlī Thought and History,* ed. Farhad Daftary. Cambridge: Cambridge University Press, 1995.

Baird, Robert D. *Category Formation and the History of Religions.* The Hague: Mouton & Co., 1971.

Barbour, Ian G. *Myths, Models, and Paradigms.* New York: Harper & Row, 1974.

Bharati, Agehananda. *Hindu Views and Ways and the Hindu–Muslim Interface.* New Delhi: Munshiram Manoharlal, 1981.

Bosworth, Clifford E. *The Medieval History of Iran, Afghanistan and Central Asia.* London. Variorum Reprints, 1977

Chand, Tara. *The Influence of Islam on Indian Culture.* Chandigarh: Chandigarh University, 1976.

Chunara, Ali, J. *Noorun Mubin.* Rev. by Jafferali N. Sufi. Bombay: Ismailia Association for India, 1951, 3rd ed.

Coulson, Michael. *Sanskrit: An Introduction to the Classical Language.* London: Hodder & Stoughton, 1976.

Coward, Harold, & David Goa. *Mantra: Hearing the Divine in India.* Chambersburg: Anima Books, 1991.

Culley, Robert. "An Approach to the Problem of Oral Tradition." *Vetus Testamentum,* 13 (1963): 113–125.

———. *Studies in the Structure of Hebrew Narrative.* Philadelphia: Fortress Press, 1976.

Daftary, Farhad. *The Ismāʿīlīs: Their History and Doctrines.* Cambridge: Cambridge University Press, 1990.

———. *The Assassin Legends: Myths of the Ismāʿīlīs.* London: I. B. Tauris & Co., Ltd., 1994.

Darghawala, Syed S. *Tawārīkh-i-Pīr.* Navsari: Published by Author, 1914.

Davies, C. Collin. *An Historical Atlas of the Indian Peninsula.* 2nd ed. Madras: Oxford University Press, 1959.

Dawlatshāh b. ʿAlāʾ al-Dawla. *Tadhkirat al-Shuʿarāʾ.* ed. E. G. Browne. Leiden-London: 1901.

de Beaugrande, R., & W. Dressler. *Introduction to Text Linguistics.* London: Longman Inc., 1981.

Deshpande, Pandurang. *Gujerati–English Dictionary.* Ahmedabad: University Book Production Board, 1978.

Dowson, John. *A Classical Dictionary of Hindu Mythology and Religion, Geography, History and Literature.* London: Routledge and Kegan Paul, 1961.

Dubois, J. A. *Hindu Manners, Customs and Ceremonies,* trans. H. Beauchamp. Delhi: Oxford University Press, 1906, 251–270.

Dundes, Alan. "From Etic to Emic Units in the Structural Study of Folktales." *Journal of American Folklore,* 75 (1962): 95–105.

Eaton, Richard. "Sufi Folk Literature and the Expansion of Indian Islam." *History of Religions,* XIV (1974–5): 117–127.

Eaton, Richard. *Sufis of Bijapur.* Princeton: Princeton University Press, 1978.

Eliade, Mircea. *Rites and Symbols of Initiation,* trans. Willard Trask. New York: Harper & Row, 1958.

Esmail, Aziz. "Satpanth Ismailism and Modern Changes Within It: With Special Reference to East Africa." University of Edinburgh: Ph.D. dissertation, 1972.

Esmail, Aziz, & Azim Nanji. "The Ismāʿīlīs in History." *Ismāʿīlī Contributions to Islamic Culture,* ed. S. H. Nasr. Tehran: Imperial Academy of Philosophy, 1977, 227–260.

Ewing, Katherine. "The Politics of Sufism: Redefining the Saints of Pakistan." *Journal of Asian Studies,* 42, no. 2 (1983): 251–268.

Ewing, Katherine P., ed. *Sharīʿat and Ambiguity in South Asian Islam.* Berkeley: University of California Press, 1988.

Fausbōll, V. *Indian Mythology.* Varanasi: Bharati Vidya Bhavan, 1972.

Finnegan, Ruth. *Oral Poetry: Its Nature, Significance and Social Context.* Cambridge: Cambridge University Press, 1977.

Fyzee, Asaf ʿAli Asghar. *Cases in the Muhammadan Law of India and Pakistan.* London: Oxford Clarendon Press, 1965.

Gala, L. R. *Viśāl Śabdakoś: Gujarātī–Gujarātī–Angrejī Koś.* Ahmedabad: Gala Publishers, n.d.

Garrett, John. *A Classical Dictionary of India.* Delhi: Oriental Publishers, 1975.

Geertz, Clifford. *Islam Observed: Religious Developments in Morocco and Indonesia.* Chicago: University of Chicago Press, 1968.

Gold, Daniel. *Comprehending the Guru.* Atlanta: Scholars Press, 1988.

Gonda, Jan. *Change and Continuity in Indian Religion.* The Hague: Mouton & Co., 1965.

Graham, William A. *Beyond the Written Word: Oral Aspects of Scripture in the History of Religions.* Cambridge: Cambridge University Press, 1987.

Granoff, Phyllis, & Koichi Shinohara. *Monks & Magicians: Religious Biographies in Asia.* Oakville: Mosaic Press, 1988.

Gupta, Shakti. *From Daityas to Devatas in Hindu Mythology.* Bombay: Somanya Publications Ltd., 1973.

Hamdani, Abbas. *The Beginnings of the Ismāʿīlī Daʿwa in Northern India.* Cairo: Sirovic, 1965.

Hardy, Peter. *Historians of Medieval India.* London: Luzac & Co., 1960.

Hawley, John S., & Mark Juergensmeyer. *Songs of the Saints of India.* Oxford: Oxford University Press, 1988.

Hefner, Robert W. *Hindu Javanese: Tengger Tradition in Islam.* Princeton: Princeton University Press, 1985.

Hodgson, Marshall G. *The Order of Assassins: The Struggle of the Early Nizārī Ismāʿīlīs against the Islamic World.* The Hague: Mouton & Co., 1955.

———. "The Ismāʿīlī State," *The Cambridge History of Iran,* vol. 5, ed. J. A. Boyle. Cambridge: Cambridge University Press, 1968, 422–482.

———. *The Venture of Islam: Conscience and History in a World Civilization.* 3 vols. Chicago: University of Chicago Press, 1974.

Hollister, John N. *The Shia of India.* London: Luzac & Co., 1953.

Hooda, Vali N., trans. "Some Specimens of Satpanth Literature." *Collectanea,* vol. 1, ed. W. Ivanow. Leiden: E. J. Brill, 1948, 55–137.

Husain, Yusuf. "The Influence of Islam on the Cult of Bhakti in Medieval India." *Islamic Culture,* 7 (1933): 640–662.

Ibn Ḥazm, Abū Muḥammad. *Kitāb al-fiṣal fī'l-milal.* Partial English transl., I. Friedlaender,"The Heterodoxies of the Shiites in the Presentation of Ibn Ḥazm." *Journal of the American Oriental Society,* 28 (1907): 1–80; 29 (1908): 1–183.

Ikram, S. M. *History of Muslim Civilization in India and Pakistan.* Lahore: Star Book, 1961.

Irwin, Joyce, ed. *Sacred Sound: Music in Religious Thought and Practice.* JAAR Thematic Studies 50/1. Chico: Scholars Press, 1983.

Ivanow, Wladimir. "Some Muhammadan Shrines in Western India." *Ismaili: Golden Jubilee Number,* (reprint) January 21 (1936): 1–12.

———. "The Sect of the Imam Shah in Gujerat." *Journal of the Bombay Branch of the Royal Asiatic Society,* 12 (1936): 19–70.

———. "A Forgotten Branch of Ismailis." *Journal of the Royal Asiatic Society,* (1938): 57–79.

———. "The Organisation of the Fatimid Propaganda." *Journal of the Bombay Branch of the Royal Asiatic Society,* 15 (1939): 1–35.

———. "Satpanth." *Collectanea,* vol. 1. Leiden: E. J. Brill, 1948, 1–54.

———. *Brief Survey of the Evolution of Ismailism.* Leiden: E. J. Brill, 1952.

———. "Shams Tabriz of Multan." *Professor Shafi Presentation Volume,* ed. S. M. Abdullah. Lahore: Majlis-e-Armughan-e-Ilmi, 1955, 109–118.

———. *Ismaili Literature: A Bibliographical Survey.* Tehran: Ismaili Society, 1963.

———. *Ismailitica I and II.* Memoirs of the Asiatic Society of Bengal, VII (1922): 1–76.

Jamani, Hasina. "*Brahm Prakāsh:* A Translation and Analysis." McGill University: M.A. thesis, 1985.

al-Jāmī. *Nafaḥāt al-Uns.* Tehran, 1918.

Juwaynī, ʿAlāʾ al-Din ʿAṭā-Malik. *Taʾrīkh-i jahān-gushāy,* ed. M. Qazvīnī. Leiden-London: 1912–1937. English transl. John A. Boyle, *The History of the World Conqueror.* Manchester: Manchester University Press, 1958.

Jūzjānī, Minhāj al-Dīn ʿUthmān b. Sirāj. *Ṭabakāt-i-Nāṣirī: A General History of the Muhammadan Dynasties of Asia.* Trans. Henry G. Raverty, vols. 1 & 2. Delhi: Oriental Books Reprint, 1881.

Kalani, K. L. "Saint Literature in Gujerat." *Indian Literature.* New Delhi: 19, 36–48.

Kassam, Tazim R. "Syncretism or Synthesis: The Narrative Gināns of Pīr Shams." Boston: Annual Meeting of the American Academy of Religion, 1987, unpublished paper.

Kassam, Tazim R. "Syncretism on the Model of Figure-Ground: A Study of *Brahma Prakāśa.*" *Hermeneutical Paths to the Sacred Worlds of India,* ed. Katherine K. Young. Atlanta: Scholars Press, 1993, 231–242.

Katre, S. M. *Introduction to Indian Textual Criticism.* Poona: Deccan College, 1954.

Khakee, Gulshan. "The *Dasa Avatāra* of the Satpanthi Ismailis and Imam Shahis of Indo-Pakistan." Harvard University: Ph.D. dissertation, 1972.

Kini, K. Srinivasa, & B. Shanker Rao. *Oxford Pictorial Atlas of Indian History,* 10th ed. Madras: Oxford University Press, 1967.

Krentz, Edgar. *The Historical–Critical Method.* Philadelphia: Fortress Press, 1975.

Lakoff, George, & Mark Johnson. *Metaphors We Live By.* Chicago: University of Chicago Press, 1980.

Lawrence, Bruce. "Islam in India: The Function of Institutional Sufism in the Islamization of Rajesthan, Gujerat and Kashmir." *Contribution to Asian Studies,* 17 (1982): 27–43.

Levering, Miriam, ed. *Rethinking Scripture.* Albany: SUNY Press, 1989.

Lewis, Bernard. *Origins of Ismāʿīlism.* Cambridge: Heffer & Sons, 1940.

Lord, Albert. *The Singer of Tales.* New York: Atheneum, 1976.

Maclean, Derryl N. *Religion and Society in Arab Sind.* Leiden: E. J. Brill, 1989.

Madelung, Wilferd. "Khodja." *Shorter Encyclopaedia of Islam.* Leiden: E. J. Brill, 1961.

Madelung, Wilferd. "Shiism: Ismāʿīlīyah." *Encyclopedia of Religion,* vol. 13, ed. Mircea Eliade. New York: Macmillan, 1986, 247–260.

Majumdar, R. M. *Cultural History of Gujerat.* Bombay: Popular Prakashan, 1965.

Makarem, Sami N. *The Doctrine of the Ismailis.* Beirut: Arab Institute for Research, 1972.

Martin, Richard C., ed. *Islam in Local Contexts.* Leiden: E. J. Brill, 1982.

———, ed. *Approaches to Islam in Religious Studies.* Tucson: The University of Arizona Press, 1985.

Miller, David. "The Guru as the Centre of Sacredness." *Studies in Religion,* 6/5 (1976–7): 527–533.

Mishra, V. B. *Religious Beliefs and Practices of North India During the Early Medieval Period.* Leiden: E. J. Brill, 1973.

Misra, S. C. *Muslim Communities in Gujerat.* London: Asia Publishing House, 1964.

Morgan, David. *The Mongols.* Oxford: Basil Blackwell, 1986.

Munshi, K. M. *Gujarat and Its Literature.* Bombay: Bharatiya Vidya Bhavan, 1967.

al-Mustanṣir bi'llāh. *al-Sijillāt al-Mustanṣiriyya,* ed. ʿAbd al-Munʿim Mājid. Cairo: 1954.

Nanji, Azim. *The Nizārī Ismāʿīlī Tradition of the Indo-Pak Subcontinent.* New York: Caravan Books, 1978.

———. "Ismāʿilism." *Islamic Spirituality,* ed. Seyyed H. Nasr. New York: Crossroad, 1987, 179–198.

———. "*Shariʿat and Haqīqat:* Continuity and Synthesis in the Nizārī Ismāʿīlī Muslim Tradition." *Sharīʿat and Ambiguity in South Asian Islam,* ed. Katherine P. Ewing. Berkeley: University of California Press, 1988.

Nicholson, R. A. *Selected Poems from the Dīvān-i-Shams-i-Tabrīz.* Cambridge: Cambridge University Press, 1898.

Nida, Eugene, & C. Taber. *The Theory and Practice of Translation.* Leiden: E. J. Brill, 1969.

Niẓām al-Mulk. *Siyāsat-nāma* (Siyar al-Mulūk), ed. H. Darke. 2nd ed. Tehran: 1968. English trans. H. Darke, *The Book of Government or Rules for Kings.* 2nd Ed. London: 1978.

Nizami, Khaliq A. *Some Aspects of Religion and Politics in India during the Thirteenth Century.* Bombay: Asia Publishing House, 1961.

Noorally, Zawahir. "Catalogue of Khojki Manuscripts in the Collection of the Ismailia Association for Pakistan." Karachi: Ismailia Association for Pakistan, 1971 (typed manuscript).

———. "Hazrat Pir Shamsuddin Sabzawari Multani." *Great Ismaili Heroes.* Karachi: Ismailia Association for Pakistan, 1973, 83–86.

———. "Khojki Manuscripts." Karachi: Manpower Training Project, n.d. (typed manuscript).

al-Nuʿmān b. Muhammad, al-Qāḍī Abū Ḥanīfa. *Iftitāḥ al-Daʿwa,* ed. W. al-Qāḍī, Beirut: Dār al-Thaqāfa, 1970.

———. *al-Majālis waʾl-Musāyarāt,* ed. al-Ḥabīb al-Faqī, Tunis: 1978.

Parrinder, Geoffrey. *Avatar and Incarnation.* New York: Oxford University Press, 1982.

Patel, Madhubhai. *Folksongs of South Gujarat.* Bombay: Indian Musicological Society, 1974.

Petrushevsky, I. P. "The Socio-Economic Condition of Iran under the Īl-Ḵhāns." *The Cambridge History of Iran,* vol. 5, ed. J. A. Boyle. Cambridge: Cambridge University Press, 1968, 483–537.

Poonawala, Ismail K. *Biobibliography of Ismāʿīlī Literature.* Malibu: Undena Publications, 1977.

Propp, V. *Morphology of the Folktale,* trans. Laurence Scott, 2nd rev. ed. Austin: University of Texas Press,1968.

Rahimtoola, Jaffer. *Khojā Komno Itihās.* Bombay: Published by Author, 1905.

Raghavan, V. *The Great Integrators: The Saint–Singers of India.* New Delhi: Government of India Press, 1966.

Rattansi, Diamond. "Islamization and the Khojah Ismāʿīlī Community of Pakistan." McGill University: Ph.D. dissertation, 1987.

Reynolds, Frank E., & Donald Capps. *The Biographical Process.* The Hague: Mouton & Co., 1976.

Rizwi, S. A. *A History of Sufism in India.* Delhi: Munshidas Manoharlal, 1978.

Roy, Asim. *The Islamic Syncretistic Tradition in Bengal.* Princeton: Princeton University Press, 1983.

Sachedina, Abdulaziz A. *Islamic Messianism.* Albany: SUNY Press, 1981.

Sadikali, Mumtaz. "Imam Shamsud-din Muhammad." *Ilm,* vol. 6, no. 4 (1981): 28–36.

Said, Edward. *The World, the Text and the Critic.* Cambridge: Harvard University Press, 1983.

Saunders, J. J. *A History of Medieval Islam.* London: Routledge and Kegan Paul, 1965.

Schackle, Christopher, & Zawahir Moir. *Ismaili Hymns from South Asia: An Introduction to the Gināns.* London: School of Oriental and African Studies, 1992.

Schimmel, Annemarie. *Islam in the Indian Subcontinent.* Leiden: E. J. Brill, 1980.

Schomer, Karine, & W. H. McLeod. *The Sants: Studies in a Devotional Tradition of India.* Berkeley: Religious Studies Series & Motilal Banarsidass, 1987.

Schubel, Vernon J. *Religious Performance in Contemporary Islam: Shīʿī Devotional Rituals in South Asia.* Columbus: University of South Carolina Press, 1994.

al-Shahrastānī, ʿAbd al-Karīm. *Kitāb al-milal waʾl-niḥal.* Partial English transl. A. K. Kazi & J. G. Flynn, *Muslim Sects and Divisions.* London: Kegan Paul International, 1984.

Shihāb al-Dīn Shāh al-Ḥusaynī. *Khiṭābāt-i ʿĀliya,* ed. H. Ujāqi. Bombay: Ismaili Society: 1963.

al-Shūstarī, al-Qāḍī Nūr Allāh. *Majālis al-Muʾmunīn.* Tehran: 1955–56.

Smith, Cantwell. *The Faith of Other Men.* New York: New American Library, 1963.

Stern, Samuel M. "Ismāʿīlī Propaganda and Fatimid Rule in Sind." *Islamic Culture,* 23 (1949): 298–307.

———. "Heterodox Ismāʿīlism at the Time of al-Muʿizz." *Bulletin of the School of Oriental and African Studies,* 17 (1955): 10–33.

Stutley, Margaret & James. *Harper's Dictionary of Hinduism.* New York: Harper & Row, 1977.

Troll, Christian W., ed. *Muslim Shrines in India.* Delhi: Oxford University Press, 1989.

Wade, Bonnie C. *Music in India: The Classical Traditions.* Riverdale: The Riverdale Co., 1987.

Walker, Benjamin. *Hindu World.* vols. 1 & 2. New York: Frederick A. Praeger, 1968.

Walker, Paul E. "Eternal Cosmos and the Womb of History: Time in Early Ismaili Thought." *International Journal of Middle Eastern Studies,* 9 (1978): 355–366.

Williams, Michael A., ed. *Charisma and Sacred Biography.* JAAR Thematic Studies 47, no. 3 & 4, 1982.

Williams, Raymond B. *Religions of Immigrants from India and Pakistan.* Cambridge: Cambridge University Press, 1989.

Vansina, Jan. *Oral Tradition as History.* Madison: The University of Wisconsin Press, 1985.

Vaudeville, Charlotte. *Kabir.* Oxford: Oxford University Press, 1974.

Young, Katherine K. "Tīrtha and the Metaphor of Crossing Over." *Studies in Religion,* vol 9, no. 1 (1980): 61–68.

Zahid, Ansar. "Ismaʿilism in Multan and Sind." *Journal of the Pakistan Historical Society,* 23 (1975): 35–41.

Index